International Issues
in Energy Policy, Development,
and Economics

Published in cooperation

with the East-West Center
Program on Resources: Energy and Minerals
Honolulu, Hawaii

International Issues
in Energy Policy, Development,
and Economics

EDITED BY

James P. Dorian
and Fereidun Fesharaki

Westview Press

BOULDER • SAN FRANCISCO • OXFORD

333.79
I616

Copyright © 1992 by Westview Press, Inc.

Published in 1992 in the United States of America by Westview Press, Inc., 5500 Central Avenue, Boulder, Colorado 80301-2877, and in the United Kingdom by Westview Press, 36 Lonsdale Road, Summertown, Oxford OX2 7EW

Library of Congress Cataloging-in-Publication Data
International issues in energy policy, development, and
    economics / edited by James P. Dorian and Fereidun Fesharaki
    p. cm.
    Includes bibliographical references.
    ISBN 0-8133-8621-7
    1. Energy policy.   I. Dorian, James P.   II. Fesharaki,
Fereidun.
HD9502.A2I585   1992
333.79—dc20   92-34954
                                                                         CIP

Printed and bound in the United States of America

The paper used in this publication meets the requirements
of the American National Standard for Permanence of Paper
for Printed Library Materials Z39.48-1984.

10   9   8   7   6   5   4   3   2   1

Contents

PART THREE: ENERGY, ENVIRONMENT, AND ECONOMIC DEVELOPMENT

Acknowledgments

The editors wish to express their appreciation for the generous support from the East-West Center, notably Mr. David Puhlick, Dr. Kerry Jackson, Ms. Patricia Wilson, and Ms. Julia Culver-Hopper, Technical Editors; Ms. Lois Bender, Publications Assistant; Mr. Russell Fujita, Graphic Artist; and Mr. David Miller, Production Assistant. Mr. David Puhlick is personally recognized for his many years of service and devotion to the East-West Center; his skills and kindness will be missed by Center staff members. This book is dedicated to him.

James P. Dorian
Fereidun Fesharaki

Contributors

John ASHWORTH is a Senior Analyst at the Meridian Corporation, Alexandria, Virginia.

Douglas F. BARNES is an Economist in the Industry and Energy Department, The World Bank, Washington, D.C.

Stuart BEIL is an Economist in the Australian Bureau of Agricultural and Resource Economics, Canberra.

Sharon BELANGER is a Senior Analyst at Applied Energy Services Incorporated, Arlington, Virginia.

Mark BERNSTEIN is the Director of the Center for Energy and the Environment, University of Pennsylvania, Philadelphia.

Ruth CAIRNIE is a Senior Analyst with the Oil Market Dynamics Group, Shell International Petroleum Company, London.

Leonard L. COBURN is the Director of the Office of Competition, U.S. Department of Energy, Washington, D.C.

Quentin CROFT is an Economist in the Australian Bureau of Agricultural and Resource Economics, Canberra.

Carol A. DAHL is a Professor of Mineral Economics, Mineral Economics Department, Colorado School of Mines, Golden, Colorado.

James P. DORIAN is a Research Associate in the Resources Programs, East-West Center, Honolulu, Hawaii.

Ramon ESPINASA is a Senior Advisor, Strategic Planning Coordination, Petroléos de Venezuela, S.A. (PDVSA), Caracas, Venezuela.

Fereidun FESHARAKI is the Director of the Resources Programs, East-West Center, Honolulu, Hawaii.

Brian S. FISHER is the Executive Director of the Australian Bureau of Agricultural and Resource Economics, Canberra.

Donald I. HERTZMARK is a Senior Analyst based in Washington, D.C.

Mike HINCHY is an Economist in the Australian Bureau of Agricultural and Resource Economics, Canberra.

George HORWICH is a Professor of Economics, Purdue University, West Lafayette, Indiana.

Andrea N. KETOFF is a Staff Scientist in International Energy Studies, Energy and Environment Division, Lawrence Berkeley Laboratory, Berkeley, California.

Eugene M. KHARTUKOV is the Chief of the World Energy Analysis and Forecasting Group (GAPMER), Ministry of Foreign Affairs, Moscow Institute of International Relations, Moscow, Russia.

LIU Qian is an Economist in the Industry and Energy Department, The World Bank, Washington, D.C.

Robert A. MARSHALLA is Vice President at Decision Focus Incorporated, Los Altos, California.

Daniel J. McKAY is the Executive Editor of Octane Week, Information Resources, Incorporated, Washington, D.C.

Robert N. McRAE is a Professor and the Head of the Department of Economics, University of Calgary, Alberta, Canada.

Bernard MOMMER is a Senior Advisor, Strategic Planning Coordination, Petroléos de Venezuela, S.A. (PDVSA), Caracas, Venezuela.

Roger NAILL is Vice President at Applied Energy Services Incorporated, Arlington, Virginia.

Dale M. NESBITT is a Senior Analyst, Decision Focus Incorporated, Los Altos, California.

Anthony D. OWEN is the Director of the Centre for Applied Economic Research, University of New South Wales, Kensington, Australia.

Eric PETERSEN is a Senior Analyst, Office of Economic Analysis, U.S. Department of Energy, Washington, D.C.

Eric H. M. PRICE is the Undersecretary and Chief Economic Advisor, Department of Energy, London, United Kingdom.

Ralph D. SAMUELSON is an Associate, Decision Focus Incorporated, Los Altos, California.

Harry D. SAUNDERS is the Director of the San Francisco Bay office, Decision and Risk Analysis, Incorporated, Danville, California.

Menahem SPIEGEL is a Professor at the Center for Energy and the Environment, University of Pennsylvania, Philadelphia.

Kazushi UEMURA is an Associate Professor of Political Economy, Sophia University, Tokyo, Japan.

Mine K. YÜCEL is a Senior Economist, Federal Reserve Bank of Dallas, Texas.

1 Introduction and Background

James P. Dorian and Fereidun Fesharaki

The complexities of the world energy industry became nowhere more evident than in the autumn of 1990, following Iraq's seizure of Kuwait. Though crude oil prices did not escalate to levels originally feared, they reached US$41 a barrel by mid-September of that year. Politics, economics, and history each played an important role in guiding global energy markets during this tumultuous period.

Unprecedented political and economic changes continued worldwide in 1991, verifying once again the intricate relationships between societal developments and the global energy markets. The breakup of the Soviet Union, the world's largest energy producer and second largest consumer, injected a high level of uncertainty and confusion into forecasting models of the global energy system. In 1988, when both output and exports reached their highest levels ever, the Soviet Union accounted for 20.5 percent of total world production of oil, making it easily the world's largest producer. It also was responsible for 14.4 percent of worldwide consumption of oil, second only to the United States.

This book provides a systematic overview of the dynamic issues of energy policy, development, and economics affecting today's fast-changing world. The objective of the volume is to illuminate the factors influencing the energy policies of key energy producing/consuming nations around the world, and to examine current trends in energy development, planning, technology, and trade. Important interactions between energy utilization and the environment are also analyzed. The authors have varied backgrounds in the energy field, and make up a cross-section of senior representatives from government, industry, and academia.

For easy reference, the book is divided into three parts, namely, Global Energy Markets and Policy, Energy Issues and Trends, and Energy, Environment, and Economic Development. Part I provides a perspective on the status of the international energy market and the lessons learned from the recent Gulf War, a review of energy policies and issues in Saudi Arabia, the former Soviet Union, Australia, and Brazil, and an assessment of energy demand in Asian developing economies. Eight chapters are presented in Part I, including one by Kazushi Uemura of Tokyo's Sophia University, who examines Saudi Arabia's oil policy in terms of the Saudi-U.S. coalition. By understanding the nature and framework of the coalition between these parties, the responses of the United States and Saudi Arabia during the recent Gulf Crisis can be explained. The chapter analyzes coalition theory and applies the lessons to the future world oil market. The author concludes that the long-term security of global oil supplies will be a function of the effectiveness of the existing Saudi-U.S. coalition.

Ramon Espinasa and Bernard Mommer, Senior Advisors with Petroléos de Venezuela, S.A., authored Chapter 9 which evaluates Venezuelan oil strategies for the long term. Their chapter describes the main phases of Venezuelan oil policy in the context of the country's contemporary economic development. The analysis is based on the systematic differentiation between oil as a productive activity—the oil industry—and oil as a source of rent for the nation. In 1978, the Venezuelan economy entered a crisis as a consequence of the inherent limitations of oil as a rent multiplier (Dutch disease), together with the collapse of oil as a productive activity. Venezuela's new oil policy seeks to make compatible the rent per barrel, and thus prices, with sustained growth of national oil production. In the long term, Venezuela's oil industry will become more global and diversified and oriented toward joint ventures both in Venezuela and abroad where value added exists, while enjoying a substantial increase in production/refining capacity.

Part II surveys critical issues related to energy economics and planning, and examines the long-term prospects of reformulated gasoline. As recently as three years ago, few could have predicted the development of reformulated gasoline. The very term was not coined until June 1989, at which time no one knew what the composition of such a gasoline would be. However, since its appearance in a proposal by United States' President Bush in June 1989, the concept has jolted the imagination of thousands of professionals involved in motor fuels research, refining and marketing around the world. Chapters 13 and 14 examine historical events leading to the development of reformulated gasoline, and prospects for its usage in the future. Daniel McKay of *Octane Week* concludes his chapter with a projection of the growth of reformulated gasoline in the United States through the 1990s.

The final chapter in Part II, Options Market for Electricity: A Proposal, examines whether a long-term options market can provide incentives for investment in new electricity capacity. Such a market instrument is appropriate to the special characteristics of the electricity industry and capable of providing incentives to producers and consumers for optimum behavior. A principal concern with the U.S. electricity supply is future capacity requirements, as there are persistent predictions of capacity shortfalls in the near future.

Part III of the book addresses the important issue of energy use and environmental quality, including an evaluation of the effectiveness of energy conservation on global warming. An increasingly environmentally conscious world has facilitated a number of studies on how industry can better manage energy utilization and development to coincide with environmental concerns. The prospect for further industrialization in the former Soviet Union and East European nations is of tremendous significance to any long-term forecasts of environmental conditions in Europe and surrounding regions. In his chapter, Eric H. M. Price, the United Kingdom's Energy Undersecretary and Chief Economic Advisor, examines the energy sectors and macroeconomics of the former Soviet Union and the East European Six and their likely impacts on world energy conditions, economic growth, and the environment. Price correctly suggests that the colossal task of restructuring their industries, reforming their societies, and reshaping their economies confronting the former Soviet Union and the East European Six will be a painful and lengthy process.

In statements of governments and in the popular press, one often sees energy conservation touted as the prescription for global warming. With minimal or no loss of economic welfare, so the argument goes, conservation can curb fossil fuel use, hence CO_2 emissions and global warming. Yet it may not be so, according to Harry Saunders of Decision and Risk Analysis Incorporated, of California. While controversial, Saunders' views point to the need for further studies on the economic soundness of various conservation measures promoted by policies to combat global warming.

The world energy market is heavily dependent on hydrocarbons, with nuclear and hydropower accounting for just 12 percent of primary energy consumption in 1991. Despite several oil shocks and the recent Gulf Crisis, active policies to reduce energy use through efficiency gains, and the environmental debate on the problems identified with the consumption of fossil fuels, hydrocarbon consumption has continued to increase. The global energy outlook for the remainder of this decade will depend on assumptions of economic growth, energy prices, energy efficiency, and tightening environmental standards. The following chapters highlight recent developments in the global energy markets, as well as critical issues facing today's energy producing and consuming nations. The variety of subjects covered in the book exemplify an intricate world energy industry influenced by economic forces and societal concerns.

PART ONE:
GLOBAL ENERGY MARKETS AND POLICY

2 Energy Demand in Developing Asian Countries

Robert N. McRae

INTRODUCTION

This paper presents econometric estimates of energy demand† in several Asian developing countries, namely Malaysia, Pakistan, the Philippines, Taiwan, Thailand, and South Korea. Why these countries? Here economic activity has grown much faster than in the industrialized countries of Western Europe and North America. With the exception of the Philippines, so has energy demand. There have been numerous conjectures made about the growth of energy demand in the developing countries, but very few empirical studies in the analysis.

Understanding the determinants of energy demand growth for these countries is going to become increasingly important as their share of world energy consumption continues to increase. Although presently quite small (10% for oil in 1987), the energy share for the Asian developing countries continues to increase, unlike that of the developed countries.

Cross-country studies of this sort have the potential to shed some light on the relationship between energy demand and the pattern of economic development. The economies of these countries are representative of different stages of development. For instance, the per capita gross domestic product (GDP) in 1987 ranges from a low of US$345 in Pakistan to a high of US$4844 in Taiwan. These countries have different levels (and rates of growth) of urbanization and industrialization: variables that, at least in a rudimentary manner, indicate the stage of development. As far as energy policy is concerned, these countries have chosen different approaches to energy pricing. These

---

†The use of non-commercial energy fuels (like firewood and animal waste) is important for developing countries (see Ref. 1). However, these data are not available and so are not included in the analysis.

7

differences in the degree of industrialization, urbanization, income and in energy pricing provide the basis for an interesting cross-sectional study.

Energy demand is estimated for each country separately, and by pooling the countries together. As well as estimating energy demand for the aggregate economy, it is estimated by end-use sector. These sectors are industrial, residential/commercial, and transportation. The response of energy demand tends to differ substantially amongst the end-use sectors, so separate sectoral estimation is important.

DATA

A consistent set of time series data for estimation is available over the period 1973 to 1987 from the Asian Development Bank.[2] The inter-country pooled estimation required comparably measured GDP and prices, which were obtained from Summers and Heston.[3] These data are portrayed in Table 2.1, and in Figs. 2.1 to 2.9.

The contents of Table 2.1 show the variation in energy consumption, economic structure and economic activity between 1973 and 1987 for the six countries under study. The data demonstrate the inter-country differences in population, income, urbanization, industrialization, energy demand, fuel shares, and sectoral end-use shares. Generally, those countries with high growth rates in per capita GDP (and urbanization) usually have a high growth in per capita energy consumption. Those countries with a large transportation component in energy demand also have a large share of oil in the fuel mix. Oil dominates all other energy fuels in the mix (50–90%) for all countries; natural gas is important in Pakistan; coal is important in Taiwan and South Korea; and for the remaining countries, electricity is the only other fuel of importance. The industrial and transportation end-use sectors are the largest, and together amount to between 50 and 85 percent.

Country-specific energy demand per capita, shown in Fig. 2.1, can clearly be grouped according to GDP per capita. There is a one-to-one correspondence in the ranking of the country's energy per capita and GDP per capita, and the countries with the largest average annual growth of GDP per capita (South Korea and Taiwan) also show the largest growth in energy per capita.

The overall real energy price for each country is shown in Fig. 2.2, whereas country-specific energy fuel prices for oil, electricity, coal and natural gas (which are used to generate the overall energy price index) are shown in Figs. 2.3 to 2.5. These figures dramatically demonstrate the differences in energy pricing by country. As far as oil prices are concerned, the sample seems to be divided into those countries that held prices low (Malaysia, Taiwan, and South Korea) and the others. Taiwan has kept its electricity price consistently below those of the other countries. By comparing the fuel prices for oil, electricity, coal and natural gas in dollars per ton of oil equivalent (toe), it is

Table 2.1.
Energy and economic data for some Asian developing countries

	Korea		Malaysia		Pakistan	
	1973	1987	1973	1987	1973	1987
population (mn persons)	34.1	42.1	11.3	16.5	66.9	100.
avg. annual growth (%)	1.5		2.7		2.9	
per capita GDP ($US)	399.	2883.	678.	1878.	101.	345.
avg. annual growth (%)	15.2		7.5		9.2	
urbanization (%)	45.0	67.6	29.0	39.8	25.8	30.6
industrialization (%)	24.7	30.3	15.8	22.4	16.3	17.5
per capita energy (toe)	0.64	1.59	0.50	0.86	0.12	0.21
energy fuel share (%)						
oil	55.0	53.1	90.9	72.8	50.0	45.7
natural gas	0	0.4	0.8	11.3	32.0	32.9
coal	39.3	36.2	0.8	3.3	9.7	10.2
electricity	5.7	10.3	7.4	12.6	8.3	11.2
energy sector share (%)						
residential/commercial	37.8	32.4	9.8	13.0	11.2	19.2
industrial	36.6	37.5	45.2	37.2	39.7	34.3
transportation	11.2	17.3	41.9	39.4	21.3	26.3
agriculture	n/a	n/a	n/a	n/a	7.5	3.6
other	14.4	12.9	3.1	10.5	20.3	16.7
	Philippines		Taiwan		Thailand	
	1973	1987	1973	1987	1973	1987
population (mn persons)	40.0	57.4	15.4	19.5	39.4	53.6
avg. annual growth (%)	2.6		1.7		2.2	
per capita GDP ($US)	268.	603.	690.	4844.	267.	890.
avg. annual growth (%)	6.0		14.9		9.0	
urbanization (%)	34.5	40.7	62.1	75.5	14.4	20.9
industrialization (%)	24.5	24.5	42.4	43.5	16.4	21.6
per capita energy (toe)	0.24	0.22	0.91	1.96	0.22	0.36
energy fuel share (%)						
oil	91.3	77.2	52.5	61.5	91.4	80.3
natural gas	0	0	10.8	3.4	0	0.3
coal	0.2	4.1	21.1	15.6	0.8	4.6
electricity	8.5	18.6	15.5	19.5	7.7	14.9
energy sector share (%)						
residential/commercial	10.2	16.5	9.6	11.1	4.6	12.1
industrial	48.3	47.8	53.5	48.4	29.8	23.9
transportation	37.5	30.5	12.8	17.4	46.6	55.1
agriculture	n/a	n/a	5.5	3.6	11.7	5.9
other	4.0	5.1	18.7	19.5	7.2	3.1

clear that electricity is the most expensive, followed by oil (about one-half of the price of electricity), coal (about one-tenth of the price of oil), and finally, natural gas in Pakistan (about one-half of the price of coal). Those countries with indigenous sources of energy (oil in Malaysia, coal in Taiwan and South Korea, and natural gas in Pakistan) have set fuel prices rather low.

Real GDP per capita, shown in Fig. 2.6, again brings out the differences amongst the countries. The 1980/81 recession had a severe impact only in

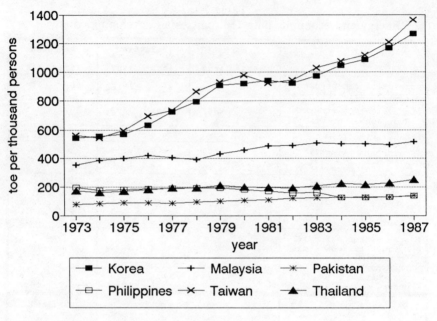

Fig. 2.1. Energy demand per capita.

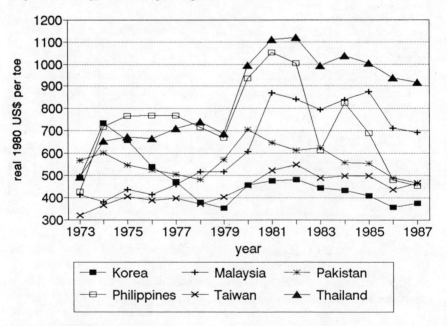

Fig. 2.2. Energy price.

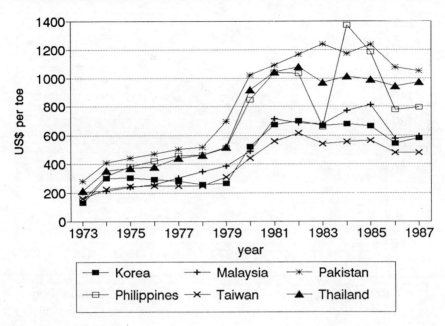

Fig. 2.3. Oil price.

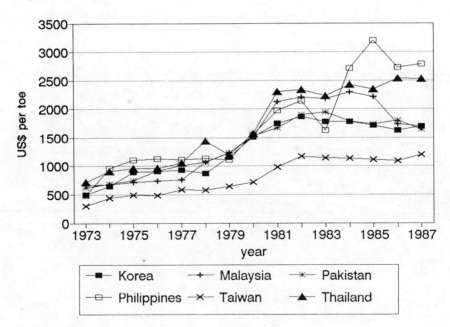

Fig. 2.4. Electricity price.

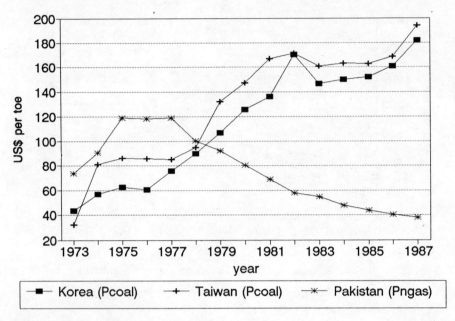

Fig. 2.5. Coal and natural gas price.

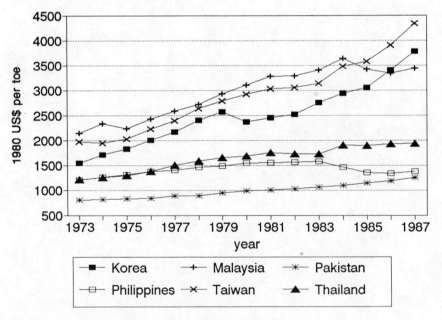

Fig. 2.6. Real gross domestic product per capita.

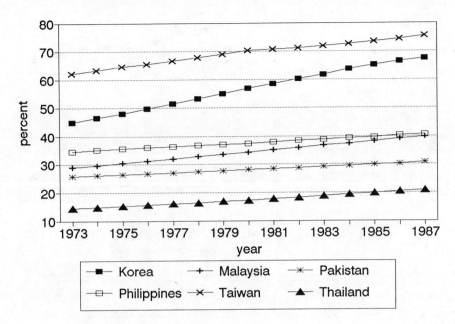

Fig. 2.7. Urbanization rate.

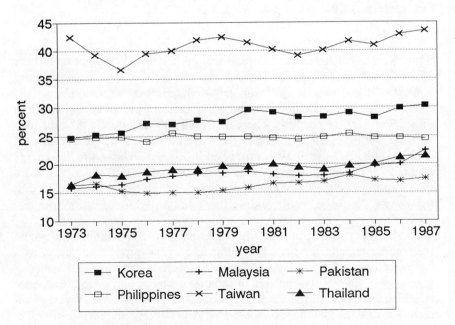

Fig. 2.8. Industrialization rate.

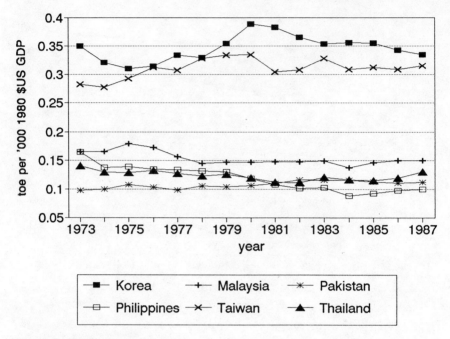

Fig. 2.9. Energy per real GDP.

South Korea. The decline in international oil prices in 1986 appears to have adversely affected Malaysia. The real income gap between the richest and poorest of the countries approximately doubled over the period.

The rates of urbanization and industrialization by country are shown in Figs. 2.7 and 2.8, respectively. There is virtually no variation in the urbanization rate within each country, but there are differences across countries.

Energy demand per GDP is portrayed in Fig. 2.9. This ratio, like energy demand per capita, exhibits a strong correlation with GDP per capita. With the exception of the Philippines, the Asian developing countries included in the sample do not generally feature the gradual decline of energy per real GDP observed in many developed countries over the same time period.

Finally, using data from British Petroleum,[4] Fig. 2.10 exhibits oil demand for broader regions in Asia. The decline in oil consumption in Japan (average annual rate of −.014) is typical of developed countries in North America and Western Europe. The pattern in Japan is in stark contrast to the increase in oil consumption in the developing countries of South Asia (average annual rate of +.05) and those of South East Asia (average annual rate of +.04).

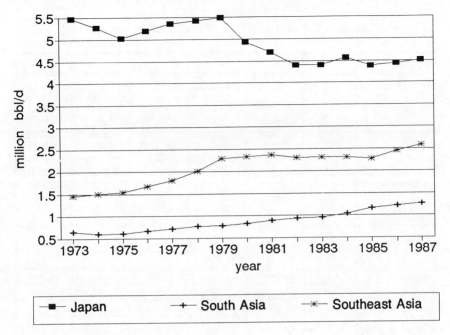

Fig. 2.10. Oil demand by region in Asia.

METHOD

The demand for aggregate energy per capita is econometrically estimated in each country for the whole economy (all-domestic sector), the industrial sector, the transportation sector, and the residential/commercial sector. The independent variables used in the model are real GDP per capita, real price of energy, the rate of urbanization and/or industrialization. A lagged-dependent variable model was estimated for each sector to test for the presence of long-run adjustment dynamics. The models are estimated using ordinary least squares (ols), unless a Cochrane-Orcutt autocorrelation correction (auto) is required. Several functional forms were tested, and the preferred models reported in Tables 2.2 to 2.5.

Aggregate energy consists of different fuels in the various countries—for instance, energy consists of oil and electricity in Malaysia, the Philippines and Thailand; oil, electricity and coal in Korea and Taiwan; and oil, electricity and natural gas in Pakistan. The price of energy for each country is calculated as a quantity-weighted average of the above-mentioned fuels. Fuels other than those mentioned above are used in these countries. They have been

Table 2.2.
Demand for energy per capita: all-domestic sector

independent variables & statistics	Korea	Malaysia	Pakistan	Philip-pines	Taiwan	Thailand
constant	1.273 (2.24)	1.757 (1.01)	1.985 (3.31)	5.535 (6.67)	3.917 (4.47)	-2.082 (-1.39)
ln(GDP/pop)	.272 (2.40)	.463 (1.71)	1.189 (12.2)	.812 (4.07)	.296 (.76)	1.005 (4.93)
ln(P_{energy})	-.151 (-2.84)	.0144 (.13)	.188 (2.13)	-.420 (-6.55)	-.268 (-2.65)	-.259 (-6.04)
urbanization	-	.0130 (1.10)	-	-	.0582 (2.18)	.00295 (.21)
industrial-ization	-	-	-	-	-	-
ln(De/pop).$_{1}$	.807 (6.78)	-	-	.316 (2.82)	-	-
method	ols	auto	ols	ols	auto	auto
rho (auto)	-	.375	-	-	.853	-.23
observations	14	15	15	14	15	15
R^2	.9917	.9314	.9704	.9547	.9901	.9618
adjusted R^2	.9893	.9127	.9655	.9411	.9874	.9514
DurbinWatson	-	1.49	1.76	-	1.73	2.00
Durbin h	-.10	-	-	-1.26	-	-

Notes:

- The demand for energy consists of oil and electricity in Malaysia, Philippines and Thailand; oil, electricity and coal in Korea and Taiwan; and oil, electricity and natural gas in Pakistan. All energy quantities are measured in Mtoe (thousands of tons of oil equivalent). The dependent variable is in logarithmic form.

- The real price of energy (P_{energy}) is a quantity-weighted average energy price, measured in 1980-based local currency per toe.

- Real GDP is measured in 1980-based local currency.

removed from the analysis, however, because their prices are not reported, and they represent only a small share of total energy consumption.

Table 2.6 reports the estimation results for each end-use sector when the data from all six countries have been pooled together. Predicating such analysis is the need to convert energy prices and GDP, denominated in local currency, to a common unit. The exchange rate could be used to convert them to US$; however, problems arise, especially when governments control the value of the exchange rate. As an alternative, we use purchasing power parity data and real GDP per capita data calculated by Summers and Heston.[3] The pooled model employs dummy variables that are used to disentangle struc-

Table 2.3.
Demand for energy per capita: industrial sector

independent variables & statistics	Korea	Malaysia	Pakistan	Philip- pines	Taiwan	Thailand
constant	2.107 (1.37)	.724 (.29)	2.259 (1.94)	4.823 (3.50)	2.485 (3.13)	1.826 (.95)
ln(GDP/pop)	.158 (.86)	.797 (1.74)	.448 (2.18)	1.493 (3.29)	1.107 (9.55)	.622 (2.23)
ln(P_{energy})	-.190 (-1.53)	-.302 (-1.19)	-.168 (-1.04)	-.401 (-5.13)	-.142 (-1.63)	-.441 (-2.89)
industrial- ization	.0306 (1.46)	-	.0307 (1.79)	.0111 (.22)	-	-
ln(De/pop)$_{-1}$	.701 (3.21)	-	.425 (2.24)	-	-	-
method	ols	auto	ols	auto	auto	auto
rho (auto)	-	.441	-	.539	.745	.364
observations	14	15	14	15	15	15
R^2	.9739	.2973	.9630	.8701	.9731	.4680
adjusted R^2	.9623	.1802	.9466	.8347	.9687	.3794
DurbinWatson	-	1.57	-	2.02	1.46	1.79
Durbin h	-2.88	-	1.62	-	-	-

Notes:

- The demand for energy consists of oil and electricity in Malaysia, Philippines and Thailand; oil, electricity and coal in Korea and Taiwan; and oil, electricity and natural gas in Pakistan. All energy quantities are measured in Mtoe (thousands of tons of oil equivalent).

- The dependent variable is in logarithmic form.

- The real price of energy (P_{energy}) is a quantity-weighted average energy price, measured in 1980-based local currency per toe.

- Real GDP is measured in 1980-based local currency.

tural differences (unrelated to the economic explanatory variables) in energy demand per capita between the countries.

ECONOMETRIC RESULTS

The econometric results are contained in Tables 2.2 to 2.6. The short-run and long-run price and GDP elasticities of demand are reported in Tables 2.7a and 2.7b. Both the short-run and long-run elasticities are given only for those equations with a lagged-dependent variable. The elasticities for the static

Table 2.4.
Demand for energy per capita: transportation sector

independent variables & statistics	Korea	Malaysia	Pakistan	Philippines	Taiwan	Thailand
constant	1.187 (.70)	-1.429 (-.60)	1.556 (1.75)	2.912 (6.66)	1.605 (1.59)	1.370 (.44)
ln(GDP/pop)	1.040 (4.64)	.916 (3.52)	.328 (.88)	.584 (3.72)	.157 (.48)	.459 (1.10)
ln(P_{energy})	-.436 (-4.19)	-.134 (-.46)	-.191 (-1.42)	-.316 (-5.85)	-.142 (-1.70)	-.343 (-5.20)
urbanization	-	-	-	-	-	.0944 (3.16)
ln(De/pop)$_{-1}$	.363 (2.63)	-	.912 (4.22)	.663 (13.4)	.835 (3.44)	-
method	ols	auto	ols	ols	ols	ols
rho (auto)	-	.532	-	-	-	-
observations	14	15	14	14	14	15
R^2	.9600	.8100	.9720	.9801	.9912	.9700
adjusted R^2	.9480	.7784	.9635	.9741	.9885	.9618
DurbinWatson	-	1.84	-	-	-	2.32
Durbin h	-1.41	-	-1.64	-1.17	-.471	-

Notes:

- The demand for energy consists of oil products used in transportation, except jet fuel. All energy quantities are measured in Mtoe (thousands of tons of oil equivalent).

- The dependent variable is in logarithmic form.

- The real price of energy (P_{energy}) is based on oil products only, and is calculted as a quantity-weighted average, measured in 1980-based local currency per toe.

- Real GDP is measured in 1980-based local currency.

models are reported as short-run, although in fact they are similar to the long-run elasticities (obtained from models estimated, but not reported).

In general, the statistical fit of the equations is excellent. Two-thirds of the models have an adjusted R^2 over .95, and only 5 equations (out of 28) have an adjusted R^2 below .90. Only three coefficients have an incorrect sign (energy price for all-domestic in Malaysia, for all-domestic in Pakistan, and for residential/commercial in Korea). For the country-specific models, about 40 percent of the coefficients for GDP and about 50 percent of the coefficients for energy price were statistically insignificant at the 95 percent confidence level. I attribute at least some of the statistical insignificance to lack of sufficient degrees of freedom. In the pooled models, with their large degrees of

Table 2.5.
Demand for energy per capita: residential/commercial sector

independent variables & statistics	Korea	Malaysia	Pakistan	Philip-pines	Taiwan	Thailand
constant	-1.183 (-2.19)	-6.817 (-2.43)	1.410 (2.53)	2.638 (8.17)	1.675 (2.06)	-22.18 (-7.28)
ln(GDP/pop)	.641 (5.35)	1.418 (3.08)	.637 (1.83)	.683 (4.42)	.221 (.97)	2.878 (5.56)
ln(P_{energy})	.211 (2.66)	-.312 (-1.89)	-.173 (-2.11)	-.208 (-2.55)	-.140 (-1.77)	-.264 (-.91)
urbanization	-	.0397 (2.25)	-	.0292 (2.09)	-	-
ln(De/pop).1	-	-	.749 (5.03)	-	.735 (3.68)	-
method	auto	ols	ols	ols	ols	auto
rho (auto)	.375	-	-	-	-	.349
observations	15	15	14	15	14	15
R^2	.9683	.9475	.9858	.6629	.9912	.9256
adjusted R^2	.9630	.9332	.9815	.5710	.9886	.9132
DurbinWatson	1.43	2.49	-	2.23	-	1.80
Durbin h	-	-	-.83	-	-.97	-

Notes:

- The demand for energy consists of oil and electricity in Malaysia, Philippines and Thailand; oil, electricity and coal in Korea; and oil, electricity and natural gas in Pakistan and Taiwan. All energy quantities are measured in Mtoe (thousands of tons of oil equivalent).

- The dependent variable is in logarithmic form.

- The real price of energy (P_{energy}) is a quantity-weighted average energy price, measured in 1980-based local currency per toe.

- Real GDP is measured in 1980-based local currency.

freedom, none of the GDP or energy price coefficients were statistically insignificant. Examining coefficients by country, one notices that energy price is statistically insignificant for all sectors in Malaysia and Pakistan, and for most sectors in Taiwan; and real GDP per capita is statistically insignificant for most sectors in Pakistan and Taiwan.

I was disappointed that the rate of industrialization and/or urbanization variables were not more useful. Their inclusion in the models was often rejected due to statistical insignificance, the wrong sign, or superior performance of an alternative model. Frequently, a choice had to be made between a model with these variables and a dynamic model—with the latter often being chosen. Whenever the urbanization or industrialization variable is included

Table 2.6.
Demand for energy per capita by end-use sector (six country pool: Korea, Malaysia, Pakistan, Philippines, Taiwan, Thailand)

independent variables and statistics	all-domestic	industrial	transport	residential/ commercial
constant	-.312 (-1.33)	-.373 (-1.14)	-1.357 (-2.71)	-.519 (-1.54)
dummy variable, Korea	.359 (6.40)	.757 (7.55)	.0103 (.18)	.261 (3.46)
dummy variable, Malaysia	.0818 (2.78)	.452 (6.03)	.0949 (1.49)	.00511 (.14)
dummy variable, Philippines	-.0119 (-.35)	.290 (3.88)	-.0413 (-.61)	-.0552 (-2.12)
dummy variable, Taiwan	.319 (6.08)	.662 (4.72)	.0591 (1.10)	.0744 (1.36)
dummy variable, Thailand	.0600 (2.55)	.0883 (1.91)	.156 (3.22)	-.0127 (-.22)
ln(GDP/pop)	.377 (6.92)	.451 (7.57)	.583 (6.20)	.247 (3.86)
ln(P_{energy})	-.103 (-5.61)	-.177 (-7.47)	-.189 (-5.94)	-.0842 (-5.64)
urbanization	-	-	-	.00144 (.72)
industrial-ization	-	.00957 (1.68)	-	-
ln(De/pop)$_{-1}$	.656 (14.0)	.473 (8.51)	.588 (8.66)	.781 (17.7)
method	pool	pool	pool	pool
observations	84	84	84	84
Buse R^2	.9992	.9989	.9945	.9975
Durbin h	.23	-.03	.34	.01

Notes:

- The same notes as for other Tables, except real P_{energy} and real GDP are converted to 1980-based international currency ($I).

in the model, it leads to smaller (absolute) values for the GDP and energy price coefficients.

In the pooled models about one-half of the dummy variables are statistically insignificant at the 95 percent confidence level. Statistical insignificance implies no difference in the constant term (for the sectoral energy demand per capita) between Pakistan and the particular country being represented by the dummy variable. Not surprisingly, most of the insignificant dummy variables are in the transportation and residential/commercial sectors.

Table 2.7a.

Price elasticities of demand by country and end-use sector

	Korea	Malay-sia	Pakis-tan	Philip-pines	Taiwan	Thai-land	pooled
all-domestic							
short-run	-.15*	.01	.19	-.42*	-.27*	-.26*	-.10*
long-run	-.78			-.61			-.30
industrial							
short-run	-.19	-.30	-.17	-.40*	-.14	-.44*	-.18*
long-run	-.64		-.29				-.34
transport							
short-run	-.44*	-.13	-.19	-.32*	-.14	-.34*	-.19*
long-run	-.68		-2.17	-.94	-.86		-.46
residential/ commercial							
short-run	.21*	-.31	-.17	-.21*	-.14	-.26	-.08*
long-run			-.69		-.53		-.38

Table 2.7b.

GDP elasticities of demand by country and end-use sector

	Korea	Malay-sia	Pakis-tan	Philip-pines	Taiwan	Thai-land	pooled
all-domestic							
short-run	.27*	.46	1.19*	.81*	.30	1.01*	.38*
long-run	1.41			1.19			1.10
industrial							
short-run	.16	.80	.45	1.49*	1.11*	.62*	.45*
long-run	.53		.78				.86
transport							
short-run	1.04*	.92*	.33	.58*	.16	.46	.58*
long-run	1.63		3.73	1.73	.95		1.42
residential/ commercial							
short-run	.64*	1.42*	.64	.68*	.22	2.88*	.25*
long-run			2.54		.83		1.13

* Indicates that the elasticity is derived from a variable which is statistically significant at the 95 percent confidence level.

Surprisingly, only one-half of the models are of the dynamic form. For those models, Tables 2.7a and 2.7b contain both short-run and long-run elasticities. With only one exception (long-run transportation in Pakistan), all price elasticities are inelastic. Not surprisingly, the residential/commercial sector is the least price elastic. Generally, the transportation sector is the most price elastic.

Slightly over one-half of the GDP per capita elasticities are elastic. There do not appear to be any consistent patterns across sectors or countries for the GDP elasticities.† When comparing the GDP elasticities, it is useful to remember that those models which include either the urbanization or industrialization variable will have lower GDP elasticities. In fact, all the low GDP elasticities in Table 2.7b are from such models. The results of the pooled models show long-run GDP elasticities of .86 in the industrial sector, 1.13 in the residential/commercial sector, and 1.42 in the transportation sector.

CONCLUSION

Some of the counter-intuitive results are due to the stage of economic development for the economy (see Ref. 5). For instance, rural electrification programs in countries like Thailand have led to problems identifying significant energy price effects on energy demand. Similar problems have arisen in countries like South Korea where residential consumers are shifting away from coal to oil for the sake of convenience despite the relative prices.

The fact that urbanization and/or industrialization do not seem to play an important part in explaining energy demand per capita was disappointing. This seems to imply the need to look deeper into the nature of the sector in each country if one is to identify development-specific factors affecting energy demand. However, it is encouraging that Jones,[6] using 1980 cross-sectional data, was successful in finding urbanization (and sometimes industrialization) to be statistically significant.

It is beneficial to be able to examine the sectoral demand elasticities from so many developing countries. The diversity and extent of results, however, make it difficult to generalize. Since the pooled models have the strongest econometric properties, I will concentrate on them. The long-run (short-run) price elasticities of demand are contained in a tight range of −.30 to −.46 (−.08 to −.19). The long-run (short-run) GDP elasticities of demand are somewhat more diverse, ranging from .86 to 1.42 (.25 to .58). Finally, it is obvious that the all-domestic sector (aggregate economy) elasticities are different from the individual sector-specific elasticities, which reinforces the need for separate sectoral estimation.

ACKNOWLEDGMENTS

I wish to acknowledge the financial support of the Social Sciences and Humanities Research Council of Canada.

---

†It should be pointed out that real GDP per capita is not the best "income/activity" variable to use in the residential and transportation sectors, but it is the best available.

REFERENCES

1. R. Bhatia, "Energy Demand Analysis in Developing Countries: A Review," *The Energy Journal: Special LDC Issue,* 8, pp.1–33 (1987).
2. Asian Development Bank, *Energy Indicators of Major Developing Member Countries of ADB,* Manila (May 1989).
3. R. Summers and A. Heston, "A New Set of International Comparisons of Real Product and Price Levels: Estimates for 130 Countries, 1950–1985," *The Review of Income and Wealth,* 34, 1, pp. 1–25 (March 1988).
4. British Petroleum, *BP Statistical Review of World Energy,* London (1988).
5. Asian Development Bank, *Energy Policy Experiences of Asian Countries,* Manila (1987).
6. D. W. Jones, "Urbanization and Energy Use in Economic Development," *The Energy Journal,* 10, 4, pp. 29–43 (1989).

3 Energy Policy, Oil Markets, and the Middle East War: Did We Learn the Lessons of the 1970s?

George Horwich

INTRODUCTION

After a decade of quiescent world oil markets, interrupted only by occasional, warmly received price collapses, supply was sharply disrupted in August 1990 when Iraq stormed into Kuwait. A world embargo brought exports from both countries to a halt and sent crude oil prices skyrocketing 118 percent by October.† The suddenness and acceleration of the price rise exceeded that of the 1979–80 shock, though prices following the invasion of Kuwait neither rose quite as much nor remained as high as long as they did after the Iranian revolution. Nevertheless, there was plenty of opportunity this time to repeat the policy mistakes of 1973–81 or, indeed, to avoid them. How did we do during this crisis and after?

I offer the following appraisal of our performance. On the positive side: (1) paradoxically, we did not, just as we did not in the 1970s, resort to arms to secure the Persian Gulf oil supply. Although we quickly mobilized and went to war in January, oil security and oil prices were not our military objectives. We stood ready this time, as in the past, to make our primary response to the rise in oil prices an economic one. And even though there may be economic benefits from our military intervention, they were not the motivating force; (2) we avoided the whole panoply of price ceilings and mandatory al-

I thank Sam Kazanow, who provided computer support and valuable advice at various stages of the research.

†Wherever possible, I use the average quarterly acquisition cost of oil imports by all member nations of the International Energy Agency as my source for oil prices since 1985. See Table 3.1.

locations that marked our dismal 1970s response. Although excessive "jaw-boning" by the administration may have inhibited some price movements of petroleum products, domestic crude oil and product prices were essentially free to approach market clearing, which they did; and (3) we (and our allies in the International Energy Agency) discreetly avoided implementing the oil sharing provision of the International Energy Program, even though, by the rules, the loss of world oil supply was sufficient to trigger it. Indeed, data I have collected confirm the continuing ability of the uncontrolled international crude oil market to adjust to shocks with reasonable speed and efficiency that no international allocating authority could hope to exceed or even match.

On the negative side, I consider (4) the failure to immediately and vigorously draw down the U.S. Strategic Petroleum Reserve—in pure economic terms, a costly error. Doing so could have kept oil prices from rising very much at all last fall. Not doing so, I believe, will eventually be charged with lopping off some measurable chunk of the GNP. But there could have been non-economic, indirect economic, and essentially strategic reasons for the failure of drawdown, and these are discussed.

I will address each of these four points, although not in the enumerated order.

NO BLOOD FOR OIL

I think I would have a difficult time convincing critics of the American military effort in the Middle East that we were not there to secure access to the region's oil. Even defenders of our policy saw the security of oil supply as one, if only one, of several legitimate reasons for our intervention. One implication of the conventional wisdom, voiced endlessly in Congress, the media, and on college campuses, is that the war would not have been necessary if we were less dependent on oil imports, bought less oil from the Middle East, and had a national energy policy that reduced energy use overall.

The belief that access to oil was the linchpin of our military effort or was even a contributing factor to it does not stand up under scrutiny. The assumption that a 118 percent rise of the world price of oil was sufficient to merit a military response must explain why the 12-fold nominal increase from 1973 to 1981 was not sufficient. Throughout the earlier period (during or just before which OPEC appropriated private oil properties on a vast scale), as Islamic fundamentalism descended on Iran and threatened its neighbors, and Iraq attempted to seize Iranian oil fields, few voices were heard in favor of sending a U.S. expeditionary force to the Persian Gulf in order to stabilize the price of oil. Neither Republican nor Democratic administrations nor Congress seriously entertained a military initiative for that purpose.

Painful as the oil price shocks were, they were viewed as economic disturbances to which the only appropriate response was an internal economic adjustment. And adjust we did. Once domestic crude oil and petroleum product prices were permitted to rise, we substituted alternative fuels and conserved our use of all energy to an extraordinary degree. Between 1973 and 1986, real GNP grew by over one-third—$1.1 trillion on a base of $3.1 trillion in 1986 prices—without the use of any additional energy. The energy/GNP ratio fell by one quarter. At the same time, we, along with our Western European and Japanese allies, built an enormous strategic oil reserve as protection against future supply interruptions.

What was different about the 1990 disruption in the Middle East? Iraq's invasion of Kuwait and the subsequent United Nations embargo cost the world four million barrels per day (b/d) of oil exports (about eight percent of noncommunist world supply) and, as noted, caused the price of oil to somewhat more than double. The production cutback and price rise would have been less in the absence of the embargo and, in any case, prices rose less than in 1973-1974, when crude oil prices quintupled, or in 1979-81, when they rose by 150 percent. The 1990 increase, moreover, was added to a real price of oil that had fallen during most of the 1980s to a level that was only about double the 1973 pre-disruption price.

So why did we respond militarily? Clearly, if Iraq, Kuwait, and, for example, Saudi Arabia had peaceably and voluntarily agreed to restrict their combined oil exports by four million b/d, we would have as in the past denounced the action, hurled verbal missiles of unerring accuracy, and not mobilized a single troop. As before, we would have tightened our belts and made the necessary adjustment: rapidly and smoothly, if we allowed prices, tempered only by drawdown of the strategic reserve, to rise freely; slowly and fitfully if, by mandatory controls and price ceilings, we chose to prolong the agony.

What was plainly new was the perception of Saddam Hussein as an unrestrained aggressor with de facto or potential possession of the most lethal weapons of destruction imaginable—weapons that in the near future could be directed at us, as well as Saddam's neighbors. The only direct relevance of oil to our decision to fight was the collateral effort to deny *him* the use of Kuwait's oil revenues to finance his arsenal. It was not oil for *our* use that explains our military response. The suggestion of some that we would not have mobilized in support of a Kuwait that produced soybeans instead of oil misses the point. Saddam would not be likely to seize a soybean kingdom unless soybeans, like oil, commanded a rent capable of sustaining his war machine.

In spite of all this, President Bush and others in his administration argued that keeping the planet's most plentiful oil reserves out of Saddam's hands was critical to "jobs" and the general economic welfare of the world community, further justifying our military response. The President was probably correct, but only because a more secure oil supply was a fortuitous by-product of the destruction of Saddam's ability to wage war.

Even tyrants, constrained by the market, tend to produce and price their exports so as not to discourage too many buyers or encourage too many competitors.[1,2]† But Saddam's ruthless pursuit of his imperial goals could easily have suppressed any normal price-optimizing behavior on his part and destroyed any recognizable stability of the world oil supply. Once again, I believe market forces, supplemented by the world's strategic petroleum reserves, were perfectly capable of offsetting and adjusting to instability without requiring us to intervene militarily. Nevertheless, having prevailed over Saddam in war also promises to stabilize the supply, but only incidentally and without thereby becoming the real goal of our military initiative.

Ironically, the coalition might plausibly have linked its military move to the security of oil supply if it had guessed that Saddam would torch Kuwait's oil wells, that the resulting fires would rage for months before being extinguished, and that the fields might suffer permanent damage as a result. In this light, the interventionist argument could have been that Saddam, a perennial aggressor, would constantly expose the fields of any number of Persian Gulf countries to destruction by either himself or someone else and that it would be best to wrest control from him sooner rather than later. But I submit that no one anticipated this scenario. I did not believe that the wells could be so readily or severely and permanently damaged, and that surely was the conventional wisdom.[3]

NO FORMAL INTERFERENCE WITH THE MARKET

Our second good policy deed was not to impose the price controls and mandatory allocations that proved so destructive of the fuel production and distribution system in the 1970s. At its height, the price of gasoline rose 24 percent, reflecting the rise in the price of crude oil. Consumers grumbled and bought less fuel, the White House tilted at the oil companies and debated endlessly, but did nothing else. Most important, with one passing exception (discussed below), the fuel system remained intact: there were no queues, early closings, delayed deliveries, nor any visible signs of interference with free-market activity at the user or wholesale level. The public, for the most part, seemed to understand that Saddam Hussein, and not the American Petroleum Institute or the corner gas station, was responsible for the price increases and that massive government regulations would not reduce the costs. All this

---

†Henderson speculated that Saddam would aim at most for a $30 per barrel price, hardly a basis for war.

was in marked contrast to the panicked, counterproductive, and Byzantine regulations that government in the 1970s imposed in a vain attempt to punish the American oil companies; or to the behavior of the American president who, in 1979, ignored the advice of his energy policy team and his own better judgment and listened instead to his political advisers who urged him not to remove the price ceilings on gasoline, as he was free to do, because doing so would cost him the next election.

Petroleum product prices, however, did not rise last fall as much in the United States as in Europe and Japan, despite the relative uniformity of world crude oil prices (described below) and the absence of price controls in this country. Philip Verleger[4] first called attention to the smaller increases in gasoline and light fuel oil prices in the United States than in Europe both on the spot market and, net of taxes, at retail. Verleger attributed the price discrepancy to the administration's "jawboning," which, he argued, was excessive and amounted to de facto control of the prices of major petroleum products. He also cited the administration's strongly negative attitude toward product exports, which increased briefly in the fall and, if continued, would have contributed to price equalization.

As a general proposition, however, one has to question the assumption that lighter products, such as gasoline and light fuel oil, are really part of an international market. Oil tankers have to be scrubbed before they can be loaded with gasoline and other light products, a time consuming and expensive procedure. Because of that and the fact that refineries are located almost everywhere, very little of these products move in international waters other than from nearby offshore sites. Accordingly, not only would the prices of light products around the world fail to move synchronously, it is unlikely that their levels would be equal even after adjustment for differences in national tax rates.

The data confirm the relative geographic disparity of gasoline prices. As a benchmark against which to compare these prices, we examine the dispersion of crude oil prices paid by the six largest importers in the Organization for Economic Cooperation and Development (OECD). The prices are taken from the analysis of the crude market during the 1990 crisis described in Table 3.1 (see also Ref. 5). For the period 1985:2 (second quarter of 1985) to 1991:1, the mean quarterly coefficient of variation of crude oil prices is 3.5 percent, taking the coefficient as the ratio of the standard deviation to the mean price of each quarter, and 9.8 percent, using the range (the highest price minus the lowest price of each quarter) instead of the standard deviation. During this period, the comparable coefficients for gasoline prices, net of taxes, were 55.3 percent and 180.1 percent. The markedly smaller dispersion of prices in the crude oil market is reflective of a market that is truly international and one that has exhibited a reasonably rapid rate of adjustment following disturbances.[6]

Table 3.1. The mean price of crude oil and the range of prices paid by major importers in four normal (N) and four shock (S) periods, quarterly, 1985–1991 (in dollars per barrel, except where noted)

	Mean price (1)		Price range (2)	Ratio: (2)/(1) (percent) (3)	Adjusted price range (3)−.052(1) (4)	Ratio: (4)/(1) (percent) (5)
1985:1	27.82	(−0.7)*	1.31	4.7	−0.14	−0.5
N 1985:2	27.65	(−0.6)	0.80	2.9	−0.64	−2.3
1985:3	26.78	(−3.1)	1.13	4.2	−0.26	−1.0
1985:4	27.44	(2.5)	1.81	6.6	0.38	1.4
1986:1	21.49	(−21.7)	5.06	23.5	3.94	18.3
1986:2	13.21	(−38.5)	0.86	6.5	0.17	1.3
S 1986:3	11.74	(−11.1)	2.02	17.2	1.41	12.0
1986:4	13.54	(15.3)	0.89	6.6	0.19	1.4
1987:1	16.93	(25.0)	1.23	7.3	0.35	2.1
1987:2	18.02	(6.5)	0.51	2.8	−0.43	−2.4
N 1987:3	18.58	(3.1)	0.61	3.3	−0.36	−1.9
1987:4	17.90	(−3.6)	1.28	7.2	0.35	2.0
S 1988:1	16.05	(−10.3)	2.76	17.2	1.93	12.0
N 1988:2	15.77	(−1.8)	1.09	6.9	0.27	1.7
1988:3	14.49	(−8.1)	1.41	9.7	0.66	4.5
1988:4	13.14	(−9.3)	1.11	8.4	0.43	3.2
S 1989:1	16.16	(23.0)	1.77	11.0	0.93	5.8
1989:2	18.29	(13.2)	1.26	6.9	0.31	1.7
1989:3	17.12	(−6.4)	.78	4.6	−0.11	−0.6
N 1989:4	18.18	(6.2)	1.49	8.2	0.54	3.0
1990:1	19.40	(6.7)	0.99	5.1	−0.02	−0.1
1990:2	15.86	(−18.2)	2.07	13.0	1.25	7.8
S 1990:3	21.86	(37.8)	5.28	24.2	4.14	19.0
1990:4	31.57	(44.4)	4.66	14.8	3.02	9.6
1991:1	20.94	(−33.7)	3.40	16.2	2.31	11.0

*This column indicates percent change over previous quarter.

Source: International Energy Agency, Energy Prices and Taxes, various quarterly issues.

During the three crisis quarters, 1990:3, 1990:4, and 1991:1, net gasoline prices (dollars per liter) changed in the United States by $.034, $.050, and −$.062, while, in the next six largest OECD countries, by an average of $.111, $.114, and −$.080 (see Ref. 5). Several factors could easily account for the smaller increases in U.S. prices. Between August 1 and December 31, 1990, privately held U.S. petroleum stocks declined from 1,062 million barrels to 995 million barrels, a reduction of 6.3 percent.[7] In OECD Europe during the same period, stocks rose from 1,120 to 1,133 million barrels, and in Japan from 557 to 577 million barrels.[7] Clearly, U.S. stock adjustments tended to depress prices, while the opposite occurred in other OECD countries.

A second factor tending to depress U.S. gasoline prices relative to those overseas was the weaker U.S. economy during fall 1990, and hence demand for petroleum products. In 1990 the real GNP growth rates in the United States, the European Community, and Japan were, in order, 0.9, 2.9, and 6.1 percent (see Ref. 8, p. 411). Finally, the dependence of Europe and Japan on Kuwaiti refinery output, which, of course, was completely cut off, may have contributed to their greater price increases.

Verleger's claim that administration "jawboning" imposed de facto price ceilings on U.S. petroleum products is also inconsistent with the almost total absence in fall 1990 of the familiar market pathologies (shortages, queuing) that accompany binding controls. Whether prices are held down by edict or voluntarily by sellers while supply quantities remain at profit-maximizing levels, demand will exceed supply. Buyers, whether at wholesale or retail, will scramble for the limited supply and eventually dissipate the gain of low-priced purchases in additional costs of search.

An alternative explanation of the industry's response is that the larger refiners and distributors decided during the crisis both to limit their price increases and to supply more than the profit-maximizing quantity. Prices then fell to a lower level at which markets cleared. Companies, in effect, would have traded current profits for what they hoped would be freedom from direct government control and greater long-run profits.

This last scenario is not implausible, although it contains a number of critical links that will not be easily identified in the data. In one well publicized case of price restraint at the retail level, the outcome was a shortage and a scramble, not the smooth lower price and greater market-equilibrium quantity described above. In late August, ARCO announced that it would freeze gasoline prices at its service stations, which are located in five Western states. It did so and experienced a massive onrush of profit-maximizing consumers, many of whom may still contribute to a greater ARCO market share. The pandemonium and the policy ended two weeks later when ARCO ran out of supplies and was forced to replenish inventories at spot prices that exceeded the pump price. Thereafter ARCO considered freezing its profit margins, but before actually doing so, again announced a price freeze, this time on the eve of the U.S. air strike. The price of crude oil plunged $10 on that occasion, however, rendering all extraordinary price-moderating initiatives superfluous.

DRAWDOWN OF THE RESERVE

The record with respect to use of the Strategic Petroleum Reserve (SPR) is, on its face, unsatisfactory. Only 21 million barrels of the 600 million in the reserve were sold. A sale of 3.9 million barrels was carried out in October and November 1990 as a drawdown demonstration exercise. Later 17.3 million barrels were sold under an arrangement coordinated by the International Energy Agency (IEA) and timed to coincide with the outbreak of hostilities in January 1991. Members of the IEA other than the United States drew an equal amount.[9]

The IEA governing board had originally planned to draw twice as much oil as it did, with a view to compensating for any war-related interruptions of supply. But when the price of crude oil dropped $10 on the opening day of the allied air strike, no bids beyond the original 34 million barrels were accepted.†

The return to normalcy in world oil markets, despite the loss of Iraqi and Kuwaiti supplies, was essentially the result of surge production by Saudi Arabia and Venezuela and a softening of world demand in response to weakening economies. Prices were in the $30 range, however, until the end of the year. For five months, August through December, prices on average were thus about 90 percent higher than they had been in the three months prior to the Iraqi invasion of Kuwait. That was a sizable price shock for which econometric models of the 1970s and 1980s would predict a GNP loss of roughly $50 to $100 billion.‡

Early and vigorous SPR drawdown could have flattened the price trajectory.§ But the President, who has the responsibility for initiating drawdown, resisted the pro-drawdown advice of his energy secretary. The explanations coming from the White House were bizarre. A recurring pronouncement claimed that there was no oil "shortage." If that term referred to the technical economic definition of an imbalance between ex ante supply and demand,

---

†An action equivalent to drawdown was the failure of the Department of Energy to acquire any oil for the SPR after July 1990. At recent rates of acquisition, that could amount to 12 million barrels during the five months, August through December 1990.

‡Most econometric models found a GNP/price of oil elasticity of −0.02 to −0.04. For a 90 percent increase in the price of oil during a five month period, or an average annual increase of $5/12 \times .90 = 0.38$ percent, the impact on GNP in 1990 would be 0.38 (−.02) to 0.38 (−.04) or −0.8 to −1.5 percent. The fall in a $5.5 trillion GNP would thus range from $44 billion to $82 billion. See Ref. 10.

§The SPR has a drawdown/delivery capacity of 3.5 million b/d. At that rate, the reserve could have replaced 87.5 percent of the four million b/d Iraq-Kuwait shortfall for almost six months. As a practical matter, a drawdown of half of capacity—1.75 million b/d—would have significantly limited the price increases and strengthened the general economy. At the same time, it is highly unlikely that the roughly equivalent reserves of other IEA countries would not have also been drawn, with or without a formal agreement (see below).

the claim was true precisely because the administration had not prevented prices from rising to their market-clearing levels. But there *was* a shortfall or supply reduction and, more to the point, a sharp price increase that is the true measure of the cost of the disruption.† At other times the White House announced that SPR drawdown would amount to "price control," in which the administration wanted no part. But this confuses the control of prices through ceilings that prevent markets from functioning with the moderating of prices and the smoothing of market adjustment that comes from adding to supply out of stocks. Responsible decision makers do not confuse these two policies.

We can only guess why the administration failed to put the reserve to its intended use. Early in the crisis it might have delayed drawdown out of fear that the Saudi fields would fall to Iraq. But by late September or early October the Saudi frontier was protected. At that juncture, one might suspect the role of the military, whose legendary appetite for fuel sometimes seems unlimited. But it is hard to believe that the Department of Defense wanted to retain the entire SPR, a roughly equal strategic reserve held by the other IEA members, the Saudi fields, and a healthy line of credit that could be converted into oil almost anywhere in the world as backup for the total military requirement in the Middle East of 500,000 b/d. I think the explanation for SPR hoarding must lie elsewhere.

One possibility, which I offer as pure conjecture, makes the failure of drawdown defensible and the convoluted rhetoric of the White House somewhat understandable. I suggest that the administration was well aware of the power and the value of timely SPR use. But it chose instead to allow fuel prices to remain high as long as possible to help persuade American and world opinion of the menace of Saddam Hussein to world peace and stability. It is easy to forget the administration's determination to destroy Saddam's military

---

†Non-economists tend to be misled by the fact that following a supply loss, the market *quantity* supplied may be unchanged or even somewhat higher. This does not mean the disruption has been offset. In the petroleum market, where the short-run schedules tend to be relatively steep, a leftward shift of supply, when traced along demand to a new equilibrium, will result in a substantial increase in price and a small reduction in quantity. Even though at the pre-disruption price, the loss of Iraqi-Kuwaiti exports is four million b/d, the sharp price increase induces an upward movement along the disrupted supply schedule (the increase in Saudi and other production) that will replace much of the lost exports. In addition, in the absence of SPR drawdown the supply shock could trigger increased private stockpiling, shifting demand to the right and further increasing price and the quantity supplied. At this point, it is possible that there is no *net* reduction in the observed market quantity.

In all this the only reliable indicator of the cost of disruption is the rise in price. Increases in quantity supplied induced by the rise in price are desirable and in fact limit the price increase. But it is unlikely that the quantity level will be maintained as absolute supply and demand elasticities increase over time and any induced stockpiling runs its course. The rise in price is still the bottom-line impact to which the economy must ultimately adjust.

capability and the unlikely prospect of securing Congressional and United Nations support for such an undertaking in fall of 1990.

An alternative explanation some have mentioned is that SPR drawdown would have violated an implicit agreement with the Saudis. In exchange for a period of high prices, it is said, our desert hosts promised to maintain their surge production for the entire period of the embargo and any military engagement that followed. In the 1979–80 disruption, the Saudis had cut back production three or four months after the fall of the Shah, thereby maintaining prices at the higher crisis level for an extended period.

With the benefit of hindsight, I seriously doubt that the Saudis, fighting for their national existence, wanted or were able to exercise this kind of leverage over their protectors. For the first time, moreover, temporarily higher prices may have been in our common interest. As noted, we may have wanted high prices for strategic purposes. And, even more concretely, those prices were financing very substantial Saudi outlays in support of the allied mobilization. In fact, Saudi incremental revenues, from August through December, earned at prices above the July level, are almost exactly equal to the Saudi pledge of $16.8 billion in support of the military effort![1] For a while, high oil prices belonged equally on both sides of our balance sheet!

A final consideration bearing on SPR use is the almost universal belief that drawdown creates inordinate benefits for other countries at our expense. This administration, no less than its predecessors, sees coordinated drawdown among all IEA members as essential to spreading the costs. And the effort to achieve coordination may have been a factor in the 1990 failure to draw down promptly and expeditiously.

Although more drawdown is usually better than less, nations benefit differentially from a decrease in the price of oil and have different preferred mechanisms for bringing about that decrease.[2] I seriously doubt that coordination can be economically justified for every nation or any particular nation, even if it did not promote delay. On a first approximation, the cost of a disruption to a nation is the change in price times its total quantity of energy used.[10] Crude oil price tends to equalize for all users with relative speed in the world oil market (see below). As a fraction of GNP, energy use varies widely and is much higher for the United States than for any advanced country in the world except Canada. Our per capita economic benefits from our stock drawdown and the induced price decline are thereby as great as, and generally much greater than, anyone else's.

Although unilateral use of SPR will benefit others, along with ourselves, so will private stock drawdown, reduced demand, and all other adaptive measures that reduce the price of oil undertaken by other countries. Free ridership is not a problem because it applies to every price-mitigating action taken by everybody and nobody can afford not to take such actions in some degree.

Unilateral drawdown by the United States is, in fact, more likely than not to trigger drawdown by others, who stand to get lower prices from any future sale of their reserves. Coordinating drawdown with the IEA countries may have become an excuse for inaction, as many of us feared it would.[12] It is also one more political element in a decision that in general should be based on economic and strategic considerations.

To meet economic goals, it is a mistake to burden government with the sole responsibility for initiating drawdown. Private traders have a sense of future economic conditions as good as or better than anyone else, including government. On this basis, their access to the SPR should be guaranteed and continuing through the sale of options to buy the reserve oil. These options should be convertible at a strike price some specified level above the price prevailing when the options are purchased.[13]

Depending on likely levels of the strike price, conversion of the options will tend to occur only in periods of sharply rising prices. In the present disruption, as well as all past disruptions, such periods are of limited duration (and, I believe, will be even more limited if we draw the reserve quickly and unilaterally). Thus, even if options were to be sold and converted into the SPR maximum drawdown capacity of 3.5 million b/d, there would still be plenty of the nearly 600 million barrel reserve left for government-initiated strategic use.[14] And if, for any reason, government wanted to use the SPR in the politically strategic sense described above, it could set the strike price at a high level that would reduce access by the private sector and enlarge government's discretionary role.

AVOIDING OIL SHARING

All IEA members deserve high marks for not once mentioning in public the oil-sharing provisions of the International Energy Program. Premised on the notion that the world oil market adjusts slowly, oil sharing reallocates oil according to a complex formula following a reduction of world supply of seven percent or more (Iraq-Kuwait removed eight percent).† The research of several colleagues and myself has convinced me that oil sharing is a flawed concept.[16] It imposes international mandatory allocations on the consuming nations at a price below market clearing. The controls may spread to the domestic economies. And the requirement that members stay within their supply "rights" under the plan will most likely lead to oil import quotas, which,

---

†A second objective frequently advanced in support of oil sharing is to limit the increase in spot prices following supply disruptions. The argument is that, even if the adjustment of markets is rapid geographically, there is a tendency for rigid contract prices to cause a disproportionate rise in spot prices. See, for example, Cooper (1988).[15] Weimer and I have criticized this contract/spot price connection on analytical grounds. See Ref. 6, pp. 286–90.

in an oligopolistic world market, could easily increase the world price, the very opposite of the program's intent![7]

The strongest argument against oil sharing is the empirical fact that it is not needed. Our reading of the 1970s persuaded us that the world market adjusts quite adequately and much more speedily than the necessary time involved in gathering the relevant data, voting, and finally implementing the sharing agreement. Joe Anderson ran many regressions which indicated that there was no significant difference in the way most major petroleum variables behaved in disruption vs non-disruption periods in the 1970s![8] David Weimer and I looked at the quarterly prices of imported oil paid by the seven largest buyers in the 1973–85 period![9] The speed of market adjustment is reflected in the rate at which the various prices converge after a price shock. We took as our measure of adjustment speed a coefficient of price dispersion: the difference between the highest and lowest price paid by the seven countries in any quarter divided by the mean price. A disruption quarter was defined as one in which the mean price rose 7.0 percent or more. In 35 normal or non-disrupted quarters from 1973 to 1985, our coefficient of variation averaged 7.4 percent. This dispersion presumably reflected differences in grades of oil, in transportation costs, and any other factors, including a possible failure of arbitrage to equalize the price paid by all buyers in non-disruption circumstances.

In disrupted quarters, which we limited to the 1979–80 and 1981 episodes because the data for 1973–74 were incomplete, the average variation was 15.3 percent or 7.9 percentage points above the normal amount of 7.4 percent. This did not strike us as an extraordinary magnitude, particularly because prices were rising from under $15 per barrel to over $37 at quarterly rates as high as 19 and 24 percent. The difference between the highest and lowest price paid by the major importers, subtracting the average normal or non-disruption difference, was never more than $3 and generally only $1 or $2 among prices whose average level was $25 to $30. Equally significant is that the price dispersion attributable to the disruption dropped to trivial amounts in any non-disruption quarter following a huge price increase.

A similar pattern of price behavior emerges in the data for 1985-91, which are entered in Table 3.1.† In this period, prices (column 1) fluctuated both up and down, starting at a quarterly average of almost $28 in 1985:1, falling to troughs of roughly $12 in 1986:3 and $13 in 1988:4, and rising to a peak of almost $32 in 1990:4. A "shock" (S) quarter was defined this time as one in which the mean price rises *or* falls 7.0 percent or more. In the 11 normal (N) or non-shock quarters, our coefficient of variation (column 3) averages

---

†The price data for 1985–91 differ from those of the earlier study for 1973–85 (Ref. 6) in that the prices paid by France, which is not an IEA member, are omitted.

5.2 percent; in the 14 shock quarters, it is 13.0 percent, leaving 7.8 percent attributable to the shock. The three percentages are each lower than the comparable percentages in 1974–85.

In column 4, the price range of each quarter is reduced by the average price range of non-shock periods, which is .052 times the quarter's mean price. In general, column 4 should thus be close to zero except in shock quarters. Column 5 expresses the adjusted price range as a percentage of each quarter's mean price.

Although the average quarterly price range during shocks is less in 1985–91 than in 1979–81, the *variability* of the mean price (column 1) and of the price ranges across shock quarters (columns 4 and 5) is greater in the recent period than in the 1979–81 disruptions. For example, in 1986:1 when the mean price fell 21.7 percent, the adjusted price range was a substantial $3.94. In the succeeding quarter, 1986:2, when prices fell a dramatic 38.5 percent, the adjusted price range was a mere $0.17. The market adjustment would appear to have been relatively sluggish in the first quarter of the shock but almost instantaneous in the second. With two exceptions (1986:3 and 1988:1), none of the remaining adjusted price ranges of shock quarters through the end of 1989 was as much as $1.00, despite quarterly price increases as large as 25.0 and 23.0 percent.

In 1990:3, when Iraq moved into Kuwait, the adjusted price range was a sizable $4.14 on a price base of $21.86, but fell to $3.02 even while prices rose 44.4 percent to a level of $31.57, compared to the 37.8 percent rise of the previous quarter. In 1991:1, when prices dropped by a resounding 33.7 percent to $20.94, the adjusted price range fell to $2.31. I see this as a market that continues to equilibrate despite shocks of increasing magnitude. I find it implausible that the oil sharing plan, which cannot take less than three or four months to implement[20] and carries a heavy load of non-market price-fixing interventionist baggage, can improve on the observed unfettered market.

CONCLUSION

My assessment gives the administration high grades for its reliance on nonmilitary solutions and essentially free markets in responding to oil supply disruptions. Although we went to war following the Iraqi invasion of Kuwait, I find no plausible connection at the time between that move and any desire to secure access of the consuming countries to Persian Gulf oil. Meanwhile, our reliance on free markets, while possibly marred by excessive "jawboning," appeared quite adequate both domestically and internationally.

Where we failed, at least economically, was in our meager, largely inconsequential use of the strategic petroleum reserve. The cost of that non-use could exceed the entire cost to the coalition of the war against Iraq. On the other hand, it might be argued that the administration avoided using the SPR so as to maintain high fuel prices in its psychological campaign against Saddam and as a critical source of Saudi revenues directed to war-related funding.

What I have not discussed in this survey is the role of monetary policy, which, in a widely held view among economists, exacerbated the costs of the 1973–74 and 1979–80 disruptions.[21-24] Prior to each disruption, central banks of all the industrial countries were in the process of tightening money in an effort to control inflation. The problem, however, was that the banks responded to the additional inflation caused by the oil shocks by tightening money further. The conventional wisdom, to which I subscribe, is that commodity shocks, such as that of oil, should be accommodated by the monetary authorities. Non-accommodation tends to enlarge the loss of real output and employment, which some argue exceeded any direct loss due to the oil shocks themselves.

I do not yet have a careful reading on how the Federal Reserve performed in the recent crisis. My guess is that it leaned towards accommodation, allowing the inflation rate to rise somewhat above its pre-crisis target. In general, I believe Alan Greenspan has a finer analytical appreciation of the distinction between demand-pull and supply-push inflation and the appropriate response to each than did either of his two predecessors in the chairman's post.

REFERENCES

1. D. R. Henderson, "Sorry Saddam, Oil Embargoes Don't Hurt Us," *Wall Street Journal* (Aug. 29, 1990).
2. D. R. Henderson, "Do We Need to Go to War for Oil?," *Foreign Policy Briefing* 4, Cato Institute, Washington, DC (Oct. 24, 1990).
3. B. Rosewicz, "Iraqis Set Fire to Oil Sites in Kuwait; Effects Limited," *Wall Street Journal* (Jan. 23, 1991).
4. P. K. Verleger, Jr., "Understanding the 1990 Oil Crisis," *Energy Journal* 11, 4, 15 (1990).
5. *Energy Prices and Taxes,* International Energy Agency, Paris (Quarterly since 1984).
6. G. Horwich and D. L. Weimer, "International Oil Sharing and Policy Coordination: A Critical Summary," in *Responding to International Oil Crises,* G. Horwich and D. L. Weimer, eds., American Enterprise Institute, Washington, DC (1988).
7. *Monthly Energy Review,* U.S. Department of Energy, Washington, DC.
8. Council of Economic Advisers, *Economic Report of the President, February 1991,* Superintendent of Documents, Washington, DC (1991).
9. S. Greenhouse, "Emergency Oil Release Plan is Set," *New York Times* (Jan. 12, 1991).
10. B. G. Hickman, H. G. Huntington, and J. L. Sweeney, *Macroeconomic Impacts of Energy Shocks: A Summary of Findings,* North-Holland, Amsterdam (1987), p. 5.

11. J. Miller, "Diplomats Say Saudi Aid in Crisis is Generous, Even Fiscally Risky," *New York Times* (Jan. 11, 1991).
12. G. Horwich and D. L. Weimer, "The Economics of International Oil Sharing," *Energy Journal* **9**, 4, 17 (1988).
13. G. Horwich and D. L. Weimer, *Oil Price Shocks, Market Response, and Contingency Planning,* American Enterprise Institute, Washington, DC (1984), chapter 4.
14. Ibid., pp. 129–132.
15. R. N. Cooper, "An Analysis of the International Energy Agency: Comments by a Sometime Practitioner," pp. 272–273, 280, in *Responding to International Oil Crises,* G. Horwich and D. L. Weimer, eds., American Enterprise Institute, Washington, DC (1988).
16. G. Horwich and D. L. Weimer, *Responding to International Oil Crises,* American Enterprise Institute, Washington, DC (1988), chapters 2, 3, 4, 7, 9.
17. G. Horwich and B. A. Miller, "Oil Import Quotas in the Context of the International Energy Agency Sharing Agreement," in *Responding to International Oil Crises,* G. Horwich and D. L. Weimer, eds., American Enterprise Institute, Washington, DC (1988).
18. J. M. Anderson, "Empirical Analysis of World Oil Trade, 1967–1984," in *Responding to International Oil Crises,* G. Horwich and D. L. Weimer, eds., American Enterprise Institute, Washington, DC (1988).
19. G. Horwich and D. L. Weimer, "International Oil Sharing and Policy Coordination: A Critical Summary," pp. 290–293, in *Responding to International Oil Crises,* G. Horwich and D. L. Weimer, eds., American Enterprise Institute, Washington, DC (1988).
20. R. T. Smith, "International Energy Cooperation: The Mismatch Between IEA Policy Actions and Policy Goals," in *Responding to International Oil Crises,* G. Horwich and D. L. Weimer, eds., American Enterprise Institute, Washington, DC (1988).
21. R. W. Hafer, "The Impact of Energy Prices and Money Growth on Five Industrial Countries," Federal Reserve Bank of St. Louis *Review,* 19 (March 1981).
22. E. S. Phelps, "Commodity-Supply Shocks and Monetary Policy Revisited," *American Economic Review* 74, 38 (1984).
23. K.M. Carlson, "Explaining the Economic Slowdown of 1979: A Supply and Demand Framework," Federal Reserve Bank of St. Louis *Review,* 15 (Oct. 1979).
24. R.M. Solow, "What to Do (Macroeconomically) When OPEC Comes," in *Rational Expectations and Economic Policy,* S. Fischer, ed., University of Chicago Press, Chicago, IL (1980).

4 Medium-Term Oil Markets: Beyond the Gulf Crisis

Ruth Cairnie

OVERVIEW

The invasion of Kuwait by Iraq in August 1990 led, following the imposition of United Nations sanctions, to the loss of over 4.5 million barrels per day (b/d) of oil exports. This and consequent uncertainties about supply availabilities led to high and extremely volatile prices for both crude and certain products. An unexpectedly strong response in terms of incremental production by both non-OPEC countries and OPEC members (especially Saudi Arabia) led, however, to all the 'lost oil' being replaced. Although regional and product imbalances were present at times, by the end of 1990, total stocks had been built up to seasonally high levels and, in the absence of War Premia, the market would have been reacting to the stock overhang.

Meanwhile, in 1990 global oil demand showed the smallest annual increase (0.3 million b/d) since 1985. Although the invasion of Kuwait was an important influence, leading to higher prices and consumer uncertainty in the second half of the year, more significant was the mild weather that depressed demand by nearly 0.5 million b/d compared with normal. The other main influence was the marked economic slowdown in English-speaking countries of the Organization for Economic Cooperation and Development (OECD). Overall, demand weakness was an important factor in ensuring that oil supplies were adequate during the crisis.

Over recent months, many of the key factors in the oil markets have signaled a return to normality. For example, attention has focused on Soviet production and exports, the possible effects of the North Sea maintenance program, and the degree of tightness or otherwise projected for the U.S. gasoline season. Looking ahead, the aftermath of the crisis will certainly reemerge as an influence: possibly through concerns about tightness of crude and product supplies to meet the coming winter's demand, or conversely, concerns about excess supplies of crude once exports from Iraq and/or Kuwait need to be accommodated. This paper considers the extent to which the effects of the crisis will extend into the longer term—say, five years—particularly on the fundamentals of supply and demand.

ECONOMICS

The Gulf crisis contributed to economic weakness in many countries in 1990/91, with recession in the United States and the United Kingdom and an increasingly marked slowdown in many other European countries. High oil prices were, however, fairly short-lived and the major impact was through lowering business confidence, as uncertainty relating to future oil supplies and prices reinforced underlying economic concerns.

Our present base case forecasts reflect an early reversal of the present economic downturn, with good growth in 1992. The recovery is sustained in the medium term but fairly subdued—a little over 3 percent average annual income (aai) for the 'free' world—in contrast to previous post-recession bounces. The East continues to outperform the rest of the world, with Japan leading the industrialized nations as growth fundamentals reassert themselves following the present monetary tightening, leading to annual growth around 4 percent, and newly industrialized economies (NIEs) and Pacific Basin lesser developed countries (LDCs) combining to nearly 7 percent growth each year.

The main risks for slower world economic growth relate to the possibility that high real interest rates delay or inhibit economic recovery; that conflict in trade negotiations leads to greater protectionism; and that political and economic breakdown in the Soviet Union cause tension among OECD countries in agreeing on policy responses and in meeting a growing economic burden. In contrast, the risk of sustained high energy prices is considered low, and vulnerability of the OECD economies to rising oil prices has been greatly reduced by improvements in oil intensity (33% reduction 1978/90). Accounting for all the downside risks, 'free world' economic growth should still average better than 2.5 percent each year as a sensitivity case. This is well above the 1.8 percent aai in 1978/83, which was the lowest average 5-year growth in the last 30 years but resulted from many converging factors including high oil prices, a simultaneous cyclical downturn in all the major economies, and the LDC debt crisis.

OIL INTENSITY

The Gulf crisis has rekindled concerns around the world about economic and strategic dependence on oil. As a result, there is a sharpened focus on alternative energy sources and renewed interest in energy conservation. The supply security concerns may be reinforced by synergy with environmental issues, making action more likely.

Some responses to the crisis have already reflected the concern to 'save' oil. The U.S. National Energy Strategy (NES) is promoting gas and possibly nuclear developments. There are new proposals for nuclear research by European countries and, in Japan, the Ministry of International Trade and Industry's (MITI's) long-term supply plan emphasizes conservation and increased use of nuclear power. Initiatives in developing countries are based on coal and gas, or renewable energy, particularly for rural areas. A substantial increase in use of gas in the Middle East is expected to moderate growth in fuel oil demand, and a shift toward alternatives is expected to make some headway in the East.

Over the next half decade or so, however, there is little likelihood of a material change from the situation prevailing before the invasion of Kuwait. It is improbable that nuclear power will enjoy a long-lived respite from environmental pressures, and a desire to move away from oil in most sectors was already the confirmed trend. At most, the crisis may lead to some acceleration in investments in non-oil capacity; but the rate of replacement will be limited by lead times and by the availability of supplies and infrastructure to use alternatives.

On the conservation front, the U.S. NES calls for measures to reduce oil consumption, but is short on firm proposals. Nonetheless, some action to tighten legislated car efficiency (CAFE) standards seems increasingly likely and U.S. gasoline demand growth is expected to be marginal. In Europe, there is growing momentum for energy tax increases to combat global warming, but it is unlikely that general implementation will be rapid. In many non-OECD countries, there were significant delays in passing through to consumers the increases in international market product prices experienced after the invasion of Kuwait, but the eventual increases have since been maintained, dampening demand growth trends. In countries such as India, which suffer from foreign exchange shortages, input of oil into the economy is likely to be restricted through measures such as price increases or rationing, leaving demand unsatisfied and constraining economic growth.

The combination of conservation and fuel diversification measures is expected to result in saving in 'free world' oil intensity of somewhat under 2 percent aai to be achieved, in contrast with the last oil crisis when a nearly 4.5 percent average annual decline was achieved between 1978 and 1983. However, over half of the 6 million b/d decline in oil demand over that period was fuel oil backed out of power generation as new nuclear and coal-fired plants came on stream. This is not repeatable over the next five years given the much lower starting level for oil uses with viable alternatives (53% of 'free world' demand now being for transportation), and long investment and construction lead times. The nuclear and coal expansions were planned well before the 1978/79 price shock.

DEMAND

Global oil demand is expected to increase by approaching 5 million b/d between 1990 and 1996. Outside the East Bloc, average annual growth of almost 1.5 percent will be driven by the economic expansion, population growth, industrialization, lifestyle changes, and many other factors, countered by efforts to limit oil dependence. Aggregate oil demand in the LDCs will overtake demand in the United States by 1994. Half of the 1990–96 demand increase is for middle distillates (gasoil and kerosene). Over 50 percent of the demand increase is for transportation fuels, predominantly road and aviation. The growing call for liquid feedstocks for bulk petrochemicals also plays an important role. Demand in the 'East Bloc' countries may be over 0.7 million b/d lower in 1996 than 1990, with the main influence being economic upheaval in the Soviet Union.

Geographically, demand growth will be rapid in the Eastern hemisphere and relatively sluggish in the West. Thus the Pacific Basin countries which represent about one-third of current demand will contribute more than half of the projected growth.

In the Atlantic Basin, demand growth will be dominated by gasoline (mainly in Europe) and gasoil for commercial transport. In the Pacific, these products are also important, as is kerosene for domestic use as urban populations grow and as increasing wealth in some countries leads to higher requirements for comfort and convenience. Numbers of private cars are expected to increase, with perhaps an additional 5 million units in Japan by 1996 and with South Korea's car population doubling.

The demand barrel will whiten everywhere, but less rapidly in the East. In some of the rapidly growing and industrializing economies, fuel oil demand will have to increase to meet energy needs, despite the underlying wish to reduce oil input. In the mid-1990s, the demand barrel in the East will still have a significantly higher proportion of fuel oil than elsewhere.

Product quality remains an important issue, driven by environmental concerns. In the Atlantic Basin, reformulated gasoline in the United States following the Clean Air Act Amendment will reduce the volume of gasoline to be manufactured from crude oil by around 0.2 million b/d by the mid 1990s, while creating a call for oxygenates well in excess of current production capacity. Reformulated gasoline may be adopted elsewhere, either through legislation or, more likely, commercial initiatives. Another major issue over the next five years will be the scaling down of sulfur content in diesel to 0.05

percent. In the Pacific, these trends are likely to be followed but somewhat later. Over the next few years, important developments will be the increasing penetration of unleaded gasoline and of premium grades.

SUPPLY

In the wake of the Gulf war, all approaches to reducing the vulnerability of oil-importing nations to further supply disruptions are under review. These include attempts to lessen instability in the Gulf through construction of political and military security systems, and strengthening of the defenses provided by strategic stocks. In addition, all governments can be expected to reinforce policies that encourage the development of domestic energy resources, including oil, and as a result an increase in non-OPEC production (outside the East Bloc) of around 1 million b/d is expected by 1996. This is higher than had been foreseen a year ago, and is partly the result of new technologies—for example, horizontal drilling. This is playing an important role in stemming to some extent the decline of U.S. production. Reductions in the United States and Canada will be offset by increases elsewhere, especially in the North Sea.

Developments in non-OPEC capacity may be limited to some extent by increasing pressure on oilfield equipment resources, resulting from reconstruction of Kuwait's oil-producing infrastructure as well as expansions in OPEC. In addition, environmental concerns will continue to play a constraining role, although in the United States the possibility that the NES will eventually lead to production from the Arctic National Wildlife Reserve demonstrates the ongoing interplay between environmental and economic/security concerns.

Perhaps the major uncertainty for non-OPEC supply is production prospects in the Soviet Union. Lack of investment in recent years and growing political and financial chaos have resulted in a severe reduction of about 0.8 million b/d in both 1990 and 1991. The giant fields that have historically provided the bulk of production are in decline and major investment will be needed to limit the rate of production loss. The present economic and political turmoil is inhibiting injection of foreign capital and expertise and impeding both current production and field development. Our base case forecasts assume that a slowing of the decline is achieved over the next two years, with the need to preserve hard currency earnings securing an increasing priority for the oil industry. Nonetheless, production is expected to decline to perhaps 9.5 million b/d by 1996 from the present estimated 10.8 million b/d. With Soviet demand also declining (and even more uncertain to predict), net exports will decline by less. Total net East Bloc exports are expected to fall by 1 million b/d from their current levels, offsetting the production increases in other non-OPEC countries.

CALL ON OPEC CRUDE AND CAPACITY

The projected developments in oil demand and non-OPEC production lead to the crude oil balances shown in Table 4.1. From Table 4.1, it can be seen that the increase in demand over the period will need to be met largely from OPEC crude production, with an expected call in 1996 around 26.5 million b/d compared with current sustainable capacity a little below 25 million b/d excluding Iraq and Kuwait.

Whether the rising call on OPEC crude will result in a tightening market depends critically on developments in production capacity. Before the invasion of Kuwait, plans existed to expand total OPEC capacity to some 34 million b/d by the mid-1990s, but some scaling down of these plans, leading to perhaps 32 million b/d by 1995, was anticipated because of question marks over the ability and will to finance the full effort.

Following the invasion and the surprisingly rapid capacity expansion in the 'OPEC 11' countries, the main issues for the short and medium term are the speed and degree to which the capacity of Kuwait and Iraq will become available, and the extent to which expansion plans may be modified in a future of lower demand growth and greater financial stringency.

The timing of exports from Kuwait and Iraq is subject to much uncertainty. It seems likely that some exports from Kuwait will resume during 1992 and in our base case we have assumed that capacity will be built up to a plateau around 2 million b/d by 1994. Exports from Iraq remain constrained by political considerations (at the time of writing). It has been assumed that, when UN sanctions are lifted, exports could resume quickly from stock and via Turkey, but exports via the IPSA-2 pipeline and Iraq's southern terminal will await damage repair. The former production potential of some 3.5 million b/d is assumed to be regained by 1993, but further expansion, some of which was underway before the invasion, could be subject to legal and practical constraints.

For the remainder of OPEC members, the main expansion plans are for the Gulf, especially Iran and Saudi Arabia. Large financial commitments over the next five years tend to argue against major investment in capacity that will not be employed, but conversely the strong voice in the formation of OPEC's pricing and production policies conferred by control of significant spare productive capacity will continue to provide the incentive for expansion. An additional motive is the desire to be in a position to take advantage of any temporary surge in demand for crude, plus the ability if needed to protect oil revenues in the short term by raising output.

Allowing for financial and technical constraints, OPEC crude oil capacity is expected to rise to over 34 million b/d by 1996, resulting in a capacity overhang of some 7 million b/d. Thus the oil market fundamentals would suggest that, once exports from Kuwait and Iraq build toward pre-invasion levels,

Table 4.1. World demand and supply and call on OPEC

	1989	1990	1991	1992	1993	1994	1995	1996
WORLD OIL DEMAND								
WOCA (1)	51.6	52.3	53.2	54.3	55.3	56.2	57.0	57.8
East Bloc	13.1	12.8	12.1	11.7	11.6	11.7	11.8	12.0
Total world demand	64.7	65.1	65.3	66.0	66.9	67.9	68.8	69.8
WORLD OIL SUPPLY								
Non-OPEC (WOCA)	25.8	26.4	26.8	27.1	27.1	27.3	27.7	27.7
East Bloc	15.3	14.7	14.0	13.6	13.4	13.3	13.1	13.0
OPEC NGL	2.0	2.0	2.0	2.3	2.4	2.4	2.5	2.6
Stockdraft (build)	(0.2)	(1.0)	(0.3)	(0.4)	(0.2)	(0.2)	(0.2)	(0.2)
Call on OPEC crude	21.8	23.0	22.8	23.4	24.2	25.1	25.7	26.7

(1) WOCA: world outside communist area.

oil prices will be subject to the same sort of downward pressures experienced in the last five years. Quotas will still be needed, and a great deal of leadership will be required to prevent disruption to the market by overproduction. The low profile of such leadership within OPEC in recent years may have ended with new perceptions of roles for individual members following the crisis. One aspect of this will be the role of political considerations in determining the pricing preferences for individual countries. The expectation is for crude prices to remain volatile but generally in the range $15 to $20 per barrel (US$ 1990) for Gulf-type crudes, toward the higher end of the range if Gulf politics have a relatively strong influence.

REFINING PRESSURES

Outside the East Bloc, operable distillation capacity is currently assessed to be over 56 million b/d. This will increase over the next few years as capacity in Iraq and Kuwait is restored, and as firm plans for capacity construction, much of it in the Far East, come to fruition. Nonetheless, the capacity increments are expected to fall below demand growth, so that utilization of primary capacity may increase to over 85 percent in 1996.

Major investments in conversion capacity are also planned, but again the demand increases and whitening demand barrel could lead to high utilization rates, perhaps close to 90 percent, with especial tightness during seasonal peaks or as a result of unscheduled shutdowns.

Supply of middle distillates may be tight in both the Atlantic and Pacific Basins, reflecting the strength of demand. Pacific Basin demand could absorb all Middle East availabilities, leaving little scope for movements West while European refiners will have to cover both incremental demand and declining Soviet gasoil exports. Such problems would be exacerbated by any delays to the restoration of Kuwaiti refining capacity and by the need to meet lower sulfur specifications.

Gasoline supplies could be finely balanced in the Far East, but in the Atlantic Basin supplies will become easier with the introduction of reformulated gasoline in the United States—at the expense of tightness in oxygenate supplies.

A crucial factor for product supply balances will be the prospects for exports of fuel oil and long residue from the Soviet Union. All the existing and planned incremental conversion capacity in the Atlantic Basin may be needed to absorb possible increases in exports as the Soviet economy declines.

The implications are that refiners' complex margins could be above pre-invasion trends in both the Far East and Europe, but weaker in the United States. However, the recent very strong margins in the wake of the crisis are not expected to persist, and there remains the risk of downward pressures if more capacity investments are made. In the East, the Japanese strategy for refining and product imports may be pivotal. Adequate return on capital from investments in refining may still prove to be elusive.

5 How the World Oil Market Could Avoid Another Supply Shock: Examination of the Saudi Oil Policy in Terms of the Saudi-U.S. Coalition

Kazushi Uemura

INTRODUCTION

Despite much speculation that the world oil market would encounter a severe oil shortage and world oil prices would rise to as much as $60 a barrel either immediately after the Iraqi invasion of Kuwait or upon outbreak of the Gulf War, the world oil market did not face another supply shock and oil prices stayed at about $15–20 a barrel between September 1990 and February 1991. This is mainly because, Saudi Arabia being under direct threat from Iraq, the United States quickly deployed its forces in Saudi Arabia and in response Saudi Arabia increased oil production from 5.4 million barrels a day (b/d) in July 1990 to 8.4 million b/d from September 1990 to February 1991. These responses by the United States and Saudi Arabia were not surprising, but were to be expected given the nature and framework of the coalition of these parties. In this paper, I apply a coalition theory and explain the Saudi response in terms of the Saudi-U.S. coalition.

A COALITION THEORY

K. J. Holsti has examined many kinds of coalition or alliance behavior of nations and has suggested a few conditions for an effective coalition or alli-

I am indebted to Professor George Lenczowski for providing me with an opportunity to do research on this topic at the University of California-Berkeley in 1979.

ance. Among others, four conditions are most important for an effective coalition or alliance.

- Governments that seek to construct permanent diplomatic coalitions or military alliances assume that they cannot achieve their objectives, defend their interests, or deter perceived threats by mobilizing their own capabilities. They thus rely upon, and make commitments to, other states that face similar external problems or share similar values.
- Common perceptions of threats and widespread attitudes of insecurity are probably the frequent sources of alliance strategies. . . Alliances have also bolstered weak regimes and served essentially domestic political purposes rather than defend against external threats. . . Political units have offered their military capabilities to other states in order to help maintain friendly governments in power or perpetuate a particular dynasty against internal and externally supported rebellion or subversion.
- (Alliances) attempt to increase diplomatic influence on some issue or problem or create a deterrent effect by combining capabilities. . . However, there is no automatic guarantee that even the most solemn undertakings will be fulfilled if those commitments are in conflict with the prevailing interests of different governments.
- Presumably any military coalition will be more effective to the extent that its members agree on the major objectives to be achieved, help each other diplomatically, and trust that once the *casus foederis* arises, the partners will in fact meet their commitments!

According to Holsti, countries that have complementary capabilities, hold common perceptions of threat, expect positive net benefits from the alliance, and make clear commitments to one another and hold confidence in each other's commitments, are likely to construct an effective coalition and survive as an effective organization. Naturally, lack of any one of these conditions may "cause strains in alliances, impairing their effectiveness both as deterrents and as fighting organizations."[1]

THE SAUDI-U.S. COALITION

Constructing a Coalition

Irvine Anderson has described the coalition formed during the Cold War between the four parent companies (Socal, Texaco, Exxon, and Mobil) of the former Arabian American Oil Company (Aramco); Saudi Arabia; and the United States.

It was clear that with the onset of the Cold War and the sale of a 40 percent interest in Aramco to Jersey (Exxon) and Socony (Mobil) in 1948, a concert of interests had coalesced around Saudi oil. The military wanted increased production to conserve Western Hemisphere strategic reserves; the Department of State wanted economic stability in the area to guard against the spread of communism; Socal and Texaco wanted increased markets to secure the concession; Jersey and Socony wanted additional sources of supply; and 'Abd al-'Aziz wanted more revenue and modernization of his country. Truman's precipitous recognition of the state of Israel had the effect of increasing State's concern over relations with Arab states, and made State especially supportive of oil company projects such as Tapline. The members of the coalition all saw Aramco as an instrument for their own purposes . . . Noticeably absent from the coalition were the Federal Trade Commission, the Anti-Trust Division of the Department of Justice, and nonparticipating American oil companies—especially the Texas independents.[2]

We used Holsti's theoretical framework to formalize the three parties' coalition as described by Anderson (see Table 5.1).

In this coalition, all three parties perceived communism to be the common threat.† Of course, each party had its own objectives. The Saudi royal family needed to secure its regime and wanted to modernize the country based on its oil. The United States intended to contain communism and also to maintain and expand its leadership in the "free world" and in the Middle East. Aramco parent companies needed guaranteed business profits. Alone, each party could not achieve its objectives. By combining their strengths, they could move towards their respective objectives (see Fig. 5.1).

- The U.S. government provided the Saudi royal government with military protection and military supplies, and the four Aramco parent companies with military protection.
- The Saudi royal government provided both the Aramco parent companies and the U.S. government with a secure supply of oil to the non-communist world and not to the communist bloc.
- The Aramco parent companies provided the Saudi royal government with a continuous oil export and a flow of oil revenues, and the U.S. government with an assurance that oil would be sold by the Americans to the non-communist world, rather than to the communist bloc.

In addition to the existence of Holsti's first two conditions for a successful coalition, there was obviously a basis on which these parties could develop confidence in each other's commitments. The two American oil companies (Socal and Texaco) had long operated in Saudi Arabia and established a good business relationship with the Saudi government. According to Lenczowski:

---

†For an analysis of Saudi Arabia's anti-communism, see George Lenczowski, *The Middle East in World Affairs*, p. 591, Cornell University Press, Ithaca, NY (1980).

Table 5.1.   Objectives and necessary complementary capacities of Saudi
Arabia, the United States, and the four Aramco parent companies after the Second World War

Objectives, capacities	Saudi Arabia	United States	4 Aramco Parent Companies
Perceived common threat	•Communism	•Communism	•Communism
Individual objectives (policy)	•Survival (secure national integrity •Modernization	•Leadership in the "free world" and the Middle East (contain communism)	•Oil profit
Necessary capacities	•Military† •Revenues	•Military† •Secure oil supply to the non-communist world	•Secure oil supply sources •Oil technologies‡ •Military†
Capacities possessed	•Huge oil supply sources	•Military†	•Secure oil sources •Military†
Capacities not possessed	•Military† •Oil technologies	•Secure oil supply to the non-communist world	

†Military means military protection and/or military supplies.
‡Oil technologies includes marketing techniques, exploration and
development technologies and financial resources for these
activities.

One of the first steps of the concessionaire (Socal and Texaco) was to give a
loan of £30,000 in gold sovereigns to the Saudi Arabian government. The loan
came in the nick of time, when Saudi Arabia was suffering from a decrease
in pilgrim traffic, caused by the world depression. The American company did
it entirely at its own risk, which, considering the strangeness and remoteness
of Saudi Arabia and the lack of official American interest, was considerable.
Yet it paid handsome dividends in good will and soon proved economically
justifiable as well. . . Oil in commercial quantities began to be extracted in the
late thirties, and a new concession agreement was signed between Aramco and
Saudi Arabia on May 31, 1939.[3]

It is reasonable to believe that the three parties were able to take advantage
of this good business relationship and constructed a coalition on that basis.

The question remains whether the three parties could get net positive
benefits from the coalition. It is obvious that this coalition "created deter-

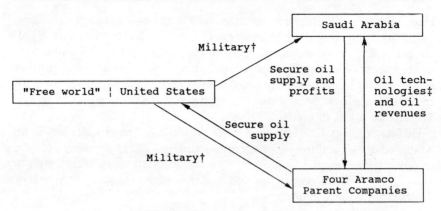

†Military means military protection and/or military supplies.
‡Oil technologies include marketing techniques, exploration and
 development technologies and financial resources for these
 activities

Fig. 5.1.   Exchanges of capacities between Saudi Arabia, the United
States and the four Aramco parent companies.

rent effect by combining capabilities'' particularly against communism. But ''these cordial relations were marred by one problem only, the problem of Zionism.''[4] This problem could have made the Saudis think that a coalition with the United States might isolate them from the Arab world. Similarly, the Americans also could have been in a difficult diplomatic position if Israel and Saudi Arabia, both allies, should get into a conflict. In fact, ''the United Nations partition resolution of 1947 and the American pro-Israeli policy produced tension, which was temporarily reflected in the negotiations concerning the extension of the Dhahran air base lease. But these matters never caused a break in relations,''[5] at least until the early 1970s.

Surviving the Coalition

Anderson has shown that the coalition survived in the late 1940s when the 50–50 profit sharing agreement was negotiated between the three parties.[6] I find no reason to believe that the basic nature and framework of this coalition has changed since then. There are several stages at which the coalition suffered strains that might have impaired its effectiveness as a deterrent or as a fighting organization, but it managed to survive until August 1990. These critical periods are analyzed below.

The Oil Embargo in 1973. Following the outbreak of the October war in 1973, the Arab oil embargo caused the first major strain in the coalition. In the early 1970s when the Palestinian problem became one of the major issues in the Middle East, Saudi Arabia felt that it needed to concentrate on regional affairs. Saudi Arabia most likely thought that a coalition with the

United States would isolate it from the Arab world and that such a coalition might not bring about net positive benefits to its national interests. Saudi Arabia pulled out of its commitment to the United States and embargoed its shipments of crude oil to the United States and other major industrialized countries in the non-communist world. This of course reduced American confidence in the Saudi commitment to guarantee a continuous oil supply. The coalition was in a crisis.

However, diplomatic efforts were made between the United States and Saudi Arabia and the coalition was reconstructed. Particularly important for the reconstruction were the Saudi-U.S. top-level negotiations in Washington in June 1974 and the agreement that followed these negotiations. *The New York Times* reported at the time:

> The United States and Saudi Arabia today signed a wide-ranging military and economic agreement that both said 'heralded an era of increasing close cooperation' . . . Mr. Kissinger said, 'We consider this a milestone in our relations with Saudi Arabia and with the Arab countries in general.' Prince Fahd said that the accord was 'an excellent opening in a new and glorious chapter in relations between Saudi Arabia and the United States.' The agreement establishes two joint commissions, one on economic cooperation and the other on Saudi Arabia's military needs. . . The two Governments also agreed to consider setting up an economic council to foster cooperation in the private sector. The Treasury Department and the Saudi Arabian Ministry of Finance and National Economy 'will consider cooperation in the field of finance' the agreement said. . . [T]he agreement did not mention the word oil. Both sides wanted to avoid the impression that these were bilateral talks on oil. American officials, however, have made no secret of their hope that Saudi Arabia will take the lead in increasing production of oil.†

As the agreement shows, the United States stated its commitment to assist Saudi Arabia militarily. In exchange it was hoped that Saudi Arabia would continue to supply the non-communist world with adequate oil. In fact, Saudi Arabia continued to supply oil until the second quarter of 1979.‡

The Camp David Agreement and the Iranian Revolution. The second major strain in the coalition arose in the autumn of 1978 at the time of both the Camp David agreement and the Iranian Revolution. The U.S.-mediated bilateral peace agreement between Egypt and Israel surprised most of the Arab countries, including Saudi Arabia, which expected a unilateral settlement of the

---

†*The New York Times,* p.12, (June 8, 1974). For the full text of the agreement, see The Middle East Journal, pp. 305–307 (summer, 1974).

‡In addition to the reconfirmation of the original commitments of the United States and Saudi Arabia, the two countries appeared to agree to exchange U.S. economic/technical assistance for Saudi Arabia's oil dollars. But a discussion of this addition of new complementary capacities is beyond the scope of this paper.

Palestinian issue. Therefore, there was a strong anti-U.S. sentiment in Saudi Arabia with regard to the American initiatives. The Saudis were also apparently disappointed at the American failure to protect the Shah of Iran, another U.S. ally in the Middle East. As a result, Saudi Arabia again pulled out of its commitment to provide an adequate oil supply and suddenly cut its oil production from 9.5 million b/d to 8.5 million b/d at the beginning of the second quarter of 1979, worsening the shortage that had been created by the Iranian Revolution.[7] The U.S. government lost confidence in the Saudi commitment to secure oil supply and the coalition was in another crisis.

The coalition narrowly managed to survive, thanks to the emergence of a new common enemy, Iran. Saudi Arabia feared that the Iranian Revolution might spread and threaten the Saudi Arabian royal regime. With the hostage crisis, the U.S. government was particularly hostile towards the new Iranian government. The coalition was reshaped to cope with the new Iran.

The United States reassured Saudi Arabia of its commitment to defend it. For example, the Carter administration sent U.S. Defense Secretary Brown to Saudi Arabia in February 1979 to discuss Saudi security, and the U.S. also decided to sell F-5 and F-15 jet-fighters to Saudi Arabia.† Of course, the discussion was not only on Saudi security but also on Saudi Arabia's oil production. Newsom has pointed out that

> [d]uring the Carter administration, for instance, some of the most significant business deals with Saudi Arabia were carried on between Secretary of Defense Harold Brown and the Saudi Arabian Minister of Defense and between Secretary of Energy Charles W. Duncan and Sheikh Zaki Yamani, the Saudi Minister of Petroleum. The U.S. Ambassador was included in some, but not all, of these conversations.[8]

Saudi Arabia reconfirmed its commitment to supply adequate oil. At the beginning of the third quarter of 1979, President Carter received a personal commitment from Crown Prince Fahd that Saudi Arabia would increase its crude oil production substantially "for a significant and specific time period."‡

Saudi Arabia's 100 Percent Participation in Aramco. Aramco participation negotiations had started by the early 1970s and Saudi Arabia's 25 percent participation in Aramco was completed by 1973 and a 60 percent participation by 1974, with full participation completed in 1980.

---

†As noted, the Saudis were unhappy about the Camp David agreement and the U.S. failure to protect the Shah of Iran and Saudi-U.S. relations were very poor. Brown's mission to Saudi Arabia was very complex. (See, for example, *The Christian Science Monitor,* p. 1 (December 29, 1978); p. 9 (August 21, 1979)).

†As noted above, the Saudis cut their oil production from 9.5 million b/d in March to 8.5 million b/d in April, 1979, which worsened the shortage in the world oil market suffering from the production decrease in post-revolution Iran (*The Christian Science Monitor,* p. 2 (July 10, 1979)).

The coalition underwent another major strain at the time of Saudi Arabia's 100 percent participation in Aramco. The major issues in the above negotiations were (1) that the technological assistance to Saudi Arabia's oil production and other related oil operations was to be provided by the four Aramco parents and (2) what quantities of Saudi oil were to be supplied to the four American oil companies. It is clear that the four American oil companies and Saudi Arabia still had complementary capabilities and thus needed each other. First, if Saudi Arabia wanted to continue producing oil and to secure a continuous flow of oil revenues, it still needed technological assistance from the American oil companies. Second, if the American oil companies wanted to stay in business and make certain economic profits, they needed to be guaranteed a continuous large supply of Saudi oil. The two parties agreed to remain in the coalition. Saudi Aramco reported of new agreements with the four former Aramco parents as follows:

> In many respects, the agreements only confirm. . . Saudi Arabia will benefit under the agreements by keeping the oil companies' accumulated expertise in exploration, production and refining, and worldwide marketing, and from the stability that firm, long-term purchase agreements bring. The American companies involved—and through them the United States as an oil importing country—will also benefit from the new agreements. Their access to large quantities of Saudi Arabian oil will be guaranteed.[9]

Thus Saudi Arabia, although it had achieved a high degree of independence in its oil operations, chose to be assisted in its key oil operations by the personnel of the former Aramco parents. For example, it still receives 115 "loanees" from the former Aramco parents for Saudi Aramco's "key operations."[†] In exchange, the four American oil companies, which used to export 70 to 90 percent of Saudi crude oil[‡] (see Fig. 5.2), were guaranteed the "long-term purchase agreements." And, even now, there is no evidence that the above "long-term purchase agreements" have been terminated. A majority of Saudi oil is still sold to the former Aramco parents. For example, Chevron (former Socal), Exxon, Mobil, and Star Enterprise (a 50–50 Saudi-Texaco joint refining and marketing company) handled 64 percent of crude oil imported from Saudi Arabia to the United States in 1989.[10] Thus, the four American oil companies still generate a large and continuous flow of oil revenues to the Saudi government as was expected in the original coalition framework.

---

†Personal communication, Saudi Aramco official at the IAEE International Conference in Hawaii on July 8, 1991.

‡The four Aramco parents handled about 90 percent of Saudi crude oil exports between June 1974 and April 1976 (*The Petroleum Economist,* p.140, (May 1976)). These companies handled about 80 percent of Saudi crude oil exports between April 1976 and March 1979 (*Petroleum Intelligence Weekly,* pp. 2–3, (May 14, 1979); p. 7, (August 4, 1980)). Their portion was cut to about 70 percent in April 1974 (*The Wall Street Journal,* p. 2, (May 10, 1979)).

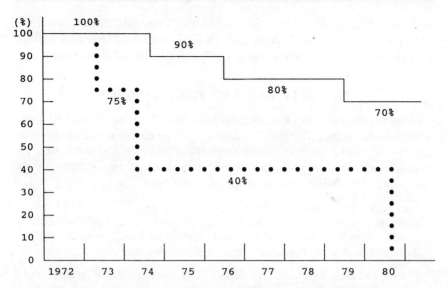

Note: The dotted line shows the equity share of the four
          American oil companies in Aramco.
Sources: *Petroleum Economist,* p. 140 (May 1976); *Petroleum
          Intelligence Weekly,* p. 2-3 (May 14, 1979); pp. 2-3
          (Aug. 4, 1980); *Wall Street Journal,* p. 2 (May 10,
          1979).

Fig. 5.2. Estimated percentage share of Saudi crude oil exported by the four American oil companies.

The Iran-Iraqi War. The fourth strain to the coalition was brought about during the eight year Iran-Iraqi war. For the first time, the coalition faced a major *casus foederis* and each party in the coalition was put in a position to meet its commitments.

At the early stage of the war, Iraqi oil facilities in the Persian Gulf were destroyed by Iranian air attacks and Iraqi oil production went down from 3.4 million b/d to less than one million b/d, creating a shortage in the world oil market. This necessitated an increase in Saudi Arabian oil production to make up for the shortage. Furthermore, when the Iranians started an offensive attack into Iraq after 1982, Iran emerged as a more direct threat to Saudi security. Similarly, when the "tanker war" intensified in the Persian Gulf after 1984, the security of American oil companies was at stake. At these critical times, each party made efforts to meet its commitments and the coalition managed to operate and survive.

As the Iran-Iraqi war escalated, the Reagan Administration expressed concern about Saudi security, and, as part of its commitment to Saudi Arabia, decided to sell five AWACS aircraft to Saudi Arabia in April 1981. In exchange, Saudi Arabia maintained a high level of oil production of nine million b/d in the first half of 1981. The U.S. government "escorted" both Kuwaiti and American tankers in the Persian Gulf in 1987 and thus showed its seriousness about protecting American oil companies from military attacks.

THE GULF WAR AND THE COALITION

Following the Iran-Iraqi war, the Gulf crisis brought about the second major *casus foederis* to the coalition. The response of the coalition to Saddam Hussein's invasion of Kuwait was surprisingly swift and effective. Both the United States and Saudi Arabia quickly perceived Iraq as the common enemy. *The Asian Wall Street Journal* reported at the time:

> American officials said Iraqi troops occupying Kuwait had consolidated their positions close to the Saudi border, moving in equipment that would be needed to support an invasion, and White House spokesman Marlin Fitzwater flatly declared that Iraq now poses a 'threat' to Saudi Arabia.[11]

The United States very quickly deployed its forces in Saudi Arabia. Saudi Arabia also fulfilled its commitment and increased its oil production from 5.4 million b/d to 8.4 million b/d in a few months and made up for the loss of oil from Iraq and Kuwait. Further, there is no evidence that the four American oil companies, fearing Iraqi air attacks, refused to purchase Saudi oil or that many of the important 100 or so "loanees" from the former Aramco parents fled Saudi Arabia during the Gulf crisis.†

The coalition particularly owed its effective operation to the strong initiative of President Bush. From the beginning of the crisis, Mr. Bush claimed that Saddam Hussein was not only a threat to Saudi Arabia but also to the "free world" and took an uncompromising attitude to Iraq. There are several reasons for this strong response. The U.S. experience was that Saudi Arabia is of vital interest to the world economy. Bush was reported to have said in a press interview: ". . . the U.S. won't let one so ruthless as Mr. Hussein dominate the world oil market."[12] As Vice President, Bush had already visited Saudi Arabia and established a good relationship with King Fahd. He may well have reassured the Saudis about the U.S. commitment to Saudi defense on his visit during the Iran-Iraqi war in 1986. In one sense, Bush had already had a rehearsal to cope with a real *casus foederis* for the coalition when as Vice President he had negotiated a mini-*casus foederis* during the Iran-Iraq war.

---

†There were 1,500 to 3,000 Americans working for Saudi Aramco in January 1991. Only one to two percent of them left Saudi Arabia from September 1990 to January 1991 (*The Asian Wall Street Journal*, p. 24, (August 24, 1990); p. 1, (September 3, 1990); p. 7 (January 25, 1991)).

CONCLUSIONS AND FUTURE IMPLICATIONS

I have shown that the increase in Saudi oil production after the August 1990 Iraqi invasion of Kuwait, which saved the world oil market from another supply shock, was carried out in response to the deployment of U.S. forces in Saudi Arabia. That Saudi response was well expected given the nature and framework of the historical three party coalition that had been originally constructed against the communist threat. On this occasion, Saddam Hussein was the common threat.

To sum up, the world oil market did not face another supply shock after the Iraqi invasion of Kuwait because Saudi Arabia was able to increase and continue producing oil at the most critical moment; one of the most important conditions for such a response was the security of Saudi Arabia; and the three party coalition proved quite effective in defending Saudi Arabia from Iraq and achieving a secure oil supply.

Applying these lessons, we can draw the following implications for the future world oil market.

(1) The future supply security of the world oil market will most likely be a function of the effectiveness of the three party coalition.

(2) Leaving aside unexpected difficulties such as the massive Iraqi oil spills, the future world oil market can expect a secure supply of oil as long as Holsti's conditions for an effective coalition are met: (a) the three parties have a common enemy (if no longer communism or Iraq, then Iran or an "externally supported rebellion" in Saudi Arabia; (b) there is no major change in the complementary capabilities of the coalition partners. If Saudi Arabia accelerates its endeavors to acquire the oil companies' accumulated expertise, it may not need the American oil companies but it will still need U.S. military protection;† (c) the three parties see positive net benefits in the coalition, so that it is especially important that the Palestinian problem should not mar the relationship; and (d) the three parties continue to make clear commitments and hold confidence in each other's commitments, as in the past.

---

†Indeed, the three party coalition has been strengthened now that they have shown that they would meet their commitments. The United States and Saudi Arabia are planning to develop a "peace shield," a radar system covering the entire Saudi Arabia (*The Nihon Keizai Shimbun,* p. 9, (July 5, 1991)). The two countries are also reported to have discussed a formal security treaty (*The Nihon Keizai Shimbun,* p. 8, (August 2, 1991)).

REFERENCES

1. K. J. Holsti, *International Politics,* pp. 111–127, Prentice-Hall, Englewood Cliffs, NJ (1977).
2. Irvine H. Anderson, *Aramco, the United States and Saudi Arabia,* p. 178, Princeton University Press, Princeton, NJ (1981).
3. Lenczowski, pp. 577–580.
4. Lenczowski, p. 584.
5. Lenczowski, p. 584.
6. Anderson, pp. 179–197.
7. Kazushi Uemura, "The Two Saudi Oil Decisions During the Second Quarter of 1979 and Their Implications towards the Future Saudi-U.S. Relationship," *The Journal of International Studies* 4 (1981).
8. David D. Newsom, "Miracle or Mirage: Reflections on U.S. Diplomacy and the Arabs," *The Middle East Journal,* p. 305 (summer 1981).
9. Ismail I. Nawwab, *Aramco and Its World,* p. 238, Aramco, Washington, DC (1980).
10. *The Middle East Economic Survey,* p. D5 (March 5, 1990).
11. *The Asian Wall Street Journal,* p. 1 (August 8, 1990).
12. *The Asian Wall Street Journal,* p. 22 (September 13, 1980).

6 Long-Term Oil Developments in the Former Soviet Union: Domestic Issues and International Implications

Eugene M. Khartukov

INTRODUCTION

The dissolution of the former Soviet Union has raised many questions about the quantity and quality of future Soviet trade in oil. How much oil will be produced, consumed domestically, and exported in a reformed Soviet Union? What will be the international implications of market-oriented developments in the petroleum sector of the largest oil-producing economy in the world? These are just a few of the questions that not only are proving to be more difficult to answer since perestroika but are proving to be even more important in light of the latest military conflict in the Middle East. These "post-perestroika" issues are the focus of this paper.

Clearly, under the growing pressure of market-oriented reforms, all the factors affecting the oil export equation (i.e., indigenous supplies, domestic requirements, and the export policy itself) are no longer determined only by predictable physical constraints and the policies of a less predictable command structure, but by an emerging economic market, and social forces so well defined by Adam Smith. Such market forces are familiar to the Western world but little understood in the eldest centrally planned economy, particularly in terms of domestic oil developments.

Despite the seemingly unpredictable nature of Soviet oil industry development, Soviet energy experts are capable of making reliable forecasts, even under conditions where the country's oil outlook is determined by the speed and depth of market reforms.

When considering Soviet energy prospects, many Western analysts underestimate the impact of internal political, economic and social factors on domestic oil supplies and energy demand, and attribute diminishing exports of Soviet oil to depleted wells and corroded pipelines. Although the producing oil fields are indeed substantially depleted and badly waterlogged (the national average water-cut reached the level of 75 percent) and at least one-third of existing oil pipelines require immediate replacement, it is the lack of incentives to work or work harder that poses the most serious problems. To complicate matters, worsening working and living conditions tempt Soviet oilmen to go on strike. These critical problems were brought to light because of glasnost, and the situation was exacerbated by perestroika, which triggered an avalanche of misguided hopes and disillusionment. If successful, the political and economic reforms that have already been implemented will tangibly improve the Soviet economy's efficiency in all business spheres, including the development and utilization of its enormous energy resources. In this respect, the author supports the notion put forward by a well-known expert on Soviet and East European energy issues that the likely net result of the political and economic transformation of the Socialist world to a market-oriented regime is a very large-scale expansion of its ability to export energy materials to the rest of the world.[1]

Thus, to assess possible impacts of future Soviet oil developments upon the world petroleum market, the Moscow-based World Energy Analysis & Forecasting Group (GAPMER) focused on three medium-term scenarios. General assumptions were made concerning the speed and depth of the marketization of the economy and oil industry of the former Soviet Union.

GAPMER's first scenario is somewhat pessimistic. Mainly extrapolated from the trends between 1970 and 1979, the scenario assumes that no more moves towards marketization will occur, with the political and economic changes of 1990-91 being regarded as temporary deviations from past trends. This "business as usual" scenario, which is based on limiting extremes, points to a continued rapid decline of indigenous oil production from 11.5 million barrels per day (b/d) in 1990 down to less than 9 million b/d in 2000, and a steady growth of wasteful consumption (from 8.5 to 11 million b/d) with net oil exports drying up by 1995 (see Table 6.1).

·GAPMER's second scenario is more optimistic. Considered a bound-building extreme, it proceeds under the assumption of rapid marketization of the Soviet economy. This basically means the Soviet economy's radical decentralization and demonopolization, with inevitable, extensive privatization, full convertibility of the ruble by 1995, steadily rising domestic fuel prices aimed at reaching international parity by 2000, an unconstrained influx of Western capital and technology into the Soviet oil industry (both upstream and downstream), and energy conservation projects. These rosy scenarios suggest fairly quick stabilization and subsequent slow growth of the national aggregate output of crude and condensate to almost 12 million b/d by the year 2000. At the same time, because of higher "market" prices, domestic

Table 6.1. Scenarios of Soviet oil development: 1990–2000 (million barrels per day)

Scenario	1990	1991	1992	1993	1994	1995	1996	1997	1998	1999	2000
A. Business as usual:											
Production (1)	11.5	10.1	10.2	10.1	9.9	9.7	9.4	9.2	9.0	8.8	8.7
Domestic consumption (A)	8.5	8.2	8.5	9.0	9.3	9.7	10.0	10.2	10.5	10.8	11.0
Net exports	3.0	1.9	1.7	1.1	0.6	0.0	-0.6	-1.0	-1.5	-1.9	-2.3
B. Rapid marketization:											
Production (A)	11.5	10.3	10.5	10.8	11.1	11.3	11.4	11.5	11.6	11.7	11.8
Production (B)	11.5	10.3	10.5	10.8	11.1	11.3	11.4	10.7	10.3	9.9	9.5
Domestic consumption	8.5	8.1	8.3	8.5	8.4	8.2	7.7	7.2	6.8	6.4	6.0
Net exports (A)	3.0	2.3	2.2	2.3	2.6	3.1	3.8	4.3	4.9	5.4	5.9
Net exports (B)	3.0	2.3	2.2	2.3	2.6	3.1	3.8	3.5	3.5	3.5	3.5
C. Slow marketization:											
Production	11.5	10.2	10.4	10.5	10.5	10.4	10.3	10.2	10.2	10.1	10.1
Domestic production	8.5	8.2	8.2	8.4	8.5	8.6	8.7	8.5	8.3	8.2	8.0
Net exports	3.0	2.1	2.2	2.2	2.0	1.8	1.6	1.7	1.8	2.0	2.1

(1) Here and below including gas condensate. (2) Here and below including direct and own use, loss and change in stocks of crude and products. (A) Without any restrictions on potential production or export level. (B) Taking into account probable restrictions on net oil exports, possibly at a level of 3.5 million barrels per day.

Note: Figures may not add due to rounding.

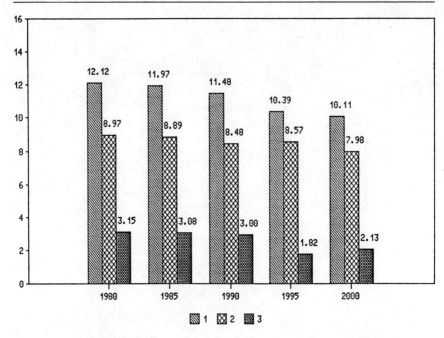

Fig. 6.1. Soviet oil balance—slow marketization scenario: 1980–2000 (million b/d).
1 - production; 2 - domestic consumption; 3 - exports

oil consumption drops from a peak of 8.5 million b/d in 1993 to less than 6 million b/d in 2000. The resultant surplus would allow for an increase in exports to nearly 6 million b/d. Restrictions imposed on net oil exports, however, would probably limit the level to 3–4 million b/d. Nevertheless, at such a level of exports, it makes sense to curtail production of crude oil to 9.5–10.5 million b/d in 1997, and to 8–9 million b/d in 2000, which corresponds to the figures for average aggregate, crude and condensate, restricted output shown in Table 6.1.

GAPMER's best-guess, "slow marketization" scenario assumes gradual increases in domestic fuel prices in line with estimated marginal costs, the introduction of external convertibility of the ruble by 1995 and full convertibility by 2000, and limited involvement of Western oil companies until the probable end of their present "wait-and-see" attitude by the mid-1990s. Under these more probable conditions, by the end of the century Soviet oil production declines to 10 million b/d, domestic oil consumption (after peaking at 8.7 million b/d in 1996) falls to 8 million b/d, and exports recover from a 1996 low of 1.6 million b/d to more than 2 million b/d (see Table 6.1 and Fig. 6.1).

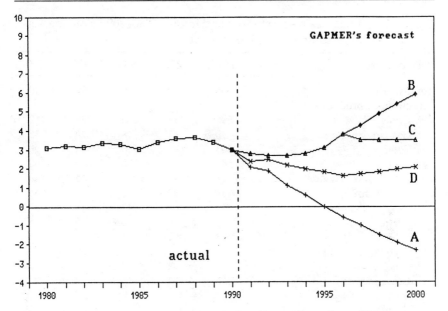

Fig. 6.2. Scenarios of Soviet net trade in oil (crude and products):
1980–2000 (million b/d).
A - business as usual; B - rapid marketization; (C - with restrictions); D - slow marketization

Admittedly, future developments of the Soviet economy and its oil industry are not limited even to this reasonable scenario. However, GAPMER is confident that the future realities of the emerging national oil market, where actual exports are to an ever larger extent determined by the market rather than by the government, will not greatly deviate from the slow-marketization path (see Fig. 6.2). The following discussion assumes the slow-marketization scenario as a base case. Table 6.2 outlines the slow-marketization scenario.

In assessing the international implications of possible developments in the oil industry of the former Soviet Union, it is assumed that the world petroleum market will not remain indifferent to the outcome of market reforms in the largest oil-producing country. Moreover, the impact of perestroika-induced increases in supplies (or decreases in supplies) of Soviet oil could easily overshadow another, say, medium-size crisis in the Middle East. To put GAPMER's conclusions into a frame of reference, it is helpful to describe the analytical tools and general assumptions used to predict world oil market developments to the year 2000. GAPMER's medium-term forecasting system is based on an original multi-equation stepwise model, built on the general premise of a competitive world oil market. The main feature of the model is the concept of objective upper and lower limits to OPEC crude oil production that re-

Table 6.2. Oil balance of former Soviet Union—1980–2000 slow marketization scenario (million tonnes)

Balance item	1980	1985	1990	1995	2000
Total supply	608	610	580	530	520
Indigenous production:					
Crude oil	593	583	552	487	462
Gas condensate	10	12	18	28	38
Total	603	595	570	515	500
Russia	547	542	518	430	380
Tyumen Region	308	361	353	285	240
Kazakhstan	19	23	23	52	85
Azerbaijan	15	13	13	15	17
Turkmenia	8	6	6	5	5
Uzbekistan	1	2	2	5	5
Ukraine	8	6	5	5	4
Belorussia	3	2	2	2	2
Gross imports:	5	14	10	15	20
Crude oil	3	12	8	13	17
Refined products	1	2	2	2	3
Total demand	608	610	580	530	520
Refinery throughput	467	472	456	450	440
Other crude oil					
Requirements (1)	21	18	15	15	15
Refined products					
Consumption (2)	427	425	407	410	380
Gross exports:	160	167	159	105	125
Crude oil	119	117	109	63	62
Refined products	41	50	50	42	63
Trade balance (net export):	156	152	148	90	105
Crude oil	116	105	100	50	45
Refined products	40	48	48	40	60

(1) Oil industry's and direct use, losses, and stock change. (2) Including refinery fuel, losses, and stock change.
Note: Figures may not add due to rounding.

strict the organization's ability to forestall sharp price swings at the market's
margins—that is, when demand for OPEC crude approaches its productive
capacity or approaches the Member Countries' minimally required crude
production, which is determined mainly by the Member Countries' economic needs (Fig. 6.3). Other major determinants in the model's real price equation are inter-fuel competition and political tensions in the Middle East.
    For the purpose of predicting and simulating world oil market conditions

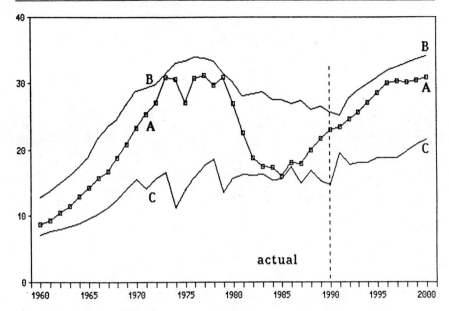

Fig. 6.3. OPEC crude oil production (A) and its upper (B) and lower (C) limits: 1960–2000 (million b/d) (moderate growth case).

in the next decade, GAPMER initially proceeds from three medium-term scenarios that assume no further serious military conflicts in the Middle East at least until the year 2000, and that differ mainly in acceptable growth rates for the developed market economies. Particularly, in the "lower growth" case, it is assumed that the OECD countries as a whole would remain in recession, which could lower their real economic growth to 1.0 percent in 1991 and −0.5 percent in 1992, with an average annual growth rate of 2.0 percent for the period 1991–95. The economic outlook for 1996–2000 is somewhat more promising—average real GDP growth of 2.25 percent for the OECD Member Countries was taken in this gloomy scenario. The result of a related model simulation, which can be seen in Figure 6.4 (curve A), points to possible gyrations of real (1990 dollars) prices of Arab Light of between $15.00 and $18.00/b, until it begins to rise steadily from about $16.00/b in 1993, to just above $20.00/b in 2000.

Naturally, higher world oil prices would result from the more optimistic assumptions of OECD economic performance, which are used in GAPMER's "higher growth" case: on the average, 3.15 percent for 1991–95 (including 2.5% for 1991) and 3.8 percent for the rest of the century. In this scenario, the real market price of Arab Light, after dropping to less than $17.00/b in 1991, would rise to more than $27.00/b in 1995 and stabilize at about $36.00/b by the year 2000 (Fig. 6.4, curve C).

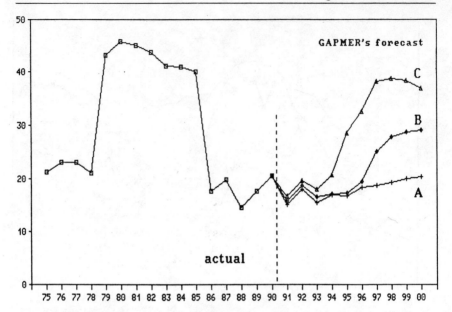

Fig. 6.4. Real market price of Arab Light under various OECD GDP
growth rates: 1975–2000 (in 1990 $/b).
A - lower growth case; B - moderate growth case; C - higher
growth case

Perhaps a more realistic and rather optimistic scenario is the "moderate
growth" case, which is based on December 1990 OECD predictions of 2.0
percent GDP growth for OECD countries in 1991, and 2.5 percent real increase in 1992.[2] Average yearly growth is assumed to be 2.75 percent from
1996 to 2000. As Figure 6.4 (curve B) shows, such assumptions yield an average 1991 price of $16.00/b, which rises to nearly $19.00/b in 1992, and climbs
from around $17.00/b in 1993–95 to $29.00/b in 2000 (in constant 1990
dollars).

   In attempts to designate the highest price level attainable in 1991, GAP-
MER tested a range of predictions for postwar recovery of the damaged Kuwaiti and Iraqi oil industries (with available estimates of their aggregate
end-1991 output potential varying from 0.8 to 2.5 million b/d). Even given
the most favorable combination of slow reconstruction of destroyed production facilities on the one hand and high assumed economic growth in the
OECD countries on the other, prices fail to move higher than an average of
$17.00/b.

   As for the output potential of the OPEC countries, GAPMER defines their
available crude oil capacity at the end of 1990 at about 24 million b/d, and

assumes that it would increase by the end of 1991 to a probable level of nearly 27 million b/d in line with the latest (March 1991) predictions of the London-based Centre for Global Energy Studies. This suggests a yearly average OPEC capacity of 25.7 million b/d in 1990 and 25.2 million b/d in 1991, which is reflected in Table 6.3.

The future path of world oil prices will be affected by a variety of market developments, some of which are regarded as virtually unpredictable even in a medium-term perspective. For example, GAPMER believes the degree of political tension in the Middle East, which tends to erupt every 6 to 10 years, is unpredictable. With a view toward "politicizing" its projections, GAPMER assessed the impact of a hypothetical oil supply disruption of 1.5 million b/d, which could result from a limited one-year military conflict in the world's main oil-exporting region. GAPMER assumes hypothetically that such a disruption will occur in 1994, 1996, or 1998. As shown in Figure 6.5 (which reflects the conflict elasticity of the simulated world oil price in our "moderate-growth" case), the impact of such a supply disruption is tolerable if it happens in 1994, or even in 1998. However, if it occurs in 1996, when the model-fitted call on OPEC crude dangerously approaches the level of available production capacity in the member countries (see Fig. 6.3), it may bring about economic disruption comparable to the oil shocks of 1973–74 and 1979–80.

Now that the world oil market is seemingly shaped with no perturbations from behind the collapsed "iron curtain," this author would like to demonstrate the impact on world oil prices of possible upward and downward deviations of USSR net trade in oil, which may be caused by differing degrees of marketization of the national economy. To this end, we present here what can happen to the simulated world oil price (as it was predicted in our moderate-growth case—see Table 6.3 and curve B in Fig. 6.4) if slower or quicker perestroika (as compared to our base case) brings about just half (50%) of the possible changes in Soviet oil trade which could result from the realization of our most pessimistic or most optimistic scenarios of marketization. As Fig. 6.5 shows, by the end of the century, faster marketization (curve A) would gradually pull the world oil price down from $29.00/b in the base case (curve B) to $22.00/b, while slower reform (curve C) would raise the price to about $36.00/b (all in constant 1990 dollars).

Thus, we conclude that the impact of the conceivable changes in the speed of Soviet market transformation will be greater than that of the tested oil supply disruptions in the Middle East (see Fig. 6.6). This close scrutiny of the changes demonstrates that examination of such changes is fairly comparable to the examination of corresponding effects of the possible differences in OECD economic growth rates (see Fig. 6.4). In other words, regardless of actual outcomes of the market reforms that have been initiated, current and future energy developments in the former Soviet Union evidently deserve no less attention by Western analysts than that which is traditionally paid

Table 6.3. Moderate-growth scenario of the World Oil Market: 1990–2000

	1990	1991	1992	1993	1994	1995	1996	1997	1998	1999	2000
FW(*) oil consumption (1), mmbd	51.6	52.0	52.8	53.7	54.8	56.1	57.5	57.7	57.5	57.7	58.1
Non-OPEC oil production, mmbd	25.8	25.6	25.3	25.1	24.8	24.6	24.4	24.2	24.1	24.1	24.3
CPE(**) net oil exports, mmbd	1.6	1.0	1.1	1.1	1.0	0.9	0.7	0.9	1.0	1.1	1.3
of which USSR..........	3.0	2.1	2.2	2.2	2.0	1.8	1.6	1.7	1.8	2.0	2.1
OPEC NGL production, mmbd	1.9	1.9	2.0	2.1	2.2	2.3	2.4	2.5	2.6	2.7	2.8
Call on OPEC crude (2), mmbd	22.3	23.5	24.4	25.4	26.8	28.3	30.0	30.1	29.8	29.7	29.8
Stock change, mmbd	0.8	0.0	0.1	0.1	0.2	0.3	0.4	0.4	0.2	0.2	0.2
OPEC crude production (3), mmbd	23.1	23.5	24.5	25.5	27.0	28.6	30.4	30.5	30.0	29.9	29.9
Available capacity (4), mmbd	25.7	25.2	27.9	29.0	29.9	30.8	31.8	32.3	32.8	33.5	33.9
Minimum requirements, mmbd	14.8	19.6	17.8	18.0	18.1	18.7	18.7	18.3	19.6	20.9	21.8
Market price of Arabian Light, fob Ras Tanurah, $/b:											
- in real terms (1990 $)	20.7	16.0	18.9	16.5	17.1	17.3	19.6	25.2	27.9	28.8	29.2
- in nominal terms (5)	20.7	15.7	19.8	17.4	18.8	19.7	23.6	33.3	39.0	41.8	44.0
Major assumptions:											
OECD GDP growth rate, %	2.8	2.0	2.5	2.3	2.7	3.0	3.5	2.5	2.1	2.7	3.0
Middle East political instability (1988 = 100)	140	135	115	100	100	100	100	100	100	100	100

mmbd: million barrels per day.
(*) Free World (excluding former centrally planned economies). (**) Centrally Planned Economies (including East Germany).
(1) Excluding refinery gains. (2) Including oil stock movements. (3) Assumed to balance world oil demand and supply with regard to normal changes in oil stocks. (4) Yearly averaged. (5) Inflated by export price index for developed market economies (1990 = 100).
Note: Figures may not add due to rounding.

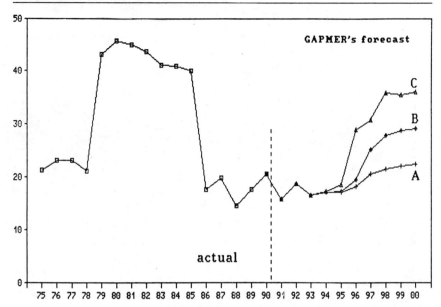

Fig. 6.5. Real price of Arab Light under various scenarios of perestroika: 1975–2000 (in 1990 $/b).
A - faster marketization; B - slow marketization; C - slower marketization

to other major oil-exporting regions of the world. Moreover, a detailed quantitative analysis of Soviet oil trends with a view toward assessing the country's export potential and determining its physical impact on the global supply and demand should be supplemented with a comprehensive qualitative examination of the institutional (regulatory) patterns of Soviet oil trade, which is becoming more and more decentralized. Indeed, the former monopoly of the USSR oil-exporting and importing agency Sojuznefteexport (SNE), the world's leading oil trader, is now undermined by the growth of independent sales which are effected by other trading companies (both national and partly foreign-owned) or directly by Soviet oil producers. In particular, last year some 10 percent of all the exported Soviet oil (more than 320,000 b/d out of 3.2 million b/d) bypassed SNE, which was not involved in the decentralized deals even as a broker or commissioned agent. It is noteworthy that every fifth barrel of these decentralized deliveries was counter-traded through barter deals, with the estimated "shadow" prices being on average four times lower than the corresponding world market prices that prevailed in 1990.

It is apparent that the recent breakup of the Soviet Union and ongoing market reforms is facilitating the gradual (if not rapid) transformation of the present quasi market situation towards a competitive marketplace. This trans-

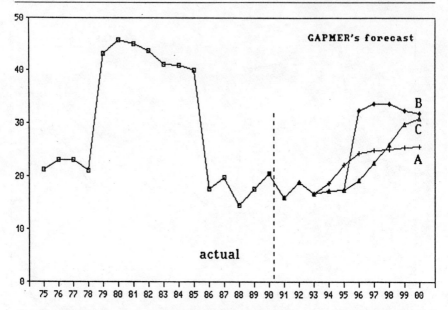

Fig. 6.6. Real market price of Arab Light under conditions of the 1.5 million b/d supply disruption occurring in 1994 (A), 1996 (B), or 1998 (C) (in 1990 $/b) (moderate growth case).

formation is likely to radically change the current patterns, terms, and conditions of Soviet oil supplies.

In this context, the possibility remains that further decentralization of the Soviet oil trade industry will facilitate greater competition among national producers desperate for hard currency, which, unless controlled by sensible government regulations or production-sharing agreements with their foreign partners, may flood an already unstable world oil market with underpriced crude oil and products, thus triggering another damaging price war.

An important question remains, however, as to whether perestroika-induced Soviet oil exports will bring desirable relief, or whether the unbound marketization of the largest oil-producing economy will unleash economic turmoil. The answer, unfortunately, depends heavily on the vagaries of almost unpredictable and barely controllable global oil developments, as well as much needed multilateral cooperation to stabilize the world energy market, a market in which the post-perestroika Soviet Union has yet to find its proper place.†

---

†Further information about GAPMER's WOM Forecasting System and its regularly updated market forecasts can be obtained from: Prof. E. M. Khartukov, GAPMER, IBS/MGIMO, 76 Vernadsky Ave., Moscow 117454, Russia. Telex: 412172 MGIMO SU; fax: (095) 936 22 42; phone: (095) 422 55 45 or (095) 434 92 53.

REFERENCES

1. Marian Radetzki, "USSR Energy Exports Post-Perestroika," *Energy Policy* 19, 4 pp. 291–302 (May 1991).
2. *OECD Economic Outlook* 48 (December 1990).

7 Oil Self-Sufficiency for Australia

Anthony D. Owen

INTRODUCTION

Australia is relatively well endowed with a wide range of energy resources. The comparative advantages conferred by this resource endowment has enabled Australia to become a significant net energy exporting nation as well as a preferred location for certain types of energy-intensive industry such as aluminum smelting. It is the world's largest exporter of coal, a significant exporter of uranium, and, within its region, an important exporter of refined petroleum products. Exports of liquid natural gas (LNG) began in 1989, and LNG has since become a major source of export revenue.

In energy value terms, black coal, brown coal, and uranium make up about 95 percent of Australia's demonstrated economic resources of non-renewable energy (Table 7.1). Although there is currently no domestic demand for uranium, and this situation is unlikely to change in the foreseeable future, coal offers a very long-term security of supply.

However, apart from a couple of years in the mid-1980s, Australia has been a net importer of petroleum, and crude oil is the country's largest single primary commodity import. Because of the distance of some markets (for example, Darwin, in the Northern Territory) from domestic refineries and freight cost differentials, similar refined petroleum products are both imported to and exported from Australia. While the country is overall a crude oil importer, significant quantities of crude oil and other refinery feedstocks are exported.

To the year 2005, Australia's energy exports are projected to increase substantially (Table 7.2), but so are net imports of petroleum as domestic crude oil production is projected to fall and demand to rise. In terms of energy values (that is, petajoules [PJ] for the purpose of this paper), Australian exports considerably more energy than it consumes. Despite projected increases in (net) oil imports, this situation is expected to continue through the current decade largely due to substantial expected increases in coal exports over the

Table 7.1. Australia's identified recoverable resources of energy minerals and fuels (as of 31 December, 1989)

| Commodity | Unit | Demonstrated resources | | Inferred Resources | Production 1989/90 | Resource life at current rates of production (years) |
		Economic	Subeconomic			
Black coal	Mt	50,800	2,000	very large	158	322
Brown coal	Mt	41,800	2,600	183,600	46	909
Crude oil and ORF	GL	379	73	na	32	12
Natural gas	TL	955	1,174	na	20.3	47
LPG	GL	114	48	na	3.8	30
Shale oil	GL	—	4,544	40,719	—	na
Uranium	kt(U)	474	58	390	3.5	135

Source: Bureau of Mineral Resources, Geology and Geophysics, Australian Bureau of Agricultural and Resource Economics

Table 7.2. Projections for Australia's energy trade; Energy Content (PJ); 1990–2005 (financial years, ending June 30)

Commodity	1990	1995	2000	2005
Exports				
Black coal	2,966	3,497	3,910	4,049
Crude oil and ORF	248	242	293	282
LPG	56	36	19	11
LNG	109	343	351	462
Uranium (1)	1,750	2,585	4,700	4,700
Other (2)	121	147	156	164
Total exports	5,250	6,850	9,429	9,668
Imports				
Crude oil and ORF	449	751	746	884
Other (3)	176	159	184	203
Total imports	625	910	930	1,087

Notes:
(1) Assuming a once-through cycle with no reprocessing.
(2) Includes brown coal, coke, and petroleum products.
(3) Petroleum products.
Source: Australian Bureau of Agricultural and Resource Economics

period. Currently, exports of energy minerals account for around 20 percent of Australia's total exports of merchandise.

Domestically, oil self-sufficiency is perceived to have both strategic and financial benefits for Australia, although the importance of the former is frequently exaggerated. Financially, however, the (net) oil import bill places a substantial (additional) strain on Australia's external trading account. This paper assesses future oil supply potential for Australia and the resulting requirement for oil imports to 2005.

BACKGROUND

The first commercial discovery of oil in Australia was made at Moonie in south east Queensland in 1961. There followed considerable exploration activity nationwide during the 1960s and further important discoveries were made in the Northern Territory and Western Australia. But these were soon overshadowed by the discovery of the vast oil and gas fields in Bass Strait (Gippsland Basin) beginning in the late 1960s, particularly Barracouta, Marlin, Halibut, and Kingfish. More recently, important discoveries have been made at Jabiru, Challis and Skua in the Timor Sea (Bonaparte Basin), and Echo,

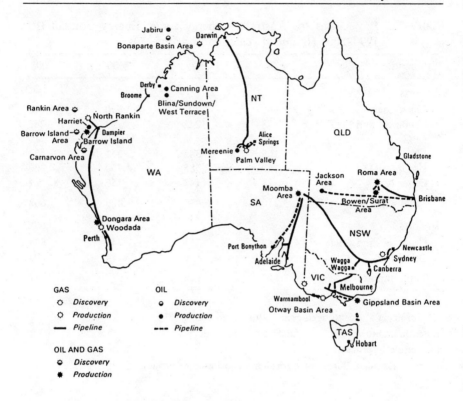

Source: Australian Bureau of Agricultural and Resource Economics

Fig. 7.1. Australia's oil and gas deposits.

Wanaea, and Cossak off the North West Shelf (Carnarvon Basin). The locations of Australia's oil and gas bearing basins are shown in Fig. 7.1.

Annual production of Australian crude oil and condensate is shown in Fig. 7.2. Commercial production started from the Moonie oil field in 1964, and increased substantially when production from Bass Strait began in 1969. From 1972 to 1983 production was running at approximately 400,000 barrels a day (b/d), but it subsequently increased to over 500,000 b/d when exports of domestic crude were permitted, commencing in 1983.

Since the mid-1980s, annual domestic oil production has remained relatively static, at around 200 million barrels. Over this period, a significant fall in production from the Bass Strait has been offset by the start of production in Timor Sea fields and significant increases in production from fields offshore Western Australia (that is, the Carnarvon Basin) and the Moomba area (the Cooper Basin). These changes are illustrated in Fig. 7.3.

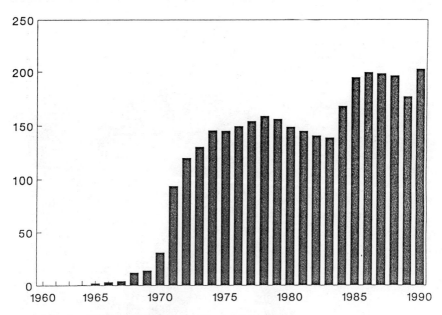

Source: Australian Bureau of Agricultural and Resource Economics

Fig. 7.2. Crude oil and condensate production (million barrels).

Over the same period, consumption of petroleum products remained relatively stable, which meant that Australia has been able to maintain a relatively high degree of self-sufficiency since the mid-1980s.

DOMESTIC SUPPLY PROSPECTS

Over the past 30 years, some four billion barrels of oil have been discovered in Australia, the great bulk of which was found in the Gippsland Basin.

In January 1990, the Bureau of Mineral Resources (BMR) estimated that Australia's remaining undiscovered crude oil and condensate resources would lie in the range of one billion to six billion barrels, with an average estimate of three billion barrels. About 60 percent of this estimate was attributed to the Carnarvon and Bonaparte Basins off northwest Australia.

Significant oil reserves are also estimated for Australia's North East Shelf, although the very deep water in this area presents a disincentive to petroleum exploration.

Projections of domestic demand for petroleum products to 2005, made by the Australian Bureau of Agricultural and Resource Economics (ABARE), and BMR estimates of future levels of domestic oil production are given in Fig. 7.4. The BMR estimates are provided at various probability levels to reflect

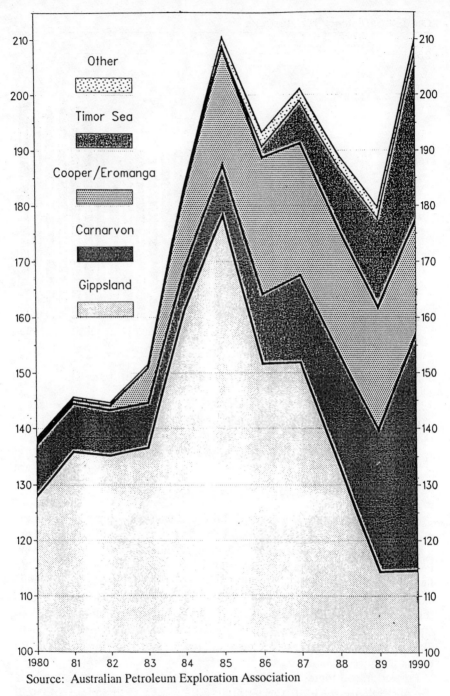

Other

Timor Sea

Cooper/Eromanga

Carnarvon

Gippsland

Source: Australian Petroleum Exploration Association

Fig. 7.3. Crude oil and condensate production, 1980–1990 (million barrels per year).

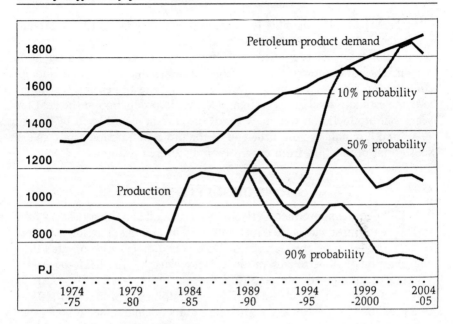

Source: Australian Petroleum Exploration Association

Fig. 7.4. Liquid petroleum production and demand.

the uncertainty surrounding future discoveries and the development of discoveries. For example, a production estimate at the 90 percent probability level means that there is a 90 percent chance of production being at least as high as the figure shown. The higher the probability level, the more conservative the assumptions made concerning reserves in identified fields; the number of identified but currently unproductive fields that will be brought on stream over the period; and the extent and success rates of future exploration activity. Future levels of production from undiscovered resources are more uncertain than production from identified fields, as is seen from the greater spread between the production estimates at the various probability levels.

In the median estimate, total crude oil and condensate production is estimated to remain at about the current level, on average, over the period to 2004–2005. A fall in production occurs in the next few years, due to the effects of the continuing decline in Bass Strait production; but new developments, particularly in the northwestern offshore region, then boost production as fields that have been identified but not yet developed are brought on stream. Production reaches record levels by the late 1990s. Thereafter, as production from the presently identified fields diminishes, that from as yet undiscovered fields becomes sufficient to keep overall output roughly steady.

At the 90 percent probability level, the estimate shows a decrease in production rates in the early 1990s, before an increase corresponding to the period when fields that have been discovered but not yet developed are brought on stream. Thereafter, however, production falls away and there is only a minor contribution from as yet undiscovered fields. At the 10 percent probability level the estimate shows only a slight decrease in production in the next few years, but production is well in excess of the current record levels by the late 1990s and it remains so until the end of the projection period as a result of substantial production from currently undiscovered resources.

PROJECTIONS OF SUPPLY SHORTFALL

Liquid petroleum products derived from crude oil and other refinery feedstocks are the most widely used fuels in Australia, and this situation is projected to continue over the period to 2005. The average rate of growth in consumption of all petroleum products is projected by ABARE to be around 1.8 percent through to that year (Fig. 7.4).

As the result of the widening gap between domestic production (50 percent probability estimate) and petroleum product demand, net annual liquid petroleum imports (including crude oil, LPG and refined products), are expected to rise by 250 percent over the period to 2005 (from 30 million barrels a year to 108 million barrels in 2005). At projected oil prices and exchange rates this level of imports would cost around A$3 billion (1990 dollars) by 2005. To put this figure into context, it is equivalent to about 6.5 percent of total Australian exports of merchandise in 1990, a not inconsiderable amount.

In order to retain the current level of production to 2005, the Australian Petroleum Exploration Association (APEA)[2] maintains that the domestic oil exploration industry will have to find and develop up to two billion barrels of crude oil and condensate. This task is likely to require an investment (in 1990 dollars) of over A$12 billion in exploration and A$14 billion on development.

SUMMARY

This paper has provided a brief assessment of Australia's oil self-sufficiency through to 2005. The estimates included a component of production from fields which are as yet undiscovered. Without any further oil discoveries, Australia's level of self-sufficiency is estimated to decline dramatically by 2005.

There are a number of sources of uncertainty in the estimates of production from undiscovered fields, but the main areas are the underlying level of Australia's petroleum prospectivity, the real price of oil, and the efficiency of exploration. The most significant factors are the prospectivity in terms of the number and size of the undiscovered fields and the assumed rate of future drilling of new-field wildcat wells. Assumptions about future discovery rates (the measure of exploration efficiency) and lead time between discovery and production can also have a significant effect on the estimate, but are of lesser importance.

REFERENCES

1. Australian Bureau of Agricultural and Resource Economics, *Projections of Energy Demand and Supply,* Australia 1990-91 to 2004-05, Australian Government Publishing Service, Canberra (1991).
2. Australian Petroleum Exploration Association Limited, "Australia's Offshore Exploration in Perspective", Sydney (April 1991).

8 Overcoming Barriers to Energy Efficiency in Transportation: The Case of Brazil

Andrea N. Ketoff

INTRODUCTION

Transport absorbs more than 50 percent of total Latin-American oil demand, and is responsible for about 40 percent of carbon emissions originating from energy use, a share that is equivalent or higher than in most industrialized countries. With prospects for fuel substitution being limited and costly, the introduction of energy efficiency is generally considered the primary response for containing fuel demand—and carbon emissions—in the sector.

A great number of studies published in recent years indicate that great potential exists to improve vehicle efficiency. In most cases these improvements would prove highly cost-effective! Progress in the efficiency of new cars in the last decade is promising, and major vehicle manufacturers have now developed prototype cars running in the range of 4.0 to 3.0 liters per 100 km (i.e., 60–75 miles per gallon).[2]

The concentration of the international automotive industry could lead to the assumption that future efficiency improvements expected for Europe, Japan, and the United States will be automatically transferred to developing countries. However, in many developing countries the cost of efficiency improvements might be prohibitive, and the potential savings might be substantially limited by the infrastructural inadequacies (e.g., bad roads, poor fuel quality) which characterize the developing world.

This study analyzes the prospects for and barriers to bringing about long-term efficiency improvements in Brazil, a country with a well-developed transport system, and where there is much interest in energy-related issues. Brazil has one of the highest levels of private car ownership in the developing world. As illustrated by the nation's well-developed car-manufacturing industry, Brazil's economic development strategy has long emphasized the local production of cars (as well as other durable consumer goods) for both domestic and foreign markets. Moreover, the country's fuel-switching policy, which promotes the substitution of sugarcane alcohol for gasoline, makes it an interesting case to analyze in view of the interaction between alternative fuel use and energy efficiency.[3]

TRANSPORT AND DEVELOPMENT: THE STRUCTURE OF MOBILITY

Transport energy demand in Brazil has increased at an average rate of 5 percent per year during the last two decades (annual growth rates peaked at over 10% in the early 1970s and the mid-1980s), reflecting a strong demand for both freight and personal mobility.[4] However, the growth of energy consumption for transport followed very closely the patterns of economic growth (Fig. 8.1), suggesting that freight transport, which is more directly related to economic activity, accounts for a large share of total consumption.

The increasing urbanization of the Brazilian population has largely contributed to the rapid growth of transport demand. The share of the population living in urban areas expanded from 56 percent in 1970 to more than 80 percent today, or from 50 to 120 million in less than 20 years. (In Brazil, rural/urban is determined by the dominant activity, not the size of the cities.) Brazil has 12 cities with more than 1 million people and two cities with more than 10 million.

Cities of such size require extensive public transport systems to guarantee personal mobility. In the city of São Paulo, more than 6 million passenger-trips are serviced every weekday by the public transport system.[5] At the country level, the number of buses grew at a rate of 7 percent per year between 1970 and 1988, increasing from 1 per 2000 inhabitants to 1 per 1000.

Despite this growth, Brazil's public transport system has had trouble satisfying the increasing demand for mobility. The high cost and low quality of the service has repeatedly been the source of social tension, particularly in the recession years of the 1980s, marked by a considerable increase in urban poverty. During the 1980s, Brazil's gross domestic product (GDP) grew more slowly than its population, resulting in a net drop in real income per capita (−5.5% lower in 1990 than in 1981). By 1986, 58 percent of the population lived below the poverty level.[†][6] With disposable income dropping in the last 10 years, transportation expenditures constitute an increasing share of household budgets. In 1980, one monthly minimum salary could buy about 1000

---

†*Poverty* level is defined in the CEPAL report (Ref. 6) as a household income below two "basic baskets" per month. Households whose monthly income was below one "basket" (17% in Brazil in 1986) are considered *indigent*. The value of the "basic basket" in Brazil was, in 1988, US$28.50.

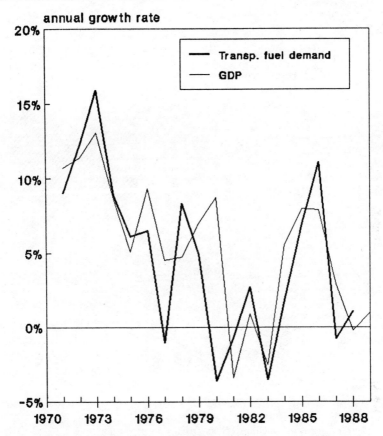

Fig. 8.1. Transport energy and economic activity.

bus fares in São Paulo; by 1990, its purchasing value was limited to fewer than 200 trips.[7]

In the period 1970–1989, while total Brazilian population grew 70 percent and the urban population 140 percent, freight tonnage increased by a factor of three. In the same period, the truck fleet increased by a factor of five, as the share of freight transported on wheels continued to grow. In 1990, 56 percent of total ton-km of freight was road-based.[8] Although lighter trucks have come to comprise a larger share of the fleet (Fig. 8.2),[9] the increase in truck traffic has led to the rapid deterioration of street and highway paving, adding a high cost of road maintenance to the investment requirements for more urban and suburban highways.[10]

Few investments have been channeled towards improving the nation's old and underutilized railway system, which has about 30,000 kilometers (km) of track.[11] Despite the mountainous terrain, railways could play a significant

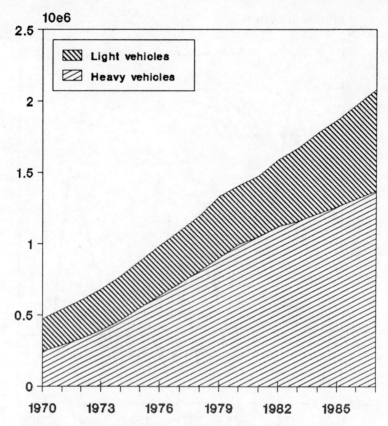

Fig. 8.2. Commercial vehicles fleet (buses and trucks).

role along the coast, particularly since 85 percent of the population resides along a 6,000 km strip that is 200 to 300 km in width. In addition, the sparsely populated interior of the country has more than 35,000 km of waterways that remain underdeveloped. Despite these opportunities, major efforts have been focused instead on developing controversial cross-country highways that have difficulty surviving the forces of nature without substantial maintenance.†

Apart from buses and the recently constructed subway systems in São Paulo and Rio de Janeiro,‡ personal mobility is satisfied by a car fleet of almost

---

†The Transamazonian highway, running through the north of the country, is now interrupted in several points due to lack of maintenance. The abandonment of the regions linked by the highway is considered a failure of that project developed under the military governments of the 1970s. Further controversy is raised by the more recent project to link southern states of the Amazonian basin with Peru through the Andes.

‡At present, subway systems extend over 90 km in São Paulo and 40 km in Rio de Janeiro. Both systems are undergoing further expansion.

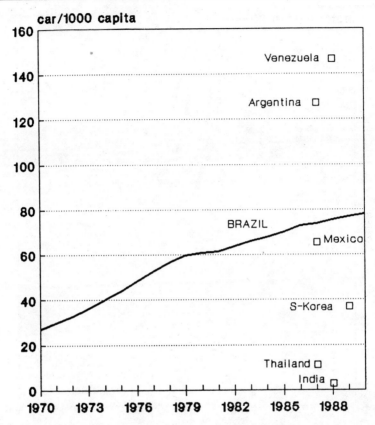

Fig. 8.3. Automobile saturation.

12 million.[12] Levels of car ownership increased rapidly in the 1970s and somewhat more slowly in the 1980s (Fig. 8.3). By 1990 there was almost one car per every 12 persons, which is very low when compared to the United States or Italy (one car per 1.8 and 2.5 persons, respectively) but double the level in South Korea (Fig. 8.3). As in other Latin American countries, the dramatic urban sprawl and the important role played by car manufacturing in the country's industrialization process have contributed to the high penetration of private cars in Brazil.

Motorcycles, on the other hand, are less common, as dangerous traffic conditions, poor road quality, long distances, and heavy tropical rains do not favor their use. However, their saturation rose significantly after 1978, revealing the potential for an enormous market in the future (see Fig. 8.4). Currently, the most popular models are 125 to 150 cc motorcycles aimed at lower-income buyers, although manufacturers are switching their production to more powerful models for young higher-income customers, as the low-

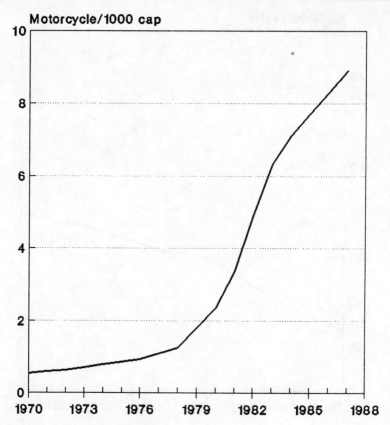

Fig. 8.4. Motorcycle saturation.

income market has been hard hit by the economic crisis.[13] If a young generation of Brazilians overcomes the safety and comfort limits of motorcycle (and
moped) riding, use of these vehicles in large metropolitan areas may increase
dramatically.

TRANSPORT AND FUELS

In 1989, the transport sector was responsible for 31 percent of total commercial energy use in Brazil and 50% of the consumption of oil derivatives.[14]
Diesel fuel, gasoline and alcohol—the three fuels used for road transport—
together account for 90 percent of the total energy demand in this sector (Fig.
8.5). Jet fuel is used for airplanes, fuel oil for ships, diesel fuel for most railways, and electricity for most subways.

In the late 1970s, Brazil addressed the increasing demand for oil products
and the growing cost of imports by implementing a major fuel-substitution

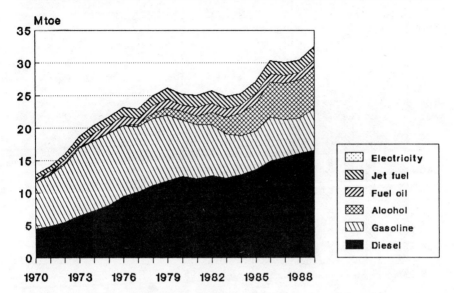

Fig. 8.5. Transport demand by fuel.

program (Pro-Alcool) to encourage the use of sugarcane alcohol in vehicles. Alcohol was introduced into the transport sector in two forms: gasohol, which is a mix of gasoline with 20 percent of ethanol, for traditional gasoline-fueled vehicles; and hydrated alcohol for appropriately converted vehicles.† By 1989, alcohol accounted for 19 percent of total transport energy use and half of the energy used for cars—a considerable success for the Pro-Alcool program.

The manufacture and sale of cars running on hydrated alcohol was promoted strongly starting in late 1979. By 1983, 90 percent of all new cars were alcohol-fueled (Fig. 8.6); the recent drop in the sale of alcohol-fueled cars is discussed later in this article. Thanks to the rapid diffusion of a technology developed by local manufacturers, more than 30 percent of the car fleet is now running on hydrated alcohol, and the rest on gasohol.[15, 16]

Even before alcohol replaced gasoline in the light-vehicle fleet, diesel had in the early seventies become the mandatory fuel for heavy trucks and buses. Diesel overtook the whole truck market, except for part of the light-vehicle fleet that now uses alcohol engines (Fig. 8.7). As a result, the share of diesel in total transport energy demand rose from one third in the early 1970s to about 50 percent by 1980, a share which it has maintained since. Gasoline trucks, which accounted for over 75 percent of sales in the early 1970s, almost disappeared from the market by 1983.[17]

---

†Ethanol-blended gasoline in the United States contains 10 percent of ethyl alcohol.

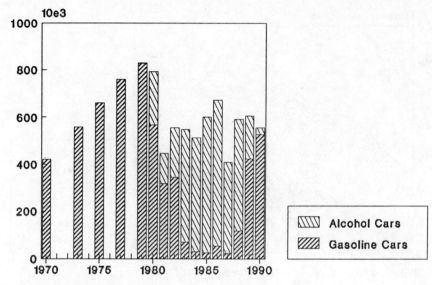

Fig. 8.6. Car sales by fuel type.

The combination of the increased use of both diesel and alcohol caused the consumption of gasoline to drop considerably. Gasoline share of transport fuels fell from over 56 percent in 1970 to less than 18 percent in 1988. Total consumption of oil derivatives fell from a peak of 99 percent in 1976 to 80 percent in 1989 (Fig. 8.5). This is an important achievement for a country that imports half of its crude, and extracts the other half from depleting—and expensive—deep-sea oil fields.[18]

While the containment of oil imports had positive effects on the Brazilian trade balance, the fuel-switching policy has weakened the country's ability to satisfy the fuel demand of its transport sector. Most alcohol producers are "re-converted" sugar producers. Since the majority of the alcohol-producing facilities also produce sugar, the level of alcohol production is dependent on the price of sugar. When the international price of sugar rose in the late 1980s, sugar became so much more lucrative than alcohol that most Brazilian producers chose to lower the levels of alcohol production in favor of sugar. As a result, alcohol shortages have occurred, even though the government increased subsidies to the producers. The government has tried to contain shortages by reducing the quantity of alcohol in the gasohol mix. Nonetheless, shortages of alcohol have persisted. With the first signs of alcohol shortages in 1988, new car buyers switched to purchasing gasohol cars that had a lower chance of being left dry at the pump. Alcohol cars, which constituted over 90 percent of new sales between 1983 and 1988, dropped to 5 percent in 1990.

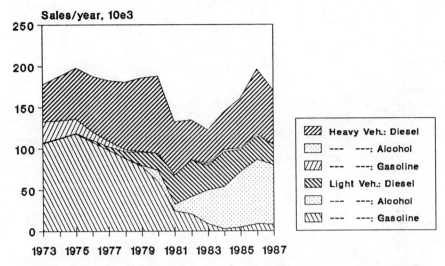

Fig. 8.7. Fuel switching in trucks: sales of light and heavy vehicles by fuel.

In the case of diesel, its use in trucks and buses increased to the point that the Brazilian refining system became unable to satisfy the country's demand for petroleum fuels. Diesel accounts for more than 45 percent of the country's demand for oil derivatives, 80 percent of which goes to the transport sector. Around 35 percent of the crude refined is devoted to diesel production at present (up from 24% in 1974). Despite the demand pressure for heavier fuels (i.e., fuel oil, diesel), Brazil is importing light crude on the basis of long-term intra-governmental trading agreements and "barter" contracts.[19] Due to the present characteristics of the country's refining system and to the quality of crude oil imports, the share of diesel-to-crude could not be increased, and Brazil became a net diesel importer in 1989.[20] Excess gasoline is exported, but the practice is difficult to maintain in a slow international market for oil products. If the present demand patterns are to be continued, the country's refineries need to be reformed and the profile of oil imports requires major changes.

The inadequate supply of alcohol and diesel have indirectly contributed to higher levels of local pollution and poor vehicle efficiencies. To stretch the diesel supply, PETROBRÁS, the national oil company and sole supplier to a number of distributors, has been altering the specifications of diesel oil, thus affecting its burning characteristics.[21] By international standards, diesel oil should correspond to the intermediate oil distillates with boiling temperatures of between 180 and 360 degrees centigrade, and their correct proportion permits optimizing the combustion in diesel engines. As shown by the distillation curve in Fig. 8.8, Brazilian diesel includes distillates with boiling

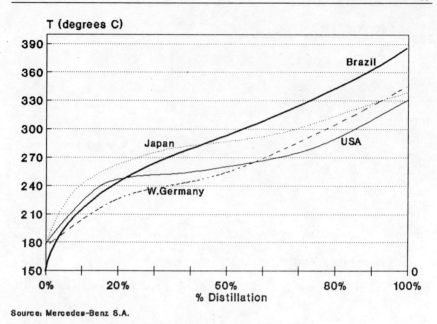

Source: Mercedes-Benz S.A.

Fig. 8.8. Distillation curves (average values 1985/86).

temperatures ranging from 150 to 390 degrees, and has a particularly large proportion of the highest temperature distillates, which leads to increased emissions of NO_x and particulates, as well as to the carbonization of the diesel injectors.[22] Additionally, Brazilian diesel standards are much lower than those in the United States or Europe, particularly regarding the content of sulfur (which is allowed to reach 1.3% of weight, compared to 0.1% in the United States and 0.2% in the European Community) and water (0.1% of volume, compared to none in the United States and Europe).[23]

The low quality of diesel fuel causes engines in trucks and buses to run improperly—using more fuel, requiring additional maintenance and emitting large quantities of particulates (black smoke), mostly within densely populated cities.† According to a recent estimate, 30 percent of total diesel demand for road transport is used for urban trips (combining freight and passengers), while the rest goes to inter-city transport (Fig. 8.9).[24] Considering that each inter-city trip originates and ends in cities—where efficiency is reduced by traffic—it can be estimated that about 50 percent of diesel oil is actually burned within urban communities.

---

†The Secretaria Industria Comercio e Tecnologia (SICT) has recently launched a nationwide program to tune-up city buses with scheduled regularity. Extending the program to trucks is presently under discussion.

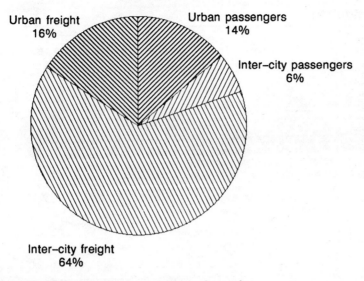

Fig. 8.9. Diesel use by mode and type of travel.

Similarly, the inconsistent quality of gasohol, varying in alcohol content between 5 percent and over 30 percent depending on the alcohol supply, results in the improper tuning of most of the car fleet, which is calibrated on the standard 20 percent mix.[25]† Conscious of the problems created by the inconsistent quality of fuels, car manufacturers produce vehicles with larger engines and wider carburetor jets, resulting in overall higher fuel consumption. Manufacturers avoid introducing more efficient vehicles into the market, as those would require consistent fuel quality to operate properly.[26]

EFFICIENCY PROGRESS AND BARRIERS

While the diversification of fuel sources in the transport sector certainly has reduced the need for oil imports, it has had an effect on the efficiency of the vehicle fleet. But how efficient are Brazilian cars and trucks? Data limits notwithstanding, there is evidence of a reduction in energy intensity of both cars and trucks.‡ As shown in Fig. 8.10, energy use per vehicle dropped

---

†According to several sources (Secretaria Ciencia e Tecnologia, Petrobras, Shell Brasil, Fiat do Brasil), variations in alcohol content are both seasonal and regional.

‡Intensities calculations are aggregated for trucks and buses. The lack of proper data makes it difficult to evaluate the energy efficiency progress of vehicles in Brazil, as no reliable estimate is available to separate gasoline consumption in cars from that occurring in trucks, particularly in the 1970s when the freight fleet was largely using gasoline. No survey is available to date on usage patterns of private vehicles, i.e., kilometers driven and load factors.

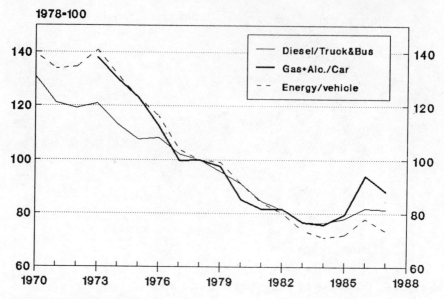

Fig. 8.10. Vehicle intensities.

by almost 50 percent since 1973.† However, this index aggregates cars, buses, and trucks (both heavy and light), and therefore does not take into account the structural shift toward a lighter fleet where cars and light trucks have a larger share. A more reliable index, attributing all diesel consumption to heavy trucks and buses, indicates a drop of more than 30 percent in their intensity in the same period, which can be considered reasonable given that much effort was put into improving maintenance and freight management in the late 1970s and early 1980s when diesel price almost doubled. However, even though the trend in vehicle energy intensity appears clearly in a downward direction, this index is not sufficiently accurate to reflect the efficiency of the fleet of heavy vehicles, as it lacks the necessary consideration of load factors.

Correspondingly, assuming that all gasoline and alcohol was used by cars and light commercial vehicles, and considering that the average distance driven per car (in kilometer/year) dropped considerably between 1973 and 1987, the resulting intensity indicator for the car/light-truck fleet indicates a significant improvement during the 1970s (of almost 40%), followed by a rebound in the 1980s (Fig. 8.10). According to these estimates, the average light vehi-

---

†In calculating this index it was considered that part of diesel is used for trains and boats (10% up to 1978, 6% afterwards). Starting in 1979, alcohol consumption was added to the calculation.

cle was running at around 6 km/liter (13 MPG) in the early 1970s and improved to 8.5-10 km/liter (20-23 MPG) in the late 1980s.†

While indications of reduced intensity during the 1970s are hampered by the lack of proper separation of gasoline use between trucks and cars, the progress observed for the 1980s is supported by the good information available on the efficiency of new cars. Accurate records on fuel efficiency of new vehicles, available since 1983, indicate definite improvements in both the new gasohol and alcohol models. On average, efficiency of new cars (as measured in performance tests) improved by 11 percent for gasohol cars (10% for alcohol cars) between 1983 and 1987, but then slightly rebounded in the following two years. Fig. 8.11 depicts total averages for new gasohol and alcohol cars as well as the evolution of average efficiency for the four major manufacturers, namely, Fiat, Ford, General Motors, and Volkswagen. The 1983 government directives on energy efficiency—Programa de Economia de Combustivel (PECO)[28]—certainly played a role in the progress observed, although some manufacturers have improved the average efficiency of their production more dramatically than others. In the case of Ford, the major drop was the result of adding smaller models to their production line. However, the bottoming of efficiency improvements around 1987 appears to be common to all car companies, indicating reduced interest in efficiency from both consumers and manufacturers.

The profile of the Brazilian buyer of new cars has in fact changed in recent years. As a result of slackening economic growth and uneven income distribution, a shrinking number of households can afford to enter the market for new cars. Less than 10 percent of the buyers of new cars are purchasing their first vehicle and therefore entering the market with the choice of a small car. The rest of the buyers are mostly exchanging their old vehicles for a larger and more powerful model (Fig. 8.12).[29] As only the highest income households can afford to buy new cars, large, more powerful models are in high demand. This shift in the characteristics of the market is increasing the average engine size of the country's fleet of new cars and forcing a rebound of previous progress in efficiency. On the other hand, used cars are driven less and for more years. Recent estimates indicate that around 50 percent of automobiles are still running after 18 years, and 20 percent go beyond 24 years.[30]

---

†A linear reduction in average distance driven was assumed here, from 16,000 km/year in 1974 to about 100,000 km/year in 1987. Others have estimated those values to be higher and dropping faster, from 25,000 km/year in 1974 to about 12,500 km/year in 1987.[27] More work needs to be done in this area to refine these efficiency estimates, particularly since a significant drop in distance driven might have occurred as a result of the economic crisis of the 1980s and would then be reversible. The rebound of energy intensity after 1984 seems to confirm this possibility. Another difficulty in calculating car performance in Brazil is the co-existence of a fleet fueled by gasohol, which has an energy content of 34.9 GJ/liter, and a fleet using alcohol, 23.5 GJ/liter.

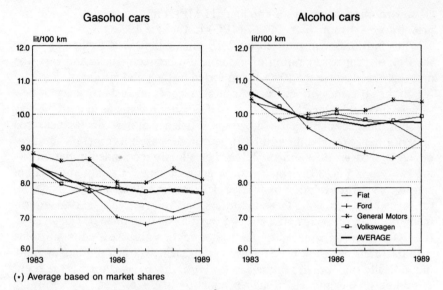

Fig. 8.11. Efficiency of new cars.

The structure of the Brazilian car manufacturing industry did not help the progress of efficiency, either. The four companies are competing in a market that has been shrinking since 1979 and is therefore of reduced interest to the major international corporations to which they are linked. Until recently, the government protectionist policy also reduced any threat of international competition from other manufacturers, particularly from Japan. As a result, improvements in manufacturing processes and in the quality of the final product have been lagging behind what has been achieved in Europe, Japan, and the United States in the same period. The only independent producer, Gurgel, is producing technologically innovative mini-jeeps that could serve the purpose of providing the lower/middle-income family with a sturdy and efficient vehicle. However, the competition of the "auto-giants" and an unprecedented economic crisis have considerably reduced the prospects of success of this interesting initiative.

The protectionism of the Brazilian car manufacturing industry originates in the difficulty of operating in a country where the product needs to be adapted to the characteristics of the local market. And most of the "adaptations" work against energy efficiency. It was mentioned above how the inconsistent quality of fuels has induced manufacturers to increase engine size and limit efficiency improvements. Poor conditions of roads and highways also play an important role in making cars less efficient, as reinforcements of chassis and suspensions become necessary and therefore increase the weight of the

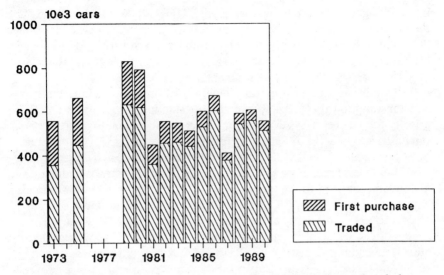

Fig. 8.12. New car sales by purchaser type ("First car" vs. "traded or second car").

vehicle.† On the other hand, a long-lasting policy of import limits is blamed for limiting the introduction of technological innovation in vehicles, particularly the use of electronic injection, which remains limited to few luxury models. As a result, Brazilian cars are heavier and less powerful than their sister European models. According to two major local manufacturers, the additional cost for larger engines and stronger structures on "Brazilian versions" is around 25 percent more than the original models, while the efficiency is around 20 percent lower.[31]

As a result of all these conditions, the consumer's choice is very limited when it stands to fuel efficiency. In 1990, the best available Brazilian car had an average performance of 16 km/liter (36 MPG),[32] while the best model available in the United States reached 20 km/liter (23 km/liter in Japan).

PROSPECTS AND POLICIES

Prospects for improvements in vehicle efficiency in Brazil appear bleak under the present economic conditions with limited capital available for renovating the industry, improving road quality, and reforming the supply system

---

†The "Brazilian version" of a popular Fiat model weighs 15 percent more than its sister European model.

in order to guarantee a reliable fuel quality. Unless these "inefficiencies" of the system are addressed, the introduction of efficient vehicles has in fact little chance of being effective. Only a combination of actions in these areas can lead to capturing the evident potential for energy savings and the related opportunities for reducing environmental impacts.

Fuel quality is such an important determinant in reducing both emissions and consumption that the improvement of standards appears as a definite priority for the sector. As expressed by several vehicle manufacturers, better standards would serve as reference for research, foster the development of new engines, and ultimately help establish vehicle emission and efficiency standards comparable to those in Europe or the United States.[33] Reducing the present variations in fuel quality through a tight control system would also have a positive effect on the running fleet, reducing oil imports, containing greenhouse gas emissions, and lowering the level of urban pollution.

Fuel prices, which dropped considerably in the 1980s (Fig. 8.13), would require a substantial adjustment if they were to reflect fully the social and environmental cost of private transportation in cars. Alcohol prices are now equivalent to the price of gasohol, after being kept lower for some years to encourage the purchase of alcohol-fueled vehicles. On the other hand, it should be considered that, in a market dominated by high-income buyers, prices have little effect on the purchase of more efficient new cars. As for diesel, its price was originally subsidized to stimulate fuel switching from gasoline trucks, but an adjustment is now seriously considered to reflect social costs and encourage a more rational freight transport system.[34]

The Alcohol Program also requires some substantial changes to maximize its effectiveness with regard to energy conservation and protection of the environment. There has been much debate about the continuation of the program and the possible expansion of the alcohol fleet. At present, the cost of producing alcohol is between $40 and $60 per barrel depending on the region of production. A recent study indicates that the elimination of government subsidies could lead to a progressive "regionalization" of the alcohol fleet into the states where alcohol is available (mostly in the southeast) and where high population density raises higher environmental concerns. In these regions, the alcohol fleet could increase to a much higher share of the total, while gasoline could remain dominant in the rest of the country.[35]

Trade barriers play an important role in limiting competitive innovation, thus restraining the diffusion of more efficient vehicles. A long tradition of protectionism is making the Brazilian manufacturing industry particularly weak with respect to foreign products, and this is especially true for cars and appliances. The new Brazilian government is moving toward an opening of the economy, allowing foreign products to compete with those manufactured locally. While the indiscriminate opening of the markets is seen as a risk to destroy the local industry, a consistent government policy liberalizing the

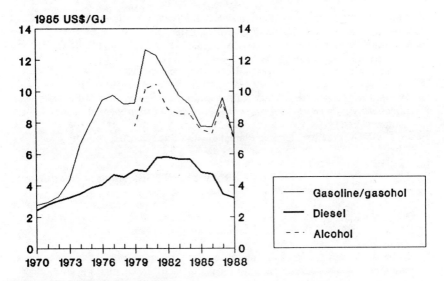

1985 US$/GJ

Gasoline/gasohol
Diesel
Alcohol

Alcohol price accounts for efficiency

Fig. 8.13. Fuel prices.

Brazilian market could favor long-term investments in increased productivity and efficient products. Under new conditions, Brazil could abandon an industrialization policy based on import substitution and undertake an exporting strategy of products that would be highly competitive on international markets. The know-how to improve engine efficiency does not need to be imported and could be rapidly developed by local manufacturers.

Overall, the inroads of energy efficiency in the transport sector will be considerably restrained if major structural reforms are not undertaken in the country. Some of the changes, such as improving fuel standards and opening of technological markets, might be relatively simple to pursue. Others, such as a flexible refining system, improved road quality, and developing alternative transport modes, might prove very expensive, but are necessary for the overall development of the economy.

REFERENCES

1. OECD, Proceedings of the International Conference on "Tomorrow's Clean and Fuel-efficient Automobile: Opportunities for East-West Cooperation," Berlin (1991).
2. D. L. Bleviss, *The New Oil Crisis and Fuel Economy Technologies,* Quorum Books, New York, (1988); D. L. Bleviss and P. Walzer, "Energy for Motor Vehicles," *Scientific American,* **263,** 3, pp. 102–109 (September 1990); A. Lovins and H. Lovins, "Global Climate Stabilization," *Annual Review of Energy* 16 (1991).
3. G. M. G. Graca and A. Ketoff, "Carbon Dioxide Savings in Brazil: The Importance of a Small Contribution," *Energy Policy* 19, London (December 1991).

4. Ministerio de Energia e Minas, *Balanço Energetico Nacional*, Brasilia (1990).
5. Estado de São Paulo, *Anuario Estadistico* (1990).
6. Comisión Económica para America Latina (CEPAL), "Magnitude da Pobreza na America Latina nos Anos 80," Santiago de Chile (1991).
7. Prefectura de São Paulo, personal communication (1991).
8. Grupo Executivo do Programa Nacional de Racionalização da Producao e do Use de Energia (GERE), *Relatorio final do grupo de trabalho sobre "Racionalização do uso de energia em rodovias—Trafego de caminhões e ônibus,"* Brasilia (January 1991).
9. GEIPOT-Empresa Brasileira de Planejamento de Transportes, *Anuario Estadistico* (1989).
10. GERE, op. cit. (1991).
11. Instituto Brasileiro de Geografia e Estatistica (IBGE), *Anuario Estatistico do Brasil*, Rio de Janeiro (1990).
12. GEIPOT, op. cit. (1989); C. Feu Alvim and O. Campos Ferreira, "Avaliação da Frota Nacional a Gasolina e a Alcool," Commissão Nacional de Energia (1989).
13. Honda do Brasil S.A., personal communication (1990).
14. Ministerio de Energia e Minas, op. cit. (1990).
15. S. Trinidade and A. Vieira de Carvalho, Jr., "Transportation Fuels Policy Issues and Options: The Case of Ethanol Fuels in Brazil," in D. Sperling, ed., *Alternative Transportation Fuels: An Environmental Energy Solution*, Quorum Books, New York (1989).
16. A. Vieira de Carvalho, Jr., "Evolution of Energy Inputs and Rationalization Efforts in the Brazilian Transportation Sector," *Revista Energetica*, OLADE, Quito (January-April 1990).
17. Associação National dos Fabricantes de Veiculos Automotores (ANFAVEA), *Anuario Estatistico 1957/1988*, São Paulo (1989).
18. Ministerio de Energia e Minas, op. cit. (1990).
19. GERE, op. cit. (1991).
20. Ministerio de Energia e Minas, op. cit. (1990).
21. GERE, op. cit. (1991).
22. Mercedes-Benz do Brasil S.A., *Os Veiculos Comerciais e o Meio Ambiente* (1989).
23. Shell Brasil, personal communication (1990).
24. GERE, op. cit. (1991).
25. GERE, op. cit. (1991).
26. Fiat-Auto, Italy, and Autolatina, Brasil, personal communications (1990).
27. G. M. G. Graca and V. Rodriguez, "Electricity Production, Private Transportation and CO_2 Emissions: The Five Highest Energy Consumers of the Developing Countries," Workshop on Human Dimensions of Global Climate Change, Montebello, Canada (1990).
28. Secretaria de Tecnologia Industrial, "Escolha certo: Guia de consumo do seu carro," Brasilia (1986).
29. Associação Nacional de Fabricantes de Veiculos Automotores (ANFAVEA), personal communication (1991).
30. C. Feu Alvim and O. Campos Ferreira, op. cit. (1989).
31. Fiat do Brasil, Autolatina, personal communication (1990).
32. Secretaria de Ciencia e Tecnologia, personal communication (1990).
33. Mercedes-Benz do Brasil S.A., op. cit. (1989).
34. GERE, op. cit. (1991).
35. M. Arouca, "O Alcool e a Politica de Combustiveis Automotivos," *V Congreso Brasilieiro de Energia-Anais*, Rio de Janeiro (1990).

9 Venezuelan Oil Policy in the Long Run

Ramon Espinasa and Bernard Mommer

ORIGINS OF RENT NATIONALISM†

To understand Venezuelan oil policy it is necessary to differentiate two aspects of the generic term "oil": oil as a *productive activity* and oil as a *source of rent*. Capital, labor and land are the three factors of production that come into play in the production of oil. The first two factors of production form what we shall refer to as the productive activity; the latter, land or the natural resource, has historically been responsible for oil as a source of rent. Since oil deposits are state property in Venezuela, oil as a source of rent was first the responsibility of the Ministry of Development. However, given the extraordinary importance oil has acquired as a source of rent, a new ministry was created: the Ministry of Mines and Hydrocarbons—today Energy and Mines.

Toward the end of the 19th century, notwithstanding Venezuela's Spanish colonial roots, the Venezuelan mine laws were a carbon copy of the French, which were then considered the most modern. The crux of this legislation was to protect the potential or actual producer against the rent-seeking, private landlords; this was achieved by declaring the oil deposits a state property. The mining laws were framed to serve the producer; for instance, the Prologue of the 1909 Mining Law reads:

> . . . the goodness of a mining law is to be seen in the level of security it offers to the exploiters in their concession; in the extension of the freedom it gives them to act, since the fewer obstacles, the better; and, finally, in the number of incentives provided to acquire mining concessions.[2]

Moreover, the concessionaires of the mines had to pay no more than ordinary taxes:

---

†Parts of this section have appeared in different form in other publications authored by Bernard Mommer; see Ref. 1.

The principles which demand that taxes be moderate as well as equal for all contributors is well known. . .[3]

In conformity with the legal situation, the first oil concessions of importance, granted between 1907 and 1912, did not establish any rent. The landowners, however, exerted pressure to appropriate the mines or at least a rent. This pressure resulted in an article in the 1909 mining law that provided for a payment of one-third of the profits accrued through the exploitation of a mine on private property land, notwithstanding that the mine itself continued to be considered state property. The Minister of Development made the following objections to this article:

> Such a precept constitutes an obvious restriction since nobody should provide the money, credit, intelligence, activity, perseverance, in short, the whole material, intellectual and moral affluence required for success in undertakings of this sort only to find that subsequently, no less than a third of the utilities has to be handed over to a partner who is forced upon the management and who neither works, contributes, nor risks anything.[4]

The government subsequently appealed this article and it was deemed unconstitutional by the Supreme Court.

Thus, the beginning of Venezuelan oil history is characterized by the concept of *free state property:* the simple negation of territorial private property. Under this conception the state *administers* the mines to the benefit of the actual or potential producers, protecting them from the rent-seeking landlords.

However, the development of the productive activity of oil in Venezuela was initiated by foreign companies dancing to the drums of an international market. In the period we are considering, oil had a very small domestic market and Venezuela was in no condition to pursue the productive activity on its own. The oil industry was thus perceived as little more than an enclave.†

But mining laws favored *foreign* producers and *foreign* consumers. Thus, as soon as the exceptional riches of the Venezuelan oil deposits became evident, the government began to take a stance consistent with its consciousness as owner of a natural resource—that is, as a landlord.

A few years after oil was first exported in 1917, the Minister of Development, Gumersindo Torres, observed critically:

> taxation is a different concept from that of a payment derived from contractual stipulations in return for the use of national property . . . in Venezuela there are taxes yet the companies pay nothing for the *exploitation right itself. . .*[5]
> [Italics added].

---

†Despite this perception, the oil industry, from its beginnings, had important multiplier effects on the national economy, especially in the labor market and the infrastructural development of the country.

Torres had accumulated some knowledge of how in the United States, the cradle of the oil industry where private property of the oil deposits prevailed, the leasing contracts included a payment of rent to the landlords. The American example gave way to a new *national* rent-seeking aspiration. Vicente Lecuna, president of the Banco de Venezuela,† presented the original formulation: the state should aspire, at least, to a royalty of 15.50 percent that he estimated as the average of what was charged in the United States.

The concept of rent-seeking nationalism was then born and that of free state property left behind. During the following decades a new concept, which could be termed *sovereign national state property,* began to develop.

The analysis of the development of this concept in opposition and, finally, in contradiction to the productive activity and how it is presently transcended is the object of the remainder of this paper.‡

FIRST PERIOD: 1920–1942

Oil as a Productive Activity

Capital accumulation is an *indicator* of the historical development of oil as a productive activity.§ In Figs. 9.1, 9.2, and 9.3, we can observe the growth of the capital stock, employment, and the production of oil. In 1928, Venezuela was the world's leading oil exporter with a volume of 276,000 barrels per day (b/d). The rate of capital accumulation in the oil sector was very high, though interrupted by the Great Depression and the Second World War.

Fig. 9.4 indicates a downward trend of prices during this period. Nevertheless, between 1936 and 1942 the profitability of capital was very high, averaging about 9.7 percent of the stock¶ (see Figs. 9.5 and 9.6).‖ The drop that is observed in 1942 was caused by the presence of German submarines that hindered the shipment of exports.

---

†This is a private bank, not to be confused with the official Banco Central de Venezuela.

‡For a first draft see B. Mommer (1989), Ref. 6.

§A more accurate measure should be based on the cost of production. Such a measure may be called non-rent oil GDP. See A. Baptista and B. Mommer, Ref. 7, and B. Mommer, Ref. 8.

¶The concept of capital stock is based on the use value of its components, and not on the book value. The latter one usually represents less than half of the former. For details on the concept, see J. A. Gorman et al., Ref. 9.

‖Disposable rent takes into account, from 1974 onwards, the movement of public external debt. Sources of the data on profits are the Ministry of Energy and Mines, and Baptista and Mommer, Ref. 7.

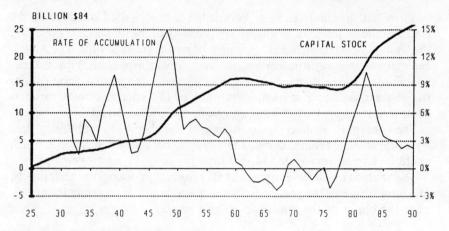

Fig. 9.1. Oil industry: capital stock.

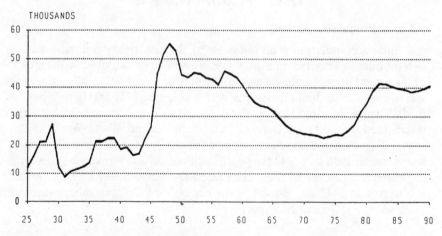

Fig. 9.2. Oil industry: direct employment.

Oil as a Source of Rent

The fiscal revenue will be the indicator we shall be using for oil as a source of rent.† In Fig. 9.4, observe the declining rent per barrel up to 1932. This, however, is a statistical phenomenon. The high levels of rent per barrel during the first years is a consequence of the initial payments stipulated in the concession contracts and of the low levels of production. Then, the rent per

---

†This indicator overestimates the real rent, as no adjustment is made for the concept of normal
taxes to be paid by all economic agents. For a more accurate measurement, see Baptista and
Mommer, Ref. 7.

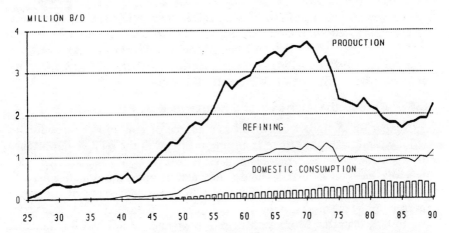

Fig. 9.3. Oil industry: production, refining, and domestic consumption.

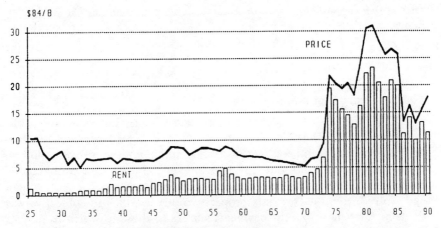

Fig. 9.4. Average price and rent per barrel.

barrel followed an ascending trajectory caused, initially, by the legislative reforms that made new concessions fiscally more lucrative. Also, the devaluation of the dollar in 1934 while the bolivar—the national currency—remained at its old peg caused a substantial increase in rent since an important portion of rent payments was stipulated in bolivars (Bs). For instance, the first concessions established a payment of Bs 2.00 per ton, which represented $0.38 before the devaluation and $0.65 after.†

---

†Venezuela was one of the few countries that did not follow the dollar's devaluation in 1934. By not devaluing, the rent in dollars increased. See B. Mommer, Ref. 10.

The growing volume of exports determined, in absolute and relative terms, an ascending trend in the oil rent (Figs. 9.5 and 9.6). The rent rate—that is, rent as a fraction of the capital stock of the oil industry—averaged 4.3 percent between 1925 and 1943. However, during this period the rent rate approached the profit rate of the tenant oil companies.

Oil as a Productive Activity and a Source of Rent

Comparing the indicators of oil as a source of rent and as a productive activity we observe that there is an upward trend in the relative importance of the former. However, there is no sign that such a gain was accompanied by a weakened oil industry. The development of oil as a productive activity in those years can be explained completely by the movement of the world market and by the higher natural productivity of Venezuelan oil deposits relative to U.S. deposits. Moreover, the rent payments established for the most advantageous concessions toward the end of this period still were substantially lower than the usual rent in the United States. Consequently, the profit rates of the companies in Venezuela were much higher than those in the United States.

SECOND PERIOD: 1943–1957

The Petroleum Legislation Reform of 1943

In 1936, after the death of the despot, Juan Vicente Gomez, a modernization process, from which the oil industry was not exempted, began in Venezuela. First, the concession contracts were incompatible with those of a modern nation. For example, not only royalties but general taxes were contractually established. Second, there existed a mosaic of concessions. The legal system had evolved from the free state property to one in which the objective was to claim for Venezuela rent payments similar to those to which owners of the deposits in the United States were entitled. Henceforth, the rent established in new contracts increased with time. Third, Venezuela would no longer tolerate the expansion of refining facilities just off its shores in the Netherlands Antilles by Exxon and Royal Dutch Shell.

The years between 1936 and 1942 were characterized by a great deal of controversy. The oil companies, backed by the Supreme Court, tried to protect what they considered an acquired right, while the government insisted on the need to mold the judicial, political and economic structure of the oil industry to suit the modernization process now under way in the country. This confrontation led, in 1938, to a halt of the granting of new concessions.

Thus, a project of reform emerged, finally encouraged by the importance of Venezuelan oil acquired during the Second World War. Ultimately, the companies had no option other than to give in.

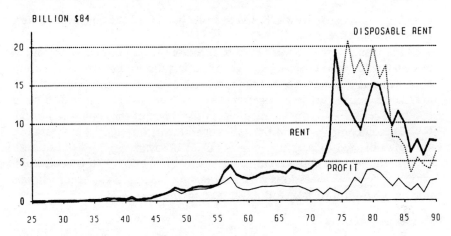

Fig. 9.5. Oil sector: profit and rent.

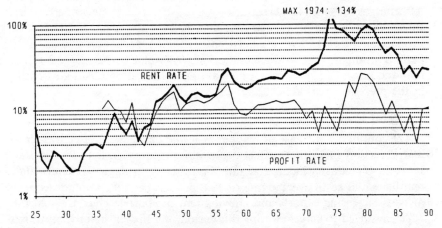

Fig. 9.6. Oil sector: profit and rent rates.

The reform affected the oil companies in three ways: First, they recognized Venezuela's fiscal sovereignty,† that is, the unilateral and sovereign right of the legislature to impose import fees and an income tax on company profits.

Second, the parties renegotiated the royalties. They were to keep their contractual character, but the companies accepted an overall increase to one-sixth,

---

†It is worthwhile to note that up to 1973 Venezuela was the only OPEC member where concessions were subject to national law and sovereign taxation. In all other countries the concession contracts were subject to international law and arbitration, and all taxes were contractually established by the concession contracts.

bringing them to par with U.S. levels; in exchange, all the concessions were
extended for 40 years until 1983.

Third, realizing the nation's need to increase the oil productive activity in
its own territory and the resulting dynamic effect this would have on the economy, Venezuela demanded that the refineries of Curaçao and Aruba should
not be developed further. Moreover, the companies were required to build
two huge refineries in the country within five years of the conclusion of the
war. The oil companies and the U.S. government, through its ambassador,
strongly objected to such a demand, but to no avail.

Once the relationship was adjusted to the satisfaction of the Venezuelan
government, new concessions were awarded in 1943 and 1944. Venezuela was
now in a position to take full advantage of the post-World War II boom.

Productive Activity

This period is characterized by sustained growth in investment and production stimulated by the high price of oil and by the construction of the two
refineries, as convened in 1943. During the construction of the refineries, direct
employment by the oil industry reached its historic peak: 55,200 in 1948.
Production increased five-fold between 1943 and 1957. Toward the end of the
period, production reached 2.8 million b/d, of which 25 percent was refined
in the country. The profit rate, which averaged 12.4 percent, was greater than
in the preceding period.

Source of Rent

The continuous increase of rent per exported barrel was caused by increasing prices and their direct effect on royalties. Moreover, between 1945 and
1948, the oil industry income tax rate was raised to the high U.S. levels.† Total
rent increased at an average rate of 12.8 percent per year as a consequence
of both increasing exports and growing rent per barrel. Thus, the rent rate,
which averaged 16 percent during this period, was higher than the profit rate.

Productive Activity and the Source of Rent

Between 1943 and 1957 the coexistence of high rates of rent and profit was
made possible by the booming world petroleum market.

The Venezuelan oil industry now operated under legal conditions very similar to those of the United States, and the tax and rent levels were also similar.
Given the higher productivity of the Venezuelan oil deposits, this situation
was still very advantageous for the oil companies. They had to recognize,
however, the Venezuelan state not only as the owner (via payment of the

---

†There was a good reason for this. The American oil companies had to pay the U.S. Treasury,
in any case, the difference between the lower Venezuelan and the higher American income
tax rate.

royalty) but as sovereign (via payment of the income tax). This peaceful coexistence was expressed symbolically by the 50–50 profit split, anticipated in the Prologue of the Law of Hydrocarbons of 1943 and formally established by the creation of an 'additional tax' of 50 percent in the Income Tax Law of 1948.†

THIRD PERIOD: 1958–1973

OPEC

In the United States, land property is subordinated to capital. This is reflected in leasing contracts. These are signed before exploration takes place—that is, before knowing with certainty of the existence of oil. Moreover, the contracts last until the definite exhaustion of the deposits, ensuring that the landlord has no second chance for increasing the rent once the existence of oil is proved.

The Venezuelan state, owner and sovereign at the same time, was not willing to accept such a subordinate position. The state was inevitably going to use its sovereign power to maximize its right as an owner. The process through which both rents and income taxes were increased to U.S. levels was only the first part of the rent-maximizing process.

After the fall of the dictator Pérez Jiménez in 1958, Venezuela faced a fiscal crisis. In December of that year, the president, Edgar Sanabria, increased radically the income tax rate leaving behind the 50–50 arrangement assuring instead a 64:36 profit split in favor of Venezuela. With this increase, the income tax rates in Venezuela surpassed those in the United States.

This tax hike marked the end of the first phase of the rent-seeking Venezuelan oil policy, which consisted in extracting as much as possible of pre-existing extraordinary profits—what is called, in American literature, a 'windfall.' Up to this point Venezuela did not concern itself with oil prices: these were determined internationally by the high cost of U.S. oil production. Furthermore, prices were not only determined by the market but by the International Petroleum Cartel, with the informal cooperation of domestic regulatory authorities in the United States.

At the time Sanabria's decree was proclaimed, however, the price structure of oil gave signs of imminent collapse. Facing dwindling oil prices, in 1959 the United States took a protectionist stance to save its marginal producers from bankruptcy. Thus, oil prices in the world market lost their base. Given the low production costs in the oil-producing countries, competition threatened to lead to a sharp fall in prices.

---

†For an exhaustive analysis of the 50–50 profit-sharing system and its meaning in the relationship between the landlords and the tenants, see B. Mommer, Ref. 1, chaps. 3 and 4.

For this reason oil prices then became the main preoccupation of Venezuelan oil policy, as they determined the rent per barrel. This led to the creation of the Organization of the Petroleum Exporting Countries (OPEC) in 1960, with the important participation of the Venezuelan Minister of Mines and Hydrocarbons, Juan Pablo Pérez Alfonzo. The declared objective of this cartel of landlord states was to invert or slow down the downward tendency of prices. This was not to happen during the 1960s; however, the downward tendency was slowed down by defending the rent per barrel against the drop in prices.

In the first half of the 1960s, the OPEC countries created *Fiscal Reference Prices,* a legal instrument that converted the income tax based on the market prices into a *tax per barrel,* that is, an excise tax. These "prices" were predetermined in negotiations between the governments and the oil companies. Later, with the changing conditions in the world market in the 1970s, these reference prices were adjusted upward in negotiations taking place in Teheran, Lagos, and Tripoli. In Venezuela, however, such negotiations never took place. Venezuela's sovereign congress authorized the Executive to set them unilaterally: Venezuela was not limited by any contractual relationships, but only by the objective conditions of the market.

Source of Rent

Despite the tax increase of 1958, there was a drop in the rent per barrel in 1959 and 1960; afterwards the rent per barrel increased slightly throughout the decade in spite of falling prices. However, in 1970 the prices began to rise and, thus, so did the rent per barrel. The increase in rent per barrel was so significant that it compensated for the collapse in production and exports that began in 1970. During this period the rent rate averaged 26.4 percent.

Productive Activity

This period was characterized by negative net investment. The building of desulfurization facilities in refining was the only important investment. Direct employment fell by half: from 44,700 in 1958 to 22,200 in 1973. Production, however, maintained its upward trend until 1970 when it reached 3.7 million b/d, its highest historical level. This increase in production was sustained by more intensive exploitation of the natural resource and not by the development of the productivity of capital and labor. The consequences became evident after 1970. Despite the increase in prices that took place at the end of that year, production levels fell drastically. By 1973, production had decreased to 2.4 million b/d. The profit rate averaged 10.5 percent, much lower than in the preceding period.

Source of Rent and Productive Activity

In this period, oil as a source of rent and as a productive activity no longer lived in peaceful coexistence; as a matter of fact, they contradicted each other.

The defense of oil as a source of rent during the 1960s put pressure on company profits,[1] eroding the role of oil as a productive activity. To protect their profits, the oil companies intensified the exploitation of the existing oil fields without making new investments.

Furthermore, the most important concessions were to expire by 1983 and 1984. The Law of Hydrocarbons provided for the possibility of a renewal of the concessions for 40 years once half the life of the concessions had elapsed— in this case, from 1963 and 1964 on. This provision of the Law was designed to make possible an uninterrupted flow of investment. However, by then Venezuela had adopted a staunch position of *no more concessions* that was part of its rent-maximizing oil policy. By 1959, there had already emerged a confrontation between the Ministry of Mines and Hydrocarbons and the oil companies about the reversion to the nation of the concessions. The heart of this confrontation was that the Ministry denied the companies' right to re-export machinery; the government considered them an integral part of the concessions to expire in 1983 or 1984, to be passed on to the state by this date without indemnification.

The situation in the other OPEC countries was similar although not as extreme. Worldwide oil production investments were hindered in the most productive areas and were concentrated in the least productive lands located in the developed, oil-consuming countries. The outcome was the oil crisis of the 1970s![2]

The most important weapon of the international oil companies against the ever-growing demands for rent of the Third World oil-exporting countries was the international control and manipulation of oil production. The reduction or the threat of reducing production in the countries that demanded higher rents while increasing production in other countries (including the United States which by then had high spare capacity) had been effective in checking the ambitions of the exporting countries during the 1950s and 1960s. This weapon was no longer effective after 1970 when excess capacity around the world disappeared, largely due to the rent-seeking strategy of OPEC.

As a result, OPEC advanced rapidly between 1970 and 1973. With the third Arab-Israeli war and the restrictions imposed on exports by the Arab countries, OPEC's strategy reaped its reward. Rent per barrel and the volume of production were subjected to the sovereign decision of the member countries; hence, the explosive increase in rent per barrel at the end of 1973.

With the sovereign control over volume of production and rent per barrel, *de facto* nationalization of international tenant capital had taken place. Legal nationalization took place in Venezuela on January 1, 1976. With the nationalization, the international companies were replaced by state-owned companies that were completely subjugated to the governments' rent-maximizing interests. Maximization of rent was the real purpose of nationalization.

The policy of obstructing the development of productive activity, particularly evident in Venezuela, had contributed to create an additional surplus: a monopolistic rent of landed property.†

FOURTH PERIOD: 1974–1986

The extraordinary increase in rent per barrel in 1974 was followed by another caused by the overthrow of the Shah of Iran and Iran's subsequent war with Iraq. However, this second increase did not compensate for the volumetric decrease in Venezuelan oil exports. Therefore, maximum rent and the highest rent rate was achieved in 1974 when it reached 134 percent. The tendency of total rent and the rent rate, despite a pronounced roller coaster pattern, was downward; they finally collapsed in 1986. Still, in this period the average of the rent rate was 72.4 percent.

In their last two years of existence, the profit rate of the transnational companies just averaged 6.6 percent. Between 1976 and 1986, profit rates were well above historical levels, averaging 15.2 percent. However, the concept of profit had lost importance. The state, sole shareholder of the operating company and owner of the natural resource, appropriated any surplus beyond necessary investments and operation costs. The high profit rates of this period reflected the high level of investment that was taking place by the now nationalized oil company.

The traditional rent policy had been a success; throughout five decades rent increased continuously in both absolute and relative terms. This success seemed to reinforce the landlord state's ideology, prevalent in Venezuela during those decades and especially between 1958 and 1973. This ideology conceived oil as a non-renewable, definitely exhaustible natural resource of unquantifiable value. Consequently, the expectations of the government and of public opinion corresponded to a simple extrapolation of past trends.[13]

It was not then understood that *one* of the *two* variables that determine total rent (rent per barrel and export volume) had reached its limit. A future increase in total rent could only be possible through an increase in the volume of exports. Consequently, the process of de-investment that had taken place between 1958 and 1973 and the drop of production after 1970 had to be confronted urgently. No less worrisome were the effects the new rent levels— thus price levels—would have on the demand for oil.

Given the degree of de-capitalization, the newly nationalized oil industry started in 1977 an ambitious plan to recuperate its potential, to reactivate exploration and to upgrade its refineries to tolerate a diet of heavier crude. At the same time, however, OPEC tried to impose a price level that was the result of exceptional situations, such as the overthrow of the Iranian monarchy and

---

†In Marxist political economy this kind of monopolistic rent is called absolute rent.

the subsequent war with Iraq. Although Venezuela recovered a potential of 2.5 million b/d and increased significantly its production in 1979, lack of demand forced a cut in output in 1980. Finally, the investment programs were significantly reduced in 1983.

OPEC as a whole was forced to cut its production by half between 1979 and 1985. Venezuela, in 1985, produced only 1.7 million b/d, which was equivalent to an accumulated reduction of 55 percent as compared to 1970. OPEC had to acknowledge its blunder and by mid-1985 Saudi Arabia took the lead in announcing its net back pricing policy that led to the sharp price reduction of 1986, consequently reducing the rent per barrel by half. Even though the prices and the rent per barrel were still twice as high as in 1973, Venezuela faced both a lower rent and rent rate. The traditional rent-maximizing oil policy met its great defeat. At the apex of its power it had adopted a short-sighted stance, and now Venezuela had to confront, under very difficult conditions, a depressed world market.

THE NON-OIL ECONOMY

In its first phase, the rent-seeking oil policy was limited to collecting excess profits, while in its second phase it tried to impose a monopolistic territorial rent. This obstructed both the development of the oil industry in the OPEC countries, and world economic growth as a whole.

By extracting an international rent, the oil countries hindered and restrained the economic progress of the world capitalist system. However, their goal was to use this rent to join and grow into this system. The failure or success of this policy can be gauged by the degree to which this objective was achieved.

Accumulation of Capital and Non-Oil GDP†

In Figs. 9.7 and 9.8, the historic development of the gross stock of non-oil, non-residential capital may be observed, as well as non-oil gross domestic product (GDP) and its rate of growth. The growth rates of the periods we have been referring to are shown in Table 9.1.

The decreasing long-run tendency of capital accumulation is obvious. When looking at the figures concerning non-oil GDP we have to take into account that during the period 1920–1943 the Great Depression brought with it the collapse of traditional Venezuelan agricultural exports. In spite of this, thanks to oil, the average growth rate was 5.6 percent.

The multiplier effect of oil as a productive activity and a source of rent can be seen in Fig. 9.9 by comparing gross fixed investment in the oil industry, oil rent, and non-oil gross investment—all three as a percentage share

---

†The central ideas summarized in this section on the non-oil economy are a result of continued discussions with Asdrubal Baptista.

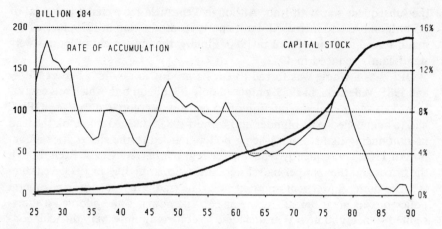

Fig. 9.7. Non-oil non-residential capital stock.

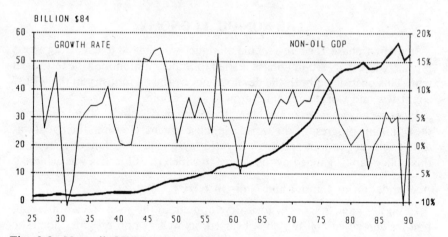

Fig. 9.8. Non-oil GDP.

of non-oil capital stock. Observe how oil as a productive activity lost importance just as oil as a source of rent was gaining momentum.

Oil and, more importantly, oil rent became the only driving force of the
development of the Venezuelan economy. As can be seen in Fig. 9.10, from
the second half of the 1950s disposable rent was superior to non-oil net investment.

During the period 1974 through 1986, the government intensified the process
of rent distribution, thus increasing demand, and non-oil GDP growth ac-
celerated. Investment responded with a lag, and when it peaked in 1977, the

Table 9.1. Average growth rate per year (%)

	1920–43	1943–58	1958–73	1973–86	1986–90
Non-oil capital stock	9.4	8.8	5.3	5.9	0.5
Non-oil GDP	5.6	9.4	5.7	4.6	0.5
Disposable rent/non-oil GDP	5.5	23.6	22.3	31.4	8.9

Note: Disposable rent takes into account, from 1974 onward, the development of public debt and its service.

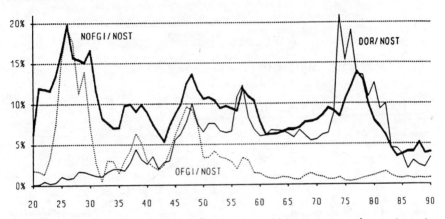

NOFGI: Non-oil, non residential fixed gross investment
NOFNI: Non-oil, non residential fixed net investment
OFGI: Oil fixed gross investment
DOR: Disposable oil rent
NOST: Non-oil, non residential gross capital stock

Fig. 9.9. Oil and non-oil investment.

growth rate of non-oil GDP was falling. The following year the collapse of the prevalent model of accumulation was evident.

The Crisis of the Oil-Rent Model of Accumulation

We can label the accumulation model that began to collapse in 1978 as a model of oil *rent* accumulation. The decline of oil as a productive activity that began in 1958 was one of the major causes of the collapse of the model. Since the end of the 1920s the oil sector was practically the only exporting sector in Venezuela. To show its importance, we can see in Fig. 9.11 oil capital as a percentage of total non-residential capital. Observe that in the past the Venezuelan economy was very open. From the end of the 1920s up to the end of the 1950s, a third of the capital of the country corresponded to export activities. Then, however, the economy became less open. Over time the per-

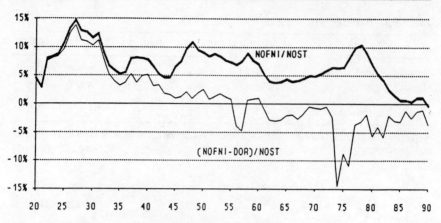

Fig. 9.10. Net non-oil investment and oil rent.

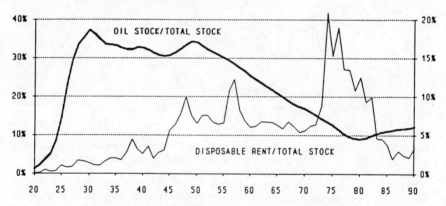

Fig. 9.11. Oil rent and oil capital stock/total capital stock.

centage of export capital to total capital dropped, falling to less than 10 percent by 1980. On the other hand, as already mentioned, direct employment in the oil industry fell from 44,700 to 22,200 between 1958 and 1973. Fig. 9.11 also shows that, thanks to rent, export earnings were higher than ever. Venezuelan foreign markets were at their minimum, while foreign earnings were at a maximum.

The absolute lack of dynamism of the external sector was the first cause of the crisis. *Sowing the oil* was oriented toward the domestic market. The massive distribution of rent took place through the overvaluation of the domestic currency and the low level of taxation, both of which were sustainable thanks to the high level of oil rent.[14] This paved the way for extraordinary growth in the domestic market, as can be seen through the rapid urbanization of the country. In 1920, 80 percent of the population (2.6 million) was rural compared to less than 20 percent of the population (19.3 million) in 1990. Immigration was another multiplier effect of oil.† First came people from Spain after the Spanish Civil War in the 1930s. Then came people from all over Europe after the Second World War. The final wave of immigrants came from all over Latin America. While the Latin American countries suffered from the continuous "brain drain," Venezuela, until the beginning of the 1980s, was the great exception[16]

The oil-rent accumulation model was a success while it consisted of importing first consumption goods, then capital goods, and finally intermediate goods to produce import substitutes. In this context, the overvaluation of the bolivar was functional and opportune. However, once the domestic market was fully developed, the model reached a dead end. High levels of profits and salaries plus inefficiencies of the rent-accelerated accumulation process of several decades made Venezuela uncompetitive in the world market. Distributed rent manifested itself now as a *cost*. The abundant rent of the 1970s was channeled to activities related to consumption and not to production. This second cause of the crisis corresponds to the syndrome known as "Dutch Disease."[17, 18, 19]

Even though the rate of growth of non-oil GDP had been decreasing since 1977, the year that investments reached their peak, the government continued its policy of distributing present and future rent via external public debt. Consumption per capita continued to grow until 1982 despite negative growth rates in GDP per capita since 1979. At the same time, and it could not be otherwise given Venezuela's low capital absorption capacity, private capital was flowing out of the country. The outcome was the exchange rate crisis of 1983, to which we must add the impact of the collapse of oil rent in 1986.

Disposable rent, which we define as rent minus foreign public debt service, is lower today than 50 years ago. Non-oil GDP per capita was reduced between 1978 and 1990 by 20 percent. The crisis is even more severe when we look at real income levels which dropped by 50 percent in the same period.

The collapse of the traditional rent-maximizing policy coincided with the debacle of the traditional *sowing the oil*.

Overcoming the Crisis

The Venezuelan Crisis, as our analysis reveals, is structural: hence its depth and duration. The metamorphosis from a crisis of abundance to a crisis of scarcity was rapid. The opportunity of a smooth transition from the oil-rent accumulation model to another was lost because of an erroneous economic policy during the years of abundance.

---

†Mansell and Percy write about the 'population multiplier' in the case of Alberta, oil province of Canada. See Ref 15.

In Venezuela, there exists, in principle, a consensus as to how to overcome the crisis: to gradually open the economy and reconstruct a dynamic external sector. Since the rent accumulation model had always been considered unsustainable in the long run,† this idea had traditionally been associated with a post-oil Venezuela. It is only since 1986 that there has been a major change of perception. It is understood that there will be no post-oil Venezuela. It became clear that the oil sector would be of paramount importance in restructuring a dynamic tradable sector and in opening the economy.

NEW OIL POLICY

Oil as a source of rent has reached an objective ceiling. The main purpose of the drastic reduction of rent per barrel by OPEC was to make OPEC oil again competitive vis-à-vis both non-OPEC oil and other sources of energy. The price of other sources of energy will determine the bounds within which the price of OPEC oil can evolve. Future increases in rent per barrel are meant to be relatively small since any large increase will be met by lower demand. Therefore, future increments in rent will only be possible through an increase in volume. The emphasis on this represents the first modification of the traditional rent-maximizing policy that since 1958 has concentrated on increasing the rent per barrel.

There is a second change of perception. Oil as a productive activity has been gaining importance. The economy was traditionally viewed as being divided into the oil sector and the non-oil sector. The new tenet, however, differentiated between oil as a source of rent and the national economy as a whole, which now includes the oil sector. The development of the oil industry is valued like that of any other industry, and it must compete for the oil rent as a source of finance. The traditional goal of *sowing the oil* now encompasses the oil sector itself.

The drop in investment by the international oil companies during the 1960s caused a decrease in exploration. The nation's oil reserves fell from 17 billion barrels in 1960 to 14 billion in 1970, which represented about 10 years of production at prevailing levels. This parameter had been falling throughout the 1960s, nourishing the national prejudice regarding the end of Venezuela as an oil country. At the beginning of the 1970s it was widely believed that the non-oil sector had to be developed urgently since oil reserves were thought to be short-lived. The massive investment plans of the Fifth National Development Plan in 1974 were born from this precept. The development of a non-oil public export industry was the axis of such development plan.

---

†However—a notable ideological phenomenon—a scientific study about this transition was never done. There was only a nightmarish general feeling about the definite exhaustion of oil.

Renewed exploration after the nationalization reversed the nation's perception towards oil reserves. By 1990, proven hydrocarbons reserves reached almost 60 billion barrels. The proven reserves of natural gas that were around 1 trillion cubic meters at the beginning of the 1960s are now 3 trillion. This does not include the practically unlimited reserves of heavy and extra heavy crude in the Orinoco Petroleum Belt, with recoverable reserves of about 270 billion barrels.

With these reserves, the production of Venezuela could be, according to technical parameters, three or four times higher than present production that stands at about 2.3 million b/d. However, given a resource base with a growing share of heavier and more acid crudes, the development of the refining process with deep conversion facilities is of utmost importance.

There are no doubts that Venezuela enjoys a comparative advantage in its oil sector. Moreover, the natural resource of the country is backed by an organizational structure and by human capital trained through seven decades. Today, the objective is no longer simply to expand volume but rather to develop the industrialization of oil to its potential, especially the petrochemical industry. It is in this context that the present plan for expanding petrochemical and coal industries should be understood. In oil production, the goal is to reach a sustainable production level of around 3 million b/d by 1996. The installed capacity of 1.1 million b/d of the country's refineries will be increased to 1.6 million b/d, augmenting substantially deep conversion capacity. In relative terms the petrochemical program is very ambitious. Its goal is to increase six-fold the present production of 2.5 million metric tons per year by 1996. The coal industry foresees an even greater relative increase in production (from 1.5 to 11.5 million metric tons per year). The planned production for 1996 of Orimulsion, a new combustible,† is 41 million metric tons per year.

To reach these ambitious targets joint ventures are already part of the scheme in the petrochemical and coal industries. An offshore gas production joint venture oriented to foreign markets is on the political agenda. The benefit of the association with foreign capital in the core of the business (exploration, production, and refining) is being widely discussed at a national level. The argument in favor of this association highlights the access to technology and markets for a resource base that is becoming more difficult to process and market. Other arguments in favor are the inability of the country to undertake these projects on its own in such a short period of time and the smaller national financial burden an association will entail.

At an international level, the tendencies toward a vertical reintegration of the international oil industry are clear. Venezuela, among other OPEC mem-

---

†Orimulsion is a mix of heavy oil (70%), water (30%) and an emulsion to stabilize the mix. This product is to compete with coal in power stations.

bers, began its internationalization policy in the early 1980s with the association of PDVSA with Veba Ol in Germany. The tendency of oil-producing countries to move downstream through the association and acquire refineries and distribution systems in oil-consuming countries to guarantee a strategic position in the market is evident. The upstream movement of capital of the oil-consuming countries into exploration, production, and refineries is a logical counterpart of the downstream movement of the oil-exporting countries. As the foundations of a reintegrated market are laid, this will lead to stability in the market favoring both parties.[20]

The expansion of the oil sector will have important horizontal and vertical multiplier effects in the economy. This will have a direct effect on the industries that supply goods and services to the oil sector. Among those affected are very dynamic industries such as the capital goods and construction industries. Therefore, we should expect the expansion plan of the oil industry to have large indirect effects. Given the large demand brought along by this plan, we should expect economies of scale to develop in national industries supplying the oil industry, enabling them to compete internationally. Finally, the dynamic effect of this oil activity will lead to a sustained and gradual expansion of the domestic market, and thus a market for national industries in general. The expansion of the oil industry will lead the way out of the economic morass the country is in. This situation was caused by the lack of dynamism of the external sector and limited capital absorption capacity of industries oriented toward the domestic market.

Judging from the past multiplier effects, the expansion of the oil activity and oil income contemplated in the 1991–1996 Plan could lead to a yearly growth rate of GDP of about 3 percent, which would imply a per capita growth rate of about 0.5 percent. Venezuela's goal, however, should be a higher growth rate.

Unlike the past, when oil was the sole driving force of the economy, new dynamic forces will be needed to propel the country to higher growth rates. Some of these forces will come from areas related, directly or indirectly, to the oil industry. Exports of oil goods and services, petrochemicals, and chemicals derived from oil could be some of the driving forces. The potential of generating thermoelectric energy associated with the higher levels of hydrocarbon production reinforces Venezuela's position as a country that has a comparative advantage in energy. This could lead to the development of energy-intensive industries, such as steel, ceramics, cement, and aluminum. In the post-rent era, the oil industry will play a stellar role in the productive activities of the country.

Given the long history of the rent-maximizing oil policy and its relationship with the question of national sovereignty, it is not surprising that the new oil policy faces many obstacles and dissenters. Above all, there is a fear that the return of foreign capital may imply both a loss of sovereignty and lower rents. But the sovereignty of the oil countries over their natural resources is no longer questioned by the international community of nations. It is true, however, that rent payments may be lowered. A maximum rent, equal to 100 percent of all the windfall, is not compatible with private enterprise. Profits must vary with prices and, most important, with productivity. This is the only way to take advantage of the dynamics of private enterprise.

Those obstacles will be overcome. Venezuela is in desperate need of a dynamic external sector. Today oil accounts for 80 percent of exports. Thus, the lack of dynamism of oil exports cannot be compensated by the remaining 20 percent. The development of non-oil exports has a long-term strategic importance that goes beyond the year 2000. The full development of the potential of oil as a productive activity is today the best, if not the only, option. Moreover, it opens excellent perspectives for the integral development of the country.

REFERENCES

1. Bernard Mommer, *Die Ölfrage,* chap. 3, Institut für Internationale Angelegenheiten der Universität Hamburg, Nomos Verlagsgesellschaft, Baden-Baden (1983); Spanish translation: *La cuestión petrolera,* Editorial TROPIKOS, Caracas (1988).
2. Quoted in Manuel R. Egaña, *Venezuela y sus minas,* p. 216, Banco Central de Venezuela (1979).
3. Manuel R. Egaña, op. cit., pp. 216–217 (1979).
4. Quoted in Angel J. Márquez, ed., *El Imperialismo petrolero y la revolución venezolana* II, p. 49, Editorial Raptura, Caracas (1977).
5. G. Torres, *Memoria del Ministerio de Fomento,* p. xviii (1920).
6. Bernard Mommer, "¿Es posible una politica petrolera no rentista?", *Revista del Banco Central de Venezuela* 4, 3 (1989).
7. Asdrúbal Baptista and Bernard Mommer, "El petróleo en las cuentas nacionales: una proposición," *Revista del Banco Central de Venezuela* 2 (1986).
8. Bernard Mommer, "Oil Rent and Rent Capitalism: The Example of Venezuela," *Review* XIII, 4, Fernand Braudel Center (Fall 1990).
9. John A. Gorman et al., "Fixed Private Capital in the United States," *Survey of Current Business* (July 1985).
10. Bernard Mommer, "La distribución de la renta petrolera. El desarrollo del capitalismo rentistico venezolano" in Omar Bello R. and Héctor Valecillo T., eds., *La economia contemporánea de Venezuela* IV, pp. 157–234, Banco Central de Venezuela, Caracas (1990).
11. Ramón Espinasa, "The Dynamics of Petroleum Price Formation," *The Petroleum Review,* London (September 1989).
12. Ramón Espinasa, op. cit. (1989), Ref 11.
13. Compare Asdrúbal Baptista and Bernard Mommer, *El petróleo en el pensamiento económico venezolano,* Instituto de Estudios Superiores de Administración, Caracas (1988)(second updated edition forthcoming).
14. Bernard Mommer, op. cit. (1990), Ref 10.
15. Robert Mansell and Michael B. Percy, *Strength in Adversity: A Study of the Alberta Economy,* University of Alberta Press, Edmonton (1990).

16. Adela Pellegrino, *Historia de la inmigración en Venezuela Siglos XIX y XX*, Academia Nacional de Ciencias Economicas, Caracas (1989).
17. Bernard Mommer, "La economia venezolana: de la siembra del petróleo a la enfermedad holandesa," *Cuadernos del CENDES* 8, CENDES/UCV, Caracas (1988).
18. J. Peter Neary and Sweder van Wijnbergen, eds., *Natural Resources and the Macroeconomy*, The MIT Press, Cambridge, MA (1985).
19. Alan Gelb and Associates, *Oil Windfalls Blessing or Curse?*, Oxford University Press, Oxford (1988).
20. Ramón Espinasa, op. cit. (1989), Ref 11.

PART TWO: ENERGY ISSUES AND TRENDS

10 Integrated Analysis of the National Energy Strategy

Eric Petersen, Roger Naill, and Sharon Belanger

INTRODUCTION

In February 1991 President Bush released the U.S. National Energy Strategy. The Strategy is a comprehensive set of more than one hundred policy actions that would, if enacted, lay the foundation for a more efficient, less vulnerable and environmentally sustainable energy future. These actions would diversify the U.S. energy supply, offer greater energy flexibility and stimulate energy efficiency. These gains would result from increased competition, expanded technology and fuel choices, expansion of R&D and support for U.S. international energy leadership. The Strategy is the product of 18 months of sophisticated and comprehensive analysis using a wide variety of tools and methods. This paper sets out the integrated analysis of Strategy actions, the Strategy integrating energy model, analysis results and energy policy insights.

ANALYSIS METHODOLOGY

The Analysis Process

The purpose of the Strategy analysis process was to provide a means to quantitatively assess proposed energy policy actions, and to determine what differences these actions could make in a comprehensive and consistent way. The process consisted of five principal steps: 1) a series of public hearings designed to solicit the views of the American people on energy policy options; 2) narrowing of those options; 3) development of 40 year baseline projections of future energy supply and demand to provide an analytical frame of reference; 4) analyses of a narrowed set of options; and 5) analytical integration of these options within a modeling framework. These steps are depicted

127

in Fig. 10.1. The first major step in the development of the National Energy Strategy was a series of public hearings. They produced a wealth of information, including several hundred energy policy options. These options, encompassing all fuels and energy consuming sectors of the economy, formed the starting point for the analysis process. A narrower set of candidate options was then identified for in-depth analysis.

Development of Baseline Energy Projections

Concurrent with the public hearings process, a set of baseline projections of future energy markets was developed with the assistance of many energy models, tools and experts. The baseline provides an analytical point of reference, while the integrated analysis estimates how far the combined actions can potentially move energy supply and demand from that baseline. Although point estimates are provided in this paper for both the baseline and the combined Strategy actions, the differences between these two cases are the critical measure of the effectiveness of the Strategy. Point projections, especially over a 40 year time horizon, are inherently inaccurate. However, comparison of the baseline and Strategy actions yields insights on the relative effectiveness of the actions. Because the purpose of the baseline is to provide an analytical frame of reference, the projections assume no changes in current Federal energy policies. As such, the baseline is characterized as the "Current Policy Base Case." Assuming no changes to current Federal policies causes the baseline to be a most unlikely portrait of the future, especially over a 40 year time horizon. However, it is a necessary assumption as a point of departure for analysis of proposed *changes* to current energy policy.

The Current Policy Base Case was developed with the aid of many diverse analytical tools and the judgments of numerous experts both inside and outside the Department of Energy (DOE). The starting point for this case was the Energy Information Administration (EIA) 1990 Annual Energy Outlook "base case forecast."[1] Department-wide modeling groups revised assumptions in that forecast and developed assumptions for extending the projections to the year 2030. Detailed sector and fuel specific models maintained by the EIA and DOE national laboratories were used to generate independent projections of long-term energy demand and supply.

These independent energy projections were then integrated through the Strategy integrating energy model. This model, Fossil2, provided price and quantity feedbacks among sectors to "clear" energy markets. (An overview of this model is provided in the following section.) The sector and fuel specific price and quantity results of this integration process were then fed back into the detailed models to provide a check on the integrating model results. In addition to energy integration, macroeconomic integration was also done, using the Strategy macroeconomic integrating model to ensure that all markets "cleared." (This tool, the DRI quarterly model of the U.S. economy, is

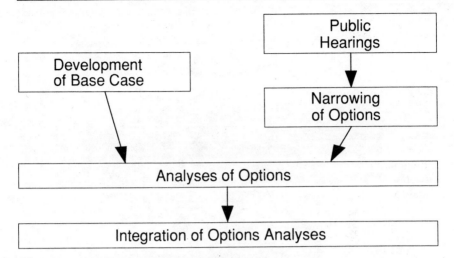

Fig. 10.1. Steps in Strategy analytical process.

described in Ref. 2 and Ref. 3.) The integration process is depicted in Fig. 10.2.

The combination of detailed models and integrating models was applied to make best use of the current set of DOE tools. It was determined that no single model existed that could both provide the level of detail necessary to develop the Current Policy Base Case as well as the integrated analysis of the full slate of energy policy actions. The modeling "system," or integrating framework, assembled for this analysis provided both sufficient detail and flexibility to produce a set of baseline projections and address important "what if" questions.

Internal consistency could be maintained within this system of models because of the nature of the models. Most of these tools are structural simulation models; this makes it possible to share not only the results of models, but the underlying assumptions and projected changes in market structure as well. That is, the underlying assumptions driving the detailed models could drive the Strategy integrating energy model as well. Information developed with the detailed models was transferred to the integrating model by calibration of the integrating model structure. In this way, the results of the detailed models could be analytically replicated in the integrating energy model. Through this type of information sharing, consistency could be maintained among the models.

Current Policy Base Case Assumptions

Many assumptions about technologies, energy prices, consumer behavior, energy resources and other factors underlie the Current Policy Base Case. As

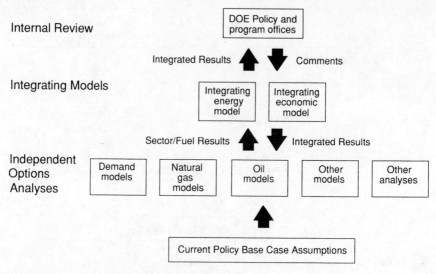

Fig. 10.2. Analytical integration process.

mentioned above, the single most important assumption is that Federal energy policies will not change in the 40 year time frame. Existing laws and regulations through September 1990 are included. Major laws enacted after that time as part of the overall Administration energy policy, including the 1990 Clean Air Act Amendments (CAAA), are included in the Strategy. A second key assumption is that market choices promote economic efficiency unless otherwise constrained. A third key assumption is economic growth rates. The U.S. economy is projected to grow on average at a 3.2 percent rate annually between 1990 and 2000, 2.7 percent from 2000 to 2010 and 1.8 percent from 2010 to 2030. These growth assumptions were provided by the U.S. Council of Economic Advisors. Additional assumptions are given in Table 10.1.[2]

Independent Analyses of Actions

The full set of National Energy Strategy actions, referred to as the Strategy scenario, covers a broad range of issues, affecting virtually every fuel and energy consuming sector of the economy. Actions were analyzed by groups of experts from the Department of Energy, DOE national laboratories and other Federal agencies, including the Council of Economic Advisors, the Office of Management and Budget, the Department of Treasury, and the Environmental Protection Agency. Because of differences in energy type, sector structure, and the nature of problems facing each sector, these groups selected models or other methodological approaches best suited for the examination of each particular action. Many different models and other tools were therefore used in the evaluation of impacts of policy actions on energy supply and

Table 10.1. Current Policy Base Case assumptions

Free market: market choices promote economic efficiency.

Economic growth rates: 2.9 percent/year (1990-2010); 1.8 percent/year (2010-2030).

World oil prices: 4.0 percent/year (1990-2010); 1.0 percent/year (2010-2030).

Technology assumptions: "cautiously optimistic;" energy efficiency improvements driven by increasing prices; overall economy becomes 20 percent more efficient by 2010.

Oil and gas reserves and resources: oil, 80 billion barrels; gas, 700 trillion cubic feet; no access to restricted areas (such as ANWR).

Alternative transportation fuels: no significant penetration without policy changes.

Nuclear power: no new nuclear plant orders; no life extension.

Clean coal technologies: penetration of demonstrated technologies due to favorable costs.

Renewable energy: steady improvements in renewable electric technologies.

No 1990 Clean Air Act Amendments (included in Strategy).

demand. The products of these analyses was a set of estimated "partial equilibrium" effects for each action. (Here, partial equilibrium represents sector or fuel specific impacts.)

The analyses used the Current Policy Base Case as the starting point for the quantitative analysis of impacts of each action on energy markets. Information on demand, supply, and prices for each type of energy from the Current Policy Base Case were used to quantify the impact of a specific action on supply and demand. For example, the advanced oil recovery technologies research and development (R&D) action analysis used the oil prices in the Current Policy Base Case in the examination of the effect of R&D programs on oil production.

Integration of Actions

Once the partial equilibrium analysis of each action was complete, the actions were integrated in order to estimate the general equilibrium effects. Many policy actions affect more than one sector or fuel; changes in one sector often affect fuel prices, which in turn affect energy demand and supply in other sectors. In addition, policy actions usually do not work in isolation from other actions; some actions work in tandem, while others work at odds with one another. The purpose of analyzing the actions in combination, or "integrating" them, is to provide an understanding of these effects. Not all Strategy actions were quantitatively integrated. In general, those actions having significant direct impacts and that could be quantified in a reasonable fashion were analytically integrated as described below. The actions integrated into the Strategy scenario, listed in Table 10.2, are the ones with major direct impacts.

The Strategy integrating energy model provided a systematic and consistent framework for the analysis of Strategy actions. Because this model has demand representations by sector and end use, supply representations by energy types, and market clearing mechanisms for demand and supply, it could simulate both the price effects and inter-fuel competition effects of each action on energy supply and demand. This detailed market structure representation in the integrating energy model made possible the integration of Strategy actions. The impacts of the combination of all Strategy actions on energy markets were evaluated by incorporating both the results and the underlying assumptions of the independent options analyses and then equilibrating supply/demand quantities and prices. In this way, the integration process could draw upon the strengths of both the detailed sector specific and fuel specific models and the more aggregate integrating models.

Key Measures

In order to quantify the effectiveness of Strategy actions, several key measures were used. These measures reflect the degree to which actions affect energy security, the environment and the economy.

The vulnerability of an economy to a disruption of oil supplies depends fundamentally upon how oil-dependent an economy is, but also upon other measures that influence the price consequences of a disruption in world oil markets. These measures include availability and use of strategic stocks, surplus production capacity, fuel switching and conservation measures. Actions that increase our ability to withstand disruptions in world oil markets can be likened to purchasing insurance for the economy; from the decision-maker perspective, the insurance should be purchased if the potential cost of supply disruptions exceeds the cost of the insurance. In economic terms, actions can be justified in terms of energy security if the net present value of the avoided reduction in GNP and other measurable welfare losses resulting from a supply disruption is positive and greater than the negative value resulting from the adoption of the actions.

For a supply disruption of a given size, the impacts on world oil prices would be smaller if total world demand for oil was relatively smaller or if total world supply of oil was relatively larger. This implies that reducing the volume and share of oil in total primary energy consumption would reduce the impacts of an oil supply disruption on the economy. The effectiveness of a Strategy action in improving energy security was therefore evaluated as its potential to reduce oil consumption, increase fuel switching capability and increase oil supply.

Table 10.2. Policy actions integrated into the Strategy scenario

---

1990 Clean Air Act Amendments.

Oil production incentives.

Advanced oil recovery R&D.

Access to the Alaska National Wildlife Refuge.

Access to restricted Federal outer continental shelf.

Natural gas regulatory reforms.

Clean coal technology incentives.

Nuclear power actions.

Hydropower regulatory reforms.

Municipal solid waste-to-energy actions.

Electric utility integrated resource planning.

Buildings efficiency standards.

Enhanced industrial energy efficiency R&D.

Alternative transportation fuels actions.

Enhanced transportation R&D.

Enhanced transportation biofuels production R&D.

Source: Ref 2.

Impacts of the Strategy on the environment were quantified in terms of changes in levels of major pollutants, including nitrogen oxides (NO_x), sulfur dioxide (SO_2) and volatile organic compounds (VOC). Emissions of greenhouse gases that may contribute to global climate change were also quantified in the Strategy using the Intergovernmental Panel on Climate Change (IPCC) global warming potential (GWP) index. This measure was used as a way to measure consistently the relative contributions of greenhouse gases to time-integrative radiative forcing. SO_2, NO_x and VOC emissions were projected with Argonne National Laboratory environmental models. Selected greenhouse gases were estimated with the Strategy integrating energy model, while global warming potential was estimated by Battelle Pacific Northwest Laboratory.

The impacts of a Strategy action on the general economy were evaluated at both the macroeconomic and microeconomic level. At the macroeconomic level, the Strategy integrating macroeconomic model was used to quantify the impacts of Strategy actions on U.S. GNP. At the microeconomic level, the net national economic benefit was assessed where possible in the individual options analyses; this was done by calculating the changes in consumer and producer surplus.

THE STRATEGY INTEGRATING ENERGY MODEL

The integrating energy analysis tool for the National Energy Strategy is a large-scale model of the U.S. energy system called Fossil2. Fossil2 is a dynamic simulation model of U.S. energy supply and demand designed to project the long-term (40 year) behavior of the U.S. energy system. The model structure, which includes all energy producing and consuming sectors, simulates the marketplace in a series of dynamic stocks and flows; the stocks include energy production facilities (for example, oil fields), energy transformation facilities (for example, power plants) and energy consuming entities (for example, houses, vehicles), while the flows include energy, prices and other macroeconomic information.

The basic structure of the Fossil2 model is shown in Fig. 10.3. The demand sector is divided into four major energy-using sectors: residential, commercial, industrial, and transportation. Each of the sectors is further divided into major end-use categories that represent different types of energy service demands. The demand for energy is determined in a "least cost/energy services" framework of total U.S. energy demand. Following this approach, the model first projects the demand for energy services (heat, light, steam, shaft power) in each end-use category, and then calculates the share of service demand captured by end-use technologies. These technologies include, for example, conservation, cogeneration, or conventional steam-generation technologies.

For most energy service categories, there are several fuels that can provide the required energy services, in addition to conservation. In a few categories (such as lighting or appliances), only electric energy services can be used. For those where there are choices of fuels, a least-cost algorithm is used to determine market shares which compares energy service costs for each fuel-technology combination.

Conservation investments are treated explicitly in the Fossil2 model. Conservation technologies are represented in supply curves that are specific to each end use and fuel type. The curves are constructed from data representing technologies currently available, and those anticipated to be available given current technical information. The conservation supply curves relate the costs and energy savings associated with customers' options for energy efficiency investments in different end-use markets. The model calculates whether a capital investment in energy efficiency is "worth" the savings in fuel costs it provides, given consumers' different investment criteria. The value of the fuel savings over the lifetime of the measure depends on the hurdle or discount rate used. The conservation technologies are arrayed in least-cost order on the curve, so the cheapest measures are assumed to be implemented first. As energy prices rise, consumers will "move up the curve," investing in high levels of conservation.

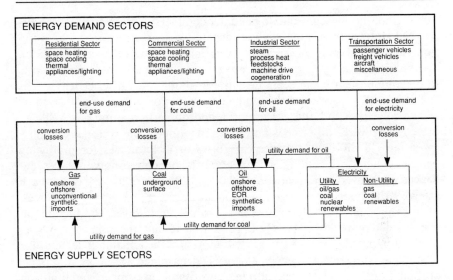

Fig. 10.3. Basic structure of the Fossil2 model.

The demand for energy determined in the demand sectors is then fed into the model's energy supply sectors. The energy supply sectors of the Fossil2 model (oil, gas, coal, and electricity) represent the decisions that lead to the commitment to new production capacity, the operation of existing production capacity, and the setting of energy prices for each of the four major fuel markets. Energy producers choose to invest in production technologies that maximize the industry's rate of return (or minimize the average cost of production). The sectors keep account of production capacity and assets, and calculate energy prices in accordance with the rules that are generally followed in each industry. These rates then feed into the demand sector, helping to determine current and future growth in energy demand. This link between supply, price and demand closes important "feedback loops," which is why the model is characterized as an "integrated" model of energy supply and demand.

The electricity generation sector of the model represents the decisions that lead to the commitment to new generation capacity, the operation of existing capacity, and the setting of electricity rates. The sector includes cost and performance characteristics for 25 different types of electric generating technologies, which compete for a share of the electricity generation market. These technologies include fossil, nuclear, and renewable technologies, as well as options for life-extending and repowering existing facilities. A "least-cost" mix of technologies is then chosen to fill the need for new capacity projected by the model (based on feedback from the demand sector). After a construction period, the chosen technologies enter commercial operation and are dispatched along with existing facilities according to an annualized load duration curve specified in the model. Operating costs are calculated based on the resulting capacity factors, and are combined with allowable capital costs to determine the average cents per kilowatt-hour price of electricity.

The oil and gas sector of the model determines oil and gas production by resource category, oil and gas imports, and domestic natural gas wellhead prices. (The world oil price is an exogenous input.) The sector is disaggregated into 13 different resource categories or technologies for producing petroleum liquids (including onshore and offshore conventional sources, enhanced oil recovery, and synthetic fuels), and 10 for producing gas. For each category, the model tracks resources from undiscovered recoverable resources, through probable (or inferred) reserves, to proven reserves. Production capacity is determined by the level of proven reserves and the estimated reserve-production profile for each category. Imports fill the remaining demand for oil and gas. Investment in each category is determined according to relative profitability, the potential magnitude of profitable investment, and limits on the availability of investment funds. The model estimates drilling and other costs based on remaining producible resources, resource find rates, and production capacity. Wellhead gas prices are calculated based on the price at which the development of new gas resources would be considered economic, adjusted to reflect market conditions.

The coal production sector simulates the operation of existing coal mining capacity and the creation of new capacity for both surface and underground mines. Coal is produced in quantities that fill the demand from the demand sectors. Coal prices are then calculated based on the average cost of production.

The model also tracks the CO_2, NO_x, SO_2, and methane emissions associated with energy transformation and consumption activities. These emissions are based on coefficients (provided by the Department of Energy) that were derived from average national observed emissions and patterns of fuel use.

Since its original development in 1978, the Fossil2 model has been subjected to a number of validity tests to examine how well the model serves its purpose of long-term energy policy analysis. For example, the model has been subjected to many "extreme value" tests where it must respond to extreme conditions, for example, the oil price shocks of 1973 and 1979-80, or very high carbon taxes. Fossil2 has participated in several different sessions of the Stanford Energy Modeling Forum (where a group of models is subjected to similar sensitivity and policy tests related to a particular issue or subject area). The model has been used to prepare policy analyses for numerous articles (for example, Ref. 4, Ref. 5) and Department of Energy reports (including all of the long-term forecasts prepared for DOE's National Energy Plans since 1979). The model's structure and assumptions are subject to ongoing reviews by energy policy experts within the DOE, national laboratories and government agencies outside of the DOE to insure its appropriateness for national energy policy analysis. Current uses include congressional energy policy analysis and global climate change policy analysis by Battelle Pacific Northwest National Laboratory.

ANALYSIS RESULTS

This section summarizes the results of the integrated analysis of the combined National Energy Strategy actions. These results are described in terms of differences from the Current Policy Base Case. Effects of the combined National Energy Strategy actions on energy markets, the environment and the economy are described.

Total Energy Use

The United States is projected in the Strategy scenario to increase the consumption of primary energy at an average rate of just under one percent per year. This is substantially less than the 1.3 percent per year rate in the Current Policy Base Case. The major factors causing this reduction are lower electricity consumption growth, fuel switching in the transportation sector and higher transportation efficiency. Total energy consumption and consumption by primary fuel are depicted in Fig. 10.4.

This figure indicates that the economy, as in the Current Policy Base Case, is expected to become substantially more energy efficient than it is today. All sectors—buildings, industry and transportation—are expected to be even more efficient than in the Current Policy Base Case. Relative to today, the economy is projected to become 32 percent more energy efficient in the Current Policy Base Case and 42 percent more efficient under the Strategy scenario.

Oil

Under the Strategy scenario, domestic oil production increases significantly relative to the Current Policy future and in fact rises absolutely in the midterm. This turnabout is due to the energy production incentives, advanced oil R&D, access to the coastal plain of the Alaskan National Wildlife Refuge (ANWR), and access to certain restricted Federal outer continental shelf (OCS) areas. Oil consumption is lower due to the combined effects of alternative fuels, transportation efficiency R&D, natural gas regulatory reforms and other oil demand reduction actions. As a result of the higher production and lower consumption levels, oil imports are sharply lower than in the Current Policy Base Case. These changes are depicted in Fig. 10.5.

The Strategy actions result in an estimated 3.8 million barrels per day (b/d) of additional domestic oil production by the 2005-2010 period relative to the Current Policy Base Case. U.S. crude oil and natural gas liquids production

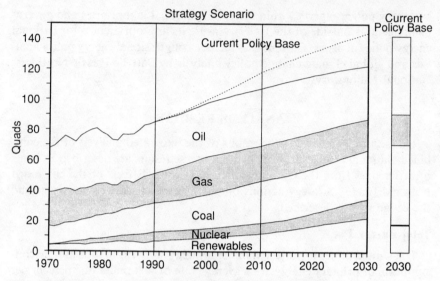

Fig. 10.4. Primary energy consumption by fuel (Strategy scenario).

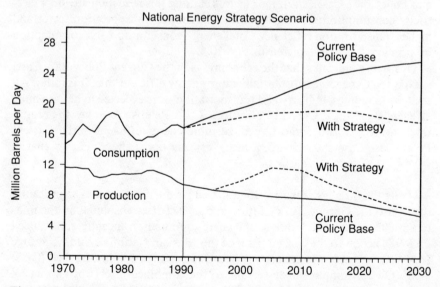

Fig. 10.5. Oil consumption and production (Strategy scenario).

is projected to rise from 8.8 million b/d in 1990 (excluding refinery gains) to 9.3 million b/d in 2000 and 10.6 million b/d in 2010. This large jump in production is the result of the oil supply actions listed above. The energy production tax incentives result in nearly 0.4 million b/d of additional production by 2000. The advanced oil R&D action results in additional oil production, including secondary and tertiary oil recovery of about 2.6 million b/d in 2005 and 2.9 million b/d by 2010. This increase is the result of an aggressive transfer of existing recovery technologies to geologic areas in which they have not been previously applied, as well as the commercialization of new technologies. The advanced oil R&D action also results in higher production from conventional lower 48 resources. Production from ANWR, based on the conditional mean resource level, reaches 0.8 million b/d by 2005 and declines slowly thereafter. Production from the restricted OCS rises to 0.1 million b/d by 2010 and reaches 0.4 million b/d by 2015. This delay is due to restrictions on Federal OCS access before 2000.

As shown in Fig. 10.5, U.S. oil consumption is projected to rise less rapidly under the Strategy scenario than in the Current Policy Base Case. Demand grows at an annual rate of only 0.6 percent per year through 2010 (less than half the rate in the Current Policy Base Case) and actually *falls* by 0.3 percent thereafter (compared to a 0.8 per year increase). Total oil demand is estimated to rise from about 17.0 million b/d in 1990 to 18.4 million b/d in 2000, 19.2 million b/d in 2010 and fall to less than 18 million b/d by 2030. This represents savings relative to the Current Policy Base Case of 1.3 million b/d in 2000, 3.4 million b/d in 2010, and about eight million b/d by 2030.

The bulk of the oil demand savings in the Strategy scenario is in the transportation sector. Projected changes in transportation oil consumption are depicted in Fig. 10.6. The alternative fuels and transportation R&D actions, together with the CAAA, result in 95 percent of the total oil savings. Overall passenger vehicle efficiency increases by 29 percent by 2010, and by nearly 80 percent by 2030 relative to the Current Policy Base Case. This is twice the rate of efficiency improvement by 2010 in the Current Policy Base Case and more than three times the rate by 2030. These long-term efficiency gains are due to successful development and market penetration of more efficient propulsion technologies after 2010. These efficiency gains are complemented by switching from oil to alternative fuels (including methanol and compressed natural gas) and substantial production of alcohol fuels brought about by a biofuels production R&D action. Alternative fuels consumption, resulting from the Strategy alternative fuels initiatives, and the use of oxygenates in reformulated gasoline resulting from the CAAA together reach 0.9 million b/d in 2000 and 2.2 million b/d by 2010.

The large reductions in oil consumption, coupled with the higher production levels in the Strategy scenario, result in substantially lower U.S. oil import levels (see Fig. 10.5). Imports are projected to rise from an estimated 7.3 million b/d in 1990 to only 8.3 million b/d in 2000, 7.8 million b/d in 2010 and 11.6 million b/d by 2030. This represents a savings of three million b/d in 2000, seven million b/d in 2010 and eight million b/d in 2030, or put

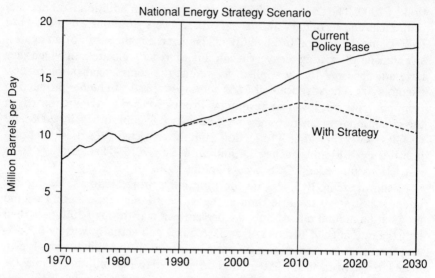

Fig. 10.6. Transportation oil consumption (Strategy scenario).

another way, over a 35 percent reduction in U.S. dependency on imported oil in 2010. The Current Policy Base Case projects importing roughly 65 percent of the oil the nation uses in 2010 and nearly 80 percent in 2030. Under the Strategy scenario, the figures are about 40 percent in 2010 and 65 percent in 2030.

Electricity

Electricity consumption rises more slowly under the Strategy scenario than under the Current Policy Base Case. Total consumption is expected to rise from 9.2 quads today to 13.7 quads in 2010 and 18.4 quads by 2030 under the Strategy scenario. This is a 12 percent reduction in 2010 and a 16 percent reduction by 2030 relative to the Current Policy Base Case. This substantial cut in future electricity demand is caused by electric utility integrated resource planning, building standards, and industrial energy efficiency R&D actions. Reductions in electricity also substantially cut future primary energy demand; energy inputs to generation fall by 4.5 quads in 2010 and about seven quads in 2030 relative to the Current Policy Base Case.

The mix of fuels used to generate electricity, shown in Fig. 10.7, is projected to change substantially in the long term under the Strategy scenario as compared to the Current Policy Base Case. In 2010, the share of coal is projected to drop from 59 percent without the Strategy to 54 percent with the Strategy, while nuclear increases from 13 percent to 16 percent and the renewables share jumps from 13 percent to 18 percent. By 2030, the coal share

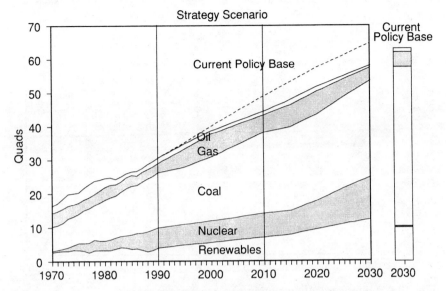

Fig. 10.7. Fuel inputs to electricity generation (Strategy scenario).

falls from about 75 percent to 49 percent while nuclear leaps from one percent to 22 percent and renewables grows from 16 percent to 26 percent. The result is a more balanced and, hence, potentially a more reliable electricity generation system as a result of the Strategy actions.

Greenhouse Gas Emissions

Emissions of greenhouse gases, which may contribute to potential global climate change, fall substantially relative to the Current Policy future. This is due to the combination of actions on nuclear power, renewable energy, integrated resource planning and the conservation actions in buildings, industry and transportation. As shown in Fig. 10.8, total greenhouse gas emissions, measured in terms of global warming potential, are estimated to stay at or below 1990 levels through 2030. Greenhouse gas emissions are projected to decline from 1990 levels after 2015, reaching a level nearly 10 percent below 1990 by 2030.

Emissions of Air Pollutants

Emissions of sulfur dioxide (SO_2) fall sharply in the Strategy scenario due primarily to the CAAA, especially in the near term. Over the long term, however, the Strategy would reduce SO_2 emissions even beyond the substantial reductions driven by the CAAA due to electricity conservation, natural gas regulatory reform, clean coal technology and nuclear power actions. Rela-

National Energy Strategy Scenario

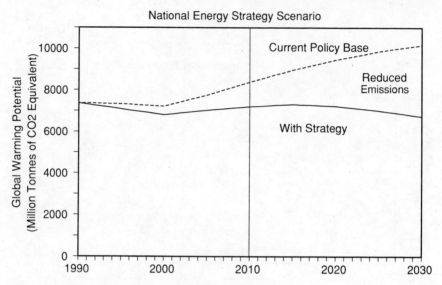

Fig. 10.8. Global warming potential (Strategy scenario).

tive to 1990 SO_2 emission levels, there is a 35 percent decrease in emissions by 2000, contrasted with a growth in emissions of seven percent in the Current Policy Base. One result of the Strategy is that electric utilities have more flexibility in meeting the emissions target of the CAAA due to the availability of cleaner, more efficient technologies. Moreover, since electricity demand is substantially lower than in the Current Policy Base Case, the cost of compliance may be somewhat reduced. SO_2 emissions are depicted in Fig. 10.9.

Nitrogen oxide (NO_x) and volatile organic compounds (VOC) emissions are also projected to be substantially lower under the Strategy scenario. Relative to 1990, NO_x emission levels are 13 percent lower by 2000, primarily because of the CAAA. VOC emissions are projected to be 24 percent lower in 2000 than in 1990, largely due to the CAAA. With increased transportation energy use by 2010, NO_x and VOC levels are projected to rise slightly from the 2000 levels, but remain lower than their 1990 levels.

Impacts on the U.S. Economy

The economic objectives of the National Energy Strategy are to maintain an economy that is second to none and to reduce the economy's vulnerability to energy supply disruptions. The National Energy Strategy results in both.

The impacts of the Strategy on the U.S. economy are projected to be positive: economic growth is estimated to be higher, and energy vulnerability lower. U.S. GNP is projected to be about $25 billion ($1990) higher by 2000 than without the Strategy. By 2010, this improvement in economic output is project-

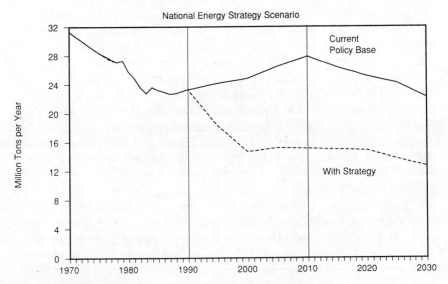

Fig. 10.9. Sulfur dioxide emissions (Strategy scenario).

ed to exceed $35 billion. These increases result from lower energy prices, which in turn are caused by lower energy demand, lower oil import bills and greater energy efficiency. These increases in economic output are quite modest. However, the important message is that the substantial improvements in energy security and environmental quality resulting from the Strategy are obtained without economic losses.

CONCLUSIONS AND POLICY INSIGHTS

The Current Policy Base Case projects that, with no new energy policy initiatives, oil imports would rise to unprecedented levels (nearly 80 percent of total oil consumption by 2030) and energy-related environmental emissions would increase substantially beyond 1990 levels. These trends would substantially worsen the U.S. energy situation; they translate into greater energy vulnerability and higher environmental stress.

Analysis of the National Energy Strategy indicates, however, that implementing the Strategy actions would significantly improve this situation by cuts in oil consumption (and hence imports), substantial reductions in emissions and modest decreases in energy costs. Furthermore, these objectives are achieved without losses in economic growth; in fact, GNP is estimated to be $25 billion higher by the year 2000 under the Strategy because of small reductions in energy costs.

This result at first seems improbable: achieving these policy goals might be expected to raise, not lower, energy costs (and thus lower, not raise, economic growth). The answer lies in the balance the Strategy strikes among policies that stimulate conservation, increase supplies, develop new technologies through cost-shared research and development (R&D) and facilitate consumer choices. The Strategy includes a number of policy actions that, if successful, would increase access to lower cost energy resources through stimulation of market forces and removal of barriers to market efficiency. Examples of these lower cost resources include conservation, oil in the ANWR, increased consumer access to natural gas, and new lower cost technologies estimated to result from increased energy R&D. The cost reductions and efficiency improvements from gaining access to these energy resources more than offset the increased costs of improving energy security and reducing future environmental damage. In addition, the Strategy does not rely on energy taxes. Strategy analysis indicated that taxes, while having the potential to reduce energy consumption significantly, would also result in substantially lower economic growth.

REFERENCES

1. U.S. Energy Information Administration, *Annual Energy Outlook 1990,* DOE/ EIA-0383(90), Washington, DC (1990).
2. U.S. Department of Energy, "National Energy Strategy Technical Annex 2. Integrated Analysis Supporting the National Energy Strategy: Methodology, Assumptions and Results," Washington, DC (1991).
3. Data Resources, Inc., *Quarterly Model of the U.S. Economy: Version U.S. 89A. Model Documentation: Theory, Properties and Coverage,* DRI/McGraw-Hill, Lexington, MA (1990).
4. Sharon Belanger and Roger Naill, "Impacts of Deregulation on U.S. Electric Utilities," *Public Utilities Fortnightly* (October 12, 1989).
5. Roger Naill, *Managing Energy Transition,* Ballinger Publishing Company, Cambridge, MA (1977).

11 Modeling Macroeconomic Impacts of U.S. Oil Protectionist Policies

Carol A. Dahl and Mine K. Yücel

INTRODUCTION

The heady days of high world oil prices, which commenced in the 1970s, finished abruptly in 1986. Except for the brief respite when oil prices spiked during the build up to the 1991 Persian Gulf War, prices will most likely remain at these lower levels. As a result, the United States, which is a high-cost producer by world standards, has seen its oil industry strongly depressed. From 1985 to 1990, the numbers of U.S. seismic crews fell by 67 percent, active rotary rigs by 49 percent, and wells drilled by 59 percent. Both the number of rotary rigs and wells drilled rebounded slightly with the higher prices in 1990, but U.S. oil production continued to fall with a total decrease of 18 percent from 1985 to 1990. At the same time, low prices stimulated oil product consumption. Although the slower U.S. economy caused a slight decrease in oil product consumption in 1990, the overall increase from 1985 to 1990 was still 10 percent. With falling production and rising consumption, nervous politicians watched imports share of consumption rise from 31 percent in 1985 to almost 47 percent in 1990, a share not seen since the peak in 1977.†

The oil price collapse in 1986 also led to calls for decreasing oil consumption or protection of the domestic industry. The three most frequent protec-

The authors would like to thank Noel Uri for comments on an earlier version of this paper but take responsibility for any remaining errors. The views expressed in this article are solely those of the authors and should not be attributed to the Federal Reserve Bank of Dallas or to the Federal Reserve System.

†Sources of industry statistics are the American Petroleum Institute (1990) Section IV, Table 1; Section VIII, Table 21; Section IX, Table 1; and Section III, Table 1; and U.S. EIA/DOE (1991), Table 5.1.

tionist proposals were a gasoline tax, an oil tariff, and a producer subsidy.† More recently, rising imports, along with oil market instability associated with the Gulf War, have renewed calls for these protectionist policies.‡ Increasing environmental emphasis also reinforces concern for high consumption of oil products, leading to policies to curtail oil consumption such as the increases in gasoline and diesel fuel taxes in the 1990 Clean Air Act.

In this article, we consider three policies to curtail imports: a gasoline tax, an oil tariff, and a domestic producer subsidy. Although all policies would decrease current imports, they would have varying effects on macroeconomic variables such as inflation, income growth, unemployment, government revenues, and the balance of payments. The macroeconomic effects of these policies are the focus of this work. Because policies to curtail imports now may increase imports later, we consider the policies in a dynamic framework that allows modeling of short-run and long-run macroeconomic effects.

In the second section of this article, we discuss the dynamic optimal control model used to simulate prices and production for the United States and OPEC. In the third section, we simulate the dynamic model with a base case and the three protectionist policies: a $0.15 per gallon gasoline tax, an equal revenue tariff, and an equal cost producer subsidy. We use the simulated price paths in the fourth section to evaluate the short-run and long-run macroeconomic effects of the three policies. We compute the direct effects of the policies on government revenues and foreign exchange savings of the policies in the short run and long run directly from the price and output paths of the dynamic models. We compute the indirect effects on inflation, income growth, unemployment, total income, and the change in the federal deficit by combining the simulated price with impact multipliers. In the fifth section, we compare these two approaches with other models that have been used to evaluate protectionist policies. We discuss conclusions, policy implications, and further research in the concluding section.

THE DYNAMIC MODEL

The dynamic model is taken from Yücel and Dahl.¹ OPEC is assumed to be a dominant firm facing U.S. total demand for oil minus both U.S. domestic production and non-OPEC U.S. imports. Domestic producers are profit-maximizing price takers on the U.S. crude oil market. Non-OPEC oil suppli-

†For example, the Senate Finance Committee proposed an oil import fee if oil imports exceeded 50 percent of demand, President George Bush in his campaign suggested a subsidy in the form of tax incentives to domestic producers (*Oil and Gas Journal,* p. 29, Nov. 14, 1988), and Rep. Dan Rostenkowski (D-Ill.) has repeatedly recommended a $0.15 per gallon increase excise tax on gasoline (*Oil and Gas Journal,* p. 3, Dec. 5, 1988; p. 4, Jan. 15, 1990).

‡Rep. Bennett Johnston (D-La.) has refiled a bill for a variable fee on oil imports when the world oil price falls below $20 per barrel (*Oil and Gas Journal,* p. 3, Feb. 4, 1991).

ers are assumed to supply the same level as in 1987, or 841.325 million barrels. The United States and OPEC maximize their profits over a 30 year period given their initial reserves. We simulated under a base case, a gasoline tax increase of $0.15 per gallon, an oil tariff of $7.70 per barrel, that brings in equal revenues over the 30 year simulation period, and an equal cost subsidy to U.S. producers of $4.92 per barrel.†

We derived price and income elasticities from econometric estimates in the literature and assumed product imports remain a constant percentage. Normalizing around 1987 prices and quantities yields the inverse demand equation used for simulation:

$$P = 136.832(Q_{us} + Q_0 + 841.325)^{-1.1}Y^{.89},$$

where P is the supply price of crude oil, Q_{us} is the quantity supplied by the U.S., and Q_0 is the quantity supplied by OPEC.

On the supply side, we assumed initial OPEC reserves are 769,214 million barrels with OPEC cost[2] equal to

$$C_0 = 23.232 - .000026\ R_0 + .016\ T,$$

where C_0 is OPEC total cost per barrel, R_0 is OPEC remaining reserves, measured in millions of barrels, and T is a time trend.

We assumed initial U.S. reserves to be 100,600 million barrels with U.S. cost[3] equal to

$$C_u = 33.13 - .0002832\ R_u + .21T,$$

where C_u is U.S. total cost per barrel and R_u is U.S. remaining reserves, measured in millions of barrels.

We assumed that income will grow 2.5 percent over the simulation period and that the real interest rate is eight percent. (See Ref. 1 for the exact specification of the maximization problem.)

SIMULATED OIL PRICE PATHS

We simulated optimal time paths beginning in 1987 for U.S. production, OPEC exports to the United States, and oil prices for a base case with no tariff or subsidy and the prevailing gasoline tax. Table 11.1 lists these simulated paths.

In the base case, oil prices rise 2.9 percent a year on average from $13.10 per barrel in 1987 to $31.47 per barrel (in 1987 dollars) in 2017. U.S. production falls by 1.4 percent a year on average and is 65 percent of 1987 produc-

---

†Revenues and costs of these policies are sums for each year discounted using an eight percent interest rate.

Table 11.1.   Simulated U.S. production, OPEC imports, and
              effective consumer oil prices (quantities in millions of
              barrels, and prices in 1987 U.S. dollars per barrel)

Year	Base case			$0.15/gal gasoline tax		
	Q_{us}	Q_{opec}	P_{oil}	Q_{us}	Q_{opec}	P_{oil}
1987	3538	2487	$13.10	3174	1835	$15.66
1989	3130	2422	$14.82	2856	1870	$17.29
1991	2848	2365	$16.46	2628	1889	$18.86
1993	2645	2317	$18.04	2461	1902	$20.37
1995	2496	2281	$19.55	2336	1913	$21.83
1997	2385	2255	$21.01	2242	1925	$23.23
1999	2302	2239	$22.41	2173	1939	$24.59
2001	2243	2232	$23.76	2124	1957	$25.89
2003	2201	2233	$25.04	2090	1978	$27.14
2005	2176	2244	$26.26	2071	2005	$28.32
2007	2164	2264	$27.41	2064	2038	$29.44
2009	2165	2294	$28.47	2069	2077	$30.47
2011	2178	2335	$29.42	2086	2125	$31.40
2013	2204	2390	$30.26	2114	2182	$32.22
2015	2242	2460	$30.95	2154	2252	$32.90
2017	2293	2549	$31.47	2208	2337	$33.42

Year	$7.70/b oil tariff			$4.92/b oil subsidy		
	Q_{us}	Q_{opec}	P_{oil}	Q_{us}	Q_{opec}	P_{oil}
1987	4863	474	$14.73	5539	2030	$10.45
1989	4053	854	$16.68	4410	2205	$12.49
1991	3525	1086	$18.49	3747	2253	$14.37
1993	3159	1240	$20.20	3317	2258	$16.13
1995	2896	1351	$21.83	3021	2250	$17.80
1997	2702	1437	$23.37	2809	2241	$19.39
1999	2557	1506	$24.84	2654	2234	$20.90
2001	2450	1567	$26.25	2542	2234	$22.34
2003	2372	1622	$27.59	2460	2240	$23.71
2005	2318	1676	$28.85	2404	2254	$25.00
2007	2284	1729	$30.02	2369	2276	$26.21
2009	2268	1784	$31.11	2352	2308	$27.32
2011	2270	1843	$32.09	2352	2350	$28.31
2013	2287	1907	$32.94	2368	2406	$29.18
2015	2323	1979	$33.64	2401	2478	$29.89
2017	2377	2061	$34.16	2450	2569	$30.42

Note: Q_{us} is simulated domestic oil production.
       Q_{opec} is simulated U.S. imports from OPEC.
       P_{oil} is simulated effective consumer price of crude oil.

tion by 2017, while OPEC imports are virtually flat, rising only two percent
over the entire 30 year period.

The policies have significantly different impacts on the oil market (see Table 11.1). All policies lower OPEC imports. The gasoline tax and the tariff
lower them over the whole sample. The subsidy lowers imports at first, but
just after the turn of the century, the effects of higher U.S. production in

Percent of Base

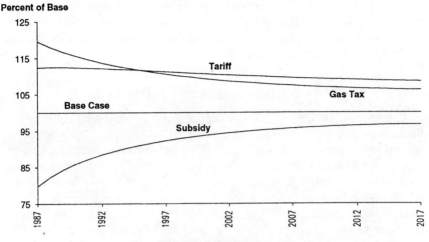

Fig. 11.1. Effective consumer oil prices.

the earlier years and higher U.S. oil consumption take effect, and OPEC imports rise over the base case. The gasoline tax lowers U.S. production over the whole sample, while the tariff and subsidy raise it over the whole sample.

The policies also have varying effects on effective U.S. consumer prices (see Table 11.1).† Because the macroeconomic effects of the policies are associated with the price of oil products, we will concentrate on these price changes. Fig. 11.1 shows the effective consumer oil price paths computed from the simulated oil prices for the three policies. For clarity, they are presented as a ratio to the base case while Table 11.1 lists the simulated values.

The effective consumer oil price paths for the three policies are quite different. The subsidy lowers prices by 21 percent at the beginning and has lower consumer prices and higher oil consumption over the whole simulation period. The gasoline tax yields the highest price at first with a 20 percent increase, but it is soon surpassed by the tariff, which chokes off OPEC imports faster. The net effect is that the tariff reduces oil consumption slightly more over the whole simulation period. The effects of the policies are largest early in the period, with prices tending to converge somewhat later.

---

†The model simulates U.S. producer prices, but the macro modeling requires the change in consumer prices. Calculating this effective oil price to consumers requires addition of the prorated gasoline tax per barrel (gasoline's share of a barrel times the tax per barrel equal to 0.4984•0.15•42) to the simulated U.S. producer price. The subsidy is subtracted from U.S. producer prices. No adjustment is needed in the case of the tariff. Because refinery margins, transportation, and other product taxes are assumed to be a constant percentage, they have no effect on the analysis and are ignored.

In the next section, we examine the short-term and long-term macroeconomic implications of these simulated output and price trajectories on inflation, income growth, income level, unemployment, government revenues, and the balance of payments cost of oil.

MACROECONOMIC EFFECTS OF THE POLICIES

We computed the direct effects of the policies on government revenues and the balance of payments using the simulated U.S. imports, U.S. production, and oil prices shown in Table 11.1.† We computed the indirect first year effects on the U.S. Consumer Price Index (CPI), inflation, the rate of income growth, and the level of income, using impact multipliers derived from the results of the Energy Modeling Forum's analysis of the macroeconomic effects of oil prices on the U.S. economy.[4] Using 14 macroeconomic models, they found a two year multiplier between oil price inflation and overall inflation of 0.046 and a two year multiplier between oil price inflation and income growth of –0.055. We assumed the one year multipliers are half as large as the two year multipliers. Using these multipliers, we translated the resultant price changes from our policies into changes in inflation, changes in income growth, and the percentage change of total income for the first year, the second year, and for the entire simulation period. Unemployment is derived from Okun's law which relates one percent unemployment to a 2.5 percent gap in Gross National Product (GNP). The Appendix gives the computational algorithms.‡

Table 11.2 shows these effects. To highlight the differences among the policies, we measured all macroeconomic variables as changes from the base case. We found that the gasoline tax has the largest negative effect on the aggregate price level in the early part of the sample, but the tariff has the largest effect in the long run. The net effect is that the average price level for the tariff is about 0.5 percent higher over the 30 year period. In contrast, the subsidy lowers the aggregate price level by 0.47 percent and 0.87 percent in the first and second year but has a smaller average effect over the whole simulation period.

All policies have the largest effect on inflation in the first two years. For the tariff and gasoline tax, the price level and inflation are both higher for the first two years. The price level is also higher for all years; however, the rate of change of this price level (or inflation) becomes and remains slightly lower after three or four years, with the converse true for the subsidy.

---

†The gasoline tax must be subtracted from the effective consumer price for oil to calculate the balance of payments savings of the gasoline tax.

‡These numbers, which are the averages from the Energy Modeling Forum's 14 models, illustrate the possible results. Readers could easily substitute their own elasticities.

Table 11.2. Changes in macroeconomic variables from policy
changes

	Impact multipliers		
	Gasoline tax	Oil Tariff	Oil Subsidy
Time period	$0.15/g	$7.70/b	$4.92/b
% change in CPI (A.3)†			
1st year	0.45	0.29	-0.47
2nd year	0.86	0.57	-0.87
30 year average	0.45	0.48	-0.34
% Change in rate of inflation (A.4) and (A.5)†			
1st year	0.45	0.29	-0.47
2nd year	0.41	0.29	-0.41
30 year average	0.01	0.01	-0.00
Net present value of income change (A.8)†			
Billions of 1987 U.S. dollars discounted @ r = .08			
1st year	($24)	($15)	$25
2nd year	($44)	($29)	$44
30 year sum	($426)	($404)	$346
% Change in rate of income growth (A.9)†			
1st year	-0.54	-0.34	0.56
2nd year	-0.50	-0.35	0.48
30 year average	-0.01	-0.02	0.01
% Change in rate of unemployment (A.10)†			
1st year	0.21	0.14	-0.22
2nd year	0.41	0.27	-0.42
30 year average	0.22	0.23	-0.16
Net present value change in government revenues (A.12)†			
Billions of 1987 U.S. dollars discounted @ r = .08			
1st year	$17.7	$10.5	($25.2)
2nd year	$15.9	$11.0	($20.7)
30 year sum	$186.0	$186.0	186.0
Net present value of change in Oil Import Bill (A.14)†			
Billions of 1987 U.S. dollars discounted @ r = .08			
1st year	($10.1)	($34.4)	($13.6)
2nd year	($9.3)	($31.2)	($10.8)
30 year sum	($116.1)	($365.7)	($84.5)

†Equation number in the Appendix that gives the computational
formula.

These patterns are also seen for income, income growth, and unemployment. In the short run, the gasoline tax has the largest negative effect, while the subsidy has favorable effect. However, except for discounted present value of the income change, the tariff tends to have the largest negative effects on these variables over the whole 30 year period. Changes in income growth are largest in the early years. However, as with prices and inflation, income is lower with the gasoline tax and the tariff over the whole sample, but this lower income grows slightly faster after two years.

The revenue effects of the policies tend to be the reverse of the effects on the macroeconomic variables. The gasoline tax raises the most federal revenue in the short run, but the tariff saves the most foreign exchange. The subsidy, on the other hand, is costly and saves the least foreign exchange over the 30 year period.

COMPARISON OF SHORT-RUN MACROECONOMIC EFFECTS ACROSS MODELS

The above modeling relies on impact multipliers because we are interested in calculating very long-term effects. In the short run, a variety of other models evaluate gasoline taxes and tariffs, which we consider below.

The short-run effects can also be computed using the simulated prices of the dynamic model as inputs into short-run macroeconomic models. This approach will hereafter be referred to as dynamic/macro modeling. The base case prices provide benchmark levels of GNP, the federal deficit, the CPI, and the unemployment rate. Feeding in the oil prices that correspond to the different policies, along with their corresponding revenues or subsidies, to the short-run macroeconomic model showed us how the above variables are changed. We present three examples of this approach.

The first two examples are prorated from Dahl and Yücel[5]† and use the Meyer model[6] and the Data Resources Inc. (DRI) model. They are labeled Meyer1 and DRI1 and are computed using the same price path as the computations for impact multipliers labeled Impact1. For the third example, we input the current simulated price paths and corresponding revenues or subsidies into the DRI model for all three policies. These results are labels DRI2, with the corresponding impact multiplier results labeled Impact2.

The runs for the macro models had the following sample periods: the Meyer1 forecasts are for 1989:III-1991:II, the DRI1 runs forecasts are for 1990:I-1991:IV, and the DRI2 forecasts are for 1991:III-1993:II. Table 11.3 gives the statistics

---

†The policies were a $0.25 per gallon gasoline tax, a $5 per barrel producer subsidy, and 25 percent oil import tariff. Since the tariff used in Dahl and Yücel (Ref. 5) was ad valorem, it is considered less comparable than the other two policies.

using the short-run macro models along with the comparable impact multiplier approach. Again, all statistics are given as changes from the base case.

The current dynamic runs for Impact2 and DRI2 used improved cost curves and a higher discount rate. They yielded a lower oil price level but somewhat larger changes in oil prices than those from Dahl and Yücel.[5] Hence, they are not strictly comparable with those earlier runs Impact1, Meyer1, and DRI1. It is therefore more interesting to make comparisons across policies and modeling types within the two modeling exercises.

In general, all models rank the policies the same. The gasoline tax has the largest negative impact on the macroeconomic variables; the tariff has a less negative impact; the subsidy has a positive impact. Some time patterns in adjustment are similar as well. The effects on unemployment and total discounted income tend to be larger in the second year than in the first year. The effects on both income growth and inflation decrease after the second year.

In other cases the models' time paths disagree. For income growth, the dynamic/macro models suggest larger first year effects for all policies, while the impact multiplier models more often suggest larger second year effects. Comparing DRI1 and DRI2, DRI1 found larger inflationary effects relative to other modeling approaches on a strong economy than DRI2 found on a weak economy. This same effect can be seen for unemployment and the change in income suggesting that policy effects are dependent on the state of the economy.

Model predictions, except for inflation, agreed more closely for the first year than for the second year. The model forecasts diverged the least for unemployment and inflation, the most for income growth and income change.

The tariff results are particularly interesting. Both DRI1 and DRI2 suggested that the tariff has very little negative impact on the domestic economy. With this small effect and foreigners absorbing a large share of the tariff, the tariff has the best short-run effect on the deficit even though the gasoline tax brings in more revenue.

The simulations reported in Table 11.2 give us an estimate of the revenues generated by the policies shown in Table 11.1. However, the macroeconomic effects offset some of the revenue changes, as can be seen by comparing the revenues with the changes in the deficit reported for comparable runs in DRI2. For example, government revenues from the gasoline tax in the first year are computed to be $17.7 billion, while DRI2 suggests that the deficit falls by only $4.7 billion. Almost three quarters of the revenue gain is canceled out by the negative effects of the policy on the economy. In contrast, the tariff, with its small negative effect on the economy, brings in $10.5 billion in the first year and reduces the deficit by roughly $7.4 billion. The subsidy costs $25.2 billion, or more than what each of the other two policies brings in. However, four-fifths of the cost of the subsidy is canceled out by its positive effects on the economy and the first year deficit only increases by $5.1 billion.

In both modeling exercises, impact multipliers ranked policies comparably to the dynamic/macro models. However, except for inflation, impact multipliers tend to have the largest effects. Because these impact multipliers were derived during analysis of energy shocks, they may be too large for the more modest price changes analyzed here. However, impact multipliers appear to be useful in making qualitative statements for short-run effects and their timing, and they allow calculation of long-run effects. The short-run results suggest that impact multipliers provide an upper bound on the total effects of policies on macroeconomic variables.

Table 11.3. Comparison of macroeconomic effects across models

	Gasoline Tax $0.15/gal	Tariff $7.70/b	Subsidy $4.92/b
Change in inflation (%)			
1 year Impact1†	0.34	0.09	-0.24
1 year Meyer1†	0.13	0.05	-0.05
1 year DRI1†	0.39	0.10	-0.25
1 year Impact2	0.45	0.29	-0.47
1 year DRI2	0.25	0.24	-0.22
2 year Impact1†	0.27	0.11	-0.12
2 year Meyer1†	0.16	0.06	-0.07
2 year DRI1†	0.52	0.16	-0.33
2 year Impact2	0.41	0.29	-0.41
2 year DRI2	0.17	0.14	-0.16
Change in average income growth rate (%)			
1 year Impact1†	-0.41	-0.10	0.28
1 year Meyer1†	-0.17	-0.01	0.12
1 year DRI1†	-0.09	-0.00	0.06
1 year Impact2	-0.54	-0.34	0.56
1 year DRI2	-0.16	-0.03	0.16
2 year Impact1†	-0.49	-0.19	0.15
2 year Meyer1†	-0.06	-0.00	0.05
1 year DRI1†	0.04	-0.00	-0.03
2 year Impact2	-0.50	-0.35	0.48
2 year DRI2	0.07	-0.01	-0.07
Change in average unemployment rate (%)			
1 year Impact1†	0.16	0.04	-0.11
1 year Meyer1†	0.04	0.00	-0.07
1 year DRI1†	0.07	0.00	-0.04
1 year Impact2	0.21	0.14	-0.22
1 year DRI2	0.03	0.00	-0.03
2 year Impact1†	0.29	0.10	-0.17
2 year Meyer1†	0.14	0.02	-0.07
2 year DRI1†	0.16	0.01	-0.09
2 year Impact2	0.41	0.27	-0.42
2 year DRI2	0.06	0.02	-0.06

(continues)

Table 11.3.   (continued)

	Gasoline Tax $0.15/gal	Tariff $7.70/b	Subsidy $4.92/b
Change in income (%)			
1 year Impact1†	-0.20	-0.05	0.14
1 year Meyer1†	-0.12	-0.01	0.07
1 year DRI1†	-0.22	-0.00	0.14
1 year Impact2	-0.54	-0.34	0.56
1 year DRI2	-0.09	-0.00	0.09
2 year Impact1†	-0.41	-0.13	0.28
2 year Meyer1†	-0.23	-0.02	0.12
2 year DRI1†	-0.39	-0.01	0.23
2 year Impact2	-1.03	-0.69	1.04
2 year DRI2	-0.13	-0.03	0.14
Total change in the deficit (+ means deficit reduction) (billions of 1987 U.S. dollars)			
1 year Meyer1†	$7.3	$11.9	($3.9)
1 year DRI1†	$8.7	$6.9	($4.2)
1 year DRI2	$4.7	$7.4	($5.1)
2 year Meyer1†	$4.9	$14.0	($2.3)
2 year DRI1†	$4.7	$7.6	($0.5)
2 year DRI2	$2.0	$5.5	($2.3)

†Computed from simulations for Dahl and Yücel.[5]

The above modeling captured the effect of policy changes across time. These changes include the extent to which the policy can be transferred to foreigners, along with the short-run macroeconomic effects of the policy. A few other studies have researched the short-run effects of protectionist policies in slightly different frameworks.† French[10] reports the macroeconomic effects of a study by the Congressional Budget Office (CBO) and three other studies using the DRI, Wharton Econometrics Forecasting (WEFA) model and the Federal Reserve Board (FRB) model of a $0.15 increase in the gasoline tax.‡ and an equal revenue tariff, while Uri and Boyd[11] analyzed a $0.15 increase in the gasoline tax using a 13 sector computable general equilibrium model. Table 11.4 lists the reported results along with comparable results from Table 11.3.

Of the four approaches, the short-run macroeconomic models used alone tended to predict the most inflation from the policies, with the tariff tending to be more inflationary than the gasoline tax. This result reverses the ranking

---

†Time and space or noncomparability did not allow inclusion of three other studies that deal with protectionist policies. (See Refs. 7, 8, and 9.)

‡Where the original study was not done on a $0.15 per gallon gasoline tax, French prorated the original study results.

of the tariff relative to the tax of the dynamic/macro models, which predicted the tariff to be less inflationary than the tax. The smaller inflation in the dynamic/macro models results from intertemporal substitution, supplier absorption of part of the tax or tariff, and the depressing effect of the policies on the macroeconomy; the tariff is less inflationary because foreigners absorb more of the tariff than the tax.

For income growth, all approaches that considered both policies agreed and ranked the gasoline tax as more negative toward growth than the tariff. The general equilibrium model with the most substitution across sectors showed small income losses for a gasoline tax, with the losses decreasing as the elasticity of demand for oil increases. However, the dynamic/macro models in some cases showed rather small losses for the gasoline tax as well.

These results on income confirm the earlier conclusion using impact multiplier models. Those models tend to rank the policies the same as other approaches, but again they tend to be in the high range for all short-run negative macroeconomic effects. Only one macroeconomic model, the FRB model, showed consistently large negative effects for both the tax and the tariff. DRI, whether used alone or in conjunction with the dynamic model, consistently showed unbelievably small income losses for a tariff, but the WEFA and FRB models, with larger losses that span the computations using impact multipliers, do not corroborate this result.

All models that address the issue conclude that the tax and tariff would raise a significant amount of revenue, and hence there would be a significant amount of deficit reduction. The general equilibrium simulations suggest that less revenue would be raised from a gasoline tax relative to the other approaches. Both dynamic/macro and macro models alone suggest significant deficit reduction, but there is significant variation in forecasts within both approaches.

CONCLUSIONS, POLICY IMPLICATIONS, AND FURTHER WORK

Three policies to curtail oil imports and protect domestic oil producers—a $0.15 per gallon increase in the gasoline tax, a $7.70 per barrel oil tariff, and a $4.92 per barrel producer subsidy—have been analyzed. These policies have varying effects across time. To quantify and compare the long-run and short-run effects of these policies, we dynamically simulated oil prices, U.S. oil production, and oil imports over a 30 year period for a base case and each of the three policies.

Our simulations suggest that all three policies decrease imports in the short run, and all but the gasoline tax stimulate domestic production. In the long

Table 11.4. Short-run macroeconomic effects from other studies

	Gasoline Tax $0.15	Equal Revenue Tariff
Change in the rate of inflation (%)		
1 year Impact1†	0.34	0.09
1 year Meyer1†	0.13	0.05
1 year DRI1†	0.39	0.10
1 year Impact2	0.45	0.29
1 year DRI2	0.25	0.24
1 year WEFA‡	-0.50	-0.60
1 year DRI‡	-0.60	-0.60
1 year FRBa‡	-0.40	-0.90
1 year FRBb‡	-0.50	
Change aggregate income (%)		
1 year Impact1†	-0.20	-0.05
1 year Meyer1†	-0.12	-0.01
1 year DRI1†	-0.22	-0.00
1 year Impact2	-0.54	-0.34
1 year DRI2	-0.09	-0.03
1 year WEFA‡	-0.23	-0.22
1 year DRI‡	-0.32	-0.07
1 year FRBa‡	-0.51	-0.50
1 year FRBb‡	-0.55	
1 year Uri and Boyd ϵ_p=-1	-0.16	
1 year Uri and Boyd ϵ_p=-.5	-0.17	
1 year Uri and Boyd ϵ_p=-1.5	-0.15	
U.S. DOE‡	-0.31	
Government revenue from policies (US$ billions)		
1 year Impact1†	$12.6	
1 year Impact2	$17.7	$10.5
1 year French§	$15.0	
1 year Uri and Boyd ϵ_p=-1	$8.8	
1 year Uri and Boyd ϵ_p=-.5	$10.8	
1 year Uri and Boyd ϵ_p=-1.5	$6.9	
Reductions in the deficit (US$ billions)		
1 year Meyer1†	$7.3	$11.9
1 year DRI1†	$8.7	$6.9
1 year DRI2	$4.7	$9.4
1 year CBO‡	$11.7	
1 year WEFA‡	$8.7	
1 year DRI‡	$4.8 to $7.3	
1 year FRBa‡	$6.3 to $11.2	

†Prorated from Dahl and Yücel,[5] tariff is not equal revenue.
‡Quoted from French,[10] original sources are French,[12] Data Resources Inc.,[13] Helkie,[14] Congressional Budget Office,[15] and Yanchar.[16]
§Average changes in government revenue from the four studies quoted.

run, however, the subsidy increases oil imports by depleting domestic production and increasing consumption. The gasoline tax raises effective consumer oil prices the most in the short run, but the tariff raises prices the most in the long run. The subsidy consistently lowers oil prices over the simulation period.

Different policies not only affect oil markets but they also affect the macroeconomy. These effects also vary across policy and time. The major goal of this article has been to quantify and compare these macroeconomic effects across time, policies, and models. The dynamic simulations are used directly to forecast balance of payments costs and government revenues from the policies. The gasoline tax raises the most federal revenue in the short run; the tariff saves the most foreign exchange over the entire 30 years. The subsidy is costly and saves the least foreign exchange.

Simulated prices are used indirectly with impact multipliers to determine the effect of the policies on inflation, the price level, income growth, and unemployment across policies and time. We find the gasoline tax to have the most negative effect on all these macroeconomic variables in the short run. On average, the tariff over the long run is more detrimental to inflation, income growth, and unemployment. However, the gasoline tax still has the most negative effect on the net present value of total income over the whole period.

The impact multiplier approach is quite easy to implement and can be used over the long time period being considered. However, to determine the robustness of impact multiplier conclusions other more complicated approaches have been considered in the short run.

Comparing the impact multiplier effects with results generated using the dynamic/macro simulations, we found that the pattern of effects was similar. The gasoline tax has larger negative impacts on our macroeconomic variables than the tariff has, while the subsidy has positive effects. The timings of the policy effects, except for inflation and income growth, also tend to mimic each other across the various models.

Using the dynamic/macro models, we found that the gasoline tax brings in the most revenue, but the tariff reduces the deficit the most.

We extended our comparison to include a computable general equilibrium model and additional short-run macroeconomic models. These additional models look at a gasoline tax and in some cases included an equal revenue tariff. They focus on a more limited set of macroeconomic indicators: inflation, income growth, and either government revenues from the policy or the deficit. In this comparison, we found somewhat more anomalous results.

All the earlier approaches ranked the policies the same. In the more diverse group, all approaches ranked the tariff superior to the gasoline tax with respect to income growth, but the strictly macroeconomic models did not rank the tariff superior with respect to inflation.

In categorizing various short-run approaches, we found the impact multiplier models to have the largest effects, and the computable general equilibrium model to have smallest effects. The dynamic/macro models have smaller effects than the macro models alone. The policy effects in the macro models seem to be dependent on the stage of the business cycle, with smaller effects during recession.

There are several relevant policy conclusions from the above comparisons. Although there is a lot of quantitative disagreement over the effects of the policies, there is broad qualitative agreement across models to suggest that the subsidy would benefit the macroeconomy but at a high cost to taxpayers. The tariff would be better for the macroeconomy, would most likely bring in less revenue, but might have the best effect on the deficit. However, there was some contradictory evidence on the deficit. The larger reduction in the deficit from the tariff results from the small negative effect of the tariff on the economy. Because the DRI model from which this estimate is derived consistently forecasted lower negative effects than the other macroeconomic models, this result needs further examination.

The long-run policy conclusions are generally similar to the short-run conclusions except that the subsidy raises imports by the end of the period, and the tariff has more negative effects than does the gasoline tax later in the simulation period. These long-run results are heavily dependent on the dynamic simulation, which in turn is based on the premise that OPEC is a dominant firm that dynamically optimizes. We found that the results were robust across the two cost scenarios that had been considered for the dynamic model. However, future work should be done allowing for other market structures such as static monopoly as well as competitive behavior. More sensitivity testing across parameters should be done to further check the robustness of the results.

APPENDIX

Please refer to Table 11.1.

The consumer price index for each year t relative to the base case (CPI_t) under each policy (p) (p = the gasoline tax, the oil tariff, and the domestic producer subsidy) is computed as:

$$CPI_0^p = 1 + \frac{.046}{2} \frac{P_0^p - P_0^b}{P_0^b} \quad \text{and} \qquad (A.1)$$

$$CPI_t^p = 1 + \frac{.046}{2}\frac{P_{t-1}^p - P_{t-1}^b}{P_{t-1}^b} + \frac{.046}{2}\frac{P_t^p - P_t^b}{P_t^b} \quad \text{for} \quad t = 1\text{-}30. \qquad \text{(A.2)}$$

Where P_t^p is the simulated oil price for the policies and P_t^b is the simulated oil price for the base case.

The percentage change in consumer price index relative to the base case is computed as:

$$(CPI_t^p - 1)100 \quad \text{for } t = 0\text{-}30. \qquad \text{(A.3)}$$

The change in the rate of inflation relative to the base case is computed as:

$$\Delta i_0^p = (CPI_0^p - 1)100 \quad and \qquad \text{(A.4)}$$

$$\Delta i_t^p = \frac{CPI_t^p - CPI_{t-1}^p}{CPI_{t-1}^p}100 \quad \text{for } t = 1\text{-}30. \qquad \text{(A.5)}$$

Income in the base case is computed as:

$$Y_t^b = Y_0^b e^{.025t} \quad \text{for } t = 0\text{-}30. \qquad \text{(A.6)}$$

Income for each policy is computed as:

$$Y_0^p = (1 - \frac{.055}{2}\frac{P_0^p - P_0^b}{P_0^b})Y_0^b \quad and$$
$$Y_t^p = (1 - \frac{.055}{2}\frac{P_{t-1}^p - P_{t-1}^b}{P_{t-1}^b} - \frac{.055}{2}\frac{P_t^p - P_t^b}{P_t^b})Y_t^b \quad \text{for } t = 1\text{-}30. \qquad \text{(A.7)}$$

The consumer price index for each year t relative to the base case (CPI$_t$) under each policy (p) (p = the gasoline tax, the oil tariff, and the domestic producer subsidy) is computed as:

$$CPI_0^p = 1 + \frac{.046}{2}\frac{P_0^p - P_0^b}{P_0^b} \quad and \qquad \text{(A.1)}$$

$$CPI_t^p = 1 + \frac{.046}{2}\frac{P_{t-1}^p - P_{t-1}^b}{P_{t-1}^b} + \frac{.046}{2}\frac{P_t^p - P_t^b}{P_t^b} \quad \text{for} \quad t = 1\text{-}30. \qquad \text{(A.2)}$$

Where P_t^p is the simulated oil price for the policies and P_t^b is the simulated oil price for the base case.

The percentage change in consumer price index relative to the base case is computed as:

$$(CPI_t^P - 1)100 \quad \text{for } t = 0\text{-}30. \tag{A.3}$$

The change in the rate of inflation relative to the base case is computed as:

$$\Delta i_0^P = (CPI_0^P - 1)100 \quad and \tag{A.4}$$

$$\Delta i_t^P = \frac{CPI_t^P - CPI_{t-1}^P}{CPI_{t-1}^P} 100 \quad \text{for } t = 1\text{-}30. \tag{A.5}$$

Income in the base case is computed as:

$$Y_t^b = Y_0^b e^{.025t} \quad \text{for } t = 0\text{-}30. \tag{A.6}$$

Income for each policy is computed as:

$$Y_0^P = (1 - \frac{.055}{2} \frac{P_0^P - P_0^b}{P_0^b}) Y_0^b \quad and$$

$$Y_t^P = (1 - \frac{.055}{2} \frac{P_{t-1}^P - P_{t-1}^b}{P^{t-1^b}} - \frac{.055}{2} \frac{P_t^P - P_t^b}{P_t^b}) Y_t^b \quad \text{for } t = 1\text{-}30. \tag{A.7}$$

The annual change in oil import bill for each policy is computed as:

$$\Delta BP_t^{tax} = (P_t^{tax} - .15 \times 42) (Q_{opec_t}^{tax} + 841.325)$$
$$- P_t^b (Q_{opec_t}^b + 841.325)$$

$$\Delta BP_t^{tariff} = (P_t^{tariff} - 7.7) (Q_{opec_t}^{tariff} + 841.325)$$
$$- P_t^b (Q_{opec_t}^b + 841.325) \tag{A.13}$$

$$\Delta BP_t^{subsidy} = P_t^{subsidy} (Q_{opec_t}^{subsidy} + 841.325)$$
$$- P_t^b (Q_{opec_t}^b + 841.325) \quad \text{for } t = 0\text{-}30.$$

The net present value of the change in oil import costs is computed as:

$$NPV\Delta BP_t^P = \Delta BP_t^P e^{-.08t} \quad \text{for } t = 0\text{-}30.. \tag{A.14}$$

REFERENCES

1. Mine Yücel and Carol Dahl, "A Dynamic Comparison of an Oil Tariff, a Producer Subsidy, and a Gasoline Tax," (manuscript), Federal Reserve Bank of Dallas, Dallas, TX and Department of Mineral Economics, Colorado School of Mines, Golden, CO (1991).
2. Carol A. Dahl, "Cost Function for OPEC Oil Delivered to U.S. Ports," (manuscript), Department of Mineral Economics, Colorado School of Mines, Golden, CO (Sept. 1991).
3. Carol A. Dahl, "U.S. Cost Function for Oil," (manuscript), Department of Mineral Economics, Colorado School of Mines, Golden, CO (Sept. 1991).
4. B. G. Hickman, H. G. Huntington and J. L. Sweeney, *Macroeconomic Impacts of Energy Shocks,* p. 165, North Holland, New York (1987).
5. Carol A. Dahl and Mine Yücel, "Macroeconomic Impacts of an Oil Import Fee, a Gasoline Tax, and a Domestic Producer Subsidy," in *Energy Developments in the 1990s: Challenges Facing Global/Pacific Markets,* pp. 255–273, Fereidun Fesharaki and James P. Dorian, eds., Proceedings of the Fourteenth Annual International Conference, International Association for Energy Economics, Honolulu, HI (July 8–10, 1991).
6. Lorenz H. Meyer & Associates Ltd., "The Washington University Model," Washington University, St. Louis, MO (1988).
7. U.S. Department of Energy, Energy Security, U.S. Government Printing Office, Washington, DC (March 1987).
8. U.S. Energy Information Administration, *Cost and Benefit Analysis of an Oil Import Fee,* Office of Energy Markets and End Use, SR/EAFD/87-03, (1987).
9. U.S. Energy Information Administration, *Studies of Energy Taxes,* Office of Energy Markets and End Use, SR/EME-91-02 (1991).
10. Mark W. French, "Efficiency and Equity of a Gasoline Tax Increase," (manuscript), Board of Governors of the Federal Reserve System, Division of Research and Statistics, Washington, DC (1989).
11. Noel Uri and Roy Boyd, "The Potential Benefits and Costs of an Increase in U.S. Gasoline Tax," *Energy Policy* 17, 4, pp. 356–368 (August 1989).
12. Mark W. French, "Economic Analysis of Gasoline Tax Increases," Wharton Econometric Study, submitted for the record in Committee on Public Works and Transportation in conjunction with author's testimony (May 22, 1987).
13. Data Resources Incorporated (DRI), "The Macroeconomic and Regional Effects of an Increase in the Federal Tax on Gasoline," Study commissioned by the American Petroleum Institute (Sept. 8, 1988).
14. William L. Helkie, "Impact of $5 Oil Import Surcharge," FRB International Finance memorandum to Edwin Truman (Feb. 19, 1988).
15. U.S. Congressional Budget Office, *Reducing the Deficit: Spending and Revenue Options,* chapter 8, sections 23–25 (March 1988).
16. Joyce Yanchar, "Closing the Deficit: An Income Tax Surcharge Versus Energy Taxes," *Data Resources U.S. Review,* pp. 17–23 (Nov. 1987).

12 Urban Interfuel Substitution, Energy Use, and Equity in Developing Countries: Some Preliminary Results

Douglas F. Barnes and Liu Qian

INTRODUCTION

The dramatic growth of urban populations in developing countries has caused a rise in the demand for energy, food, water, and other resources. The growing number of people living in urban areas of developing nations is quite dramatic. Over 1.25 billion urban dwellers live in 360 cities that contain more than 500,000 people. Overall population growth rates for rural areas are between 1.5 and four percent per year. By contrast, the urban growth rates are even higher at between three and seven percent per year, because of high birth rates and extensive migration from rural areas to cities.

Migrants from rural areas bring with them their traditional patterns of energy use, which are mainly based on the use of wood fuels. In urban areas demand for wood products is highly concentrated, creating difficulties such as the environmental problems associated with harvesting trees around urban centers. However, the urban demand for fuels also creates opportunities for possible economies of scale in the distribution of modern fuels.

Rapid increases in demand for energy resources has been the basis for many energy-related problems in urban areas. In some countries, the poorer households that use wood fuels are affected by rapidly rising wood prices without other market choices being made available to them. In many cases consumers

This paper was prepared as part of a research project funded by the UNDP/World Bank/Bilateral Assistance Energy Sector Management Assistance Program (ESMAP) and the Research Administration Budget of the World Bank. The report does not represent the views of the Bank Group, nor does the Bank Group accept responsibility for its accuracy or completeness.

do not have a choice between wood-based and modern fuels because they are not available in the marketplace due to government policies or the relative remoteness of the urban location. The supply of modern fuels such as kerosene, LPG, and electricity to urban areas for cooking has been affected by sometimes inconsistent government policies. Even where substitute fuels are available, there can be a substantial difference between the economic cost of importing or producing the fuel and the cost that consumers actually pay. Also, the environmental externalities involved in harvesting trees for urban markets are not reflected in urban market prices of wood.[1,2] The growth in demand for wood resources around cities has caused deforested rings around some urban centers extending 100 kilometers and more (see, for example, Bowonder et al. and Allen and Barnes).[3,4]

This study systematically analyzes the dynamics of interfuel substitution in urban areas of developing countries, and explores the feasibility of substituting kerosene, LPG, or electricity for wood-based fuels. To accomplish this objective, the study examined the causes of interfuel substitution in urban areas. The research included an analysis of consumer behavior and how it is affected by urban fuel policies, urban energy availability, and socioeconomic characteristics of households within urban areas. Finally, the analysis examined the potential effect that encouraging interfuel substitution may have on income distribution and poverty.

Most studies of interfuel substitution have been of individual urban areas, and thus the transition for specific urban areas. The rewards of comparing energy use patterns *between* cities include a major step forward in understanding the energy transition in developing countries. By comparing energy use patterns between small and large cities, low and high income classes, between regions with extensive forests and regions with few trees, and between areas with government policies to subsidize modern fuels with those that tax them, a qualitative jump can be made in understanding the processes that drive interfuel substitution in developing countries. Making policy recommendations for individual countries is not the goal of this paper, but by placing an individual country in a larger transition framework, the quality of individual country studies can be improved.

The results of this study shed some light on the effectiveness of existing energy policies in developing countries, the conditions under which transitions to modern fuels can be expected to occur, and the socioeconomic and environmental impacts and consequences of interfuel substitution. As expected, the preliminary findings indicate that government policy along with income has a significant impact on residential fuels use in developing countries. A somewhat surprising finding is that many of the poorest households in urban areas of developing countries use electricity, but rarely use LPG. In addition, wood fuel use is fairly extensive in all but the largest cities. It should be cautioned that the results presented in this paper are preliminary and more analysis is needed before firm conclusions can be drawn.

MAIN POLICY ISSUES OF THE ENERGY TRANSITION

Although well known problems exist for making cross national comparisons, such comparisons overcome some of the difficulties encountered in the analysis of individual countries or cities. This paper takes the first step in analyzing the empirical patterns involved in the energy transition. The larger objectives of the current study are to examine the factors that are associated with the transition from traditional fuels to modern fuels. A different set of policies may be appropriate at different stages, whether it is to continue to use wood, to improve market access to modern fuels, or to promote a switch to modern fuels. The extent to which wood fuel demand can be reduced through interfuel substitution strategies needs are assessed. Some of the widely divergent patterns of interfuel substitution in urban areas that occur despite similarities in conditions need to be explained. Finally, the equity implications of existing fuel policies and for existing patterns of fuels use in urban areas are examined.

Much useful knowledge has been gained from the many good individual country studies which have the advantage of examining in depth the local conditions that are associated with different kinds of fuel use, focusing on income as one of the key factors affecting substitution.

Based on the findings of urban energy studies, the factors known to influence energy transitions in various ways include income, wood availability, access to modern fuels, fuel prices, and government policy. People with low incomes generally use fuelwood or charcoal as their main cooking fuel (see, for example, Munslow et al., and Leach and Mearns).[5,6] By contrast, people with higher incomes tend to use modern fuels. Higher wood availability surrounding urban areas generally leads to more use of wood as a fuel, but does not affect the fuel used in the upper income groups. Generally people in large, more urbanized areas use more kerosene, LPG, and electricity. Evidence from urban energy studies suggests that government policies tend to encourage the use of certain fuels as people switch to the fuel and continue using it longer than is expected based on their income level.[7] Not all of these issues are addressed in this paper, but they form the underlying basis for the continuing research.

The following simplified description of the energy transition has been developed from the most recent literature on interfuel substitution. This description provides a framework concerning the ways in which people are currently meeting their needs for energy in urban areas, whether there are socioeconomic problems that typically occur at different stages in the transition, and whether it is feasible or desirable in particular contexts to speed up the transition to commercial fuels. The general description is based on both *static and dynamic* inferences. It is static in the sense that a given city is represented at a fixed point in time and at a fixed stage in the transition from wood to other fuels. As a consequence, differences in energy use between cities may be due to unique characteristics of one city. But it is dynamic in the sense that cities and towns today are at different points in the energy transition.

The *first stage* is characterized by small cities with relatively low income. In such cities there is extensive use of wood as a fuel, abundant wood resources around the city, low wood energy prices, and limited availability of modern fuels. In this stage agricultural expansion and shorter farm fallows surrounding growing urban regions cause trees and bushes to be harvested from common land. At the same time, migrants are streaming into urban areas, bringing with them their traditional and mainly wood-based rural cooking habits. Although demand for wood in the urban areas is increasing quite rapidly, this demand can be met fairly easily by the wood that is being cleared for agriculture and for other uses around the urban areas. As a consequence, the price of wood compared to alternative fuels remains quite low, and there is little incentive for people to switch to alternative fuels. Even at this stage higher income households will switch to fuels such as kerosene, charcoal or LPG, since these fuels generally are more convenient and produce less smoke than wood. But the general pattern is that a high percentage of the urban population will use wood as their primary cooking fuel.

The *second stage* is characterized by medium sized cities with intermediate levels of wood use, moderate levels of wood resources around the city, wood energy prices that are at or somewhat below prices of modern alternative fuels, undeveloped fuel markets, and intermediate levels of household income. In this phase, population growth causes deforestation and degradation of land around the cities. Consumer demand for wood products exceeds the rate at which trees are regrown on common land, so the wood is rapidly cleared from around the urban areas. During this stage, trees continue to be harvested from common or fallow land, partly because the future costs of replanting and environmental consequences are not included in the relatively low market price of the fuel. The combination of decreasing supplies of wood fuels and increasing demand means that the price of wood fuels increases suddenly or even exceeds the price of competitive fuels. In this period there may be a significant substitution of charcoal and kerosene for wood. Charcoal and kerosene will replace wood as the main cooking fuel because of convenience and the growing scarcity of wood. Since charcoal is lighter than wood, transportation costs are lower than for wood. For kerosene, the fuel can be made readily available to middle class urban consumers without too much investment on their part in cooking equipment, and without too much investment by a government in a distribution system. At this stage, the ability of consumers to pay for LPG and electricity for cooking would still be quite limited, although a growing number of higher income households will begin to use these fuels.

The *third stage* is characterized by large cities with low levels of wood use, various levels of wood resources around the city, wood energy prices that are competitive with the price of alternative modern fuels, developed modern fuel markets, and high levels of household income. This stage is characterized by the switch from charcoal and kerosene to LPG or electricity. During this stage, incomes will have risen substantially in urban areas, markets for fuels will be better developed, and consumers will prefer to do most of their cooking with LPG or electricity, while charcoal will remain a fuel used for specific traditional meals. Developed countries and some high income developing countries are at this stage today. It is how, when and why people arrive at this final stage that is of particular interest.

From the extensive literature on individual cities or countries, it is obvious that the process is not so straightforward. During the transition, there is a wide distribution of energy substitution and use. In addition, distortions occur, including periods when wood might be cheap in urban areas because the prices are based only on cutting and transport costs. In order to better explain the forces that cause the wide variation in energy use, we examine the associations between government policy, city size, and income class with respect to energy prices, energy choice, and fuel use by urban households.

METHODS OF ANALYSIS

From a policy perspective it is just as important to understand how cities and towns today compare to one another as it is to understand how energy use has changed over time. The analysis here is based on careful comparisons of cities today with allowance for factors hypothesized to be important for the future fuel use in these cities. As cities evolve over time it is expected that the changes in such characteristics as income, city size, and other factors will affect changes in fuel use. The ability to analyze such changes is possible only when there is significant variation between energy use and socioeconomic characteristics of urban areas. Here we present some of the preliminary results of such an analysis.

The effectiveness of government policies to change types of fuel use can be evaluated through a comparative analysis of urban areas. As indicated, most existing studies have difficulty in dealing with the effects of country-specific policy issues, particularly the effects of subsidies or taxes on interfuel substitution. Problems arise when trying to examine the reasons for interfuel substitution in urban areas. For instance, the comparative analysis of one urban area to another within one country can be idiosyncratic because of the lack of variation in a country's policies towards fuels, a narrow range of price variation within urban areas, and relatively fixed resource endowments surrounding the city. In a single urban area, fuel policies generally do not vary for the period of the study. This can be problematic for the estimation of price elasticities because of the relatively small variation in prices for a given city at one point in time. A comparative urban research design in combination with an analysis of urban household energy use in urban areas in individual countries is able to address most of the important issues involving interfuel substitution.

Our analysis is based on actual surveys of urban household energy consumption in 11 countries of Asia, Latin America, and Africa. Because a typical urban survey includes both primary and secondary cities, there are data for about four to five cities per country (see Table 12.1) and the cities have been divided into about five income classes each. As a consequence, for the countries included in the project, a data base of about 250 representative urban income classes was analyzed. The sample contains large and small cities with significant variation across resources, along with cities that tax and cities that subsidize particular fuels. As a consequence, the analysis is able to determine the impact of these important variables on the process of interfuel substitution. For instance, countries that subsidize kerosene can be compared to countries that do not or to countries that tax kerosene.

Overall patterns of fuel use for the analyzed countries are presented first. The effect of government policy is next described by examining national aggregates of fuel profiles of consumption and prices. We then set out the effect of urban size on energy consumption. Finally, we examine the differences in energy use between different income classes.

OVERALL PATTERNS OF URBAN ENERGY DEMAND

The most striking finding when examining the average energy consumption for the 11 countries is the relatively even distribution of energy use between the various fuels. While the overall pattern of energy demand does not include the regional variation in fuel use, it gives a picture of the kinds of fuels being consumed in developing countries. To make the comparisons between cities more representative, the figures presented in this paper are weighted by city rather than the population in the cities. As expected, wood fuels are a significant percentage of urban household fuel consumption, with firewood and charcoal accounting for over 40 percent of total consumption (see Fig. 12.1). This is especially true for the cities in Africa, where both wood and charcoal are consumed in significant quantities, but it is also true for Haiti, a poor Caribbean country. Surprisingly, kerosene is not used for household purposes as much as might be expected, accounting for only one-tenth of total residential energy consumption. Coal, which is specific to China, consists of about one-tenth of total consumption. Finally, the highest value fuels

Table 12.1. Sample characteristics of the 43 urban areas in the study

	Income/ Person $/Month	Population Thousands	Energy Expenses Percent	Fuel Consumption Per Capita in KgOE per Month						
				Wood	Charcoal	Kerosene	Coal	LPG	Electric	Total
Bolivia	68.33	379	6.48	1.59	0.00	0.47	0.00	4.61	4.00	10.79
La Paz	78.52	1017	5.69	0.17	0.00	0.99	0.00	4.63	5.06	10.91
Quillacollo	59.11	36	7.33	2.66	0.00	0.03	0.00	5.12	2.88	10.95
Oruro	42.90	190	7.93	0.38	0.00	0.57	0.00	5.19	3.04	9.08
Tarija	70.27	74	6.30	2.62	0.00	0.07	0.00	5.30	4.30	12.45
Trinidad	76.34	49	6.24	3.19	0.00	0.22	0.00	3.30	3.50	10.38
Haiti										
Port au Prince	65.08	1000	16.97	0.00	8.23	0.51	0.00	1.12	2.54	12.57
Yemen	87.89	348	11.46	2.42	0.76	0.79	0.00	2.71	0.91	7.78
Sanaa	118.86	472	10.92	2.56	0.59	0.18	0.00	3.19	1.23	7.88
Taiz	48.47	161	13.79	2.60	0.82	0.69	0.00	2.70	0.45	7.48
Hodeida	41.21	182	11.16	1.95	1.13	2.38	0.00	1.53	0.44	7.73
Indonesia	24.45	4274	9.81	0.72	0.28	6.07	0.00	0.37	1.04	8.51
Jakarta	27.15	7976	8.78	0.13	0.08	6.73	0.00	0.47	1.25	8.67
Bandung	26.40	2308	9.94	0.26	0.17	6.04	0.00	0.44	1.04	7.98
Surabaya	22.26	2226	10.00	0.17	0.10	6.73	0.00	0.18	0.84	8.11
Semarange	17.12	1068	13.84	0.93	0.15	4.85	0.00	0.77	0.94	7.63
Surakarta	15.11	688	12.03	2.75	0.71	3.87	0.00	0.27	0.80	8.44
Yogyakarta	27.88	645	9.78	2.37	1.05	4.75	0.00	0.23	0.87	9.35
Philippines	60.10	6651	8.21	0.65	0.54	0.98	0.00	1.39	3.26	6.92
Manila	67.86	8150	7.87	0.24	0.32	0.93	0.00	1.61	3.79	6.92
Bacolod	37.12	360	10.07	2.73	3.36	1.33	0.00	0.56	1.27	10.14
Cebu City	32.02	674	9.78	1.51	2.01	0.94	0.00	0.58	0.92	6.03
Cagayan	27.45	312	9.84	2.57	0.11	1.16	0.00	0.37	1.55	6.31
Davao	20.24	839	9.57	2.80	0.44	1.28	0.00	0.51	0.98	6.20
Thailand	117.50	3006	7.53	0.24	1.68	0.00	0.00	3.56	5.43	10.82
Bangkok	142.21	6000	8.36	0.03	0.89	0.00	0.00	4.23	7.07	11.79
Chiangmai	102.09	150	6.20	0.58	3.44	0.01	0.00	2.72	4.04	10.96
Ayutthaya	84.45	40	6.87	0.29	1.40	0.01	0.00	3.14	3.45	8.62
Cape Verde	56.05	55	16.57	1.33	0.15	1.39	0.00	3.00	1.09	7.03
Praia	65.46	59	13.52	1.30	0.22	0.54	0.00	3.12	1.12	6.33
Mindelo	43.09	50	21.06	1.37	0.05	2.57	0.00	2.84	1.06	8.00
Mauritania	25.34	382	24.40	0.50	8.43	0.21	0.00	1.23	0.32	10.83
Nouakchott	42.57	60	22.19	0.00	5.17	0.09	0.00	2.83	0.52	8.84
Atar	33.57	35	22.00	0.00	7.62	0.43	0.00	2.05	0.30	12.45
Keadi	15.77	12	16.06	1.88	6.65	0.26	0.00	0.07	0.22	9.57
Kiffa	20.21	20	12.08	2.17	12.07	0.43	0.00	0.08	0.00	15.95
Nouakchott	24.44	550	27.46	0.23	8.62	0.16	0.00	1.26	0.36	10.45
Burkina Faso	35.12	369	12.51	8.87	0.68	0.57	0.00	0.14	.	10.48
Ouagadougou	38.71	473	13.61	8.84	0.75	0.62	0.00	0.18	.	10.60
Bobo Dioulasso	30.42	247	10.00	8.90	0.68	0.53	0.00	0.07	.	10.45
Koudougou	22.40	55	13.42	8.71	0.35	0.39	0.00	0.02	.	9.61
Ouahigouya	29.74	41	9.84	9.47	0.04	0.49	0.00	0.00	.	10.10
Zambia	23.04	324	16.31	4.05	9.42	0.82	0.00	0.00	2.07	16.48
Lusaka	28.89	704	14.70	1.51	10.75	1.35	0.00	0.00	1.80	15.62
Kitwe	27.72	360	15.70	4.18	7.92	0.62	0.00	0.00	2.95	15.73
Luanshya	16.89	149	18.60	3.34	9.17	0.74	0.00	0.00	2.24	15.43
Livingston	18.93	81	16.82	7.37	9.79	0.57	0.00	0.00	1.32	19.19
China	17.92	60	8.05	3.04	0.44	0.01	15.56	1.00	0.61	21.16
Xiushui	9.32	40	14.11	13.14	2.17	0.02	2.64	0.23	0.34	19.24
Kezuo	15.19	32	8.50	1.60	0.00	0.00	32.04	1.29	0.60	36.86
Jinayang	16.08	50	7.23	0.33	0.01	0.01	14.53	0.06	0.67	15.79
Changshu	26.30	120	3.88	0.02	0.00	0.00	11.87	1.87	0.69	14.46
Huantai	22.67	55	6.65	0.10	0.00	0.00	17.09	1.57	0.79	19.43
Average	41.82	879	11.78	2.51	2.49	1.26	1.82	1.53	1.72	11.41

Source: ESMAP Energy Studies.

Note: The figures beside the countries are the average for all households in the urban household energy survey.
   The average across all of the countries is the average for all of the cities in the study.

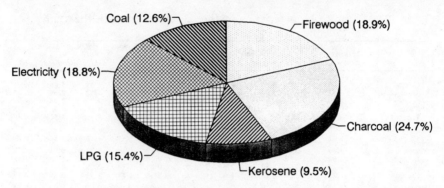

Fig. 12.1. Average household fuel consumption in urban areas of 11 developing countries.

(LPG and electricity) together account for about one-third of total consumption.

Expenditures on fuels present quite a different picture compared to consumption (see Fig. 12.2). Expenditures on wood fuels shrink to less than one-third of total expenditures of fuel, while expenditures on the high quality fuels of LPG and electricity increase to just under two-thirds. This is an indication that urban households place higher value on electricity and LPG, and higher income families will purchase these fuels if they are available to them. Also, many of the households that use wood collect part of it, and this brings down their cash expenditure on this fuel. Based on energy content, electricity is the highest priced fuel, followed by LPG. However, LPG is very price competitive with the other fuels typically used by middle income households, including kerosene and charcoal. As is explained later in the paper, the poor spend a greater percentage of their income on energy, but purchase less and lower quality energy than more wealthy households.

ENERGY POLICIES AND URBAN FUEL USE

As noted, the patterns of urban fuel use do little to explain some of the individual country variation in fuel consumption. It is evident from our preliminary analysis that government policy has a significant role to play in the fuels that people choose for use in urban households. Since most government policies that affect fuel—including whether modern fuels are taxed or subsidized—are decisions taken at the country level, in this section urban fuel use at the national aggregate is examined.

Three countries with significant subsidies in our sample are China, Zambia, and Indonesia. Several interesting points emerge about the countries that subsidize a major fuel. Subsidies appear to encourage consumption of that

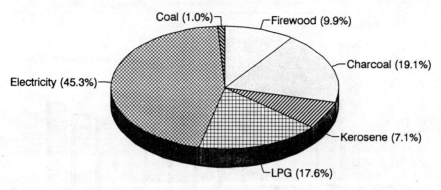

Fig. 12.2. Average household fuel expenditures in urban areas of 11 developing countries.

fuel. For instance, coal in China is the lowest price fuel for all of the developing countries in our study. As is evident from Fig. 12.3, coal accounts for a significant proportion of total energy use for the five towns and cities in our study. Energy use is high for China because heating is necessary in some of the towns in our sample, and coal is highly subsidized. An exception occurs in Xiushui, China, where wood is a major fuel because it is available from the surrounding countryside and coal is not available in large quantities because the town is difficult to reach by road. In Indonesia, government policy that makes kerosene available both to assist poor households and to prevent deforestation seems to be effective in that most people in Indonesia use kerosene for cooking. In fact, of the 11 countries in the study, Indonesia is the only country in which people use kerosene in a major way for cooking. The policy also has the effect of keeping middle class families from switching to the higher value fuels of LPG or electricity.

The countries that have a more market-oriented policy environment demonstrate a greater mix of fuels in use in urban households than those that either tax modern fuels or subsidize a major fuel. These findings hold true after controlling for income across countries. Although these countries are somewhat weighted toward the more wealthy, most of them have policies to price fuels at their international value and to make the fuels available for use in the country. The most notable case is Cape Verde, a small African island nation. In Cape Verde the mix of fuel use is quite evident, with extensive electricity, LPG, and kerosene being used by urban households (see Fig. 12.3). These fuels in Cape Verde are not subsidized and reflect their market value, and as a consequence people in the country spend a very high proportion of their income on modern fuels.

The countries with taxes on petroleum products are among the poorest countries in the study. Burkina Faso, Mauritania, and Haiti all have taxes

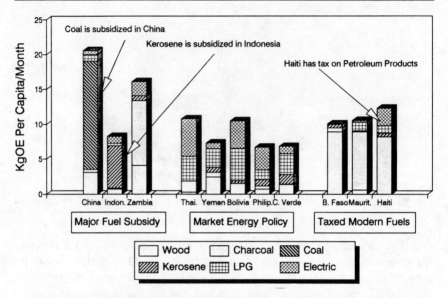

Fig. 12.3. Government policy and fuel consumption in urban areas of 11 developing countries.

on kerosene or LPG and, as indicated in Fig. 12.3, people are discouraged from using these fuels. In all three countries, people use mainly wood or charcoal for their residential energy needs. This may be a reflection of the level of income of the cities in these countries, but certainly the tax and foreign exchange constraints associated with importing petroleum products contribute to the fuel mix in these countries. Preliminary analysis controlling for income also tends to confirm these patterns.

The final point about the countries that subsidize a major fuel is that the price of other fuels in these countries is lower than in the other countries in the study. As indicated in Table 12.2, the subsidy of a major fuel seems to pull down the price of alternative fuels. As a consequence, a major subsidy does not just affect the fuel being subsidized, but rather can lead to distortions in the market prices of other fuels as well, including the price of wood fuels. Policymakers need to be aware that fuel subsidies not only have an impact on particular fuels, but also have a more widespread effect in the fuel economy.

THE EFFECT OF URBAN SIZE ON FUEL USE

The size of an urban area is expected to have an effect on both the price that people have to pay for a fuel and its availability for the local population. One reason is that smaller cities often are in more remote areas that

Table 12.2. The relationship between government policy and urban household energy consumption, choice and prices in developing countries, 1988

Energy Use and Price by Policy Type	Monthly Income US$	Firewood	Charcoal	Coal	Kerosene	LPG	Electricity
Energy Consumption (KgOE/Capita/Month)	21.80	2.61	3.38	5.19	2.30	0.46	1.24
Subsidy	77.98	1.25	0.63	0.00	0.73	3.06	2.94
Market	41.85	3.13	5.78	0.00	0.43	0.83	1.43
Taxed							
Energy Choice (%)	21.80	26.10	43.60	29.70	57.10	19.80	82.50
Subsidy	77.98	19.60	27.20	0.00	27.70	81.30	90.00
Market	41.85	39.40	66.20	0.00	64.40	27.20	50.40
Taxed							
Energy Price (US$/KgOE)	21.80	0.14	0.17	0.03	0.24	0.26	0.48
Subsidy	77.98	0.34	0.64	.	0.39	0.40	1.25
Market	41.85	0.30	0.40	.	0.55	0.85	2.24
Taxed							
Useful Energy Price (US$/KgOE)	21.80	0.97	0.77	0.11	0.69	0.40	0.56
Subsidy	77.98	2.42	2.92	.	1.11	0.61	1.47
Market	41.85	2.13	1.83	.	1.58	1.31	2.63
Taxed							
Middle Income Groups Only (US$ 20-40)							
Energy Consumption (KgOE/Capita/Month)	26.32	1.34	2.45	6.01	2.73	0.84	1.26
Subsidy	28.94	1.78	0.94	0.00	0.83	2.11	1.43
Market	29.03	4.97	4.77	0.00	0.42	0.70	0.42
Taxed							
Energy Choice (%)	26.32	12.90	29.10	35.80	53.90	30.80	86.50
Subsidy	28.94	35.30	36.50	0.00	42.60	66.70	90.20
Market	29.03	60.90	48.60	0.00	64.20	24.40	35.20
Taxed							
Energy Price (US$/KgOE)	26.32	0.13	0.21	0.03	0.23	0.26	0.51
Subsidy	28.94	0.33	0.56	.	0.35	0.35	1.05
Market	29.03	0.37	0.45	.	0.58	0.94	2.51
Taxed							
Useful Energy Price (US$/KgOE)	26.32	0.91	0.95	0.10	0.67	0.39	0.60
Subsidy	28.94	2.36	2.56	.	1.01	0.54	1.24
Market	29.03	2.62	2.05	.	1.66	1.45	2.95
Taxed							

Source: ESMAP Energy Studies

require transportation of modern fuels and higher transport costs may increase the price of the fuel. In addition, smaller cities also obviously have smaller markets, so that the distributors of modern fuels may not be as interested in targeting them for sales. The lack of fuel alternatives in the marketplace may influence the other prices in the marketplace. Another factor is that biomass is often more readily available around the boundaries of smaller cities. The combination of sheer size and the volume of demand for wood fuels around larger cities makes the local collection problematic for poor urban residents. As a consequence they purchase charcoal, kerosene, or coal for cooking and other end uses.

Our expectation was that with an increase in city size, people would have less access to wood fuels around the cities. As a consequence, their use of wood fuels would decrease. We were surprised to find that for cities up to one million people, the use of wood fuels remains fairly extensive and does not decrease (see Fig. 12.4). Although it appears that the overall pattern is that energy use is declining with city size, this is somewhat misleading because of the extensive use of coal in the small towns and cities of China that are included in the study. Once cities reach a population of one million and above, their populations switch from using biomass fuels to modern fuels, including LPG, electricity, and limited amounts of charcoal. The large cities in the study include Manila, La Paz, Bangkok, Port au Prince, and four cities in Indonesia, where very little charcoal and virtually no fuelwood is used for cooking. Partly because of the use of LPG and electricity in smaller cities in countries like Cape Verde and Zambia, the amount of these fuels used in the smaller cities is somewhat larger than expected for the total study. This is consistent with findings not reported here that useful energy for *cooking* does not appear to be dependent on city size.

The income that is spent on fuel is not significantly dependent on city size. The average share of income spent on fuel is about 12 percent, and it is slightly lower for cities above one million. The implication is that neither city size nor the mix of the fuels within different cities has much to do with percentage of income spent on a fuel for urban households. Rather, as we make clear in the next section, the important factors affecting income expenditures on fuel include the level and distribution of income within cities.

The size of the city correlates to some extent with the price of different fuels (see Table 12.3). As might be expected, the price of electricity, kerosene, and LPG declines with city size, while the price of wood fuels remains almost constant. It is clear that part of the reason people in smaller towns and cities do not use as much modern fuel as those in the larger urban areas is that the prices they pay for the fuels are somewhat higher than in the largest cities, especially those above one million people, and incomes in such towns are generally lower. A surprising finding is that the price of wood fuels is higher in the smaller cities. This is probably because some of the smaller urban areas in the sample, including those in Mauritania and Yemen, have very little biomass around them. In a later analysis, we will be able to examine the impact of biomass supply around cities on residential fuel use patterns. As indicated above, the finding that the price of the fuels is higher in smaller cities can be explained in part by the higher distribution costs for electricity and the higher transportation costs of LPG and kerosene.

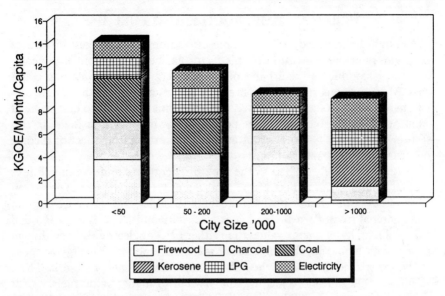

Fig. 12.4. City size and household fuel consumption in 11 developing countries.

Table 12.3. The relationship between city size and urban household energy consumption, choice and prices in developing countries, 1988

City Size	City Size ('000)	Monthly Income US$	Firewood	Charcoal	Coal	Kerosene	LPG	Electricity
Energy Consumption (KgOE/Capita/Month)								
Town	33.89	38.19	3.82	3.33	3.85	0.21	1.70	1.41
Small City	102.54	41.38	2.19	2.15	3.11	0.62	2.12	1.59
Middle City	526.98	35.74	3.41	3.08	0.00	1.40	0.60	1.27
Large City	3718.13	55.82	0.24	1.24	0.00	3.35	1.68	2.82
Energy Choice (%)								
Town	33.89	38.19	52.50	40.00	16.80	33.60	46.50	64.10
Small City	102.54	41.38	25.10	36.10	21.10	37.20	60.40	78.40
Middle City	526.98	35.74	47.90	53.30	0.00	64.50	23.00	69.50
Large City	3718.13	55.82	4.30	28.00	0.00	61.30	37.30	95.40
Energy Price (US$/KgOE)								
Town	33.89	38.19	0.27	0.29	0.03	0.45	0.53	1.64
Small City	102.54	41.38	0.26	0.57	0.03	0.40	0.48	1.23
Middle City	526.98	35.74	0.27	0.38	.	0.34	0.51	1.15
Large City	3718.13	55.82	0.22	0.29	.	0.24	0.36	0.78
Useful Energy Price (US$/KgOE)								
Town	33.89	38.19	1.92	1.33	0.09	1.28	0.81	1.93
Small City	102.54	41.38	1.82	2.60	0.12	1.14	0.74	1.45
Middle City	526.98	35.74	1.95	1.73	.	0.98	0.79	1.35
Large City	3718.13	55.82	1.58	1.32	.	0.69	0.55	0.92

Source: ESMAP Energy Studies

URBAN INCOME, EQUITY, AND FUEL USE

As might be expected, urban incomes are among the strongest influences on urban interfuel substitution. This factor has been documented in nearly all surveys conducted for urban household energy use in developing countries. Most previous studies have been for single countries with a single policy environment. As a consequence, it is sometimes difficult to determine at what point on the income ladder people will switch between fuels. In this section, we present a first attempt at trying to sort out the effect of income on urban interfuel substitution.

Income is strongly related to the type of energy use and to expenditures on fuels, but it is not related to the total quantity of energy use. The reason is simple. As households move up the income ladder, they move from wood and charcoal to modern fuels such as electricity and LPG. Both wood and charcoal have lower energy values than either LPG or electricity. Even though people with higher incomes use about the same amount of energy as those in the lower income groups, they obtain more useful energy from it. Thus, as households gain more income, they switch to higher value fuels.

The percentage of people using LPG for cooking increases from about 10 percent in the lowest income groups to just under 80 percent in the highest income groups. From the analysis we estimated that the income threshold point at which people begin to switch to LPG is about $25 per person per month, while the point at which they switch to electricity is much lower at about $5 to $10 dollars per person per month. There is a very high penetration rate for electricity even in the lowest income classes, where six out of 10 of the households use electricity, but the poor use very small quantities of it. The correlation between the quantity of electricity used and income is much stronger than the correlation with the quantities of LPG consumed, which is probably caused in part by the different ways in which the fuels are used. There are capital costs involved in cooking with LPG, including stoves, bottles, and bulk purchases. By contrast, most electricity companies do not charge large connection fees, so initial electricity consumption involves mainly household lighting in very small quantities.

Wood fuels are used in low income households, but they continue to be used even in very high income households. This finding tends to contradict many predictions based on income alone. Also, the higher income households that are still using wood fuels for cooking and other uses are not only in Africa. In addition to cities in African countries like Burkina Faso, Mauritania, and Zambia, high income households use wood fuels in the cities of Port au Prince in Haiti, Trinidad in Bolivia, Cagayan in the Philippines, and even Chiangmai, Thailand. It is obvious that income and price alone may not be enough to explain why people continue to use wood fuels in urban areas in developing countries. The explanation for the continued use may lie in other factors, such as access to local wood supplies around cities, the use of charcoal as a special cooking fuel for grilling, and distorted market access to modern fuels.

The poorest households in the poorest countries spend a high proportion of their income on household fuels, and the fuels that they purchase are mainly wood fuels. About 75 percent of total expenditures for energy in low income households are on wood fuels, including fuelwood and charcoal (see Table 12.4). Except in some of the countries that subsidize intermediate fuels such as coal or kerosene, the price of wood and charcoal in the poor countries is fairly high. For example, the price of wood and charcoal in urban markets in Burkina Faso, where a high percentage of income is spent on purchasing fuels, is almost as much as kerosene or LPG. In Mauritania, where charcoal is used extensively for cooking, the price of charcoal and wood is above that of kerosene or LPG on a useful energy basis. As indicated before, petroleum products are taxed in Mauritania. We drew the conclusion that those who are the poorest spend a significant proportion of their income on fuels, and these fuels tend to be mainly wood fuels along with a small but significant amount of modern fuels.

The affordability of the different fuels is reflected in the percentage of income spent on fuel by different income groups. The lower income groups spend approximately one-fifth of their monthly income on fuel, while the higher income groups spend just over one-twentieth of their income on fuel. The poor purchase mainly traditional fuels, while the more wealthy households purchase higher quality fuels such as LPG and electricity. The percentage of income spent on electricity is about three percent, regardless of income class. In terms of total expenditures, the poor spend less on fuels, but because their incomes are low, it represents a higher proportion of their income. Thus, the paradox of fuel expenditures is that those least able to afford it pay a higher proportion of their income on lower quality fuels, while those who spend a smaller proportion of their income on energy purchase the high quality fuels. As noted above, this is probably because the poor cannot buy the appliances that are necessary to take advantage of modern fuels.

Figs. 12.5 and 12.6 depict the relationship of urban income to fuel consumption and fuel expenditures, respectively, in the countries in our study. Income is obviously an important factor in fuel choice and use in developing countries. It is apparent that the highest value fuels of electricity and LPG are most highly correlated with income. As household incomes rise, the use of these fuels increases along with a corresponding drop in the other fuels. However, the negative relationship between income and wood fuels use is not as clear as the very predictable increasing use of LPG and electricity as incomes rise. As a consequence, we must look to other factors to explain declining use of wood as a household fuel in developing countries, including access to wood around cities and government policies.

Table 12.4. The relationship between income class and urban household energy consumption, choice, prices and energy expenditure in developing countries, 1988

Income Class (Per Capita)	Monthly Income US$	Firewood	Charcoal	Coal	Kerosene	LPG	Electricity	Total
Energy Consumption (KgOE/Capita/Month)								
Low	8.59	3.63	3.28	2.38	1.33	0.15	0.60	11.59
Mid-Low	15.51	2.57	2.66	3.21	1.73	0.42	0.82	11.59
Middle	25.02	2.10	2.20	2.83	1.50	1.25	1.15	11.15
Mid-High	41.94	2.62	2.54	0.67	1.14	2.09	1.77	10.82
High	116.95	1.66	1.79	0.00	0.60	3.70	4.15	11.62
Energy Choice (%)								
Low	8.59	55.00	54.30	14.70	67.90	10.20	61.40	NA
Mid-Low	15.51	38.70	44.00	17.00	62.80	22.40	70.10	NA
Middle	25.02	31.50	36.60	15.50	52.20	43.70	76.90	NA
Mid-High	41.94	26.10	37.30	4.70	40.70	59.80	79.30	NA
High	116.95	15.90	29.30	0.00	19.60	76.70	92.30	NA
Energy Price (US$/KgOE)								
Low	8.59	0.21	0.27	0.03	0.35	0.52	1.15	NA
Mid-Low	15.51	0.22	0.29	0.03	0.34	0.49	1.18	NA
Middle	25.02	0.25	0.41	0.03	0.35	0.45	1.15	NA
Mid-High	41.94	0.31	0.51	0.03	0.39	0.48	1.34	NA
High	116.95	0.29	0.55	.	0.39	0.44	1.23	NA
Useful Energy Price (US$/KgOE)								
Low	8.59	1.50	1.21	0.11	1.01	0.80	1.36	NA
Mid-Low	15.51	1.54	1.32	0.11	0.97	0.76	1.38	NA
Middle	25.02	1.81	1.87	0.10	0.99	0.70	1.36	NA
Mid-High	41.94	2.21	2.33	0.11	1.12	0.73	1.57	NA
High	116.95	2.09	2.50	.	1.11	0.68	1.45	NA
% Expenditure on Fuel of Energy Expenditures								
Low	8.59	20.45	30.82	7.77	19.23	3.27	18.46	100
Mid-Low	15.51	12.76	21.01	9.4	19.92	8.91	28.01	100
Middle	25.02	8.68	17.13	6.97	13.49	18.83	34.88	100
Mid-High	41.94	6.83	17.48	2.01	9.35	23.78	40.54	100
High	116.95	3.45	9.44		3.7	24.49	58.94	100
% Energy Expenditures of Total Income								
Low	8.59	4.67	6.15	0.69	3.11	0.67	2.93	17.92
Mid-Low	15.51	2.23	3.15	0.57	2.09	1.07	3.13	11.98
Middle	25.02	1.63	2.01	0.29	1.28	1.83	3.18	9.92
Mid-High	41.94	1.06	1.75	0.06	0.72	1.92	3.29	8.66
High	116.95	0.38	0.69		0.18	1.37	3.25	5.74

Source: ESMAP Energy Studies

Note: NA stands for not applicable.

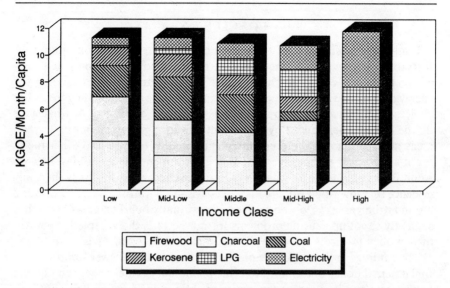

Fig. 12.5. Urban income and fuel consumption in 11 developing countries.

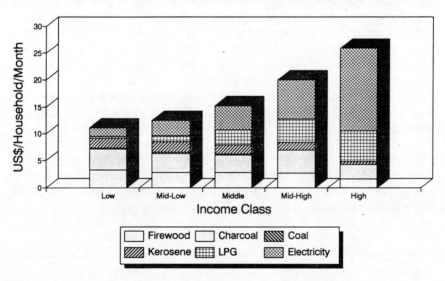

Fig. 12.6. Urban income and fuel expenditures in 11 developing countries.

CONCLUSION

Limited understanding of the nature of the energy transition hinders efforts to formulate policy concerning the most effective and economic strategy for providing energy for households in urban areas. Understanding the energy transition will help to provide a framework for understanding the policy choices for urban areas. Several questions need to be addressed. At what stage do the externalities caused by significant harvesting of wood around urban areas justify intervention to encourage households to switch to other fuels? From a least-cost perspective including environmental externalities, how do wood fuels compare to alternative fuels in the energy transition? Is there any evidence that low wood prices cause excessive and harmful harvesting of wood around urban areas? Do wood prices rise gradually in urban areas or do they suddenly shoot up causing problems for markets? Is there a role for government policy to direct the pace of the transition between fuels?

The findings in this paper are one attempt to start to answer some of these fundamental policy questions. From the preliminary evidence, we can say that government policy plays a very important role in influencing households to choose one fuel over another. Furthermore, policies to promote LPG for households with incomes that are less than about $25 per person per month are likely to lead to disappointment. Apparently electricity can be promoted at much lower income levels because of the high value urban households have for lighting, although this will require substantial capital costs by the electricity industry. In developing countries, wood fuels do not disappear completely as incomes rise since many high-income households continue to use wood, reflecting the utility of these fuels for urban households. However, they do seem to disappear from urban households in large metropolitan areas over one million, where wood apparently is very hard to obtain. The urban poor are probably affected most by urban fuel policies, since they are spending a significant proportion of their incomes on energy. Obviously, there is much more work to be completed before we fully understand the dynamic patterns affecting urban interfuel substitution in developing countries.

REFERENCES

1. Keith Openshaw and Charles Feinstein, "Fuelwood Stumpage: Considerations for Developing Country Energy Planning," Industry and Energy Department Working Paper: Energy Series Paper 16 (1988).
2. Witold Teplitz-Sembitzky and Gunter Schramm, "Woodfuel Supply and Environmental Management," Industry and Energy Department Working Paper: Energy Series Paper 19 (1989).
3. B. Bowonder, S. S. R. Prasad and N. V. M. Unni, "Deforestation Around Urban Centers in India," *Environmental Conservation* 4, 1, pp. 23–28 (Spring 1987).
4. Julia Allen and Douglas Barnes, "The Causes of Deforestation in Developing Countries," *Annals of the Association of American Geographers* 75, 2, pp. 163–184 (1985).
5. Barry Munslow, Yemi Katerere, Adrian Ferf and Phil O'Keef, *The Fuelwood Trap: A Study of the SADCC Region,* Earthscan Publications Ltd., London (1988).
6. G. Leach and R. Mearns, "Bioenergy Issues and Options in Africa," A Report for the Royal Norwegian Ministry of Development Cooperation, Energy and Development Program IIED (1988).
7. K. Fitzgerald, D. Barnes and G. McGranahan, "Interfuel Substitution and Changes in the Way Households Use Energy: The Case of Cooking and Lighting Behavior in Urban Java," Industry and Energy Department Working Paper: Energy Series Paper 29, World Bank, Washington, D.C. (1990).

13 Reformulated Gasoline and U.S. Energy Policy

Donald I. Hertzmark and John Ashworth

INTRODUCTION

Rationale for the REFORM Approach

The REFORM approach to analyzing issues of gasoline makeup uses analytical tools that are well tried in the petroleum industry. Our purpose in making yet another linear program was to gain the ability to test a number of different restrictions now included in various versions of the Clean Air Act and South Coast Air Quality Management District (SCAQMD, California) plans. The existing legislation will impose significant changes on the composition of gasoline. Earlier regulation of gasoline was intended in large measure to do two things: eliminate lead and make gasoline compatible with catalytic converter technology.

The earlier modifications of the gasoline pool were successful in making the universal adoption of catalytic converters possible in new vehicles. However, the concern with making gasoline compatible with converters did not address other issues. In particular, there are several components and characteristics of the gasoline pool that were not addressed in earlier fuel regulation. These are:

- vapor pressure of the fuel—the lower the vapor pressure (in summer) the fewer hydrocarbons will enter the atmosphere;
- aromatics, olefins, and other smog precursors;
- benzene, a powerful carcinogen; and
- oxygen, a known means of reducing carbon monoxide (CO) formation by motor vehicles.

This paper shares many assumptions and results with a longer study undertaken by the two authors for the Meridian Corporation in 1990 and 1991. This work is entitled the *REFORM Guidebook* and contains a full set of references to the Clean Air Act and to the chemistry of gasoline reformulation.

Our purpose in constructing a programming model was to take a look at different fuel content and emissions policies. In the ongoing national debate about fuel content and the Clean Air Act, we decided to create a tool which was expressly designed to look at the key levers now under discussion in the Congress. In addition, we felt that it was crucial to put together a model that would be capable of considering regional regulations, such as those in Southern California, New York, or Denver. Additionally, we wanted to be able to look at intraregional issues, especially the cost and pollution impacts of specific airshed policies such as those in Southern California, and on gasoline markets elsewhere in the region, for example, Seattle. Once data are available, we wish to use the gasoline slate that emerges from REFORM as an input to the EPA's Mobile4 model which calculates final emissions.† This effort will lead to conclusions on the cost-effectiveness of various approaches to automobile pollution control.

To discuss the changes in gasoline composition proposed in recent revisions to the Clean Air Act, it is necessary to keep in mind an image of the current composition of the gasoline pool. Table 13.1 shows the important characteristics of the key gasoline blending components and their relationships to gasoline quality and emissions levels.

Policy Issues and Industry Concerns

Government policymakers and industry executives will differ in their approaches to the determination of optimum formulations of gasoline and their relationships to desirable levels of air pollution. What REFORM does is to translate the government policies into a set of actions and expenditures by industry that will comply with the regulations at the least cost.

The rationales for reducing emissions from gasoline were alluded to in the previous section. The overall objectives of the government's policies for both fuels and vehicles might be summarized as follows:

- What combinations of fuel quality and engine technology will result in the lowest feasible level of emissions?
- How long will it take to develop the requisite technology and to make the necessary investments in mass production or fuel supply?
- What steps can be taken in the immediate future to reduce emissions from motor fuels? How are these steps, especially in fuel supply and technology, related to the long-term emission control strategies?
- What are the economic and health impacts on the general and motoring publics of such changes in fuel supply?

---

†At the current time the EPA's *Mobile4* model does not address factors other than oxygen levels in fuel. No consideration is yet given to vapor pressure, aromatics, or olefins. However, these elements will be added shortly once results are available from the Auto-Oil Study.

Table 13.1. Major gasoline blending components and their environmental constraints

Ingredient	Key characteristics	Current use (kbd)	Outlook for use in reformulated gasoline
Reformate	High aromatics and benzene, high octane	1,850	Cannot be greatly reduced due to great volumes of current use. Must be used in less severely refined form with lower aromatics.
Catalytic cracked naphtha	High olefins and octane	2,600	Will continue as key ingredient but perhaps increasingly as feed for alkylation units.
Alkylate	Benign, low aromatics, RVP and olefins, high octane	950	One of few components that will face excess demand in reformulated gasoline.
Ethers (ETBE and MTBE)	Reduces CO, raises octane, low RVP	125	Will become major octane booster; >500 kbd.
Butane	Raises octane and RVP	~250	Will fall by >100 kbd as new RVP regulations come into effect.
Toluene/xylene, benzene	Raises octane, contains high levels of aromatics	~75	Will be cut sharply by restrictions on aromatics and benzene.
Isomerate	Raises octane of light naphthas, high RVP	~300	Demand will fall in summer.

From the industry's perspective the important questions have a great deal to do with the specifics of components: which ones must rise and which ones will fall; what kinds of equipment will be needed; and how this might affect other product streams, particularly jet fuel and diesel fuel. In particular, we were interested in answering the following questions.

1. What mixes of the major gasoline pool blending components are currently feasible in terms of specifications and emissions potentials (aromatics, olefins, vapor pressure)?

2. What mixes of such components or changes in their manufacture will be required in the future to meet possible or expected specifications and regulations of gasoline content?

3. What is the role of oxygenates in the future gasoline pool? Are there distinctive roles for MTBE, ETBE, and ETOH?
4. How will refiners respond to the potential losses and reductions in some of their most important blending materials, reformates, aromatics, and butanes, as vapor pressure levels are reduced and aromatics controlled?
5. How much will the proposed steps cost refiners and motorists? Is there a way to put these costs on a comparable basis with proposed engine modifications? Can these costs be compared with the emissions reductions that accompany reduced driving, induced by higher fuel prices?

In the remainder of this paper, we lay out the method and approach used in this analysis of the proposed changes in the gasoline supply. At the end of the main text is a section with discussions of the impacts of proposed formulation changes on national gasoline content and on that in the SCAQMD.

THE NATURE OF THE REFORM ANALYTIC TOOL

Objectives of the Model

Starting from a view of oil refiners as economic agents responsive to market signals and incentives, we developed the REFORM model to highlight the key shifts in the gasoline market as federal standards regarding the composition of gasoline change. The model is intended to represent the market's view of the proposed federal or state standards. The objectives of this exercise are quite simple. They are:

1. Showing how refiners must reformulate gasoline to meet current and future specifications at the least cost to themselves and to the motoring public;
2. Making maximum use of current technologies and blending materials wherever possible;
3. Showing what materials and processes will be needed to meet future standards, regardless of the current economic feasibility of supplying such materials;
4. Maintaining sufficient flexibility to handle extreme value cases; and
5. Achieving compatibility with Mobile4 and other models.

The model is designed to approximate closely the current blending patterns in the gasoline market.† The construction of the model proceeded along the following lines.

---

†Achieving results that are congruent with the current realities of the gasoline market is a necessary step in the verification of the structure of the model. That is, can the model predict accurately the reality on which the model's assumptions and structure were based?

- The refiner wants to make the requisite specification fuel at a minimum cost. Therefore, it is necessary to compare costs of both the ingredients and the capacities.
- Set out an objective: minimize the cost of supplying gasoline of a specified octane and other characteristics. This is the essence of a linear program.
- This set of characteristics and objectives can be imbedded in a spreadsheet program and then reformulated to use one of the commercial LP packages that interfaces with the spreadsheet. Working with such a spreadsheet allows the results to be manipulated for post optimality or reporting in a simple manner. For this paper we have used Quattro Pro® as the data entry program.
- Environmental constraints on gasoline composition can be represented as constraints on the materials that can be blended into gasoline since each of the key environmental characteristics of gasolines has a quantitative dimension.
- Changing the levels of various constraints allows us to look at the capacities of upgrading equipment (reformers, hydrocrackers, alkylation units, FCCUs) and blending components, especially oxygenates, that are needed to meet strict environmental standards.
- Infeasible options can be identified. By looking at the combinations of feedstocks and equipment that are necessary to meet various specifications for the final product, we can eliminate spurious options or chart the path of increasing costs for refiners.

The Structure of the Model†

REFORM is set up as two linked linear programming files for each of the Petroleum Administration for Defense Districts (PADDs) of the United States. The first file is an overall refinery cost minimization program that takes various crudes (up to eleven) and runs them through distillation, cracking, and reforming to meet the demands for each of the major refined products. The demand for gasoline comes from the second LP which is actually a detailed gasoline blending program that meets the volume and quality specifications for gasolines at least cost. The refinery model then decides on the least-cost combination of cracking, reforming, etherification, and isomerization, consistent with the overall demands and equipment configuration.

The refinery model "produces," *inter alia,* blending materials and intermediate products for alkylation and etherification. Shipments of refined products to other PADDs are considered to be exports while inbound ship-

---

†The first part of this section is intended for readers interested in the details of the model structure and should be considered optional.

ments are imports. The system is balanced nationally by linking the regional models with a national level set of LP files that constrains the activity levels within each PADD.

With regard to the physical structure of the model itself:

- A spreadsheet format is used for gasoline blending, giving the refining requirements and major characteristics of each of the major blending components (the X vector):
  - reformate—3 kinds, full range, heavy, and "lite,"†
  - alkylate,
  - FCC naphtha—3 kinds, full range, heavy, and light,
  - oxygenates—ETOH, MTBE, ETBE,
  - butane,
  - toluene/xylene, and
  - isomerate.
- The characteristics of the blending components that comprise the gasoline pools include both qualitative constraints and policy constraints. The former include octane, vapor pressure, and oxygen while the policy constraints cover most of the same territory. Such constraints in our model include the following:‡
  - octane,
  - aromatics,
  - olefins,
  - benzene,
  - oxygen, and
  - vapor pressure.
- In addition, there is a supply constraint, now at about 7.1 million barrels per day (b/d), averaged throughout the year. The 1995 demands are expected to range from about 7.2 million b/d to 7.6 million b/d.
- The blending components draw on pools of refining equipment and raw materials. These form the physical or capacity constraints of the model:
  - reforming,
  - alkylation,
  - hydrocracking,
  - catalytic cracking,

---

†"Lite" reformate is a low severity product containing lower levels of aromatics and benzene, along with less octane. This product is not to be confused with light reformate, a component of full range reformate which has relatively low octane and high vapor pressure.

‡As this article was being written, new results from the Auto-Oil study indicated that blanket restrictions on both olefins and aromatics would be cost-ineffective and that the heavier aromatics fractions actually caused most of the hydrocarbon pollution from reformates and FCC naphthas. Results on olefins are inconclusive thus far, though the known reactivity of olefins points to some type of limitation eventually.

- gas plants, and
- light olefin feeds.

Key Assumptions of the Model

In any given run of the model, a linear program uses fixed input prices. In some of the extreme cases, it is reasonable to conclude that the cost of providing more of that capacity will rise.†

Using the standard technique of comparative statics, the appropriate way to include higher prices for blending components is to change one at a time.

The gasoline pool in each PADD is treated as a combination of the separate demand regions within that PADD, with appropriate specifications for each demand node. In the East Coast PADD, for example, there are more than ten demand nodes. This multiplicity is necessary to analyze different levels of enforcement and compliance with the Clean Air Act.

Capabilities of the Model

REFORM is designed to cover a broad range of potential policies and base conditions. Products and processes can be added or deleted, as circumstances demand, and changing crude oil prices can be accommodated easily by changes in the prices of major blending components. As in all linear programs, the constraints on the variables and the upper and lower bounds of each variable proscribe the available solutions. In addition, the results of the model are limited by history. The large investments in reforming and catalytic cracking capacities in the 1960s–1980s means that these ingredients will continue to dominate the formulations of gasoline well into the 1990s.

In the base case, without enaction of the new Clean Air Act, REFORM will provide solutions for the following ranges of environmental and performance constraints:‡

- octane—RON between 92 and 98; MON between 80 and 88;
- oxygen—between 0 and 0.5 percent of the overall pool;
- RVP—ranges from a low of 9 to a high of 11.5;
- aromatics—ranges from 40 percent down to 28 percent;
- olefins—ranges from 20 percent down to 12.5 percent;
- benzene—ranges from 1.5 percent up to 2.5 percent.

---

†For example, many of the extreme case solutions require 50–100 percent more alkylate than is currently available. From such information, it is reasonable to conclude that the price of producing alkylate will rise as the alkylation units themselves encounter heavy or even excess demand over the next five years.

‡Please turn to the section headed The Key Constraints and Their Limits for a discussion of the constraints under current and proposed gasoline reformulation regulations.

The base case provides a current reference against which the kinds of regulations proposed for the mid- and late-1990s can be compared. For the summer and winter pools, the base cases were referenced to the specifications provided by the *Oil and Gas Journal* summary of finished gasoline properties. In subsequent runs of the model, the constraints are changed so that we can see the impacts of different levels of each of the important policy and capacity constraints on gasoline composition.

A number of these constraints interact so that, for example, the octane number may be limited by the aromatics restriction (affecting reformate). Similarly, the level of olefins in the final gasoline pool is determined in part by the requirement to consume a certain amount of catalytic cracked naphtha for volume as well as for octane.

In addition to the limitations imposed by the constraint levels, each of the variables has an upper and lower bound. These bounds, though quite wide for many of the blending components, reflect the physical relations in the refinery units that comprise the gasoline refining system. Table 13.2 shows the bounds for many of the key variables.

In the short term, many potential formulations of gasoline must respect the component bounds. For example, full range reformate, with its 60–70 percent levels of aromatics, must be used at volumes of at least 1,250,000 b/d, more than 15 percent of the current gasoline pool. With lower reformate demand, the gasoline volume constraint cannot be met nor can the octane specifications be met without vastly increased imports and octane constraints.[†] For butane, the upper and lower bounds reflect the lack of alternative uses for the additive at levels equivalent to its current use in gasoline of about 175,000 b/d. In addition, for many small refiners, butane still represents a cost-effective additive for both volume and octane.[‡]

As the gasoline supply system has evolved over the years, its pieces have become integrated. Thus, a cost-minimizing linear program will choose high levels of butane in the pool in spite of its high vapor pressure because it is half the price of any other substitute and it adds octane to the pool in a highly compatible form.

Even as the RVP levels allowed in the pool are lowered under nine points, butane is a preferred additive in some solutions.

[†] In the longer term such a volume demand can be met by increased output of blending components that are more compatible with the emissions specifications, mostly ethers and alkylate. However, it is not reasonable to expect that such supplies can rise by an aggregate total of more than 150,000 b/d per year.

[‡] In general, more upgrading units in the refinery will mean more butane and propane production since these gases will be by-products of most cracking processes.

Table 13.2.　Variable bounds in the REFORM model baseline case ('000 b/d)

Component	Lower bound	Upper bound	Use in 1989
Full range reformate	750	1,500	1,450
Heavy reformate	100	400	400
Full FCCN	750	1,500	1,350
Heavy FCCN	250	625	500
Light FCCN	250	750	750
Straight run naphtha	125	350	250
Alkylate	500	1,100	850
MTBE	0	400	75
Ethanol	0	55	50
Butane	50	250	210
Isomerate	0	300	250
Raffinates (BTX) and aromatics	50	250	175

Note: Use of MTBE increased to about 125 kbd in 1990. FCCN is fluid catalytic cracked naphtha.
Sources: *Oil and Gas Journal* (June 18, 1990); REFORM printouts.

Competition Among Blending Components for Feedstocks and Refinery Processes

Feedstocks and processes interact so that outputs of some processes become inputs of others. Inputs for various processes are constrained in volume so that processes that compete for feedstocks are shown explicitly in the model. As a result, it is necessary to trade off ingredients and capacity against one another, as set out below.

- Both catalytic reforming and catalytic cracking produce LPGs. These LPGs can be used as inputs to alkylation and etherification.
- Both alkylation and ethers require light olefin feeds.
- Lowering reforming severity will reduce octane and aromatics levels in the reformate but yield fewer LPGs as well. To accommodate this reality, the model can make available a "lite" reformate to complement the heavy and full range reformates. This light product has a higher yield from the naphtha feeds but has lower octane and aromatics levels.
- Less use of reformate will make available more straight run naphtha, a lower octane product.
- Butane, with reduced demand due to lower RVP standards, can be used as a feedstock for isomerization and transformation to light olefin feedstock as isobutylene.

Variations in the Baseline Model

To achieve the kinds of specifications that have been proposed in Denver, New York, Southern California, and elsewhere, a number of the constraints and variable bounds must be changed. In particular, the following changes must be made to the current bounds and blending component supplies:

- increased supplies of oxygenates—ETOH, MTBE and, potentially, ETBE;
- reduced demand requirements (lower bound) for butane;
- reduced demand requirements for reformates (if the binding constraint is aromatics) or cracked naphtha (if the binding constraint is olefins);
- increased supplies of imported "green" gasoline to balance the gasoline barrel;
- increased supplies of "lite" reformate to meet volume requirements; and
- increased production of alkylate to provide a high octane, low emissions additive.

In addition to the changes which must be made in variable bounds, changing the specifications will require that more light olefin feedstock be made available for the manufacture of both alkylates and ethers. Although it is possible to use the olefin feed in alkylation units after it has reacted with alcohol to make one of the ethers, some of the feed will be consumed and the overall expansion in production of both products will require additional feedstocks.†

The most restrictive emissions standards for gasoline that were tested have the following constraint levels:

- oxygen—3.7 percent;
- RVP—7;
- benzene—1 percent;
- olefins—9 percent; and
- aromatics—22.5 percent.

Some of these constraints are well below the levels now under consideration in the Clean Air Act discussions. However, singly or in combination, most of these constraints have been proposed for the entire country or for specific regions at particular times of the year. Thus REFORM serves to give a number of snapshots of the gasoline supply under varying circumstances.

---

†Reduced demand for butane gives refiners a chance, born out of necessity, to further process the butane via isomerization to isobutane and then to isobutylene as a feed for ethers and alkylates.

Limitations of the Model

As with any liner program, the chief sin of REFORM is that it assumes linearity in a highly nonlinear world. Several of the key parameters of the model behave nonlinearly. These include the following:

- RVP varies nonlinearly with temperature and with concentration of a component in the base fuel;
- yields of blendstock from reformers and crackers fall nonlinearly as the limits of producing particular fractions are reached; and
- blending octane will vary, *inter alia,* with aromatics levels in the base fuel.

As an aggregated model, REFORM cannot predict the optimal mix of activities at any one refinery. This limitation is the price that is paid for compactness and quickness of solution.

REFORM starts from a palette of fixed technologies and prices. The model is incapable of modifying itself to account for the effects of excess or insufficient demand for a product or process.† As a result, modifying prices manually becomes one way of accommodating change in the world.

At the present time, the model is not yet attached to the *Mobile4* model. As a result, REFORM does not predict the emissions of various alternative blends of gasoline. It merely shows the least-cost way of meeting particular specifications for the entire gasoline pool.

BASIC ASSUMPTIONS UNDERLYING THE MODEL

Many of the assumptions that govern the running of REFORM have been discussed above. However, it is useful to go over the key operational and structural assumptions briefly. There are four key assumptions:

1. All of the functional relationships in the model are linear.
2. There is a feasible solution for each package of constraints.
3. All material flows must balance.
4. Volumes of blending components, and the capacities to produce them, are limited in the short term.

These assumptions are applied to REFORM in such a way that the model can accommodate the vast changes that will be required by the Clean Air Act and the SCAQMD and yet retain the appropriate properties for a linear program.

---

†Models that contain a price modification function from one period to the next are called recursive programming models. Such a model represents one possible extension of the current work that is made feasible in a programming sense through the spreadsheet interface.

In a blending model, the flows of materials within the refinery must be accounted for, even though this is not a full refinery linear program. These materials must be "produced" in the refining process model. In particular, butane, light olefins, and aromatics are produced in the refinery.

Capacity for each of the blending variables is constrained in the near term. There are three reasons for this:

- First, refining and upgrading capacities are limited to what now exists. Such constraints are not yet crucial for reformate and catalytic cracked naphtha but may already be limiting for alkylates, isomerization of butane, and ethers;
- Second, suitable feedstocks are limited. As the demand barrel lightens, the supply barrel, crude oil, becomes heavier. This trend produces more feed for catalytic cracking and hydrocracking units, which use heavy oil feeds but less naphthas for reformers;
- Finally, several potential blending components compete for the same feedstocks and processes. These conflicts are explained below.

The major quantitative characteristics of the key blending components used in REFORM are shown in Table 13.3. These characteristics help to determine how each of the variables relates to the constraints.

As Table 13.3 shows, the characteristics of some of the key variables differ greatly from one another. The reformates tend to have high aromatics and relatively high levels of olefins while the catalytic cracked naphtha has high olefin levels along with moderate aromatics. Only ETOH and MTBE contain oxygen. As the table shows, RVPs are low in MTBE, the heavy reformates and naphthas, and alkylate, while ethanol and butane have extremely high blending octane values.†

At the present time, the supply of alkylate in the United States is just under 1 million b/d. This component is one of the key elements of reformulated gasolines of the future. In all of the extreme cases, with severe restrictions on aromatics, olefins or RVP, alkylates are required in volumes that surpass their current levels by 50 percent or more. Characteristics of key future blending components are shown in Table 13.4.

---

†Blending values are often different from the value of a fuel in neat use. This is an example of the nonlinearity that characterized gasoline blending. For example, the Alcohol Reference Document shows that the neat RVP of ethanol is 2.3 while the blending RVP ranges from 12 to 27. Similarly, the RON of neat ethanol is 97 while the blending octane ranges from 106 to 118.

Table 13.3. Major characteristics of key blending components

Variable	Aromatics	Olefins	RVP	RON	Oxygen
Full reformate	63%	0.7%	5.3	97.7	0.0
Heavy reformate	87%	0.5%	1.3	104.9	0.0
Full FCCN	29%	29%	7.1	92.1	0.0
Light FCCN	14%	40%	9.9	92.6	0.0
Heavy FCCN	60%	17%	2.6	91.9	0.0
Naphtha	7%	2%	11.5	76.0	0.0
Alkylate	4%	5%	7.5	93.2	0.0
Ethanol	0.0	0.0	23.0	106.0	34%
MTBE	0.0	0.0	7.8	117.0	18%
Butane	3%	0.0	55.0	94.2	0.0

Table 13.4. Major characteristics of key future blending components

Variable	Aromatics	Olefins	RVP	RON	Oxygen
"Lite" reformate	35%	0.5%	5.3	90.0	0.0
Low olefin FCC	40%	15%	3.5	90.5	0.0
Naphtha	4%	5%	7.5	83.0	0.0
ETBE	0.0	0.0	5.0	119.0	16%

Note: The characteristics reported for the "lite" reformate and the low olefin FCCN are just approximations. The actual specifications may differ from one refinery to another. For ETBE, the blending RVP can vary from about 2.5 to 6, depending on its concentration in the gasoline mixture and the ambient temperature.

THE KEY CONSTRAINTS AND THEIR LIMITS

The important government constraints on gasoline composition have been discussed above. This section shows how the regulations affect the overall mix of materials available to the blending pool and what limitations might exist on the constraint values. The major impacts of changing levels of these qualities of gasoline are listed below and explained in detail in the text that follows. There are five important factors that govern the "inherent" emissions qualities of gasoline.

1. *Reid Vapor Pressure* (RVP) shows how easily gasoline can vaporize. In the summer, a high RVP can lead to fuel system problems and "vapor

lock" as well as emissions of hydrocarbons with smog-formation capabilities.

2. *Aromatics* are one of the major building blocks of petrochemicals and are both chemically and biologically active. Reducing aromatics in fuel will lower the atmospheric reactivity of exhausts and refueling emissions.
3. *Olefins,* like aromatics, are a major chemical building block and can combine with sunlight and heat to react in the atmosphere, causing smog.
4. *Benzene* is an animal and human carcinogen found in reformates and added to gasoline for its octane enhancement characteristics.
5. *Oxygen* is an additive that will "lean" out the air:fuel mixture in an engine, thereby creating less carbon monoxide after combustion.

In addition to the pollution considerations, one of the key constraints affecting gasoline is octane. Limiting the use of reformates and cracked naphthas in order to limit aromatics, benzene, and olefins affects the blend's octane numbers as well. Correspondingly, maintaining octane is a key constraint in the model. Evaluations of the significance of these key constraints is discussed below.

Octane. At the present time, the U.S. gasoline pool has an average octane (RON+MON)/2 of about 88.5–89. This range is bracketed by RON values in the 94–96 range and MON values of 83–85. Raising octane levels significantly is not necessary given the characteristics of most modern engines. Mandating large volumes of oxygenates, with their high octane numbers, will lead to an oversupply of octane, provided the requisite oxygenates can be produced.

RVP. At the present time, the summer RVP of the U.S. gasoline pool is between 9.5 and 10. In the winter, that number rises by about 1 point.† It is possible to reduce summer RVP by as much as 1 point, to the 8.75–9.25 range, without significant reformulation of gasoline. At the present time, there are proposals to cut the summer RVP by as much as 2–2.5 points, to the 7.5–8 range. While such a range is possible, given large increases in alkylate levels and even larger proportionate increases in ether supplies, the practical limits of RVP will remain in the 8–8.5 range for the remainder of this decade.‡ In a recent version of California regulations, summer limits of 7.8 and even 7 in high summer have been proposed for the Los Angeles basin. In other parts

---

†In the winter, higher vapor pressure is needed to evaporate the fuel for ignition in cold engines. In fact, commercially available "liquid gas" additives are often just methanol which raises the vapor pressure of the fuel mixture, thereby promoting vaporization and hence, ignition.

‡It is possible to provide very low RVP fuels in small regions, for example, Los Angeles, provided equally low levels are not required elsewhere. In the REFORM runs for California, it was found that a very low vapor pressure fuel could be supplied in the Los Angeles region, provided RVP levels were not controlled elsewhere in the region. To provide a summertime fuel in the 7–7.5 point range throughout the region would require imports of alkylates and ethers, if available, and exports of reformate and naphtha.

of the country, more modest summer limits of 8–9, depending on the region, have been proposed in the Clean Air Act.

Oxygen. A key element of efforts to reduce carbon monoxide levels, especially in older vehicles, is increased use of oxygenates. These fuels also have high blending octanes. As a result, the oxygenates will become key blending components as restrictions on aromatics promote the use of a "lite," lower octane reformate while olefins restrictions reduce the contributions of FCCNs to the gasoline pool.

Oxygen ranges of 0 percent to 4 percent are technically possible, while maintaining drivability. However, drivability is reduced at levels beyond 2–2.5 percent with few improvements in CO levels after that point.† The levels that are used in the model, 1.0, 2.0, 2.7, and 3.1, are important because they are specific oxygen levels that have been inserted into various versions of the Clean Air Act, now in Congressional Conference.

Benzene. This material remains attractive to refiners as an octane additive. Since benzene is formed during catalytic reforming of naphtha, there will be some impetus to reduce the severity of such reforming, thereby reducing the formation of benzene. The octane contributed is not important to the gasoline pool as a whole but is significant for certain refiners. Limits on benzene force them to purchase octane boosters from outside vendors, reducing the profitability of gasoline blending. Benzene levels that are used in REFORM vary from a high of 2.5 percent to a low of 1 percent. Results indicate that for the pool as a whole, levels of 1–1.25 percent are easily achieved. However, individual refiners, especially those lacking alkylation plants, will not be able to provide sufficient volume or octane without benzene.

Aromatics. As discussed above, aromatics are contributed to the gasoline pool largely from reformates. In addition, heavy catalytic naphtha contains significant aromatics levels of 60 percent, and almost 510,000 b/d were used in the United States last year. However, it is the reformate that is the main contributor of aromatics, since aromatics content varies directly with octane number. To reduce aromatics in the U.S. gasoline pool, the contribution from reformates will need to fall significantly. There are various ways to do this:

- Aromatics can be extracted from the reformate, especially the benzene-containing aromatics;
- Benzene precursors in the C5–C6 range can be removed from the naphtha feed;
- The use of reformates can be restricted to something less than their almost 2 Mb/d; or

---

†For an extended discussion of performance and emissions issues, see Section 6 of the Alcohol Fuels Reference Work #1, Meridian Corporation (1990).

- Reformers can be run less severely, producing a less aromatic and lower octane blending component.

Olefins. The main contributor of olefins to the gasoline pool is the FCC naphtha. Both the full range and light FCC naphthas have more than 25 percent olefin content. These compounds are believed to be highly reactive in the atmosphere and now comprise about 16 percent by volume of the nation's gasoline pool. As with reformate, FCC naphthas form such a large part of the overall gasoline pool, at approximately 2.6 million b/d, that reducing the demand for these compounds is not yet feasible with the current demand requirement of over 7 million b/d. Olefin levels in gasoline can be reduced in two ways, in addition to simply not using them.

- New catalysts are available that can reduce olefin levels in FCC naphtha, usually at the expense of octane; and
- Catalysts can select for greater output of light olefins which will then become feedstocks for etherification and alkylation units.

Table 13.5 summarizes current and proposed model constraints affecting emissions.

PRELIMINARY FINDINGS

REFORM has been used to look at winter and summer formulations of gasoline under existing and proposed specifications. The values for the important constraints affecting emissions, RVP, aromatics, olefins, benzene, and oxygen are listed in Tables 13.6 and 13.7. Values for California's SCAQMD are covered in the Annex to this paper. In each version of the model, enough capacity of the requisite sort was provided to ensure a solution. This does not mean that building such capacity will be either possible or economically feasible. Perhaps more important, the gasoline cost figures showing the impacts of the regulations on ex refinery prices should be considered *minimum* values.

Where significant additional capacity must be added, we can expect that costs will increase nonlinearly, unlike the linear assumptions used in RE-FORM. In particular, there are four areas in which costs can be expected to increase quickly as the more extreme values for the important constraints are imposed on the model. These are:

1. Alkylation capacity;
2. Light olefin feedstock and butane isomerization;
3. Ethanol and methanol supply; and
4. Etherification.

Table 13.5. Model constraints affecting emissions: current and proposed

Constraint	Current value	Proposed limit	Notes
Oxygen	0.00	3.1%	Comes from ethanol and MTBE, proposed levels require 6x increase in output or imports.
Olefins	~16%	10%	Reduction means less FCC naphtha in gasoline, more light olefin feedstocks for alkylation and ethers.
Aromatics	~33%	25%	Now produced largely in reforming units and in FCC naphtha, less severe reforming possible but at cost of reduced octane.
Benzene	~2%	~1%	Now added to gasoline for octane and a significant (~4%) element in reformates.
Octane (R + M)/2	~88.5–89	89	Pool will lose octane through losses of reformate and FCCN, more alkylate and ether production will counteract those losses.

Other constraints in the model are concerned with the interplay of various refinery units for producing reformate, alkylate, FCCN, and ethers. These constraints attempt to portray the tradeoffs in feedstocks and processing units for light olefin feedstocks for ethers and alkylation. In addition, REFORM contains a new lower severity reformate ("lite") that has the desirable environmental properties described above.

Table 13.6. Current and proposed winter gasoline standards

Standard	Current	Proposed			
		1	2	3	4
Aromatics (%)	35.0	35.0	30.0	25.0	25.0
Benzene (%)	2.0	2.0	2.0	2.0	1.0
Olefins (%)	16.0	15.0	12.5	10.0	10.0
Oxygen (wt %)	0.0	2.7	2.7	2.7	2.7
RVP (psi)	10.5	10.0	9.5	9.5	9.5

Table 13.7. Current and proposed summer gasoline standards

Standard	Current	Proposed			
		1	2	3	4
Aromatics (%)	35.00	35.00	25.00	25.00	25.00
Benzene (%)	2.00	1.10	2.00	2.00	1.10
Olefins (%)	16.00	10.00	10.00	10.00	10.00
Oxygen (wt %)	0.00	2.00	2.00	2.00	2.00
RVP (psi)	9.50	8.00	8.50	8.50	8.00

One reason that there will be such massive shifts in capacity types is that the types of constraints now embodied in proposed legislation could lead to significant changes in every major current component of gasoline. Given the vastness of the proposed changes in the gasoline pool, it is useful to view Table 13.8 as one of the possible outcomes for implementation of the Clean Air Act.

As Table 13.8 shows, there will be dramatic changes in the composition of gasoline under the currently proposed regulations. Without the regulations, (that is, based on the old Clean Air Act), the REFORM model runs indicated that the composition of gasoline would not change significantly between now and 1995.

In comparing these results with those in the baseline case (no 1991 Clean Air Act), butane use was projected to fall in the summer while MTBE use would increase to as much as 3 percent of the gasoline pool in both summer and winter. Detailed data about both winter and summer gasoline formulations are presented in the Annex. For both the winter and summer formulations, Tables 13.6 and 13.7 show how four different versions of the regulations will affect the composition of gasoline. It is important to note that *these results do not suggest that all of the possible capacity increases are feasible*. Rather, the tables show what changes in capacity will be required to meet the proposed constraints. In the model runs, it is assumed that the price of crude oil is in the range of $22 per barrel (bbl). Other components are priced correspondingly according to netback formulae.

CONCLUSIONS: REFORMULATED GASOLINE
AND U.S. ENERGY POLICY

The numerous runs of the REFORM model in each of the PADDs has provided a superfluity of data on the possible impacts of the Clean Air Act. However, several conclusions have emerged from the mass of model runs.

Table 13.8. Composition of total U.S. gasoline pool: 1990 and 1995

Component	1990 average	1995 winter	1995 summer
Reformate	29.60	19.16	17.92
FCC naphtha	41.10	31.30	29.52
Other naphthas	4.00	7.04	3.27
Alkylate	13.30	19.38	26.01
ETOH	0.56	1.62	0.53
MTBE	1.67	6.83	6.35
Other ethers	0.00	5.44	6.96
Butane	3.49	3.18	0.87

Note that the remainder of the oxygen for winter gasolines will be met by imports of oxygenated gasolines. About 50 percent or more of this MTBE will be imported, assuming it is available.

Other ethers include TAME, ETBE, ETAE, and others and the results assume explicitly that sufficient supplies of methanol and ethanol will be available. If they are not, these levels will not be achieved. REFORM model runs using projected ether capacity along with reformulation requirements of the Clean Air Act yield infeasible solutions, that is, "you can't get there from here."

- The U.S. gasoline pool will undergo a massive restructuring. Refiners will need to replace about 2 million b/d of the current gasoline pool with other materials to meet the new standards. About two-thirds of the material replaced will be reformates and FCC naphthas.
- Large-capacity expansions will be required for oxygenates and alkylation to meet the new formulations. Both materials have the desirable properties of low or moderate RVP, low or no aromatics/benzene, and good octane.
- Gasoline prices may rise by $1.50–4.00 at the wholesale level.
- There may a significant rise in gasoline imports, especially on the East and West Coasts. It is not likely that domestic upgrading capacities can rise quickly enough to provide enough oxygen and low aromatics materials.

However, the impacts that cannot be quantified are more significant than these conclusions. This can be explained by looking at some of the key features of the Clean Air Act as it pertains to the refining industry.

1. There cannot be trades of compliance or standards between or among non-attainment areas.
2. Cost considerations are not valid grounds for granting waivers for non-attainment areas.
3. The falling marginal effectiveness of various blending components, for example, O_2 for reducing carbon monoxide, will not be relevant to de-

termining waivers for non-attainment areas.
4. Other methods of reducing emissions from automobiles are not to be considered as alternatives to fuel reformulation.

This approach to regulation has a number of perverse and costly consequences for the economy. One, the increased reliance on imported finished gasolines has already been noted. However, there are a number of others that are perhaps more serious. The REFORM analysis has shown that it is possible to compare costs of compliance within and among regions and non-attainment areas. And yet, the current legislation makes such comparisons impossible. In other words, it will not be possible under the existing rules for the EPA to grant a small waiver to the Los Angeles region reducing the required oxygen levels in order to provide some winter oxygenate for Anchorage, Alaska, a CO non-attainment area. Such regulatory inflexibility ignores the small change in air quality in Los Angeles compared with a rather larger change in the air quality in Anchorage from a given volume of O_2 in the gasoline.

Numerous studies have indicated that a small proportion of older vehicles are responsible for a disproportionate amount of vehicular air pollution. Moreover, using cleaner-burning fuels for urban fleets can also have a disproportionate effect on air quality. And yet the Clean Air Act implementation of gasoline reformulation ignores the effects of the automobile fleet. Clearly, the Act makes little attempt to minimize the costs of achieving a given reduction in airborne emissions. At the same time, there is no effort to equalize the cost of similar reductions in pollution. Simply put, the Act now ignores the possibly disparate costs of fleet versus fuel supply approaches to pollution reduction.

Lastly, the Clean Air Act gives areas that are currently in compliance with either the summer or winter standards an incentive to "opt-in" to stricter standards, thereby raising the overall costs of compliance regionally or nationwide. For example, if Seattle is currently in compliance with the summer ozone standards, the region may still choose to opt-in to the stricter gasoline standards that apply to the SCAQMD. Such a move is essentially a defensive one for Seattle. By opting for the stricter gasoline formulation, they make sure that highly emissive blending streams go somewhere else. In other words, opting in to the higher air quality standards prevents the SCAQMD from acting like a giant vacuum cleaner with regards to "green" gasolines and blending materials, possibly contributing to a degradation of air quality in areas receiving the rejected blending streams.

As currently constituted, the Clean Air Act promotes a high-cost approach to improving the air quality in non-attainment areas in the United States. The Act specifically ignores elements of regional trading and cost-effectiveness comparisons that would permit more effective and efficient solutions to the pollution problems that plague many areas in the U.S.

ANNEX: APPLICATION OF REFORM TO CALIFORNIA'S SOUTH COAST AIR QUALITY MANAGEMENT DISTRICT

One of the key issues addressed by REFORM is the proposed reformulation of gasoline in California's SCAQMD.

The key element that makes this analysis unique is that the California market, along with the rest of PADD 5, is essentially isolated from the main U.S. refining centers in Texas, Louisiana, the Midwest, and the East Coast. As a result, it should be expected that the optimal solution to the pollution restrictions will differ somewhat from those found in the rest of the nation. In addition, and this is an important qualification, we have looked at cases where the SCAQMD has first call on all "green" blending materials and another case where such other cities as Seattle, San Francisco and a number of other non-attainment areas "opt in" to stricter enforcement. The relevant specifications are shown in Table 13.9.

The specifications that apply to the SCAQMD are different from those which apply to other regions in the United States. In particular, summer RVP standards are 7.8 psi for most of the summer and 7 psi for high summer; maximum winter oxygen is 3.1 percent; and ethanol supplies to PADD 5 are limited to 250 million gallons per year (16,300 b/d).

A first step to winter regulations, reductions in all classes of emissive components, indicates that the least cost formulation will rise by about $1.73/bbl.† More significantly, perhaps, the makeup of the demand barrel also shifts a great deal. Reformate and FCCN decline to about 55 percent of the barrel, while low RVP ethers, ETBE and MTBE would be called to meet about 15 percent of the demand barrel. The large increase in low RVP ethers allows a vast increase in straight naphtha use, to 13.5 percent, and continued use of butane in the mix.

Lowering the winter RVP to 9.5 adds about $0.22/bbl to the formulation and would be expected to show up as an additional $0.01 per gallon at retail. The major differences in formulation are the decline in butane from 3.27 percent of the barrel to 2.05 percent of the barrel and the concomitant increase in reformate to 26.5 percent of the demand barrel. A final possibility, increasing O_2 to 3.1 percent, would further alter the demand barrel, and total reformate and FCCN use would drop to just over 50 percent of the barrel, while straight naphtha use would rise dramatically. These results are in line with ones presented recently for individual refineries and indicate the declining

---

†This translates to about $0.06 at the retail pump.

Table 13.9. Composition of California/PADD 5 gasoline pool: 1990 and 1995 (%)

Component	1990 average	1995 winter	1995 summer
Reformate	28.50	22.50	22.50
FCC naphtha	45.40	29.60	22.90
Other naphthas	2.50	15.00	2.50
Alkylate	6.00	3.75	36.30
ETOH	0.00	0.00	0.00
MTBE	1.67	9.04	8.52
Other ethers	0.00	9.27	9.27
Butane	3.75	2.29	0.00

Note that the remainder of the oxygen for winter gasolines will be met by imports of oxygenated gasolines. About 25 percent or more of this MTBE will be imported, assuming it is available.

Other ethers include TAME, ETBE, ETAE and others and the results assume explicitly that sufficient supplies of methanol and ethanol will be available. If they are not, these levels will not be achieved. REFORM model runs using projected ether capacity along with reformulation requirements of the Clean Air Act yield infeasible solutions.

It is assumed that enough alkylate will be available for summer, perhaps through seasonal storage, as with oxygenates.

role of traditional octane-boosting reformates as benzene and aromatics restrictions are stiffened. In this extreme case, the cost per barrel would rise by $2.23, the equivalent of about $0.08–0.10 per gallon at retail.

With lower RVP in the summer, gasoline costs about $0.02-0.03 per gallon more to produce in comparison to the winter base case. The basic set of specifications for SCAQMD gasolines is expected to raise the cost at the refinery by about $3/bbl over the winter base case.† The formulation will change a great deal as well. Reformate and FCCN will fall from almost 75 percent of the mixture to just over 50 percent. Alkylate will take almost 25 percent of the blend while oxygenates contribute another 12 percent. The use of butane and toluene/xylene will cease in the summer blends.

Extending the basic summer formulation more widely in the region, to the other large cities on the coast, will increase the costs per barrel to $3.29 above the winter base case. With the apparent inability of the region's refineries to meet the demands for oxygenates and alkylate, this specification could be met only if the region were to import about 10 percent of demand, most of that in the form of oxygenated, low aromatic, etc. "green" gasoline. Without such imports the demand for the low emission gasoline cannot be met in the region.

---

†This means an increase of about $0.10 at the retail level.

A final run of the model was made to look at the case of the proposed "high summer" standards of 7 psi for the RVP. This mixture was applied only to the demand in the SCAQMD. The costs of the blend are extremely high, about $5/bbl over the winter base case. The gasoline would need to be completely reformulated so that reformate and FCCN declined to just 45 percent of the barrel while alkylates and oxygenates rose to 49 percent of the barrel.

These results are preliminary. However, they do show that the program of gasoline reformulation that has been proposed for the SCAQMD will have serious implications for investments and costs. At a minimum, the summer program will cost about $0.10 per gallon at retail. Significant additional capacity will need to be built for alkylation and etherification. This in turn will require new isomerization units to handle the surplus butane. The rest of the region will have to absorb a fuel that will have considerably higher levels of aromatics, olefins, and benzene. Application of the summer standards regionally may cost 1.5 to 2 times the application of the standards to the SCAQMD only.

REFERENCES

1. *Oil and Gas Journal,* p. 50 (June 18, 1990).

14 Reformulated Gasoline: A Brief History, a Bright Future

Daniel J. McKay

INTRODUCTION

Two years ago, few could have predicted the development of reformulated gasoline. The very term was not coined until June 1989. It originated in response to President George Bush's original Clean Air Act proposal that would have required methanol-fueled vehicles in severe ozone non-attainment areas. At the time those provisions were written, no one knew what the composition of such a reformulated gasoline would be. Since its appearance in the proposal that President Bush delivered to the nation on June 12, 1989, however, the concept has jolted the imagination of thousands of professionals involved in motor fuels research, refining and marketing around the world. Consumers, oil companies, environmentalists and politicians all have requirements that are being satisfied with the development of a cleaner version of America's most popular and widely accepted motor fuel—gasoline.

On September 1, 1989, Arco Products Company stunned the refining world with its introduction of "EC-1,"[1] a new product designed to reduce ozone smog and carbon monoxide pollution. Since then, nine other major U.S. oil companies have introduced reformulated gasoline products at the retail level, each somewhat different from the others. Because such commercial products do not meet the more stringent provisions of the Clean Air Act amendments, the term "interim reformulated gasoline" was applied to differentiate these first-step rollouts from the more fundamentally altered composition of reformulated gasoline in the years ahead.

Since EC-1, new gasoline products have featured compositions different from the fuels they replaced. Several tactics were adopted in a multitude of combinations: decrease volatility, blend oxygenates, diminish aromatics, reduce sulfur content, adjust the distillation curve, restrict distribution through wide nozzles to target older vehicles. The push to reformulate has already spread to Western Canada and Finland.

Developing these new products has given the industry some valuable experience in the reformulation process. The exercise has also given oil companies a measure of how much more work and investment lie ahead, since none of the products on the market yet meet the 1995 requirements.

Following its introduction of EC-1, Arco has earned praise and recognition from President Bush, U.S. Environmental Protection Agency Administrator William E. Reilly, the California state legislature, the California Air Resources Board (CARB), and General Motors Chairman Roger B. Smith, among others. In accepting the award, George H. Babikian, President of Arco Products Company, said, "EC-1 was not created to expand Arco's market share, but to prove that reformulation could be done."[2]

Producing and distributing the expected volumes of reformulated gasoline that will meet the Clean Air Act Amendments of 1990 will challenge refiners, pipeline companies and gasoline marketers as never before. There are likely to be dislocations and adjustments. For example, the petroleum industry is likely to have problems meeting the 1992 oxygen requirements for CO attainment with methyl tertiary butyl ether (MTBE) and downstream blending of ethanol.[3]

If history is any guide, however, the industry will rise to the occasion. At least some of the survivors of the process will reap profits. Refiners did an excellent job in the 1980s of largely removing tetraethyl lead from the U.S. gasoline market.[4] Most oil companies resisted the lead phasedown program, but the experience changed some attitudes and opinions in corporate board rooms.

Arco and other refiners have proven that gasoline composition can be changed to reduce emissions. Although the extent of further changes needed in the coming years is becoming clearer, getting there will not be easy. The potential rewards, however, are great.[5]

Over the course of two years, major oil companies have introduced "interim" reformulated products in select U.S. markets. Arranged chronologically according to rollout dates, the following sections summarize the properties and availability of these products.

ARCO'S "EC-1"

On September 1, 1989, Arco Products Company introduced EC-1 at 750 Arco stations from San Diego to Santa Barbara. EC-1, with an octane rating of 88 $(R+M)/2$, replaced leaded gasoline in these Southern California markets. Arco produces 28,000 barrels per day (b/d) of EC-1 at its 214,000 b/d Carson refinery in Los Angeles. Arco worked for more than six months to develop the new product and spent between $15 and $20 million, most of it for manufacturing costs, to develop and bring EC-1 to market. Company researchers selected the cleanest refining streams available at Carson, which enabled them to reduce the sulfur content of EC-1 by 80 percent, cut Reid vapor pressure (Rvp) from nine psi to eight psi, halve the benzene content and reduce the other aromatics by one-third. EC-1 has a 1.0 percent (wt.) minimum oxygen content, achieved by blending MTBE at 5.5 percent (vol.). MTBE makes up for octane loss incurred by eliminating tetraethyl lead.

By restricting the distribution of EC-1 to wide gasoline pump nozzles, EC-1 can be used by pre-1975 automobiles and pre-1980 trucks. Arco claimed that by using EC-1, emissions from these vehicles could be cut between 10 and 15 percent, removing an estimated 350 tons a day or more of reactive organic gases, CO, and nitrogen oxides (NO_x) from Southern California's air if every pre-1975 car used EC-1.

New conversion units at the Carson refinery played a key role in producing EC-1. A new 12,000 b/d sulfuric alkylation unit came on stream at Carson, replacing an older 10,000 b/d alkylation unit. In addition, five months after the product was brought to market, Arco commissioned a 1,900 b/d MTBE plant, providing the refinery with an internal source of oxygenate.

Although manufacturing costs to produce EC-1 are one to two cents a gallon higher than those of the leaded gasoline it replaces, Arco has kept the retail price of EC-1 the same as leaded regular. It has long been common practice for California marketers to use leaded gasoline as a "loss leader." Despite the apparent margin-slicing, Arco believes it will make a profit on the product. Arco did not patent the formula for EC-1. Instead, Arco volunteered to share the specifications with any interested refiner, including the Soviet Union.

DIAMOND SHAMROCK'S "RG-87"

In December 1989, Diamond Shamrock R&M introduced "RG-87" in Colorado's Front Range. RG-87 replaced leaded regular at the 77 Diamond Shamrock Corner Stores in Denver, Colorado Springs and along the Front Range of the Rocky Mountains in Colorado. MTBE raised the octane to 87, which is a half number higher than the (R+M)/2 of leaded gasoline sold in those markets.

Diamond Shamrock was the first company to introduce a reformulated gasoline in Colorado. Like Arco's EC-1, Diamond Shamrock's RG-87 is specifically formulated for older cars and trucks that have been using leaded gasoline.

In producing RG-87, Diamond Shamrock eliminates lead and reduces the volatility level and aromatics content. Rvp is reduced by one psi below Colorado's motor fuel requirements and the recently reduced federal level. Lower vapor pressure reduces the potential level of hydrocarbon (HC) emissions that contribute to ozone pollution.

Aromatics were reduced to half the previous level, with a maximum set at 20 percent (vol.). RG-87 contains no detergent package nor a lead-replacement additive for older vehicle engines with soft valve seats. Vehicles able to use the new fuel represent a relatively small percentage of the total number of vehicles in the state. However, recent studies in Denver have concluded that just 10 percent of cars generate about half of all CO emissions.

CONOCO'S "RXL"

In February 1990, Conoco introduced "RXL" a reformulated leaded gasoline seasonally adjusted for Colorado's varied environmental conditions to replace the company's leaded gasoline. From November through February, when the state government's program requires gasoline in the Front Range to be oxygenated, RXL has an oxygen level of 2.5 percent (wt.), achieved by blending MTBE at a level of nearly 15 percent (vol.).

In other months, RXL is not oxygenated. Instead, methylcyclopentadienyl manganese tricarbonyl (MMT) is added for octane quality. The new product, manufactured at its 43,000 b/d refinery in Commerce City, CO, is sold at more than 400 branded service stations throughout the state. The new product retains the same 86.5 octane posting as the leaded gasoline it replaced.

Emissions from vehicles using the new fuel contain less CO, NO_x, hydrocarbons and particulates, all of which contribute to Denver's unique air quality problems that include CO-induced "brown cloud" in the winter and ozone pollution in the summer. Like Arco's EC-1 in Southern California and Diamond Shamrock's RG-87 in Colorado, RXL is sold through wide-nozzle pumps for use in cars designed to run on leaded gasoline.

Seasonal adjustments to the reformulated gasoline include a 25 percent increase in oxygen content during the winter and a reduction of the Rvp to 8.5 psi during the summer. The lower summertime Rvp is one psi below the federal limit of 9.5 psi. The new gasoline will have a year-round base formula that reduces aromatics and contains DuPont's phosphorus-based "ValveMaster" lead-substitute additive. Conoco is a wholly-owned subsidiary of DuPont. Even if Conoco had not restricted distribution of RXL to wide pump nozzles, the new fuel could not be considered unleaded; EPA regulations ban phosphorus in unleaded gasoline because phosphorus poisons catalytic converters.

Conoco later began offering a separate reformulated unleaded regular gasoline, as well as its RXL leaded reformulated product, in Yellowstone National Park and other parts of Montana and Wyoming. They are produced at the company's 48,500 b/d refinery in Billings, MT.

The new unleaded regular product, like RXL, features a lower aromatics content and a Reid vapor pressure below the EPA's volatility limits. The products are available at roughly 100 Conoco branded service stations. Conoco has been the sole supplier of motor fuels in Yellowstone for nearly 75 years.

PHILLIPS' "SUPERCLEAN UNLEADED PLUS"

In February 1990, Phillips 66 Company introduced "SuperClean Unleaded Plus," a reformulated 87-octane midgrade gasoline in Colorado's Front Range. In April, a somewhat different version of the product was introduced in metropolitan St. Louis, along with the announcement of a test program to measure emissions reductions.

Unlike the "interim" reformulated products from Arco, Diamond Shamrock and Conoco, neither version of SuperClean Unleaded Plus is reserved for pre-catalytic converter vehicles designed for leaded gasoline. Although the Colorado product is provided on an exchange basis from Diamond Shamrock, Phillips produces the St. Louis product itself at its 105,000 b/d refinery in Borger, TX.

Phillips eliminated leaded gasoline and replaced it with an unleaded midgrade. In St. Louis, SuperClean Unleaded Plus contains 20 to 30 percent less olefins and aromatics and 35 percent less benzene than the average gasoline sold in St. Louis. It also features at least 2.0 percent (wt.) oxygen provided by MTBE, maximum aromatics content of 20 percent (vol.), maximum benzene content of one percent and a summertime Rvp of 8.5 psi. The fuel is sold at 125 branded service stations in the seven-county metropolitan St. Louis area. It is priced between regular unleaded and premium unleaded. Phillips is considering long-range plans to produce a reformulated product at all three company refineries. Phillips is currently building a 7,500 b/d dehydrogenation-based MTBE plant at its Borger, TX refinery.

MARATHON'S "AMARACLEAN"

In March 1990, Marathon Petroleum Company became the first in the nation to offer a full slate of reformulated gasolines: the "Amaraclean" product lineup in the Detroit metropolitan area.[6] The Amaraclean product slate, which is marketed through 161 branded service stations, consists of 87-octane "Milemaker Unleaded," 89-octane "Extra-M Plus" and 92-octane "Super-M Premium." All three products are MTBE blends with reduced aromatics and lower Rvp. The cleaner-burning gasolines, specially refined and blended at Marathon's 68,500 b/d Detroit refinery, are formulated to be particularly effective in pre-1981 vehicles which have less sophisticated emission control systems.

Amaraclean gasolines have a summer Rvp of 9.5 psi and a winter Rvp of 13 psi. These volatility levels are one psi below the EPA specification and about one-half psi below the industry average. Aromatics in the new gasolines have been reduced 16 percent. With a limit of 25 percent, the Amaraclean line has the lowest aromatics content of any gasolines now available. The average oxygen content of the reformulated gasolines is 1.8 percent, achieved by blending an average of 10 percent MTBE. The MTBE is produced at a new

900 b/d unit at the company's Detroit refinery. With lower Rvp, evaporative pollution is reduced, lessening the formation of ground-level ozone. The company estimates that HC emissions are being reduced by 20 percent and CO emissions by 14 percent.

SHELL'S "SU-2000E"

In April 1990, Shell Oil Company implemented a 10-city rollout of "SU 2000E," a premium-grade "interim" gasoline. SU-2000E is a 92-93-octane product that contains at least 5.5 percent (vol.) MTBE and has a Rvp lower than upcoming state and federal summer volatility specifications.

The 10 cities supplied with the new product are Washington, D.C., and the nine cities defined as severe ozone non-attainment areas: Los Angeles, New York, Chicago, Philadelphia, Houston, San Diego, Baltimore, Hartford, CT, and Milwaukee, WI. SU 2000E is manufactured at four Shell refineries: Norco, LA, Deer Park, TX, Wood River, IL, and Wilmington, CA. Company executives project sales of the new product in 10 markets to exceed 83,300 b/d: between 35 and 40 percent of the company's total premium gasoline sales nationwide. Company literature accompanying the introduction of SU-2000E used the term "environmentally enhanced" rather than "reformulated" to describe the new gasoline.

Some controversy accompanied Shell's rollout. Compared to the four reformulated products then on the market, SU 2000E made the fewest compositional changes from conventional unleaded gasoline. Unlike all four previously introduced "interim" reformulated gasolines, Shell made no reductions in aromatics or olefins. Also, Shell's unreformulated SU 2000 premium unleaded gasoline already contained roughly between two percent (vol.) and five percent (vol.) MTBE in certain areas of the United States, primarily in PADD I.

Shell officials stressed the broad geographic scale and unprecedented significant volumes available, rather than the degree of alteration to their fuel's composition. Company officials declined to disclose the added production cost, but outside estimates place the cost at roughly one cent a gallon higher than the cost to manufacture unreformulated SU 2000. Modeling studies performed by Systems Applications, Inc. show that 80 fewer tons of hydrocarbons and CO would be emitted into the air nationwide when Shell customers use the new product.

EXXON'S "SUPREME," "EXTRA," AND "PLUS"

In April 1990, Exxon Company, U.S.A. announced "interim" reformulated versions of its premium and midgrade products in more than 40 major markets, first along the East and Gulf Coasts, then on the West Coast. The new versions of 93 (R+M)/2 "Supreme" and 92-octane "Extra" are Exxon's premium products; "Plus" is Exxon's 89-octane midgrade. These products feature reduced Rvp and, in the New York and Los Angeles metropolitan areas, are blended with 5.5 percent (vol.) MTBE to help alleviate year-round CO problems. As with Shell's SU-2000E, Exxon made no reductions in aromatics or olefins.

Refining and marketing analysts said Exxon's announcement, following a similar announcement by Shell, brought to a boil a simmering controversy about what qualifies as reformulation. Although the new gasolines cost more to produce, the wholesale price for these products is competitive with other premium and midgrade gasolines.

In June 1990, Exxon started shipping reformulated 93-octane Supreme and 89-octane Plus from its 455,000 b/d refinery in Baton Rouge, LA. At the same time, Exxon started rolling out the new products from its 493,000 b/d refinery in Baytown, TX. Also in mid-June, Exxon introduced lower Rvp Extra in Montana, Northern Idaho, and Eastern Washington. In New York and Los Angeles, where the new products are oxygenated all year, company officials estimate a seven percent reduction in CO emissions from a typical automobile. MTBE is supplied through the company's 3,000 b/d chemical division and by spot and contract purchases. Because Spokane, WA, is a "serious" CO non-attainment area, Exxon blends 5.5 percent (vol.) MTBE in Extra sold there from November through March.

The reformulated Supreme and Plus are manufactured at three locations: Baytown, TX, Baton Rouge, LA, and at the company's 120,000 b/d refinery in Linden, NJ. The new Extra delivered to metropolitan San Francisco, Sacramento and Reno is produced at Exxon's 128,000 b/d refinery in Benicia, CA. The base fuel for the new Extra delivered to Los Angeles is produced by Ultramar at its 41,600 b/d refinery, then blended with 5.5 percent (vol.) MTBE at the terminal. The Rvp of Exxon's reformulated Extra averages 8.1 psi—a half-pound lower than the California summer industry average. California's summer Rvp limit is nine psi.

Company officials claim to be the leading producer of reduced emissions gasolines, since the lower-Rvp products are available in more than 40 markets from coast to coast. Exxon estimates sales of the new versions of these new products to be nearly 190,000 b/d, more than half of the company's branded gasoline sales in these markets.

CHEVRON'S "SUPREME"

In June 1990, Chevron U.S.A. Inc. introduced a reformulated version of its 92-octane "Supreme" in Los Angeles, San Diego and Santa Barbara, CA.

In addition to reducing Rvp to a range between 8.0 and 8.5 psi and blending a minimum of five percent (vol.) of MTBE, the new product features a tailored distillation curve for improved drivability.[7] According to company officials, this provides motorists with smoother performance in the warm-up phase for vehicles that experience stumbling, hesitation or stalling. The tailored distillation curve of the new Supreme, however, diminishes the refinery's gasoline output.

Chevron did not specify other changes, such as a reduction in aromatics content. Company officials maintain that studies of the impact of aromatics on ozone smog formation are inconclusive. A recent two-car test conducted jointly with the California Air Resources Board (CARB) indicated that reducing aromatics did not lower emissions of HC, CO, or NO_x. Others disagree. Emissions tests performed by Arco Chemical Company, Ethyl Corporation and others link aromatics reductions directly to a measurable reduction in NO_x and CO.

Chevron maintains that reducing vapor pressure will certainly lower HC emissions. Carbon monoxide emissions are reduced and the octane level is maintained by adding a minimum of 5.5 percent (vol.) of MTBE, or about one percent (wt.) oxygen.

ARCO'S "EC-PPREMIUM"

On September 6, 1990, a year after introducing EC-1, Arco Products Company introduced "EC-PPremium." The new 92-octane gasoline replaced Arco's 91-octane "Super Unleaded" gasoline at more than 700 branded retail outlets in California markets from Santa Barbara to San Diego. Like EC-1, the new product is made at the company's refinery in Carson, CA, where between 18,000 and 20,000 b/d are produced. The benzene content is one percent (vol.), overall aromatics are limited to 25 percent (vol.), and it contains 8.25 percent MTBE. The benzene level is 63 percent below the average reported for all premium gasolines in a Motor Vehicle Manufacturers Association survey of the Los Angeles area.

Arco called the fuel the "cleanest burning" gasoline available in Southern California. Compared to conventional unleaded premium, Arco said the new fuel reduced emissions of cancer-causing benzene by 36 percent, carbon monoxide by 28 percent and smog-forming hydrocarbons by 21 percent. Refinery processing changes reduce the amount of benzene produced by up to 12,600 gallons a day. Arco has also reduced total aromatics and olefins, a group of chemical components that react in the presence of sunlight to form smog, by 25 percent. In addition, Arco has lowered vapor pressure by one psi below the California state standard.

Tests show that EC-PPremium generates 28 percent less carbon monoxide, 21 percent less exhaust hydrocarbons and 36 percent less evaporative emissions than conventional premium gasoline. Arco's tests showed that the introduction of EC-PPremium will reduce emissions by 86,000 pounds (43 tons) a day.

Other tests, however, indicated that the new 92-octane product produces a 34 percent increase in emissions of 1,3-butadiene, a suspected carcinogen, from some of the feedstock sent to the fluid catalytic cracking (FCC) unit. Arco confirmed the butadiene results but said the 9.8 percent nitrogen oxide increase was based on unreliable data. Independent researchers said that even with a 34 percent increase, the 1,3-butadiene concentrations were too small to be significant. Arco researchers claim that despite the butadiene, EC-PPremium reduces overall pollutants enough that the overall cancer risk is down by 28 percent.[8]

AMOCO'S "ULTIMATE," "SILVER," AND "REGULAR"

On November 1, 1990, Amoco Oil Company introduced a reformulated product slate in Washington, D.C. and surrounding states. The Amoco lineup is the only one to meet the 1992 requirements of the Clean Air Act Amendments of 1990. Amoco timed its rollout to closely coincide with the passage of the amendments.

The product slate is available at roughly 250 branded service stations from Baltimore to Roanoke, VA. Amoco is the leading gasoline marketer in these areas, with an estimated 20 percent market share.

All grades of Amoco gasoline sold in this region feature reduced vapor pressure (9 Rvp during summer months), 0.8 percent (wt.) average benzene content, and contain 30 percent (vol.) aromatics, or less, on an annual average basis. Amoco will add 15 percent (vol.) MTBE to its gasolines in winter months to address the area's carbon monoxide levels.

Company executives anticipate capital investments of up to $2 billion for future refinery modifications to produce gasolines that comply with the 1990 Clean Air Act Amendments.

CHEVRON CANADA'S "SUPREME" AND "SUPREME PLUS"

Chevron Canada recently introduced two interim reformulated gasolines into southwestern British Columbia.

The two highest octane products of the four grades on the company's product slate now feature a reduced Reid vapor pressure (Rvp), a one percent (wt.) oxygen content provided by blending methyl tertiary butyl ether (MTBE), and an adjusted distillation curve to improve the drivability index. The new products, 94-octane (R+M)/2 "Supreme Plus" and 92-octane "Supreme," are produced at the company's 40,000 b/d refinery in Burnaby, B.C., near Vancouver.

Chevron Canada's two other grades, 87.5-octane "Regular" and 89.5-octane "Regular Plus," are unchanged unleaded gasolines. All gasoline sold in Canada is unleaded. The government has banned lead since December 1, 1990,

although leaded gasoline largely disappeared from the marketplace months
before the law took effect.

The new Supreme and Supreme Plus are available at about 150 branded
retail stations in Greater Vancouver/Fraser Valley and on Vancouver Island.
This represents more than half of the company's retail outlets. The lower Fraser
Valley has Canada's second-worst summer ozone pollution problems, after
Windsor, Ontario.

NESTE'S "CITY GASOLINE"

In early June, 1991, Neste Oil introduced a new reformulated gasoline in
southern Finland. The new product, called "City Gasoline," will produce lower
levels of aromatic compounds, benzene and sulfur than conventional gasolines. City Gasoline features a two percent (wt.) oxygen content achieved by
blending MTBE. Company officials estimate the MTBE content reduces carbon monoxide emissions by 15 percent on average. Total exhaust emissions
from vehicles using the gasoline would be cut by up to 20 percent, Neste estimated, adding that unburned hydrocarbon emissions would be cut by about
10 percent. Neste claims to be the first company in Europe to introduce a
gasoline containing a two percent (wt.) oxygen content, though similar
products have been available in the United States for a number of years.

The new fuel will initially be available only in southern Finland but could
be exported later. City Gasoline is produced at Neste's 243,000 b/d refinery
in Porvoo, Finland in both leaded and unleaded versions. The leaded products
will have octane levels of 97 and 99 (RON); the unleaded products will have
octane levels of 95 and 98 (RON).

SUN'S "SUNOCO-CL"

Sun Refining & Marketing Co. in June 1991 began introducing partially
reformulated gasolines at 141 Sunoco stations in the Baltimore-Washington
area. The new gasolines, named "Sunoco-CL," feature increased oxygenate
contents and limited levels of benzene. According to Sun officials, the introduction is a first step towards meeting the fuel composition requirements of the
1990 Clean Air Act Amendments.

In the Baltimore-Washington area, Sunoco's premium 94-octane "Ultra"
gasoline, already high in oxygen content, will not drop below the 1995 summertime requirement for two percent (wt.) oxygen. The oxygen content of
Sunoco's partially-reformulated 86-octane "Economy" is increased to one
percent, thereby also boosting the oxygen content of "Regular," "Plus," and
"Super," the three intermediate grades blended from Ultra and Economy via
the company's patented "Sundial" blending pump.

The new products are refined at Sun's 170,000 b/d refinery in Marcus Hook, PA, where the company commissioned a 2,500 b/d MTBE plant in 1989. Benzene levels in all grades of the new gasolines are limited to two percent and all grades have an additive that meets the 1995 requirements of the Clean Air Act. According to company executives, the use of oxygenates reduces emissions of both unburned hydrocarbons and carbon monoxide. The Sunoco-CL gasolines are to be priced the same as comparable non-reformulated Sunoco gasolines, even though they cost from two to five cents a gallon more to make. The company had made preliminary plans in the summer of 1990 for an introduction of an interim reformulated product in September, but the August 2 invasion of Kuwait and related gasoline price spike delayed the plan.

FORECASTS FOR THE 1990S

In this decade, a sizable share of the U.S. gasoline will be oxygenated as a result of the Clean Air Act Amendments. Oxygen-rich refiners and marketers will therefore have an economic advantage over those refiners in short supply. Table 14.1 shows a projection of the growth of reformulated gasoline through the decade.

Refiners and merchant oxygenate producers are making an all-out effort to build added capacity for MTBE and TAME. Fuel ethanol will supplement the oxygen available from these ethers. Ethyl tertiary butyl ether (ETBE), until now an oxygenate produced in a pilot plant and in test batches, may be manufactured on a commercial scale. Other forecasts include the following:

- by 1995, refiners will need over 230,000 b/d of MTBE and 120,000 b/d of ethanol to meet oxygenated fuel demand (assuming that the market for oxygenates is split evenly between ethanol and MTBE in carbon monoxide non-attainment areas, and split 65 percent MTBE/35 percent ethanol in ozone non-attainment areas under ideal distribution conditions);
- the heavy demand for oxygenates will reactivate studies of alternative compounds for blending and for cosolvents of methanol;
- more oil companies may invest in fuel ethanol production. Texaco is a joint venture partner in Pekin Energy Company and Ashland is a joint venture partner in South Point Ethanol. Fuel ethanol formulation may be attractive because it provides higher levels of oxygen per blended gallon. Arizona-based oil refiner Giant Industries, Inc., bought ethanol producer Portales Energy in May;[10]
- as much as 60,000–80,000 b/d of tertiary amyl methyl ether (TAME) units will be added to U.S. refinery operations by 1995 to help meet oxygen requirements. The first several of these units were announced in late April and early May (see, for example, Ref. 11);

Table 14.1. U.S. gasoline volumes affected by Clean Air Act legislation (b/d)

Year	Carbon monoxide areas	Extreme and severe ozone areas	Marginal and moderate ozone "opt in" areas	Gasoline sold in non-attainment areas
1992	392,485	0	0	392,485
1993	767,599	0	0	767,599
1994	773,359	0	0	773,359
1995	779,159	1,183,973	0	1,963,131
1996	785,003	1,192,851	391,389	2,369,243
1997	790,894	1,201,794	782,779	2,775,466
1998	796,823	1,210,809	1,174,168	3,181,800
1999	802,798	1,219,889	1,565,558	3,588,245
2000	808,819	1,229,041	1,956,947	3,994,808

Source: Information Resources, Inc., Washington, D.C.

- U.S. refineries will need to produce more hydrogen from sources other than the catalytic reforming unit. The need to reduce aromatics in gasoline will call for less severe reformer operations, which will reduce hydrogen output from reforming. In addition, the distillate side of the barrel will require more hydrogen for desulfurization and possibly aromatics removal;
- gasoline imports to the United States, which have provided a crucial share of the East Coast's supply, are likely to decrease as European refineries are pressed to produce unleaded gasoline in ever greater quantities; and
- some incremental expansion of processing capacity will occur at existing refineries, but new refineries are unlikely to be built in the United States because of the huge capital outlays required and the difficulties in obtaining permits to build them.

REFERENCES

1. "Arco Preparing California's First 'Clean Gasoline,'" *Octane Week* (Aug. 14, 1989).
2. "Arco Executives Receive Honor for First Reformulated Gasoline," *Octane Week,* (April 2, 1990).
3. G. H. Unzelman, F. L. Potter, J. E. Peeples et al., "The Impact of the Clean Air Act on Motor Fuels: An Analysis of Reformulated Fuels and Oxygenates, 1990–2000," Information Resources, Inc., Washington, D.C. (1991).
4. G. H. Unzelman, "Oxygenates in Gasoline—The '90 Decade," *NPRA Paper AM-91-46,* NPRA Annual Meeting, San Antonio, Texas (March 17–19, 1991).
5. G. H. Unzelman, "Environmental Problems Will Unleash Opportunities in the 1990s," *Octane Week* (Dec. 11, 1989).
6. "Marathon to Reformulate Whole Slate in Detroit Area," *Octane Week* (March 19, 1990).
7. "Chevron Rolls Out New Reformulated 'Supreme'," *Octane Week* (June 18, 1990).
8. "Smog Drop Outweighs Higher Butadiene in New Arco Fuel," *Octane Week* (Oct. 1, 1990).
9. "Sun Announces 'Sunoco-CL' Interim Reformulated Slate," *Octane Week* (May 6, 1991).
10. "Refiner Buys Portales Energy's New Mexico Ethanol Plant," *Oxy-Fuel News* (May 13, 1991).
11. "Exxon Poised for Huge Growth in TAME Production," *Octane Week* (May 13, 1991).

15 The DFI World Gas Trade Program for Analysis of Worldwide and Regional Natural Gas Trade

Robert A. Marshalla, Dale M. Nesbitt, and Ralph D. Samuelson

INTRODUCTION

The Decision Focus Incorporated (DFI) World Gas Trade Program has been designed to provide insights into, and improved ability to forecast, worldwide and regional natural gas markets over the coming decades. The World Gas Trade Program is a private multi-client activity performed by DFI and The Canadian Energy Research Institute (CERI) over the past year. The centerpiece of the program has been the development of the World Gas Trade (WGT) Model, a large-scale, market equilibrating model of regional and worldwide natural gas and LNG markets, designed to forecast the following quantities over time:

- gas prices (from wellhead to burnertip);
- production levels;
- consumption; and
- interregional gas flows (pipeline and ship);

in all major producing and consuming regions and over all major pipeline corridors and LNG routes in the world. The model distinguishes over 40 supply regions and 25 demand regions and spans a forty-year time horizon into the future. The key feature of the model is its ability to generate forecasts of *market clearing* natural gas prices and volumes, given input data on resource costs and availabilities, transportation costs, and worldwide demand functions for natural gas and competing fuels. It is, as far as we know, the first and only model of its kind.

Amoco
Chevron
California Energy Commission
Enron Gas Liquids
Esso Resources Canada
Exxon
Fina Oil and Chemical Company
Phillips Petroleum
Texaco
Shell Canada

Fig. 15.1. World Gas Trade Program: Phase 1 sponsors.

Phase 1 of the World Gas Trade Program, completed in October 1991, has produced the following products:

- the World Gas Trade Model, running on "plain vanilla" workstation and PC environments;
- a comprehensive World Gas data base that includes supply, transportation, demand, interfuel competition, government policy, and other elements;
- a rather comprehensive analysis of world gas issues using the model and data base; and
- reports and private briefings to program sponsors.

Phase 1 of the program has required approximately one year of effort and has been sponsored by the major North American producing entities indicated in Fig. 15.1. Phase 2, scheduled to begin in early 1992, will include a much broader spectrum of sponsors, expanding to other regions of the world (e.g., Europe and the Pacific Rim) and other industry segments (e.g., pipelines, service companies, and LNG-related companies).

PURPOSE

The World Gas Trade Program is designed to address issues of direct interest and business relevance to sponsors as well as to provide them with a lasting and expandable modeling capability to address emerging issues in the future. The most general statement of the program purpose is to forecast intra- and inter-regional natural gas prices, flow volumes, and capacity additions, including pipelines, LNG facilities, and gas reserve capacities. Fig. 15.2 illustrates.

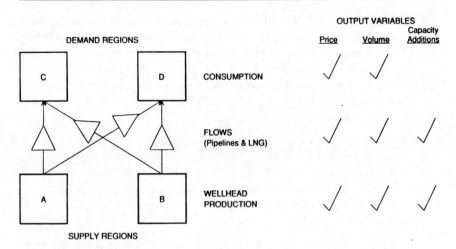

Fig. 15.2. Forecasting.

Among the more concrete *forecasting issues* addressed are the following:

* Prices
  - When will gas prices start rising? How fast?
  - Will LNG be the "backstop" in the U.S.?
* Trade
  - Will natural gas develop a world market?
  - What levels of imports and exports are likely in each region?
    . . .from whom?   . . .to whom?
* Displacement
  - What traditional supply sources and pipeline routes will be displaced by new sources and routes?
  - To what extent will gas displace oil as an industrial boiler fuel?
* Capacity Expansion
  - Where will economic forces be brought to bear for capacity expansions/additions including reserve additions, pipelines, and LNG facilities?

One of the key issues the program has been designed to address is the mid-term (5–10 years) and long-term (beyond 10 years) prospect for *world LNG trade*. At present, there are several nearly independent and rather Balkanized continental natural gas markets. Will they remain so? Will LNG trade grow in importance, thereby rendering gas a true world-scale market? If so, when?

To address such questions, we have begun with a carefully defined "pure economics" reference case: What is the logical end point toward which pure market forces might drive the world gas market. To wit, if competitive markets prevailed worldwide with no insurmountable political or infrastructure constraints, what would be the nature and timing of LNG's role in world energy markets? A pure economic case such as this has proven an ideal benchmark or reference case over which to superpose logical political or infrastructural considerations and to understand whether those considerations are likely to be sustainable and to evolve over time. Obviously, there are factors of critical importance beyond pure market forces shaping the future of LNG, including, for example:

- siting constraints for new/expanded facilities;
- trade policy constraints;
- LNG treated as a by-product of oil production or as a government policy instrument to achieve national oil or energy objectives; and
- environmental factors (methanol fueled transportation, global warming policies, air quality objectives).

Some of these factors will impede and some may accelerate development of worldwide LNG trade. The WGT Model is designed to examine the individual and collective effects of such factors and to determine how and whether they will distort the pure economic solution.

As an example of economic and policy issues the WGT Model has been used to address, consider that *electric generation,* including generation by utilities, cogenerators and other independent power producers, is seen by many as the greatest potential short- to mid-term source of gas demand growth in North America and Europe.

The WGT model has segregated electric generation customers from other noncore customers and represents competition between gas and oil, and between gas/oil based generation and other types of generation (e.g., coal, nuclear). In Phase 2 of the program, we will be exploring alternative electric generation scenarios in different countries, based both on differing economic and policy assumptions.

In addition to topical studies of issues like the roles of LNG trade and electric generation, sponsors gain a great deal of insight from straightforward sensitivity analysis. Some of the key variables driving the WGT Model are highly uncertain, and no model can eliminate that uncertainty. But the WGT Model structure presents an excellent vehicle for examining the ramifications of alternative outcomes of these variables. Some of the key variables for which we have or are performing sensitivity analyses are:

- level and cost of undiscovered recoverable gas (most interestingly, region by region, rather than for the world as a whole);
- world oil prices;
- capacity constraints (on both existing and potential new pipelines and LNG facilities);

- LNG "supply chain" costs (the total cost of liquefying, transporting and regasifying LNG); and
- demand growth (by region and worldwide).

The number of topics to which we can contribute insight with the WGT model and data base is large. *Future topics* for Phase 2 or later and/or individual sponsor studies include the following:

- global warming, air emissions policies;
- natural gas transportation scenarios—LNG, methanol, MTBE;
- Soviet development and modernization;
- trade policies;
- technological progress scenarios;
- profitability-by-region study;
- producer government development policies,
  - Middle East,
  - Nigeria,
  - Algeria,
  - Norway,
  - USA (re: Alaska);
- Consumer government energy policies,
  - Japan,
  - Korea,
  - Taiwan,
  - USA,
  - European Community (EC).

THE MODEL

Model Structure

The World Gas Trade Model is implemented within DFI's Generalized Equilibrium Modeling Software (GEMS) modeling system. GEMS permits users to construct and modify model structure by connecting process models together to form a network. Network changes to increase or decrease scope, complexity, or level of detail are easy to make. Model structure for GEMS-based models is most effectively communicated in terms of hierarchical network diagrams that graphically illustrate the actual network connections in the software.

At the highest level, the WGT Model is divided into eight global regions, such as North America and Africa, that span the entire world. The WGT global regions, along with the actual and potential trade routes between them,

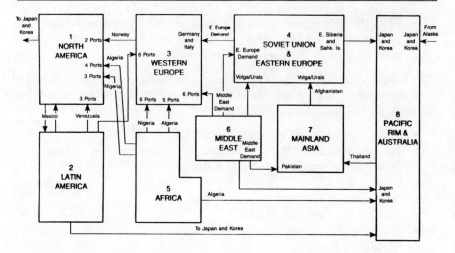

Fig. 15.3. Global regions and trade routes.

are indicated in Fig. 15.3.† In a hierarchical network, within each region or box resides a more detailed network diagram enumerating the sub-regions or activities represented within that region or box. For example, Fig. 15.4 shows the next level of network structure inside the Western Europe global region. Notice that supply and demand regions are distinguished individually. In some situations, supply and demand regions represent the same physical area, such as the United Kingdom supply and the United Kingdom demand regions. In other situations, they do not. For example, Norway is important enough to be distinguished as a separate supply region, but Norway's demand is included in the more aggregate "other Western Europe" demand region. Altogether, Western Europe is subdivided into five supply regions:

- United Kingdom;
- Norway;
- Netherlands;
- other EC;
- other non-EC Countries;

---

†The North American region has been represented by incorporating the previous stand-alone model known as the North American Regional Gas (NARG) Model into the WGT network. The NARG Model has been in widespread practical use for years in the U.S. and Canada at nearly 30 oil and gas companies, research institutes (like the Gas Research Institute, which originally sponsored its development) and government agencies.

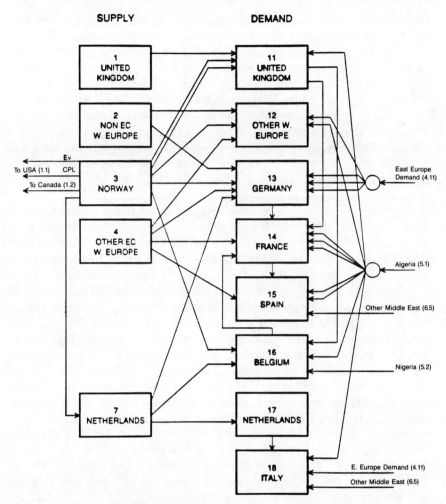

Fig. 15.4. 3—Western Europe.

and subdivided into eight demand regions:

- United Kingdom;
- Germany;
- France;
- Spain;
- Belgium;
- Netherlands;
- Italy; and
- other Western Europe.

The arrows between the various regions represent the existing and prospective future pipeline and LNG routes flowing between the various regions in the WGT Model. Arrows pointing out of the region at the left of the page in Fig. 15.4 represent export flows to other regions, while arrows pointing into the region at the right edge of the page represent imports from other regions. A similar country-level network diagram for the global region entitled "Pacific Rim and Australia" in Fig. 15.3 is shown in Fig. 15.5. A complete set of network diagrams for all of the global regions shown on Fig. 15.3 can be found in Appendix A. For simplicity, the country-level network diagrams in Figs. 15.4 and 15.5 suppress most of the LNG liquefaction and regasification related network structure in the WGT Model. This structure is shown in full detail in the appendix, however.

Inside each of the countries or sub-regions shown in the second level network diagrams is yet another level of network structure. This is the final, most detailed level of network structure in the model. The geometric figures in these diagrams correspond to GEMS "process models" (i.e., subroutines) that represent technological processes and producer or consumer behavior.

Intuitively speaking, process models correspond to industrial activities or consumption activities present within the given region of the world. For example, consider the Indonesia supply sub-region pictured in Fig. 15.5. The detailed network structure inside that sub-region is displayed in Fig. 15.6. At this final level of network structure, our convention is that hexagon-shaped figures represent wellhead production† of natural gas in a given location using a given technology. We see that Indonesia is divided into eight producing sub-regions. Triangles represent natural gas transportation, either via pipeline or LNG tanker. We see that gas is transported into the Indonesia supply region from Thailand. Circles represent markets, or "market allocation" activities, where multiple supply sources compete for market share based on price and other limiting factors such as infrastructure and existing contracts. Finally, the arrows leaving the market allocation activity show that gas produced in Indonesia, or shipped in from Thailand, can go to four places: new or existing liquefaction facilities, the Malaysia region (box 2 in Fig. 15.5), or the ASEAN countries (represented in aggregate as demand region 11 in Fig. 15.5). All of the nearly 60 bottom level supply regions in the model have a network structure similar to that shown for Indonesia, although the number of activities in each varies.

Fig. 15.7 shows where the liquefaction bound links in Fig. 15.6 go. We see that after liquefaction, the LNG can be shipped to regasification facilities in Japan, Korea or Taiwan. Some LNG sources can be transported to far more destinations. For example, LNG from Algeria can be shipped to 13 different regasification facilities.

---

†Actually, it represents the whole cycle of exploration, development and production.

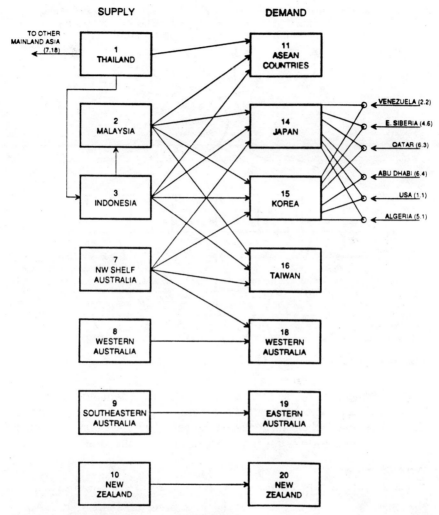

Fig. 15.5. 8—Pacific Rim and Australia.

A sample ultimate-level demand region is presented in Fig. 15.8, which represents the Germany demand region within the Western Europe global region. The network structure of this demand region is representative of the network structure in most of the four dozen or so demand regions in the model. At the lower left of the figure we see that gas can enter Germany from seven different sources. When gas reaches the market allocation labeled "1 - Gas Allocation" it is at the level of city gate delivery. From there it can be distributed to three different customer segments. Demand by customer seg-

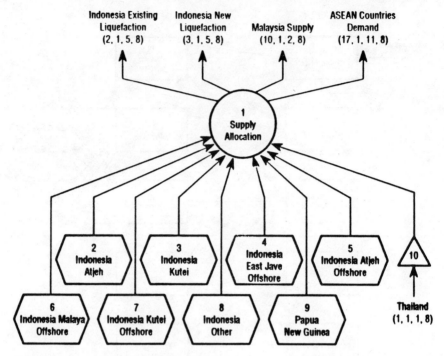

Fig. 15.6. Indonesia supply (1,3,8).

ment is represented by the tombstone shaped "final demand" activities at the top of the exhibit. We see that there are three customer groupings: core demand (for which there are no reasonable gas substitutes), non-core demand (where oil can substitute for gas), and electricity generation.

Network Structure

The network structure in the North America region is a little different than the others, because we incorporated the pre-existing stand-alone North American Regional Gas (NARG) Model directly into the WGT Model. North America has one additional level of network hierarchy compared to the other regions. It is subdivided first into the United States and Canada. This breakdown is shown in Fig. 15.9, where we also can see all of the potential pipeline and LNG import and export flows for each country, including gas flows between the United States and Canada. Individual supply and demand sub-regions are at the next level of network hierarchy inside both the United States and Canada. They are listed in Figs. 15.10 and 15.11, where we see there are 28 such regions in the United States and 10 in Canada. Because there are so many demand and supply regions in North America, we have found it easier to dis-

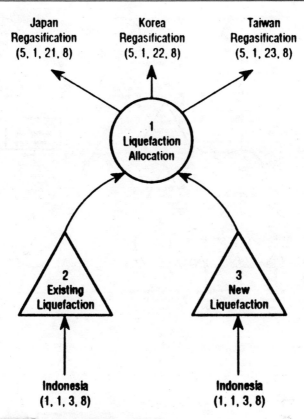

Fig. 15.7. Indonesia liquefaction (1,5,8).

play their pipeline interconnections with a map-like diagram, as shown in Fig. 15.12, instead of the conventional GEMS network diagrams we have presented in previous exhibits.

The ultimate level network diagrams showing the network structure inside each supply and demand region in North America, as well as in the other global regions, are too lengthy to include here, but they are readily available from the model developer.†

Model Data

The input data and assumptions comprising the World Gas Trade model's data base can be grouped into three general categories:

---

†The authors may be contacted at Decision Focus Incorporated for this or other additional information about the WGT Program: telephone (415) 960-3450; FAX (415) 960-3656; address: 4984 El Camino Real, Los Altos, CA 94022, U.S.A.

232

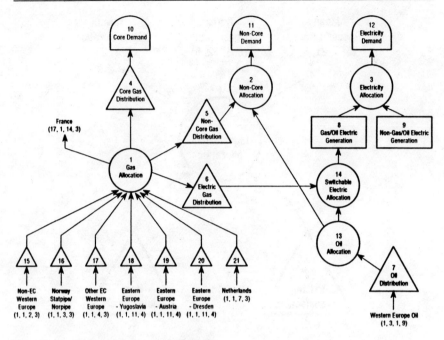

Fig. 15.8. Germany demand (1,13,3).

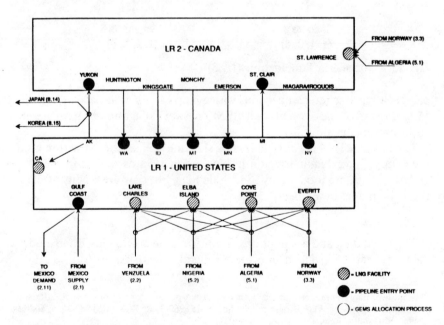

Fig. 15.9. 1—North America.

Supply — *13*

1. Alaskan North Slope
2. South Alaska
3. San Juan Basin
4. Rocky Mountains
5. Northern Great Plains
6. Anadarko
7. Permian Basin
8. Gulf Coast
9. North Central
10. Appalachia
11. Offshore Atlantic
23. Southern California
24. Northern California

Demand — *12*

15. Pacific Northwest
16. West North Central and Mountain
17. West South Central
18. East North Central
19. East South Central
20. South Atlantic
21. Middle Atlantic
25. Southern California (except SDG&E & EUR)
26. Northern California
27. SDG&E Service Area
28. Enhanced Oil Recovery Producers
29. New England

SPECIAL SECTORS — *3*

12. Mexican Imports Gateways
13. Canadian Imports Gateways
22. Oil

Fig. 15.10. GR1—North America; LR1—United States—28.

Supply — *5*

1. British Columbia
2. Alberta
3. Saskatchewan
4. Northern Canada
5. Eastern Canada

Demand — *4*

10. British Columbia
6. Alberta/Sask/Manitoba

7. Quebec/Maritimes
9. Ontario

SPECIAL SECTORS — *1*

8. Oil

Fig. 15.11. GR1—North America; LR—Canada—10.

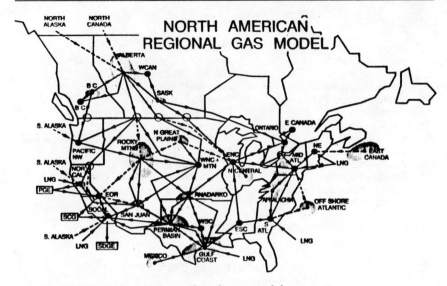

Fig. 15.12. North American regional gas model.

- supply data;
- transportation data; and
- demand data.

We will briefly summarize the most important aspects of each of these. The data for the Phase 1 study was developed by CERI. The supply data was developed in consultation with Charles Masters of the USGS and the private firm, PetroConsultants. Other data was collected from numerous published sources.

Supply Data

Supply data is critical for determining the wellhead prices and overall availability of gas by region. For each of over 200 individual supply activities (the hexagons within the model's supply regions) we input a pair of supply cost curves which represent the resource cost as a function of cumulative developed reserve additions. An illustration is shown in Fig. 15.13. "Cost" includes exploration, development and production costs. It is defined to exclude lease bonus, royalty or economic rent terms, however, as these are computed endogenously by the model. Separate curves are input for capital costs and variable operating costs. "Reserve additions" are defined as *developed* reserves *in addition to* developed reserves already in place as of the model's starting year. Developed reserves already in place as of the model's initial year represent another key input data item. Well decline profiles (or simply the normal R/P

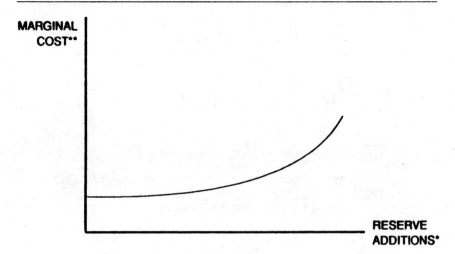

*In addition to 1990 proved developed reserves
**Excludes lease bonus, scarcity rent, any returns in excess of "normal"

Fig. 15.13. Supply data.

ratios) for each resource activity were also estimated and can play a major role in the model solution (e.g., the lower the R/P ratio, the less one has to move up a given resource supply curve to attain a given level of production). Rounding out the key supply data, the prices of alternative fuels, most importantly oil prices, are provided to the model exogenously. (The user sets the non-gas fuel price. The model equilibrium solution determines the quantities of that fuel selected by the market.) Of course, the prices of natural gas in every region, and at every point in the upstream/downstream flow, are fundamental *outputs* of the model, and are not exogenously assumed in any way. (Note that gas prices, in general, can be expected to differ significantly from gas costs for decades to come, especially outside the more well developed areas like the United States.)

The *transportation data* in the WGT Model is fairly simple. There are about 300 individual pipeline corridors and LNG route activities in the model, each denoted by a triangle-shaped figure in the network diagrams. The key functions of the transportation activity are: (1) to mark up the price of the gas flowing through it; (2) to account for fuel losses; and (3) to keep track of capacities in place. The formulas, in their simplest possible forms, for the price markups and fuel losses are presented in Fig. 15.14. Basically, within these formulas, the "markup" and the "loss rate" terms are the user inputs.

Capacities can be handled in two ways. We can assume a time-varying hard constraint on the annual flow capacity possible along any given route. Or,

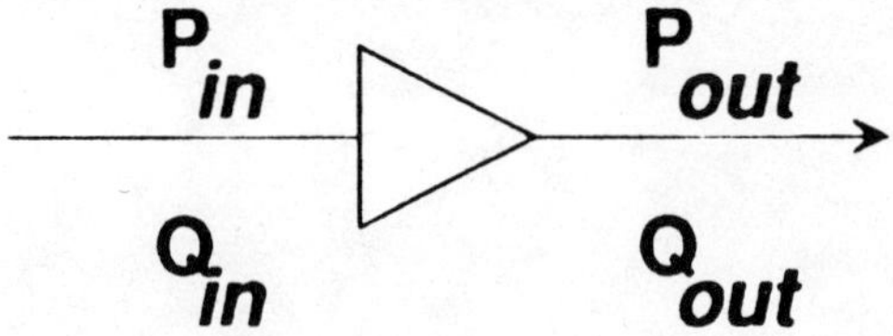

$$P_{in} \triangleright P_{out} \rightarrow$$
$$Q_{in} \qquad Q_{out}$$

$$P_{out} = \frac{P_{in}}{(1 - \text{Loss Rate})} + \textbf{Markup}$$

$$Q_{in} = \frac{Q_{out}}{(1 - \text{Loss Rate})}$$

Fig. 15.14. Transportation data.

we can assume that if market forces dictate, new capacity can be added. In the latter case, we may assume a different (usually higher) markup will apply if new capacity is added. This implies a transportation activity supply curve that looks like that in Fig. 15.15. If the market still calls for transmission along a given route even after applying the higher post-capacity-addition tariff, then the new capacity will be built. Other transportation input data include the initial capacities in place along each transportation route, as well as the change in markup, if any, for exceeding the initial capacity in place.

A final word on transportation data concerns LNG. A single transportation activity (i.e., one triangle) is usually used to represent a given pipeline or pipeline corridor. An LNG route, by contrast, is represented by a series of three transportation activities, as shown in Fig. 15.16, representing liquefaction, shipping and regasification. Despite the structure in the exhibit, a single shipping route in the model can accept LNG from several liquefaction facilities and/or deliver it to several regasification facilities.

As introduced earlier (in Fig. 15.8), demand is represented separately for three customer segments in most demand regions. Each such demand segment is represented in the network diagrams by a tombstone-shaped figure which denotes the GEMS demand process. Within each demand process, de-

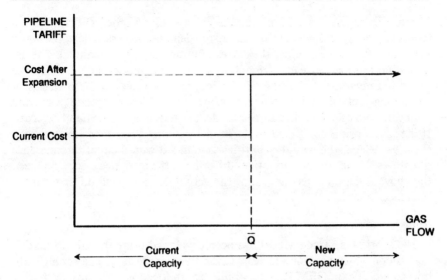

Fig. 15.15. Transmission costs before and after capacity expansion.

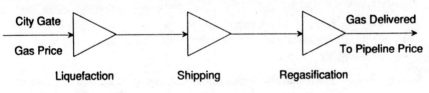

Fig. 15.16. LNG costs.

mand is determined by a simple log linear demand function of the following form:

$$\frac{Q(t)}{\bar{Q}(t)} = \left(\frac{Q(t-1)}{\bar{Q}(t-1)}\right)^a \left(\frac{P(t)}{\bar{P}(t)}\right)^e$$

where

t = this year
$t-1$ = last year
Q = actual demand quantity
$\bar{Q}$ = reference demand quantity
P = actual price
$\bar{P}$ = reference price
a = lag coefficient
e = short run (i.e., one year) price elasticity.

The rest of the model (i.e., all but the given demand process) determines a tentative price of gas, which then enters the demand process. There, the above demand function determines the corresponding quantity demanded. The *demand data* needed by each demand activity in the model include reference prices and quantities for each model period, and the values of the price elasticity and lag coefficient parameters. In effect, the reference demand prices and quantities are used to calibrate the model to an exogenous demand forecast. If the actual prices computed by the model were to equal the reference prices, then, by design, the actual quantities demanded would equal the reference quantities. If the equilibrium prices differ from the reference prices, however, the above function determines how the actual demands will differ from the reference quantities.

Model Logic

The World Gas Trade Model has been developed using the GEMS modeling system, which has some 15 years of development history. The key algorithmic capability of GEMS is the ability to endogenously compute market clearing (and where appropriate, constraint respecting) prices and quantities simultaneously:

- from wellhead to burnertip;
- across all regions; and
- across all time periods.†

In the World Gas Model, this amounts to solving some 20,000 simultaneous nonlinear equations and unknowns. The algorithm is a successive under-relaxation nonlinear search procedure developed specifically to solve GEMS-type economic models.

The WGT Model, like all GEMS models, is a network of inter-connected process models. Each process model simulates the behavior of a market participant (e.g., a gas producer) in utilizing some technology (e.g., tight sands gas drilling) to produce some commodity or service. The process models are based on fundamental microeconomics; e.g., competitive firms make investment and operating decisions to maximize profits, given their outlooks on future market conditions. Capital stocks are tracked by vintage for each process throughout time (e.g., we keep track of the amount of developed reserves added each period, and how much of each vintage remains at any point of time). Producers' required supply prices are computed based on the economics of depletable resources (i.e., the model calculates "Hotelling rents", or "user

---

†GEMS models are fully dynamic in that every price or quantity variable potentially depends on variables in all time periods, past, present and future. The model can be executed assuming participants have perfect future foresight (i.e., the rational expectations assumption), or that imperfect forecasting rules are used to generate forecasts.

costs", which are critical to determining the ultimate market clearing gas prices). And finally, the ultimate market solution is consistent with general equilibrium theory. Rather than a "macro" or econometric model, we would characterize the WGT Model as a large scale microeconomic model.

We will stop with only this terse introduction, as the economic logic and algorithms comprising GEMS and the World Gas Trade Model are well documented elsewhere[1]

SUMMARY OF RESULTS

Thus far, we have made five generations of runs of the WGT Model, each run preceded by a new generation of data. After five generations, we are becoming increasingly confident of the accuracy and relevance of the results, which we will summarize briefly here.

The reference case, a pure economic case, argues that the magnitude of LNG trade in the Atlantic and Pacific basins promises to grow to rather large levels. For example, LNG imports on the Atlantic seaboard of the United States remain below currently installed capacity until the year 2005. The domestic price of gas on Atlantic seaboard locations is below the netforward landed cost of LNG from Venezuela, Nigeria, Algeria, etc. Thereafter, however, the domestic price of gas on Atlantic seaboard locations promises to rise to the point at which the netforward landed cost of LNG is equal or lower. At this point, there is tremendous propensity of the Atlantic seaboard to substitute lower cost LNG imports for higher price domestic gas. Furthermore, since netforward LNG supply is highly elastic while domestic gas supply is not so elastic, there is growing impetus over time to import LNG. In the reference case, which we reemphasize is a pure economic case, current sites are filled to capacity by 2010 and expand to a huge 7 Tcf per year by 2020.

Where might such large magnitudes of LNG emanate? The World Gas Trade Model indicates that the preponderance of LNG imports to the United States will emanate from Venezuela (nearer term) and Nigeria (longer term). It is well to consider that Venezuela is closer to New York than Calgary, and certainly closer in an economic sense than Nigeria, Algeria, and the North Sea. Venezuela (and contiguous regions such as Trinidad) have a significant competitive advantage in Atlantic U.S. markets. Nigerian gas begins to complement and ultimately displace Venezuelan gas as the latter begins to deplete and costs rise accordingly.

We should emphasize that there is little LNG importation by the United States from Algeria or Norway. Algeria is economically contiguous to European markets; it finds much more attractive markets closer to home. Norwegian gas is likewise contiguous to European markets, and it too finds much more attractive markets closer to home. Mexican gas is more likely to be used domestically to fight severe pollution problems in central Mexico, particularly if the country develops and grows. This bodes poorly for exports of Mexican gas to the United States. Furthermore, the incremental capital requirements for Mexico to build domestic pipelines rather than LNG export facilities argues that Mexico will lean toward domestic gas development.

The model results indicate approximately 10 Tcf per year of gas imports to the United States in the year 2020. Of that 10 Tcf, just over 3 Tcf comes from Canada and the balance of just under 7 Tcf comes from Venezuela and Nigeria. This is a huge quantity of imported gas and argues that the United States gas system will fast evolve to an import economy like oil. It is important to keep in mind, pure economic forces will drive the United States in this direction, but governmental initiatives and restrictions might well retard the rate.

The model results present the overall situation in Western European markets. Notice that Europe remains largely self-sufficient in gas for 25 years. Approximately two-thirds of Europe's gas will be provided by Norway during that period with the balance from domestic sources plus Algeria. After 2010 as Norwegian gas depletes, Algeria will accelerate and Nigerian and Soviet gas will begin to increase their market shares in Europe.

It is enlightening to examine prospects for Soviet exports to Europe. It is well to consider that Soviet gas is very far from Western European markets. Not only is the physical distance long, the economic distance (i.e., cost) is high. Soviet pipelines have been abysmally inefficient, exacerbating the high cost and low throughputs. Furthermore, the major Soviet reserves lie far to the North. Production of Soviet gas is like production of Prudhoe Bay or MacKenzie Delta gas, not Gulf of Mexico gas. It is remote and hostile. Furthermore, Soviet gas pipelines are like the proposed MacKenzie Delta or ANGTS pipelines, not the Kern River pipeline. Costs of hostile Arctic pipelines are inherently higher. Our analysis suggests that Soviet gas will operate at a disadvantage in Europe relative to the more benign, less hostile, closer sources in Norway and Algeria.

The high cost of exporting Soviet gas must be coupled with the reality of Soviet economic development. Local use of gas in the Soviet economy is already very large. Any growth in the economy is sure to catalyze significant increase in domestic consumption of gas, both for economic as well as environmental reasons. Soviet producers will see much higher margins (if in fact they see margins at all) for domestic use rather than export. Export netback margins will be chronically low. In summary, the high domestic pull coupled with the low export margins for Soviet gas paint a rather pessimistic picture for exports to Europe.

Middle Eastern exports to Europe are similarly nil. While Middle Eastern gas is virtually free at the wellhead, transportation distances and costs to European and United States markets are astronomical. Middle Eastern gas promises not to be economical in Western markets for at least 25 years.

The model has provided a number of useful general insights, some of which we will summarize here. First, in the United States, we have often repeated a crucial finding: "Pipe is cheap compared to gas." It is the gas that matters most, not the pipeline or pipeline entitlement. Precisely the opposite is true in world gas markets. Gas is virtually free; there are perhaps 60 to 70 years of proved reserves known today. However, transportation to critical demand centers in Europe, the United States, Japan, and Korea is expensive and capital intensive. It is important to continually review and revise the LNG "supply chain" from the important producing regions in Venezuela, Algeria, Nigeria, and the Pacific Rim to important consuming regions. There supply chain costs dictate wellhead prices and burnertip prices and which sources of gas flow where.

Second, in the Pacific Rim, there are a tremendous number of alternative sources of supply: Indonesia, Malaysia, Australia, the Soviet Union, the Middle East, and Alaska. Prices promise to be low because of the inherently high degree of competition this multiplicity of prospective supply sources will engender. Furthermore, Pacific Rim consumers in Japan, Korea, and Taiwan will assuredly engage in multiple deals with economically contiguous producers right at home in the Pacific Rim.

CONCLUSION AND SUMMARY

This paper has presented a summary overview of DFI's World Gas Trade program, model, and data base, and has given a few results. Further information is available from the authors.

REFERENCES

1. Decision Focus Incorporated (DFI) Reports: "GEMS Overview" (1983); "NARG Reference Guide" (1991); DFI Presentation by R. Samuelson, "How the World Gas Trade Model Finds a Solution" (August 1991).

16 Options Market for Electricity: A Proposal

Mark Bernstein and Menahem Spiegel

INTRODUCTION

The recently observed trends of liberalization of electricity markets that are strongly supported by the recent changes in the legal environment encourage the departure from the traditional organization of production and distribution of electricity. Traditionally, a typical electricity market in most urban and populated regions could be characterized by a fully vertically integrated single firm controlling and performing all the activities related to the provision of electricity. This includes owning and operating the production capacity at the power plant level, the owning and controlling of the transmission lines from the power plant to the local distribution center and owning and managing the distribution of electricity to the final consumers.

As a result of technological improvements, many important changes have been observed in this industry during the last two decades. The important changes which have affected the nature of the industry are increased interutility cooperation, especially in the area of pooling capacity; more disintegration of production, including non-utility generators and independent producers; more competition; and less restricted trade in these markets.

These new arrangements call for new market instruments and arrangements to accommodate these developments. The objective of this paper is to propose a market instrument that is capable of handling the special characteristic of electricity and at the same time provide the correct incentive to producers and consumers for efficient behavior. Our suggestion is that an organized active options market for electricity output at the generating level (that is, capacity) will serve as a vehicle to more efficiently solve many of the current problems faced by the policy makers.

The economic objective served by functioning competitive markets is to provide incentives for efficient allocation of scarce resources both at a point in time and over time. Electricity, as an instantaneously perishable and non-storable good, deserves special treatment. Spot markets for electricity are efficient instruments for allocating the available (hot) generating capacity to its most valuable uses at a given point in time. But spot markets might fail to provide the appropriate long run incentives for developing and investing in new capacity and new technologies.

The futures market in electricity is limited by the fact that electricity is a non-storable good. Therefore, the proposed options market can serve as a vehicle which will promote efficient planning and capacity expansion. The current practice is that all the investment planning of capacity expansion and utilization is based on demand estimations which are done by the owners of the generating capacity. Under these circumstances the owner of the capacity is standing alone confronting the financial risks of his investment. On the other hand, the future users take very little or no financial risk at all. Having a "long-term" options market can help the producers share some of the financial burden of the estimation of future demands with the users, who are a partial source of the uncertainty. This will result in better and more efficient allocation of resources in this market.

THE OPTIONS MARKET: DESCRIPTION
OF THE INSTRUMENTS

The proposed options market is similar in its nature to a commodity futures market for a non-storable commodity, with the exception that traders are given the option to review their position and revise their decision after the initial contracting date. An option is a contractual arrangement between a prospective buyer and seller. The *call option* contract is special as it includes a back out clause for the buyer. Thus, in the case of a *call option,* the buyer has the privilege to back out of the contractual obligation. That is, the decision whether to exercise the contract is the buyer's decision.†

A typical *call option contract* in the proposed options market for electricity will have to specify the following:

a. The date of the future trade, that is, the delivery date.
b. The standardized quantity to be traded.
c. The exercise price to be paid at time of delivery.
d. The option expiration date.
e. The option price to be paid at the time of contracting.

While some of the items at the top of the list are a common part of almost any contract, the last few deserve some closer attention. The exercise price

---

†Similar kind of *put options* can be used by sellers to obtain the right to final decision. In order to keep the analysis short and simple, this version of the paper considers only call options.

is the predetermined fixed price upon which the prospective buyer and seller agree and that will be paid to the seller at time of delivery.† In the case of a call option, the option's expiration date is the last date by which the prospective buyer of electricity can back out of his contractual obligation to purchase electricity by telling the seller that he refuses to accept delivery and will not have to pay any penalty.‡ The option price states how much the prospective buyer has to pay at present for the right to buy the electricity at the fixed exercise price at a certain date in the future.

THE OPTIONS MARKET: DESCRIPTION OF THE OPERATION

Let us consider an options market for electricity where the trading is limited to agents with a direct interest in the underlying product, electricity. That is, sellers are the producers of electricity and include owners of varying power plant technologies. Electricity distribution utilities and other large consumers of electricity such as large industrial or commercial consumers buy and use the output.

In an active options market for electricity, a call option offered with all the specified information about option price, exercise price, expiration and exercise dates, implies that there is a prospective seller with the available future capacity who stands ready to sign that contract. A buyer of such a call option is a prospective buyer of electricity such as a typical distributing utility which plans to resell this power to its customers. The purchasers of the call option will sign the contract, pay the up front option price and later on, at the expiration date, will decide whether they are interested in buying the electricity at the exercise price. If interested, the exercise price will be paid and delivery accepted. If the option is refused, the producer will keep the receipt from the selling of the option. In such a case the seller will be free to sell the output to any other buyer and in particular at the spot market for electricity.

---

†In case of the volatile oil markets, the traders of options of electricity can agree on a fixed formula which will be used to determine the exercise price at the date of delivery. For example making the exercise price related to the crude oil price at a certain future date.

‡In financial markets, the buyer's call option represents the buyer's right to purchase the underlying item at a fixed predetermined price. Two types of buyer's call options are common in financial markets: the American call option and the European call option. In the American call option, the buyer can decide to exercise his option and to buy the item at *any time* within the specified period or before the expiration date. In the European call option, the buyer's decision to exercise his right to buy at the agreed price can be made *only at one* specified point in time, at the expiration date. For simplicity, the discussion here is limited to the European call option.

MARKET INCENTIVES

The call options in the electricity market, that is, the right to refuse the delivery, is valuable to the prospective buyer as it allows the buyer an additional degree of freedom to adjust planning in changing market conditions. The same call option is costly to the prospective seller (producer) of electricity as the seller needs to stand ready to supply the non-storable good which cannot be supplied out of inventories. Therefore, the buyer is willing to pay a price for this call option and the seller (producer) will be able to recover the cost of standing ready to supply.

The following is a simple example. Assume that a distribution utility (or a large consumer of electricity) expects to sell to its customers one unit of the standardized unit of electricity (say the amount of X kWh) at a certain specified time T. The utility can wait and buy this electricity at the spot market at the prevailing spot price at that time p_T. Let $E(p_T)$ denote the expected value of the future spot at time T. Alternatively, the utility can buy, at time t, a call option in the options market for delivery at time T. Let the cost of the option be $o_{t,T}$ the option price paid immediately and $S_{t,T}$ the exercise price to be paid upon delivery.

Assuming the interest cost of buying the option to be negligible and that the buyer is neutral towards risk, the expected cost of using the call option is $\alpha_T(o_{t,T}+s_{t,T})+(1-\alpha_T)o_{t,T}=o_{t,T}+\alpha_T s_{t,T}$ where α_T is the probability that the call option will be exercised at the expiration date T.† Equivalently, the expected cost of using the future spot market is $\alpha E(p_T)$. When all other things are equal, the utility will choose the minimum of $\{\alpha E(p_T), o_{t,T}+\alpha s_{t,T}\}$. In order for a typical utility to participate in the options market, it must be that $\alpha E(p_T) \geq o_{t,T}+\alpha s_{t,T}$. Otherwise, the utility will prefer to wait and use the future spot market at time T. From the demander's point of view, the equilibrium will be realized when $\alpha E(p_T)=o_{t,T}+\alpha s_{t,T}$ or when the option price is $o_{t,T}=\alpha\{E(p_T)-s_{t,T}\}$. Clearly, the option price will be proportional to the expected gain.

On the supply side (when all electricity producers are alike) the components of the long run cost of producing the standardized unit of electricity can be denoted by FC (the fixed cost) and by MC (the marginal cost). The total cost is thus FC+MC. An electricity producing firm owning a unit of capacity can sell a call option and expect the revenue of $o_{t,T}+\alpha s_{t,T}+(1-\alpha)E(p_T)$ or wait for the future spot and expect the revenue of $E(p_T)$. The firm will choose whether to sell a call option or trade in future spot markets according to the maximum of $\{\alpha E(p_T), o_{t,T}+\alpha s_{t,T}\}$.

---

†In general, α_T increases as p_T is more stable and the utility is not over optimistic in its planning process at time t about its expected demand at time T. For the simplicity of the current presentation it is assumed that α is independent of the realization of p_T.

In equilibrium, when both the spot market and the options market are operational, $\alpha E(p_T) = o_{t,T} + \alpha s_{t,T}$. The electricity producing firms will stop investing in capacity expansion once $FC + MC = \alpha E(p_T) = o_{t,T} + \alpha s_{t,T}$. Clearly, as implied from $FC + MC = o_{t,T} + \alpha s_{t,T}$, a possible equilibrium price setting is $FC = o_{t,T}$ and $MC = \alpha s_{t,T}$.

CONCLUDING REMARKS

One of the major concerns in U.S. electricity supply today is future capacity needs. There are persistent predictions of capacity shortages in the near future. At least partly these expected capacity shortages can be attributed to the current market organization where utilities and other independent power producers are hesitant to invest in new capacity. A long-term options market can provide incentives for appropriate investment in new capacity as some of the financial risk of investment can be shared between the best informed agents. The proposed options market is superior to simple long-term contracts as the total amount at "risk" is smaller and can be adjusted over time in accordance with market realizations.

Furthermore, the organized pooling and cooperation among utility and owner of non-utility generators can be improved by an active options market. That is particularly the case in expanding base load capacity which is characterized by low operating costs and eliminating to a certain degree the need to use high cost peak load.

In future work we intend to evaluate the implication of this development on electricity supply, technology efficiency and environment. We will begin to examine how this can be made operational and provide different options for organizational structure, transmission and distribution.

REFERENCES

T. W. Berrie, ed., "Spot Pricing," *Energy Journal* 116, 4 (August 1988).
Michael Crew, *Issues in Public Utility Pricing and Regulation,* Lexington Books (1980).
Michael Crew and Paul Kliendorfer, *Public Utility Economics,* St. Martins (1979).
Paul Jaskow and Richard Shmalensee, *Markets for Power: An Analysis of Electric Utility Deregulation,* MIT Press (1985).
Edward Kahn, *Electric Utility Operation Regulation and Assessment,* ACEEE (1988).

PART THREE:
ENERGY, ENVIRONMENT,
AND ECONOMIC
DEVELOPMENT

17 Energy and the Environment: Impacts of Developments in the Former Soviet Union and the East European Six

Eric H. M. Price

INTRODUCTION

The twin influences of glasnost and perestroika have had many important impacts since 1985, not only on the former Comecon countries of eastern Europe—the East European Six: Poland, Hungary, Czechoslovakia, Romania, Bulgaria, and the former German Democratic Republic—but also on the European energy scene. In the future, the further spread and development of these ideas will have substantial effects on the entire energy world. Perestroika, focusing on modernization, sought to restructure the Soviet Union's economy with the aim of building up investment, retooling, updating industry, and improving quality control standards. Glasnost sought to encourage individual initiative with more accountable bureaucracy. From these beginnings, the idea of modernizing the existing system developed into a campaign to reform the system itself. At the center of these reforms in the Soviet Union was the "Law on State Enterprises" which, among other things, replaced output targets with centrally directed orders placed with concerns to deliver specified quantities of goods. This gave enterprises greater autonomy in the use of internally generated funds, in wage payments, incentive bonuses, and other matters.

In the Soviet Union, under perestroika and glasnost and in the absence of tight macroeconomic control, various things happened: the liquidity of enterprises rose, boosted by higher retained profits; wage settlements tended to get out of control; and the newly delegated managerial decisions continued to be based on distorted and inflexible prices and costs. Further, as the tight central control and discipline of the old system loosened, social, political, and allocative problems emerged that led to distribution difficulties, railway and other transport bottlenecks, and falling oil and coal outputs.

ENERGY IMPACTS ON THE SOVIET UNION

Soviet Energy Resources

As shown in Table 17.1, the former Soviet Union holds a major position in the world energy scene. Although it has only six percent of the world's proved oil reserves, it has the world's largest gas reserves (38 percent of the total) and the second largest coal reserves (24 percent). It has reserve/production ratios, at current production levels, of 14 years for oil and 56 years for gas. In output terms, in 1990 it was the largest producer of both oil and gas, with 18 percent of world oil production, 37 percent of gas production, 16 percent of refinery capacity, 14 percent of coal production, nine percent of nuclear output, and 10 percent of world hydroelectricity output! It is the world's third largest coal producer. Overall, its energy use represents just about one-sixth of the world's total, with a similar share of its primary energy output.

The gas reserve position of the former Soviet Union is particularly strong: the Middle East and the Soviet Union together have two-thirds of the world's gas reserves. The Soviet Union, with Urengoy, has the second largest gas field in the world, with reserves equal to three times U.S. total gas reserves. With Yamburg, Bovanenkovskoye, Zapolyarnoye, and Orenburg it has the third, fourth, seventh and ninth largest gas fields in the world.

Soviet Supply Side Problems

Recently, the Soviet oil sector has suffered in two ways: the collapse of the command and control economy under which Gosplan set output levels for each enterprise, and the impact of perestroika on the Soviet oil industry that led to falling oil production.

Crude oil and condensate production fell from its peak of 624 million tonnes in 1988 by nine percent in 1990; and in the first half of 1991 it was down 10 percent from 1990.[2] This implies an output for 1991 of some 508 million tonnes, the lowest level since 1976. Moreover, oil output is expected to continue to decline in the future, possibly even making the Soviet Union a net oil importer.

The system of centrally imposed production targets has been a major reason for the premature decline of many Soviet oil fields. Oil output is falling in existing fields because of past poor oil field practices involving the use of low-key technology with oil extracted at too fast a rate. This has resulted in very poor lifetime oil recovery rates. To develop deep, high pressure hot reservoirs, the Soviet Union needs the latest western technology. The practice of water-cutting, which in the West has been in use only when the greater

Table 17.1. Soviet energy production, consumption and reserves, 1990

Resource	Quantity (mtoe)	Percent of world	World ranking
Production			
Coal	296	14	3
Oil	570	18	1
Natural gas	656	37	1
Nuclear power	44	9	4
Hydroelectric	56	10	3
Consumption			
Coal	276	13	3
Oil	403	13	2
Natural gas	560	33	1
Nuclear power	44	9	4
Hydroelectric	56	10	3
Proved reserves			
Oil	7,800	6	7
Gas	37,000	38	1
Coal	117,800	24	2

mtoe: million tonnes of oil equivalent.
Source: BP Statistical Review of World Energy (June 1991).

part of the oil has been extracted and not at the outset, has been used in the Soviet Union for a quarter of a century and has led to increasing water content of the oil from its fields. Indeed, over 90 percent of Soviet oil is produced by artificially maintaining formation pressure by water injection to oil fields.[3] Such poor methods have had a disastrous effect on the proportion of oil reserves finally recovered, considering that an eventual recovery at abandonment of only 20 percent is said to be common. As a result, 18,000 new wells are spudded every year. In contrast, only 200 were spudded in the North Sea in 1990.

Currently, some 20,000 oil wells are said to be idle due to breakdowns, lack of spares, and other supply problems. These problems are attributable in part to equipment production difficulties arising from civil disorder and strikes in Azerbaijan, where manufacture of oil field equipment is concentrated. Damage by vandals has occurred in some oil fields, notably in the Tatar Republic of the Volga Urals and in the Almeteevsk area.

Attempts at enhanced oil recovery have been expensive and of doubtful benefit. Indeed, some Soviet officials believe that the oil and gas sector has received more resources than are justified, and that provision of new capital resources should be limited. For this reason and because of supply and finance constraints, the oil sector cannot get high-pressure compressors for enhanced recovery or for pipelines. Consequently, the emphasis seems to be on opening up new fields with the balance moving from the Volga/Urals areas to western Siberia, such as the Yamul Peninsula in the Arctic.

There are supply problems for other fuels also. Most of the large coal deposits are of low-quality/high-polluting coal; yet, as oil output declines and gas is diverted to take its place, coal and nuclear power are expected to become more important. After the Chernobyl disaster, four nuclear stations were closed and plans were canceled or postponed for 26 others. Despite this, nuclear generating capacity is still planned to increase by 60 percent by 2000. Given the high capital costs of nuclear power, the perception of nuclear risks, and the difficulty of financing such investment, it seems likely that more coal generation will be necessary, thereby adding to air pollution. The coal industry, however, has its own share of problems. Miners are demanding higher wages and better conditions and have shown that they are prepared to strike. The former central government ceded the control of its massive coal fields in Siberia to the Russian Federation, thereby meeting the demands of miners who are also demanding a greater share of profits. This could well lead to similar pressures from oil workers. This is significant because the Russian Federation produced 90 percent of Soviet oil and 70 percent of Soviet natural gas.

Gas production seems to be holding up, but has difficulties that center on development and transportation. Indeed, the Soviet bulk transportation system is a subject of widespread concern. According to Cambridge Energy Research Associates, 25 percent of all Soviet oil and gas compressors need repairs, 60 percent of the gas pipelines need modernization and 10 percent need to be replaced. Apart from one massive gas explosion there, methane losses from the system annually are substantial, as much as the annual natural gas use of the Netherlands. Although the main problems appear to be equipment shortages and a deficiency of planned maintenance schedules, doubt persists concerning the quality of materials and components used.

It must be noted, however, that an alternative interpretation of these system "losses" is that they do not take place on this scale, but stem from an administrative system in which gas producers have an advantage in overestimating the quantities going into the pipelines and those receiving it at the other end have an incentive to underestimate their offtake. The limited number of reported accidents lends some credence to this interpretation.

Soviet Demand Side Problems

One of the major energy problems of the former Soviet Union and eastern Europe is the absence of valid prices and costs, since they are a necessary basis for energy planning or decision making, whether centralized or dispersed. Moreover, without a proper basis for prices, the high energy intensity of the

Soviet Union, as compared with western Europe (shown in Table 17.2), will persist.

In the Soviet Union, all energy is underpriced in relation to world markets. Electricity, for instance, is one kopek per kilowatt-hour (kWh), equivalent to 1.7 cents per kWh at the official exchange rate, 0.2 cents per kWh at authorized dealers, and perhaps 0.05 cents per kWh from illegal street currency traders. The absence of valid economic costing and pricing strongly suggests that there are substantial inefficiencies and cross-subsidies in the energy sector with more resources expended in producing and supplying energy than its value to the consumer; indeed, energy prices are said to be around one-third of their resource costs. Generally, domestic dwellings do not have individual meters for all fuels, and some are not metered even on an apartment block basis. In contrast, the former Baltic Republics—capitalist economies until the Second World War—do still seem to have domestic electricity meters.

Although the bulk of Soviet energy demand is centered on the Russian Federation, Byelorussia, the Ukraine, and the three Baltic Republics, most energy supply must be transported over vast distances from the east, southeast, or northeast. Nevertheless, the price of energy to the user is generally the same regardless of the user's location in the vast area of the former Soviet Union. For industry, energy prices are slightly higher but not markedly so, but this is of small consequence since decisions about output levels, resource allocation, pricing and wage levels are not dependent upon profit and loss accounts. Soviet workers, having a legal right to work, cannot be displaced by redundancy or by the closure of a factory. Increasingly, however, some form of profit and loss is being developed for enterprises.

Future Prospects for Soviet Energy

The energy sector, along with the agricultural sector, holds the key to the former Soviet Union's trading future. In 1991, oil and gas accounted for over 80 percent of Soviet total foreign exchange earnings. The former Soviet Union has few potential exports likely to interest hard currency areas (at least at existing exchange rates); yet, to attract the new plant, machinery and technical expertise it needs, it must either increase its exports or, failing that, demonstrate conclusively its ability to export in the future. Gas, oil and, to a lesser extent, coal are central to its export prospects.

For all these reasons, the position of the energy sector in the reformed economy has been a subject of intensive debate. The Politizdat in 1984 set out the main principles of a long-term energy program into the next century. An updated version was promised for 1989 but has not yet materialized.

One central issue, currently a subject of fierce debate, is the issue of the "gas bridge." As originally conceived, substantial increases in the output of gas would enable the transition to a market economy over a period of 10 to 15 years. The plan envisaged gas output increasing from 796 billion cubic

Table 17.2. Energy intensities in the Soviet Union and Europe, 1988 (in tonnes
of oil equivalent per thousand 1985 US$ of output)

Sector	Soviet Union	Europe-4
Total economy	0.99	0.38
All industry	1.55	0.54
Energy	2.55	2.21
Basic industry	2.09	0.64
Refineries and chemicals	1.68	0.42
Non-metallic mineral products	1.66	0.78
Basic metals	2.65	1.22
Other industry	0.59	0.14
Construction	0.15	0.02
Agriculture	0.34	0.16
Commercial transport	1.17	n.a.
Services	0.13	0.05
Residential sector (in kg of oil equivalent per square meter)	32.1	17.5

Europe-4 refers to France, Germany, Italy, United Kingdom.

Note: Services exclude commercial transport but include communication. The energy industry
includes non-energy mining and water utilities, but excludes refineries. The data for basic industry refers only to France and Germany.

meters (bcm) a year to 1,000 bcm by 2000 and to 1,200 by 2010, thereby fueling 100,000 MW of gas-fired power plants. Gazprom, however, sees gas
production leveling out at 920 to 950 bcm over the next five to 10 years as
a result of financial and environmental constraints at the points of supply.
Although enhanced energy efficiency is planned to make good some of this
shortfall, there is pressure in quarters to reinstate nuclear power as an option
and to build more stations. For example, Vitaly Konovalov, the former Soviet
Nuclear Energy Minister, has argued for the building of an extra 19,600 MW
of nuclear plants, tripling existing capacity by 2000, that is, some 20 new
RMBK reactors.[4] Whatever the outcome, it seems most unlikely that gas exports will be jeopardized as a result.

The long-term future for gas exports could be promising if the former Soviet
Union develops as a democratic market economy. In 1991, the Soviet Union
sold only seven percent of its gas production. By 2010, the European Community (EC) could be importing 50 percent of its gas from outside, and the
East European Six, 90 percent. Of course, around Europe's borders there are
ample proven reserves of gas, perhaps 80 years of supply; the problem is that
much of it is in areas that are remote or politically unstable (or both) and
the costs of bringing it to western Europe would be substantial. Overall, the

infrastructure for new gas projects is much more expensive than that for oil or coal and takes longer to develop, on average five years.

One prospect is the installation of a new pipeline to bring gas to western Europe from western Siberia. Preliminary indications of the possible costs are not promising: allowing for an acceptable profit level (such as 15 percent discounted cash flow real post tax), using construction methods of the Organization for Economic Cooperation and Development (OECD), and building it to western environmental standards, the cost of delivery to western Europe could be as high as $24 per barrel of oil equivalent (boe) for Arctic gas, plus local distribution and certain other costs to get the gas to final users. This compares with the current UK (bench) price of around $15/boe for UKCS gas delivered for sale in the UK market. Even so, in the event of rising gas prices in western Europe by 2000, Soviet gas might be able to find a place in the market, though this might be very costly and a high-risk project in physical, political, and market terms. Indeed, it has been estimated that £3 billion would be needed over 20 years to get the gas to western European markets.

Apart from the political uncertainties in eastern Europe, the prospects for the Soviet energy sector being able to generate increased exports of fuels in the near future are not good. Oil output has declined and is expected to continue to decline. Increased gas supplies will become available internally, but are seen by some Soviet officials as substituting domestically for oil within the Soviet Union. Much of the coal output is of poor quality, is not close to deep-sea ports, and is required for Soviet power generation. New nuclear capacity is exceptionally capital-intensive and hardly constitutes an optimal solution to energy problems for a country poor in capital resources (although rich in energy resources), even if Soviet nuclear technology had been proved to be safer.

The Relevance for the World Energy Scene

It is clear that, unless radical changes are made, the former Soviet Union is unlikely to be able to earn the enhanced export surplus it needs from energy sales. One consequence of the pronounced energy shortages at home and the high priority given to earning more hard currency from exporting oil to the West is that Soviet officials are seeking to decrease eastern Europe's dependence on Soviet oil, with clear implications for world markets.

The impact of Soviet energy exports, however, extends beyond eastern Europe (Table 17.3). Since 1973, one of the key factors that has constrained the power of OPEC has been the growth of hydrocarbon energy production outside OPEC, notably in the Soviet Union, Mexico, the United Kingdom, and Norway. The Soviet Union expanded its production by a third, from 452 million tonnes in 1974 to a peak of 624 million tonnes by 1987, thereby reducing OECD dependence on OPEC. In 1989, the Soviet Union exported 210 mil-

Table 17.3. Main flows of internationally traded crude oil, 1990 (million b/d)

	Output	Consumption	Net exports (imports)	Trends to mid-1990s
Soviet Union	12	8	4	Lower exports
OPEC	25	7	18	Rising exports
United States	9	16	(7)	Rising imports
Japan	—	5	(5)	Stable
European Community	2	11	(9)	Stable
Other	17	18	(1)	Rising imports
World	65	65	—	—

OPEC: Saudi Arabia, Kuwait, UAE, Qatar, Iraq, Iran, Nigeria, Libya, Algeria, Gabon, Venezuela, Ecuador, Indonesia.

lion tonnes of oil, of which 78 million tonnes went to western Europe and 89 million tonnes to eastern Europe. The immediate significance for the rest of the world of developments in the last few years in the Soviet Union is that its capacity to export oil would seem to have been reduced by as much as a third in only three years. Some observers now expect Soviet oil exports to drop to between 50 million and 55 million tonnes in 1991, against 108.6 million tonnes in 1990.[5] A few observers are even discussing the prospect of the former Soviet Union becoming a net importer of crude oil—though this may prove to be unduly alarmist. It may, however, be significant that whereas in 1990 the Soviet Union exported 97 million tonnes of oil to OECD countries, only six million tonnes were exported to them in 1976, the last year in which the oil output level was as low as the 1991 current estimate.

The former Soviet Union's future oil outputs will be crucial to oil prices in the mid-1990s and late 1990s. The future of Soviet energy developments, and the adjustment of the East European Six to the ending of the Bucharest Agreement which governed the supply and pricing of Soviet oil to eastern Europe, will have profound effects on European and world energy markets. Any tendency for supplies of oil from the former Soviet Union to become more erratic could be as important for world markets as their average levels. To date, the economics of these various influences and their impact on world oil prices have not received the attention they deserve.

Possible Solutions for the Former Soviet Union

Generally, and even before the events of 1991, Soviet energy officials were deeply pessimistic about the future of the energy sector. If economic reforms do not take place, that pessimism is fully justified; but, given continued progress towards democratic and economic reforms, the vast natural resources of the Soviet Union can be located, developed, distributed and traded to provide the hard currency surplus necessary to finance the energy sector's growth, thereby contributing significantly to the recovery and eventual prosperity of the country as a whole. The people's acceptance of initially strong and unpalatable economic medicine cannot be taken for granted, but without it, longer term political stability is far from certain and inward investment from the West might well represent good money chasing after bad. The West, after all, is still recovering from the shocks from past large-scale lending operations, notably to Third World countries, recycling the OPEC surpluses of the 1970s and early 1980s.

It is difficult for any economist to prescribe with confidence solutions for economies so alien to his or her own experience; but it appears that among actions that need to be taken within the energy sector of the former Soviet Union are those discussed below.

1) The energy sector must move rapidly towards world market energy prices—that is, fixing all prices for oil, gas and coal to reflect the opportunity cost of each energy form. The first step in this could be to equate these with delivered world prices of energy at frontiers, then deducting internal transport costs of energy to establish market-related prices throughout parts of the former Soviet Union. Where the long-run marginal production cost of energy in the former Soviet Union exceeds world prices netted back in this way, there is a need to charge prices directly related to the long-run marginal costs of production, including normal profits. Where the market cannot sustain such prices, the case for closing these production facilities needs to be addressed. The necessary price rises will increase existing prices several times. One could expect prices to vary between areas of the former Soviet Union as they do in parts of the OECD and within its member countries. There is, however, one immense difficulty in implementing price reform, that of establishing what the appropriate exchange rates are. To do this for the ruble in terms of any western currency is a daunting task. Apart from the official exchange rates, there is the newly established commercial exchange rate between the ruble and the dollar, but this is a poor guide to the free market level, that is, the relative purchasing power of the two currencies. Istvan Dobozi has shown that with a world crude oil price of $17.42 the internal wholesale price of crude oil could be anything between $5.70 and $0.17 a barrel depending on whether one uses the official exchange rate, the Hungarian ruble-to-dollar cross rate, the tourist rate, the black market rate, or the auction rate.[6] A start in reforming energy prices has already begun: in 1991 the wholesale prices of energy were increased markedly. Crude oil went up 130 percent; natural gas, 100 percent; coal, 90 percent; electricity, 40–50 percent; heat, 60–65 percent; and refined oil products, 30 percent, giving an average energy price increase of around 80 percent.[7, 8, 9] On top of these increases, President Boris Yeltsin of the Russian Federation recently promised to raise oil prices perhaps three-fold.

2) Gas and electricity meters should be installed progressively in all individual family dwellings, offices and factories. It is clear that without direct pricing and billing, energy efficiency standards approaching those of OECD cannot be achieved. The case for metering electricity can be justified by reduced need for expensive new power station capacity resulting from lower consumption expected with metering. Gas metering should result in increased hard currency earnings resulting from greater availability of gas for export. The political process of "selling" meters to the public may be achieved by offering cheaper prices for metered electricity and gas consumption than for unmetered consumption.

3) A policy should be energetically pursued towards achieving by a target date those measures that have been found to be most cost-effective and that have already been fully exploited in OECD countries.

4) Practices must be adopted in oil and gas fields to achieve maximum economic recovery of reserves. Specialists in most efficient technology should be brought in, and modern equipment, such as high pressure compressors, should be obtained.

5) The industry must attract foreign capital and know-how. This assistance will not be readily forthcoming unless foreigners have reliable legal guarantees for delivery of a predetermined quantity of oil and gas. Joint ventures will be necessary for new ventures, for example, Yamul Peninsula and other Arctic areas. The news that the Russian Federation is proposing to allow 100 percent foreign-owned companies to take part in oil projects is promising, as are the prospects that exploration acreage will be available to them and that petroleum legislation based on international standards is forthcoming.

6) Maintenance programs must be introduced, using OECD expertise, for plant and machinery in all areas of the energy sector, such as supply, transportation, and distribution.

7) The best western practices for nuclear station control and monitoring must be introduced, using high-capacity computers, computer programs for probabilistic risk analysis, electronics, and training methods and relying on key western components.

8) Energy investment options must be evaluated on a sound economic basis, involving realistic opportunity costs of capital, "netted back" external world prices where appropriate, and with appropriate wage differentials for skilled workers and managers that will provide realistic incentives and rewards for responsibility and skills.

9) Coal prices need to be differentiated, to reflect their opportunity cost whether in terms of netted back export price or marginal cost of production where higher, and also to reflect the higher pollution costs of all coal as compared with other fuels and the higher emission levels associated with high sulfur coals.

10) Realistic evaluations must be made of initial capital costs, eventual disposal costs, and likely plant availabilities of nuclear power stations. For a country in which capital is scarce relative to other factors and energy resources, it does not seem sensible to opt for the most highly capital-intensive form of energy, nuclear power. Nevertheless, it is reported that Soviet officials are seeking to reinstate the nuclear industry and to accelerate and expand the postponed nuclear reactor construction program.[10]

11) In the electricity industry, two-part tariffs should be introduced, with a large maximum demand charge for industrial and commercial loads to restrain demand and thus limit the need for massive investment in new capacity for electricity generation and associated transport.

12) The efficiency of energy use needs to be improved. This should be the foremost priority, since it offers massive scope for energy savings of as much as 40 to 50 percent of existing use. Soviet officials recognize energy efficiency is low by western standards and there is large potential for improvement of efficiency and reduction of emissions. The actions necessary to achieve these benefits may be beyond the former Soviet Union's financial capability even though the costs are far less than the investment options that face them on the supply side. Currently, the approach to improved energy efficiency appears to place too much reliance on planning, whereas to be successful, it has to be price induced.

13) Extending the use of natural gas for residential consumption if it is allowed to proceed will help to solve the environmental problem; however, the current prospect in the Soviet Union is for rising levels of CO_2 emissions.

The recent decision to cut taxes on oil and gas exports from 40 percent to three percent and on oil product exports from 35 percent to three percent could enhance incentives for enterprises to increase output and exports.

ENERGY IMPACTS ON THE EAST EUROPEAN SIX

The changes in approach associated with perestroika have spread rapidly into eastern Europe. Although it may be many years before these economies are really market-orientated, the first important steps have been taken. The impact is particularly evident in their energy industries, where drastic and far-reaching decisions have to be taken which, initially, impose hardship on their populations. Some of these difficult decisions have already been taken, notably with impressively high increases in energy prices in most countries; other decisions remain to be addressed.

In general, the prospects are poor for adequate energy availability in eastern Europe in the near future. The first impacts of the radical changes there were shortages of energy as a result of lower availability of Soviet supplies, and there have been sharp increases in energy prices. Both impacts have curtailed economic growth and this may persist for some time.

Eastern Europe, in sharp contrast to the former Soviet Union, is not well endowed with energy resources. Its oil reserves are meager, constituting only 0.1 percent of the world total. Its natural gas reserves represent only 0.7 percent of the world total and coal reserves (mainly in Poland and in the former German Democratic Republic) about eight percent. In output terms, it consumes 473 million tonnes of oil equivalent a year, six percent of the world total, but it produces only 4.5 percent. As a result, the East European Six countries remain heavily dependent on imports from the Soviet Union. For the most part, their energy policies remain characterized by extensive use of brown coal burned in low-efficiency apparatus with high levels of acid rain emissions, high and increasing dependence on Soviet natural gas and on nuclear power, and the objective of economizing in the use of oil wherever possible.

Given their traditional reliance on the Soviet Union for imported oil, gas and electricity, the events of the last few years have forced the East European Six to revise their energy plans (Table 17.4). At the start of the 1980s, they had plans to use more natural gas and Soviet-designed nuclear power in order to minimize their imports of expensive oil. However, events such as the accident at Chernobyl, the fall in the oil price in the mid-1980s, the Soviet Union's current need for hard currency, and its oil production problems have provided reasons for reevaluation of the plans.

A major factor forcing this reassessment was the ending of the Bucharest Agreement, which had applied to sales to the former Comecon countries and which contained oil pricing formulas for invoicing Soviet oil on the basis of a rolling three year average of world prices. Originally, its aim was to protect these economies from the impacts of sharply fluctuating world prices. Thus, when world prices were on an upward trend, the East European Six gained; but after the price falls in the mid-1980s, they had to pay considerably more for Soviet oil than OECD countries paid for their oil. Moreover, as the three year average price fell, eastern Europe built up balance of payments surpluses of rubles that were useless for trading outside the Eastern Bloc. To understand how these surpluses came about, one has to appreciate that the Soviet Union's trading terms for energy required eastern Europe to "participate" in Soviet energy investments to obtain long-term oil and gas supply contracts.

Because of these circumstances, the East European Six were suddenly faced with paying the full world price for their energy imports, and at the same time, because of production and distribution problems within the Soviet Union, the availability of Soviet energy for export to its former Comecon countries was declining. With the former Soviet Union now moving to settlements in dollars rather than in non-transferable rubles, exports to Comecon of soft currency oil will be reduced. Soviet oil exports to eastern Europe are now predicted by the Vienna Institute of Comparative Economic Studies to fall

Table 17.4. Soviet oil and gas exports to Eastern Europe, 1989

	Crude oil (mt)	Oil products (mt)	Natural gas (est) (bcm)
Bulgaria	11.5	1.2	6.8
Czechoslovakia	16.6	0.3	12.6
East Germany	20.0	0.1	6.5
Hungary	6.3	1.5	6.3
Poland	13.0	2.1	8.4
Romania	3.9	7.0	7.3
Total	71.3	12.2	47.9

Source: Vneshnaya Torgovlya & Cedigaz (1989)

from 56.4 million tonnes in 1989 and 39 million tonnes in 1990 to only 20 million tonnes by 1995.[1] This will probably hit Bulgaria and Romania hardest unless the combination of increased Soviet gas imports and improved energy efficiency eases the situation. Soviet gas supplies to eastern Europe are expected to increase from 32 bcm in 1989 to 47 bcm in 1995.

One consequence is that eastern Europe will seek energy supplies from other sources, probably involving barter with Middle Eastern oil suppliers, though overall they will seek to limit their oil imports to the absolute minimum. Eastern Europe is also seeking to diversify its gas imports. Norwegian, Iranian and Algerian gas and LNG supplies are being considered. Poland, Hungary and Czechoslovakia, however, assisted in the construction of the 4,500 kilometer Progress gas pipeline from the Yamburg field in western Siberia to the border of Czechoslovakia at Uzhgorod and, in view of this, will receive gas from the former Soviet Union at concessionary rates for the next two decades.

Refineries in eastern Europe are beset with problems. Designed to take Soviet crude oil as feedstock, the refineries, lacking adequate upgrading facilities, produce a heavy mix of products with too few lighter elements. Until now, this may have been appropriate, considering the limited internal markets for gasoline and diesel and the extensive use of fuel oil for power generation; but, as demand for transport energy grows with rising incomes and greater car ownership, large amounts of capital will have to be devoted to modernizing and rebalancing the refineries.

Although Poland, Czechoslovakia and Hungary produce coal, economic reforms there have disrupted production, and output has fallen. Moreover, with sharp increases in the price of coal, consumers are switching to other fuels.

Generally, the options for the energy policies of these countries are heavily constrained by their lack of indigenous resources and also by their existing foreign indebtedness and the difficulties of servicing additional debt. Their gross external debts, as given by the Institute of International Finance, are: Hungary, $20 billion; Czechoslovakia, $7 billion; GDR, $22 billion; Yugoslavia, $17 billion; Poland, $40 billion; Romania, nil (having been written off); and Bulgaria, $10 billion.

Compared with western European economies, eastern European countries use far more energy per capita in relation to their GDP than west Europe. The graph in Fig. 17.1 depicts the situation for east and west Europe. Although there are well known pitfalls in making comparisons of GDP between countries, there are good reasons for concluding that the quality of the GDP in OECD economies is higher than in controlled economies, since its components have been tested in the marketplace and hence the OECD's GDP data are not overstated. An interesting comparison can be made between the energy intensities per capita of the East European Six with those countries with broadly comparable GDP per capita in the West, such as Portugal, Greece, and Spain.

Energy use in each of the eastern European countries is markedly higher, and well above the "best fit" curve for western economies generally (Table 17.5). With such high energy intensities of these economies, sharply higher energy prices will provide strong incentives for energy efficiency improvements and optimal fuel switching. For all these economies, improved energy efficiency represents the outstanding "best buy."

Energy Strategies of the East European Six

There is some difference of view between western and eastern Europe regarding the strategies eastern Europe should adopt to resolve its energy problems. Western European countries, in the main, would like to see lignite-fueled power stations in the East—with their high emissions of pollutants—closed down, retrofitted to different fuel use, or equipped with fluidized gas desulfurization equipment. Westerners are also concerned about the many Soviet-designed nuclear stations in the region.

In practice, eastern Europe is going to become increasingly reliant on natural gas with gas-fired district heating replacing the burning of brown coal briquettes in homes. Gas will also be increasingly used to fuel power stations but the timing of this depends essentially on the extent to which the Soviet Union can make further supplies available.

Detailed assessments of the energy sectors in each of the East European Six are beyond the scope of this paper. They have many features and many problems in common, but they also have different indigenous energy resource bases, industrial structures, geographical locations, political sensitivities, foreign indebtedness, and abilities to attract foreign capital. Some key considerations that determine their individual energy strategies are described below.

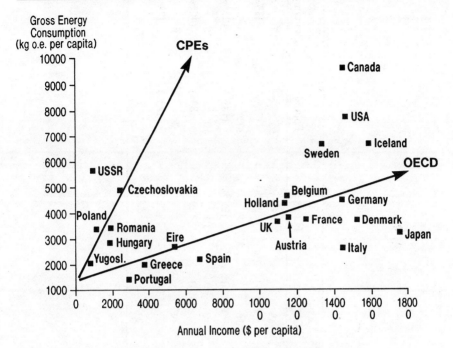

Fig. 17.1. Per capita income and energy consumption.

East Germany

East Germany has the highest primary energy consumption per capita in Europe. This is partly due to its industrial structure which is concentrated on energy-intensive heavy industry, and partly because four-fifths of its electricity is generated from coal, nearly all of which is lignite.

The existence in postwar years of large domestic lignite reserves helped eastern Germany achieve better economic performance than other eastern European countries. In 1989, for instance, 311 million tonnes of lignite were mined, meeting more than 73 per cent of the country's entire energy needs; more recently, with the decline in oil and gas supplies from the Soviet Union, reliance on domestic lignite sources has been increased. One consequence of both its energy intensity and its pattern of energy use has been heavy pollution of air and water, especially in Lower Saxony.

The contrast of energy sources in East and West Germany is interesting. In 1987, 64 percent of East Germany's fuel use was brown coal, against eight percent in West Germany. On the other hand, oil was 17 percent of total fuel in the East against 42 percent in the West, and gas use was only half (nine percent) the percentage in the West. (These comparisons show why British

Table 17.5. Primary energy use, 1989 (million toe)

	Bulgaria	Czecho-slovakia	Eastern Germany	Hungary	Poland	Romania
Coal	9 (28%)	41 (54%)	69 (71%)	7 (21%)	93 (76%)	17 (23%)
Oil	12 (38%)	16 (22%)	16 (16%)	9 (28%)	17 (14%)	20 (27%)
Natural gas	5 (16%)	10 (13%)	8 (8%)	10 (29%)	10 (8%)	30 (40%)
Nuclear/hydro	6 (19%)	9 (11%)	4 (5%)	7 (21%)	2 (2%)	6 (7%)
Total	32	76	97	33	172	73

Note: Figures in parentheses show percentages of total use.

Gas Plc. has been seeking to acquire stakes in distribution companies in the Leipzig, Halle, and Magdeburg regions, particularly as only five percent of dwellings in East Germany have central heating).

With reunification, East Germany's reliance on low-grade coal is likely to decline. A halt has been put on coal field development there and a 40 percent decline in output is planned over the next decade. This has already started: lignite and brown coal production in 1990 was 250 million tonnes, down 17 percent from 1989. The opening of economic links with West Germany might well result in a quick reassessment of its energy policy which had been heavily reliant upon polluting low-grade coals. East Germany plans to gradually replace lignite-fueled electricity capacity with new nuclear plants, but this might not be acceptable to West German environmental concerns, which have centered on the safety of the Soviet-designed reactors at Greifswald. Two Soviet-designed nuclear stations have been closed and there is fierce resistance to plans by West German electricity companies to build nuclear stations there. A more likely solution to its energy problems will be increased reliance on natural gas. East Germany's only gas field at Salzwedel produces an estimated eight bcm, though a further seven bcm is currently imported from the Soviet Union. The Schwarze Pumpe gas combine and Ruhrgas are now looking at plans to link up the East and West German gas grids to provide access to big new supply sources.

The costs involved in such undertakings could be daunting. For instance, just to upgrade and improve control of power generation and transmission to western standards on a centralized control system has been estimated to cost £10–14 billion.

The reunification with West Germany should help East Germany to solve its energy-related problems faster than its eastern and southeastern neighbors. Steps have already been taken to reform energy pricing and the opening of its industries to EC competition should rapidly restructure the economy and change energy use, with resulting environmental improvements. The ready availability of western finance, know-how and management should force the pace of change and thereby markedly reduce energy intensity.

Poland

Poland is a coal-based economy; 78 percent of its total primary energy usage comes from coal, which accounts for 95 percent of its primary energy production. In 1989, 95 percent of its generated electricity came from solid fuel, with hard coal being 60 percent of this and the balance being lignite.

Poland has substantial coal reserves, sufficient to last it some 180 years at current production rates; but production is falling: in 1990 it was down 14 percent from 1989 and there is little hope of a recovery in the short term. As a result, less coal is available for export. Foreign coal sales are estimated to have dropped from 33 million tonnes in 1989 (when Poland was the world's sixth largest coal exporter) to around 28 million tonnes in 1990, of which 60 percent went to hard currency areas. The consequent fall in hard currency earnings obviously inhibits the general process of economic restructuring in Poland.

The Polish energy sector has close links with the Soviet Union. It imports all its gas and nearly all its oil from the Soviet Union, and exports some coal to Soviet markets. The price of Soviet oil and gas at the frontier is now determined by world oil prices and paid for in hard currency.

To date, there are no nuclear plants operating in Poland, although a Soviet-type PWR rector had been under construction at Zarnowice, near Gdansk, since 1982 which has now been halted. The future of this project is far from certain since the government is undecided on whether to proceed with it.

Like other eastern European countries, Poland is energy intensive in terms of tonnes of oil equivalent per $1000 of GDP, consuming 0.78 tonnes, compared to 0.41 tonnes for the EC, though in terms of primary energy per capita it is in line with the EC.

One reason for the high energy intensity is that Polish energy prices have until recently been held down well below prices outside. Since the outset of 1990, there have been substantial price increases, but prices are still well below those in the EC and have a distorted pattern. An International Energy Agency study of Poland in 1991 estimated that energy prices would have to rise to approximate EC levels in the following amounts: natural gas in residential premises, +400 percent; electricity in residential premises, +170 percent; coal, +70 percent; electricity for industry, +60 percent; and gasoline, diesel and natural gas for industry, +20 percent.[12] These theoretical rises are in addition to the substantial price increases actually implemented between January 1990 and January 1991. These latter increases were dramatic and impressive by any standards, with household gas increasing 18-fold, in terms of money of the day; household coal and electricity, 11-fold; industrial coal and gas, 7.5-fold; and more modest increases for gasoline, diesel and industrial electricity, ranging between 3.5-fold and 4.5-fold. Of course, with inflation running at 700 percent during 1989, such increases are not as draconian as they seem. In 1991 the general inflation rate appears to be running at a little over 20 percent per year. How price increases of such magnitude will affect consumption is impossible to predict, but in the medium term the impacts are likely to transform the whole energy scene, with significant and favorable effects on pollutant emissions.

The objectives of Polish energy policy now appear to be 1) to change the pattern of energy use, increasing dependence on oil and gas to reduce dependence on coal, with some addition of nuclear power; 2) to diversify the sources of gas and oil imports away from the Soviet Union; 3) to improve energy efficiency; 4) to protect the environment by these policies and by specific measures designed to reduce pollution; and 5) to privatize Poland's energy sector, although the timetable for this is unclear.

Bulgaria

Bulgaria has extremely limited energy sources. Its only indigenous source is some poor quality lignite. Lignite production is a key problem in Bulgaria. Three-quarters of lignite output goes to electricity generation, but current plans are for lignite output and use to increase by 40 to 50 percent by the end of the 1990s; the consequent increase in pollution emissions is a cause for concern. Because of this concern, Bulgaria has been importing as much as two-thirds of energy, and all its oil and gas, from the Soviet Union. Bulgaria's economy generally has been developed to be heavily reliant on trade links with the Soviet Union. Soviet exports to Bulgaria are running at around £1.2 billion a year, of which some £0.8 billion is oil or gas, causing Bulgaria to be especially vulnerable to recent events in the Soviet Union.

The government, as a result of the ending of the Bucharest Agreement, planned to reduce oil imports. Up to 1989, Bulgaria imported 11 mtoe of oil from the Soviet Union, but in 1990 this fell to 7.8 mtoe. In 1991 an agreement for the Soviet Union to deliver five million tonnes of oil was signed, but supplies during the first quarter were well short of this. Also in 1991, the government instituted petrol rationing, cut off lighting and heating from homes for a number of hours, and stopped production in some parts of industry.

The government also stated that it would reduce energy subsidies to the user. Nevertheless, the fact that it still envisages rapid energy growth causes one to question whether price reforms of the type and magnitude of those already in place in Poland and Hungary are seriously intended. Generally, Bulgaria has been relatively slow to adopt economic reforms, compared with other countries in eastern Europe.

As elsewhere in eastern Europe, improved energy efficiency would lead to lower cost of imports and reduced pollution. Although such efficiency could be pursued with western know-how and, at least initially, with fairly modest needs for capital expenditure, its potential would be severely constrained unless the level and pattern of internal energy prices were put on an economically reasonable basis.

Currently, a major part of Bulgaria's long-term energy strategy involves nuclear energy. It has already invested heavily in nuclear power and is planning to meet over half the forecasted increase in electricity demand for 2000 from nuclear power. There are four WWER 440 MW reactors (built between 1969 and 1974) and two newer WWER 1000 MW reactors operating at the Kozlodui nuclear plant, which generates more than 35 percent of Bulgaria's electricity. However, following an incident in 1990, two of the reactors were closed down and in June, the International Atomic Energy Agency warned that the Kozlodui station was unsafe and in need of immediate corrective expenditures. The cost of these corrective repairs has been put at between £140 and £250 million and the new parts and spares would have to be paid to the Soviet Union in hard currency. A second Soviet-designed reactor is being built at Belene, with 1000 MW units imported from Czechoslovakia. This plant is due for completion in 1992-1994 but completion is now in doubt because it is located in an earthquake zone. Nuclear development in Bulgaria is uncertain; the environmental movement is strong and played its part in the resignation of the former President Tyodor Zhivkov.

If nuclear plans are reduced, gas substitution will become a major element in energy policy. Bulgaria currently imports around seven bcm of gas from the Soviet Union. In 1991 gas imports from Iran began and could rise to three bcm by the end of the decade.

Apart from improving energy efficiency, Bulgaria may be able to increase its gas imports to fuel power stations. Whether that is a real option depends on its success in increasing general exports to secure hard currency and providing exports to the Soviet Union, possibly taking gas as barter exchange or getting the Soviet Union to import Bulgarian exports on a dollar priced basis.

One major problem is that Bulgaria had to suspend payments on its foreign debt in 1990. As a result, it lacks western credit to enable it to modernize either its energy sector or the general structure of its industry.

Hungary

Partly because of its geographical location, Hungary is closely integrated into the Soviet energy export system, though it has the benefit of the Adria oil pipeline through Yugoslavia to the Adriatic. It has a good multi-fuel energy mix and produces about half of its energy needs. Even so, its net self-sufficiency could fall to as low as 40 percent by 2005. Oil production of 1.8 million tonnes is expected to decline to 1.5 million tonnes by 2000, and gas output may drop from six bcm to four bcm. Domestic coal production is also falling, partly due to the exhaustion of existing pits; it is estimated that production was between 18 million tonnes and 20 million tonnes in 1989. Currently some 30 percent of Hungary's electricity supply comes from the Soviet Union. A key problem for Hungary is its excessive reliance on Soviet supplies of oil and electricity and the risk this entails.

Hungary's strategic energy plans emphasize the importance of saving energy and seek to diversify its import sources. World Bank loans have been obtained to help finance the preparation and implementation of its conservation program.

Abandonment of the Nagymaros 440 MW hydroelectric scheme on the Danube—under pressure from environmentalists—has left a gap in projected power production. Hungary is now considering the possibility of allowing western firms to build new electricity plants in exchange for future deliveries of power to finance present construction expenditures. Securing additional supplies of gas to assist power generation is an option, with the possibility of linking into the western European gas grid.

Hungary has so far been relaxed towards nuclear power. Four 440 MW reactors at Paks currently generate around one quarter of Hungary's electricity. It is now thought unlikely, however, that plans to expand the country's only (Soviet-designed) nuclear plant there will go ahead, but this is still being discussed with western interests. One new problem—shared with Bulgaria and Czechoslovakia—is that nuclear waste from Soviet reactors can no longer be sent back for disposal in the Soviet Union without charge and they have no nuclear reprocessing or large scale storage facilities of their own.

Hungarian domestic energy prices were raised by as much as 285 percent on June 1, 1991. Coal prices went up by 176 percent on average. In contrast, annual inflation is running at around 30 percent. As a result, Hungarian energy prices are now not too far removed from world prices. This has assisted the introduction of their energy efficiency programs and enabled these to start to have an effect. Progress is also under way in restructuring manufacturing industry and privatizing parts of it with plant closures and extensive re-equipment programs.

Hungary is fortunate in not having severe air pollution problems experienced by its more northerly neighbors. It has some potential for increasing its indigenous fossil fuel output over the medium term, but like others in the region, it does not have the finance to exploit these to the full, particularly in view of its outstanding foreign debt.

Romania

Romania is the only eastern European country with appreciable reserves of oil, about 1.6 billion barrels, which constitute some 80 percent of the proven reserves in eastern Europe. Before 1939, Romania was an oil exporter; since then, with the expansion of its heavy industries and the peaking of its own oil output in the 1970s, it has had to rely on Soviet exports to make up oil supplies. The largest internal energy source, however, is natural gas, which represented 56 percent of its production in 1987, compared to 22 percent for coal and 16 percent for oil. Romania's gas reserves, like those of oil, are limited, and gas output has started to decline. Nevertheless, it remains the only significant gas producer in eastern Europe.

The Romanian economy is now in poor shape. The once thriving oil and gas industries have been neglected and the populace has been forced to endure draconian energy rationing. The immediate impact of the revolution on energy plans has been a cutback in oil exports to improve domestic supply. If the situation stabilizes and Romania opens to western companies, there could be significant opportunities for international oil companies. Oil production has fallen below 9.5 million tonnes, compared to 11 million tonnes in

1985, while gas output has slipped from 35 bcm to an estimated 25 bcm. With foreign expertise and equipment, this decline could probably be reversed. As elsewhere in the East, the main needs seem to be for compressors and other enhanced recovery equipment at mature onshore deposits. Offshore, in the Black Sea, assistance is required in assessing and developing new hydrocarbon discoveries.

Trade protocols signed during the last weeks of President Ceausescu's rule allowed for Soviet gas deliveries nearly to double, rising to 7.34 bcm; and a deal with Iran was arranged for purchases of one bcm of gas via the Soviet grid. Ceausescu also had ambitious plans to develop a nuclear power industry with five reactors in operation by 1995. At present, Romania has no nuclear generating capacity, although a plant at Cernavoda is under construction, five years after its scheduled start-up date.

Czechoslovakia

Because of its central position in Europe, Czechoslovakia has limited options for energy import sources; it receives all its oil and gas imports from the Soviet Union. With 3000 kilometers of gas pipeline crossing its territory, Czechoslovakia receives important transit fees for the large amounts of Soviet gas piped to eastern and western European customers. It also receives favorable rates for assisting the Soviet Union in building the Yamburg-Uzhgorod gas pipeline.

It has substantial reserves of both hard coal and lignite. Domestic coal mines and open-cast workings provide half of Czechoslovakia's energy, though most reserves are of low-grade lignite that causes high amounts of pollution. The best open-cast has now been exploited, and the amount of overburden increased by 44 percent from 1980 to 1989.[3]

The impact of energy use on the environment is a major concern in Czechoslovakia. Northern Bohemia is one of the worst areas for air pollution in Europe because of the extensive use of brown coal and lignite, especially for fueling power stations. This concern has caused the government to revise its energy plan. The view has been advanced that installing modern anti-pollution equipment to retrofit existing coal-fueled stations would exceed the cost of closing them and expanding nuclear power. For this reason, the government plans to expand use of both natural gas and nuclear power.

Czechoslovakia is the biggest customer of Soviet gas, importing around 12 bcm. By 2000, indigenous gas demand is expected to rise to 20 to 25 bcm. Most extra gas will come from the Soviet Union because of concessionary prices, but new gas suppliers are also being sought in Algeria and Iran.

Czechoslovakia has a substantial nuclear energy program. Nuclear plants at Dukovany and Jaslovcy Bohunice already provide about 27 percent of total electricity production. Construction of plants at Mochovce in western

Slovakia and at Temelin in southern Bohemia are under way. In 1990, a contract was signed with Bayernwerk in Munich for the sale of 1400 MW of electricity from the Mochovce nuclear station from 1994 to 1998. No significant environmental protests have been raised against nuclear power, perhaps because the Czech nuclear construction industry seems to be the most advanced in eastern Europe. Indeed, Czechoslovakia is seeking to become an important supplier of nuclear electricity to western Europe. It has an ambitious nuclear power program at a time when, elsewhere in eastern Europe, nuclear power plans and are being scrapped. With some of the worst air pollution in Europe, the Czech people seem to be prepared to accept nuclear power. As a result, the country hoped to meet 40 percent of its electricity needs from nuclear plants. Whether such plans are realistic remains to be seen, considering the high capital costs and long gestation time for nuclear plants.

Opposition to Czechoslovakia's nuclear industry seems to come from outside its borders. Austria, for example, offered Czechoslovakia £170 million in free electricity supplies to shut down its oldest Soviet-designed 440 MW reactors at the Jaslovske Bohunice station in Slovakia, and the Czech government is now understood to have agreed to close the plant.

The Czechoslovakian government has already taken major steps to liberalize its energy prices and bring them more into line with world markets, and further steps are planned. With one of the world's highest per capita electricity use levels, twice that in the EC, Czechoslovakia's efforts to reduce consumption by promoting energy efficiency and restructuring away from heavy industry are of key importance to the economy. Efforts to increase energy prices and to privatize the energy sector should bolster these aims. These steps, together with restructuring its industry and its considerable success in trading with western nations, should assist Czechoslovakia in attracting foreign capital into the energy sector.

ENVIRONMENTAL IMPACTS

A principal reason for interest in the energy sector in the former Comecon countries stems from the air pollution that results from energy use. The East European Six and the former Soviet Union have the highest fossil fuel carbon emissions per capita in the world, except for the United States, and higher carbon emissions as a percentage of GNP than any other country except China. Per capita emissions of sulfur dioxide and NO_x are high, and energy efficiency is low, judged by standards in western Europe. Eastern Europe and the Soviet Union account for over half the SO_2 emissions in Europe.

As a result of their energy intensity and heavy reliance on coal, the Soviet Union and eastern Europe annually emit about 3.6 tonnes of carbon per person (Figs. 17.2 and 17.3). This compares with some 2.3 tonnes per person

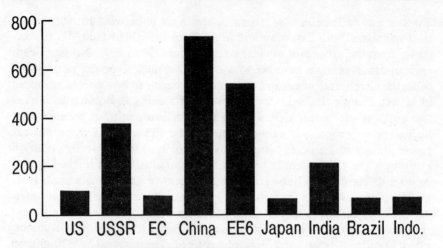

Energy data source: BP Statistical Review of World Energy, June 1989
GNP data source:The World Factbook 1989

Fig. 17.2. Fossil carbon emissions per unit GNP.
(US=100, conventional exchange rates)

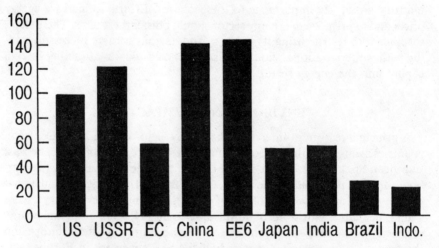

Energy data source: BP Statistical Review of World Energy, June 1989

Fig. 17.3. Fossil carbon emissions per unit RGNP.
(US=100, Purchasing Power Parity basis)

in western Europe, 2.1 tonnes in Japan, and 5.0 tonnes in the United States. The pollution intensity of the Soviet Union and eastern Europe is especially stark when adjusted for the differences in levels of GNP per capita.

The environmental problems of eastern Europe have been well publicized. The levels of exposure to the main pollutants, particularly SO_2 and NO_X in cities there exceed the standards prescribed by their governments (Fig. 17.4). One of the most highly polluted areas is the so-called "dirty boomerang" formed by Northern Bohemia, Lower Saxony and the southwest and southern regions of Poland, including Krakow and Katowice.[4]

These problems have arisen because of the geographical position and because these eastern European economies have in recent decades failed to adapt to higher energy prices by re-equipping their industries and restructuring their economies towards lighter and service activities. As a result, they have relatively high energy use per unit of GNP, high reliance on coal, including high-polluting brown coal and high shares of industrial output in GNP. Moreover, within the industrial sector, they are very dependent upon heavy industries that include chemicals, iron, steel, and other metals.

As these economies become restructured and integrated into world trade patterns, with higher energy prices, western technology, expertise, and managerial control, substantial environmental improvements should result. On the other hand, whereas car ownership in these countries today is very low by OECD standards, as incomes rise increased car ownership in the future will add to the problems of pollution with higher emissions of nitrogen oxides, ozone, and petrochemical smog.

AN ESTIMATE OF THE MAGNITUDE
OF THE OVERALL PROBLEM

It is hard to estimate the investment needs of a group of nations as large as the former Soviet Union and eastern Europe with their vast, poorly distributed reserves, their current pace of political and structural change, and their underpriced energy, but some outside observers have produced estimates. Gaffney, Cline and Associates, for instance, have estimated that the area will require more than an average £80 billion a year of investment for 15 years to meet their economic growth needs. This is based on a perception that these countries as a group will see their demands for energy rise by between 518 mtoe and 924 mtoe, that is, by 26 to 46 percent, over this period due to economic growth. Some 90 percent of the investment is needed in the former Soviet Union. The Soviet need is broken down as 50 percent for oil projects, 39 percent for gas, five percent for coal, four percent for electricity, and the balance for pipelines and refineries. Outside the Soviet Union the largest investment need was seen for the Polish coal industry. Gaffney, Cline and Associates concludes that "the implications for international oil prices of the

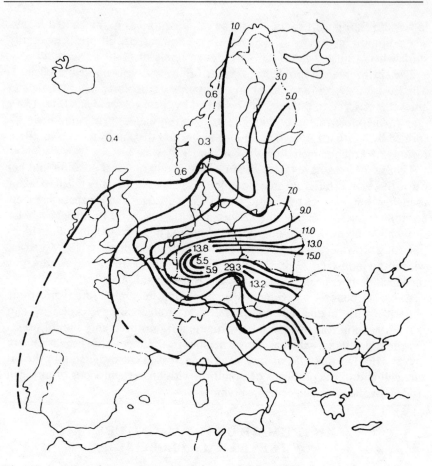

Fig. 17.4. Annual mean concentrations of SO_2, 1985 (μg s/m³).
Source: United Nations

politico-economic changes in eastern Europe is one of steadily increasing upward pressure which could manifest itself during the mid-1990s in escalating oil prices."[15]

The efficient development of the energy sectors of the East European Six and the Soviet Union will not only have a marked impact on living standards in that area, but will also have important global repercussions.

SUPPORT FROM WESTERN DEMOCRACIES

The task confronting the former Soviet Union and the East European Six of industrial restructuring, reforming their societies, and reshaping their economies is a colossal one that will be a painful and lengthy process. In judging progress, it is well to remember that western market-orientated capitalist economies were not created overnight. They, and the democratic legal frameworks which underpin them, evolved into what they are today over centuries in an interactive, trial-and-error process with successive adjustments and fine tuning. There have been few, if any, cases where a market-based economy has come about suddenly. Most of the Soviet Union has not had anything like a market economy for four generations, and eastern Europe for two or three generations. It comes as no surprise, therefore, that the developments in recent years east of the river Elbe and the Bohemian forests have not progressed smoothly.

Structural adjustment—particularly, the restructuring of state-owned enterprises—now has a high priority. Although outputs in the state sector have fallen sharply, unemployment generally has not yet risen to any marked extent; however, this will happen and, when it does, political pressures for relaxing tough reform policies will grow. With limited knowledge of the western world, how can people in eastern Europe be sure that OECD expertise is soundly based and practicable in their countries, and that pain today ensures greater prosperity tomorrow?

The need for support from the West to help the transition to market economies is clear. Various steps have already been taken, as discussed below.

The negotiation of Agreements of Association between the EC and Poland, Hungary, and Czechoslovakia is vitally important in eastern Europe, both economically and politically. There is a need to make these agreements as free trading as possible. Access to the Community's markets (including the sensitive areas of textiles, steel, and agriculture) seems necessary. A successful conclusion to these negotiations would assist the adjustment process.

In 1989 the EC's policy towards central and eastern Europe was extended beyond the negotiation of trade and cooperation agreements to include the provision of financial assistance and practical measures to support the economic reform process. It took the form of coordinating assistance from the 24 OECD countries to Poland and Hungary. Called the Poland/Hungary Aid for Restructuring of Economies (PHARE) exercise, it has since developed to cover a wide range of economic measures and projects and to include large sums of money. Moreover, at Community level, the principle has been endorsed of extending the PHARE exercise, on certain conditions, to include other central and east European countries. On February 16, 1990, the group of 24 OECD countries examined the memoranda presented by Bulgaria, Czechoslovakia, the (then) German Democratic Republic, Romania and Yugoslavia in the light of their progress towards political and economic objectives, including the rule of law, respect for human rights, the establishment of a multi-party system, free elections, and the creation of a market economy. The group expressed its support for the measures already taken or envisaged by each of these countries in their pursuit of political and economic reform. The group confirmed its readiness to coordinate assistance, adapted to each country's own situation. In this way, the PHARE operation was expanded to include these other countries. The PHARE program now has one billion ECUs, that is, £0.7 billion, for support to eastern Europe in 1992.

In December 1989, the European Council proposed the establishment of a European Bank for Reconstruction and Development, (EBRD) as part of the western response to the need for action in support of the eastern European economies. The main objective of the EBRD, now located in London, in consultation with the International Monetary Fund and the World Bank, is to finance productive and competitive investment in central and eastern European countries, to help their transitions to market oriented economies. Thirty nine countries (the OECD countries of the "Group of 24", plus the Soviet Union and central and eastern European countries) agreed to set up the Bank. The ERBD's funds are available for lending purposes and not for expenditures on technical assistance.

The European Commission, following a proposal by the Dutch Prime Minister, Mr. Lubbers, is devising a European Energy Charter designed to promote an open, liberal and non-discriminatory energy market throughout Europe to assist in restructuring the energy sectors of eastern Europe and the Soviet Union on a market-orientated basis. The Charter is designed to provide an agreed set of principles relating to energy and energy trade with a series of protocols negotiated individually, and covering specific sectors and issues attached to the Charter. These intergovernmental agreements will provide the framework and climate of confidence to encourage commercial investment from outside. These agreements will contain the details necessary for freer energy markets within and between the signatories. The UK sees two main objectives for the Charter: to assist the Soviet Union and eastern Europe in their transition to market-based economies and to increase energy liberalization in the more established democracies, both inside and outside the Community. The Charter will reduce discrimination against companies when they operate overseas and provide new commercial opportunities by removing some barriers to trade. It is hoped that getting energy policies right throughout eastern Europe and the Soviet Union will be a catalyst for the transformation of their economies and environment and hence for gains from trade throughout Europe and beyond.

The UK established "know-how funds" to supply eastern European countries and the former Soviet Union with experts and technical assistance. These mirrored other forms of EC technical support and are now under way.

Finally, companies from the West engaged in energy, finance, construction and engineering are participating in joint ventures with concerns in the former Soviet Union to unlock the energy potential of these vast regions with their currently unexploited hydrocarbon resources. So far progress has been slow.

Of 1,790 joint ventures registered in the Soviet Union through 1990, only 350 were active and only seven were in the oil and gas sector.[16] There are various reasons for this: doubts about which Soviet authorities are the appropriate ones to deal with; a tendency for new parties to seek to become involved as negotiations proceed; the lack of an appropriate basis of contract law and private ownership; and uncertainties as to whether flows of oil and gas outputs—as payment in kind—for delivery to world markets can be guaranteed in the years ahead. In addition, the political turmoil of the kind that occurred in August 1991 does not help to encourage foreign business participation. As it is ultimately only through the provision of private capital that the vast sums necessary for the Soviet energy sector can be raised, these issues represent the crucial problem that only the Soviet Union and its republics can resolve. Similar problems exists in negotiation with the East European Six, but to a lesser extent.

REFERENCES

1. *British Petroleum Statistical Review of World Energy* (June 1991).
2. Goskomstat Communique, Ekonomika i zhizn.
3. L. P. Guzhnovski, "Some economical problems of the USSR oil industry," address given at the British Institute of Energy Economics, London, (September 19, 1990).
4. *Pravda* (May 18, 1991).
5. Report by Soviet Ekon Research Group, Moscow (July 1991).
6. Istvan Dobozi, "Impact of market reforms for USSR energy consumption," *Energy Policy* **19**, 4, pp. 313–314.
7. E. Figurnov, "Kak pereity k rynku" (How to make the transition to the market), *Ekonomika i Zhizn* 15 (April 1990).
8. "Tzenoobrazovanie na toplivo i energiu" (Pricing of fuels and energy), *EKO* 8, pp. 59–80 (1989).
9. Yu Borozdin, "Tseny: Vzgliad bez illynzii" (Prices Without Illusions), *Ekonomika i zhizn* 14 (April 1990).
10. *World Gas Intelligence,* p. 3 (June 1991).
11. *Petroleum Economist* **58**, 6, p. 24 (June 1991).
12. "Energy Policies: Poland", International Energy Agency 1990 Survey, led by David le B. Jones (1991).
13. "Energetics and Environment," Table 2, Socioeconomic Institute of CSAV, USTI nad Labem, Czechoslovakia (November 1990).
14. "The State of Transboundary Air Pollution," *Air Pollution Studies* 5, p. 36, United Nations, New York, (1989).
15. "Prospects For and Opportunities in the East European and USSR Energy Markets to 2005," Gaffney, Cline and Associates (1990).
16. Report by Scottish Enterprise Ltd. (July 1991).

18 Does Energy Conservation Worsen Global Warming?

Harry D. Saunders

Energy conservation is the prescription for global warming. So says the preamble to nearly every government's energy policy. So say countless statements in the popular press. The U. S. Environmental Protection Agency, to take one of many examples, loudly promotes more energy-efficient lighting systems to profitably "reduce emissions of greenhouse gases and help curb acid rain and smog."[1] With no loss of economic welfare (or even with a gain), so the arguments go, conservation can curb fossil fuel use, hence CO_2 emissions, and hence global warming.

Yet it may not be so. Rather, energy conservation could in fact have the *exact opposite* effect: *increase* fossil fuel use, hence CO_2 emissions, and hence global warming. More generally, it could increase pollution.

This unsettling conclusion, which at first blush seems wildly counterintuitive, ends up being not so difficult to entertain as it might seem. First, however, a little background is necessary in the way of a more precise definition of conservation.

WHAT IS CONSERVATION?

To a lay person, conservation usually means using less energy to accomplish the same thing as when using more energy. The definition an economist might favor is not too different from this. The one additional question an economist might ask is: Does this gain in energy efficiency cost anything—that is, does the gain in energy efficiency reduce economic welfare in any way? Obviously, if it costs $100 billion (to take an absurd example) to heat a home in winter to the same level with one less cubic foot of natural gas, this would clearly affect one's opinion about the value of such a conservation measure.

It turns out that a useful way to understand conservation, from an economist's viewpoint, is to decide whether or not it is "price induced." By "price induced'' we mean it has somehow come about as a direct result of an energy price increase.

Figure 18.1 shows how this categorization works. To an economist, price-induced energy conservation (i.e., conservation due to higher energy prices) comes about as a result of substitution in the economy of other "factors of production" for energy, namely capital, labor, or materials. This kind of substitution may require new technologies. Energy economists have shown[2] that such substitution comes at a real net cost (i.e., it reduces overall economic welfare) since it requires using these other production factors to replace energy, instead of using them to produce more economic output (more goods and services). An example of such a phenomenon, indicated in Figure 18.1, is home insulation, which substitutes capital for energy. While it is true that such substitution maximizes economic output, given the circumstance of higher energy prices, output is not as great as it would have been without the higher energy prices. Clearly, then, this type of conservation, while it might curb energy use and therefore reduce global warming, is *not* the kind of energy conservation touted by those who claim conservation can reduce energy use without reducing economic welfare.

At the other end of the spectrum, economists think of technologies that are not used for substitution, but rather simply reflect continued improvement in human skills over time—the idea that over time society simply gets smarter about how more efficiently to use energy and other factors of production to generate output. This type of improvement in energy efficiency comes at no real cost to the economy, and therefore represents an outright improvement in economic welfare—reduced input of energy to produce economic output without having pilfered other valuable production factors. Such conservation would truly be welfare-increasing. Economists think of this type of efficiency gain (again, see Figure 18.1) as "factor-augmenting" technical progress, and this is what economists could cite as being the closest to the energy conservation championed by global warming conservationists.† This occurs even in the absence of energy price increases. An example would be an innovative control system for space heating that reduced use of all inputs—capital investment, labor, material, and, of course, energy.

In between these two extremes is a type of energy conservation that, truth be told, is the type most lay persons would tell you they mean when they speak of energy conservation. For economists, this lies in a gray area (Figure 18.1). This type of conservation (a good example is the car pooling that followed from the energy price shocks of the 1970s) is ambiguous in terms of its eco-

---

†A number of researchers have contributed to our understanding of energy productivity and its implications for global warming. Researchers in energy productivity include Schurr, Barnett, Adelman, Watkins and Berndt, Jorgenson, Berndt and Wood, and Schipper, among many others. Researchers in energy and global warming include Manne and Richels, Hogan, Williams, Nordhaus, and Hogan and Jorgenson.

Example	CONSERVATION TYPE	Economic Welfare Impact	Economic Description
Insulation (capital/energy substitution)	*PRICE-INDUCED*	Reduces welfare	Factor substitution
Car pooling?	"Fat-cutting"	?? reduces? (one-time effect)	"Free" good?
"Soft" technologies (passive solar, heat control systems)	NON-PRICE-INDUCED	Increases welfare	Energy-augmenting technical progress

Fig. 18.1. Three types of energy conservation.

nomic welfare impacts. Some people think of it as a pure tradeoff between energy use and economic welfare, and therefore as comparable to price-induced conservation. Others apparently think of it as essentially a "free good," reducing the use of energy by "cutting fat," as it were, meaning, presumably, that the activity could have been carried out just as easily—with no loss of productivity, real economic activity, or convenience—using less energy.† However, there are two problems with this type of conservation from a global warming perspective. First, it is not clear whether this type of conservation is truly costless or whether it instead reduces economic welfare—for instance, to accommodate a car pool, workers might choose to leave work earlier than they would if they had full freedom to choose a departure time, thus reducing production. Second, if it is a free good, it is at most available on a one-time basis. Once the waste has been eliminated, it cannot be eliminated again. It should not be looked to as a mechanism providing endless opportunities for reducing energy consumption without cost.

Therefore, the only mechanism that holds out such promise is the welfare-increasing, factor-augmenting technical progress form of energy conservation. Let us call it here "pure" energy conservation.

"Pure" Energy Conservation

As a potential mechanism for controlling long-term global warming due to energy use, this "pure" conservation would seem the ideal candidate. This

---

†I am grateful to Ed Chilton of Chevron for distinguishing so articulately for me this category of conservation.

type of conservation reduces energy consumption per unit of economic activity without reducing welfare. However, this is where the story becomes curious.

Khazzoom[3] and Brookes[4] have raised the possibility that this "pure" type of energy conservation, if encouraged, might in fact have the perverse effect of actually *increasing* overall energy consumption. (By the way, both of these energy economists somewhat bemusedly credit Jevons[5] with having "scooped" them in a paper published in 1865!) Grossly stated, this Khazzoom-Brookes[6] effect might occur if:

1. this technical improvement in energy efficiency, by reducing the "effective" price of energy, causes energy use to expand due to elastic substitution; or
2. the new economic opportunities created by such technical progress generate enough additional economic activity (and associated energy use) to offset the energy efficiency gains, leading to an overall *increase* in energy consumption, even if energy consumption per unit output drops; or
3. both of these occur.

As it happens, the best way to describe all of this is to look at the Khazzoom-Brookes effect from the perspective of "neoclassical growth theory," a theory espoused largely by Nobel Prize-winning economist Robert Solow[7] that explores how economies grow in the presence of factor-augmenting technical progress. But, don't be put off. The arguments are quite simple and intuitive. All it takes is a little patience with some relatively straightforward math.

NEOCLASSICAL GROWTH THEORY AND ENERGY CONSERVATION

In this section, neoclassical growth theory is used to show how "pure" energy conservation—technical progress in energy use—affects the growth in energy use in the long run.

Neoclassical Growth Without Energy Conservation—the Mathematics

We begin by describing economic growth in the absence of energy conservation (or technical progress of any kind). The basic math is simple.

At its root, growth theory simply combines *a production function:*

$$Y = F(K,L,E)$$

where Y = real economic output,
              K = capital; L = labor; E = energy,
and *an assumption about investment:*

$$I = \frac{\delta Y}{\delta t} = sY$$

where   s = the savings rate.

With standard assumptions, all the results of growth theory then follow.

Neoclassical Growth Without Energy Conservation—the Results

In the absence of technical progress, neoclassical growth theory predicts that **energy consumption will grow at the same rate as economic output**, and energy intensity will stabilize—at fixed energy prices, that is. (Remember that we are talking about **non**-price-induced conservation here, so we are fixing energy prices.) This is shown in Figure 18.2, which charts the results from a simulation of the above set of equations. In fact, it can be seen that **all** factors of production—capital, labor, and energy—grow at the same rate as output.

Neoclassical Growth with Energy Conservation—the Mathematics

But we are concerned with what energy conservation does to energy consumption. The "pure" energy conservation we are considering is factor-augmenting technical progress. It occurs in the absence of energy price rises, and increases, rather than decreases, economic welfare. It is easy to incorporate such technical progress explicitly in the production function.

$$Y = \tau_N F(\tau_K K, \ \tau_L L, \ \tau_E E)$$

where
$$\tau_N = e^{\lambda N t} = \text{neutral technical progress}$$
$$\tau_K = e^{\lambda K t} = \text{capital-augmenting technical progress}$$
$$\tau_L = e^{\lambda L t} = \text{labor-augmenting technical progress}$$
$$\tau_E = e^{\lambda E t} = \text{energy-augmenting technical progress}$$

Neoclassical Growth with Energy Conservation—the Results

The results depend on the form of the production function used. But the Khazzoom-Brookes effect is dramatically illustrated when the most commonly-used production function, the Cobb-Douglas production function, is employed.

With a standard Cobb-Douglas production function, conservation (energy-augmenting technical progress) **increases** energy consumption more than would occur otherwise. Figure 18.3 shows the increased growth rate in energy use due to energy-augmenting technical progress.

In fact, an even more powerful conclusion can be drawn about the impact of technical progress on energy use. As shown in Table 18.1, *all* forms of technical progress (whether neutral, energy-, labor-, or capital-augmenting) increase energy consumption given Cobb-Douglas production. In other words,

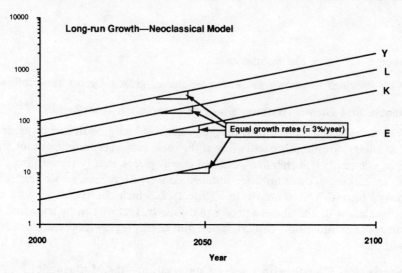

Fig. 18.2. Long-run growth—neoclassical model, with no conservation (Assumes fixed real energy price).

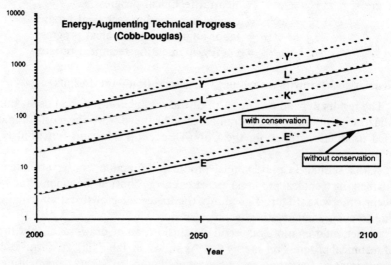

Fig. 18.3. Energy-augmenting technical progress (Cobb-Douglas) increases energy use (Assumes fixed real energy price).

Table 18.1. Simulation assuming all technical progress rates = 1.2 percent/
year and fixed real energy price

	Annual growth rate (%/year)			
Form of technical progress	$\dot{Y}$	$\dot{K}$	$\dot{L}$	$\dot{E}$
None	3.0	3.0	3.0	3.0
Neutral	4.8	4.8	3.0	4.8
Capital-augmenting	3.5	3.5	3.0	3.5
Labor-augmenting	4.2	4.2	3.0	4.2
Energy-augmenting	3.1	3.1	3.0	3.1

the smarter we become at using inputs more efficiently to produce economic output, the **more** energy the economy will use—given the standard Cobb-Douglas description of production, that is.

For different production functions, the story is more complex. Figure 18.4 shows an example that uses a type of production function called a nested CES production function and applies neutral technical progress. In this case, technical progress **increases** energy use as before, but it increases output even more, reducing energy use per unit output (the macroeconomic measure of conservation). More generally, with this type of production function, whether conservation increases or decreases energy consumption can depend on the value of parameters.

Example: Nested CES production function (after Manne and Richels)

If   m = annual growth rate of energy consumption
           r = annual growth rate of economic output
           λ_N = annual rate of neutral technical progress
           λ_E = annual rate of energy-augmenting technical progress
           σ = energy elasticity of substitution

Then $m = r + (\sigma - 1)(\lambda_N + \lambda_E)$.

So if the energy elasticity of substitution is greater than unity, technical progress will result in energy consumption growing even faster than the growth of output; that is, energy intensity will increase. (Note that r is always greater than n, the rate at which energy use would grow without technical progress of any kind.) For this CES example, energy-augmenting technical progress can cause a *decrease* or an *increase* in energy use, depending on the substitution elasticity. This is shown in Figure 18.5.

Conservation Increases Energy Use—A Hypothetical Example

A hypothetical example may help to explain how conservation can increase energy consumption. Such an example is shown in Figure 18.6.

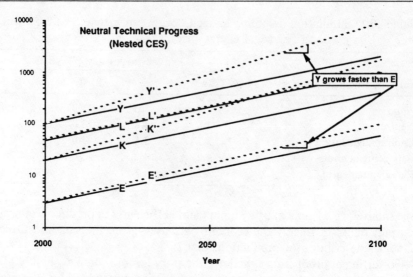

Fig. 18.4. Neutral technical progress (Nested CES) increases energy use (Assumes fixed real energy price).

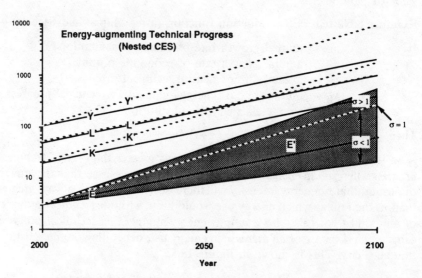

Fig. 18.5. Energy-augmenting technical progress (Nested CES) can increase or decrease energy use (Assumes fixed real energy price).

Example: A new "diesel pill" is developed that turns a 50/50 diesel/water mix into pure diesel fuel

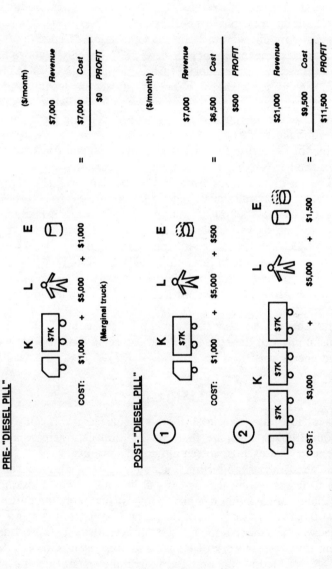

Diminishing returns eventually limit profit.

Fig. 18.6. Hypothetical example shows how conservation can increase energy consumption.

Consider an owner of a fleet of tractor trailer trucks used for transporting consumer goods between San Francisco and Los Angeles. Some of her trucks are more profitable than others. Her marginal truck transports $7,000 worth of goods monthly, and she pays $1,000 monthly payments on the truck, $5,000 per month for the driver, and $1,000 per month for diesel fuel. Her net profit on this marginal truck is therefore $0. When considered in production function terms, inputs are capital (the truck), labor (the driver), and energy (the diesel fuel); economic output is the transportation of goods.

Now suppose someone invents a "diesel pill" that can be added to a 50/50 mixture of diesel fuel and water to turn it into pure diesel fuel. This would be "pure" energy conservation, or energy-augmenting technical progress. It has not resulted from a diesel price increase, does not come by substituting capital or labor for energy, and it is not due to "cutting fat"; however it increases economic welfare.

Initially, the owner finds that costs on her marginal truck have dropped by $500 since her fuel bill has been cut in half from $1,000, increasing her monthly profit on this truck from $0 to $500. However, she discovers that by adding two additional trailers to the rig she can do even better. With three trailers she can triple the transportation of goods to $21,000 per month. Her payments for the rig will triple to $3,000, but her cost for the driver stays the same at $5,000. Her fuel cost triples compared to its level immediately after she began using the "diesel pill," but it is still only $1,500. One result is that her profit increases to $11,500. (Ultimately, diminishing returns will limit how many trailers she can profitably add to a single rig, even if regulations do not.)

But the other result is that the "diesel pill" causes her to triple her profitable consumption of diesel fuel. "Pure" conservation, in other words, has increased energy use.

CONCLUSIONS

We have shown how neoclassical growth considerations can reinforce the Khazzoom-Brookes postulate that conservation can increase, rather than decrease, energy use, thus worsening global warming.

If the Cobb-Douglas production function is a reasonable model of the economy, all forms of technical progress will increase energy consumption, including energy-augmenting technical progress (arguably the purest form of conservation). With other forms of the production function, parametric values determine whether conservation increases or decreases energy use. Importantly, the recent econometric work of Hogan and Jorgenson[8] shows that the form of the U.S. production function and its parameters are such that technical progress probably does increase energy use.

Therefore, policies aimed at encouraging conservation could backfire, thereby increasing long-run energy consumption, hence CO_2 emissions, and hence global warming.

ACKNOWLEDGMENTS

This paper benefited greatly from preliminary discussions with Robert Solow, Massachusetts Institute of Technology, and Thomas Burns, Chevron Corporation, to both of whom I am indebted. In addition, helpful comments were received from Alan Manne, Sam Schurr, Hill Huntington, Lee Schipper, Daniel Khazzoom, Leonard Brookes, Michael Grubb, Ed Chilton, and Robert Kleinbaum. Of course, any errors are mine, not theirs.

REFERENCES

1. EPA full-page advertisement in *Discover* magazine, April 1992.
2. See, for example, Hogan, William W. and Alan S. Manne (1977). "Energy-Economy Interactions: The Fable of the Elephant and the Rabbit?" in Energy and the Economy, *Energy Modeling Forum,* Stanford University.
3. See, for instance, Khazzoom, J. Daniel (1980). "Economic Implications of Mandated Efficiency Standards for Household Appliances." *The Energy Journal* 11(2): 21–40.
4. For example, Brookes, Leonard (1990). "Energy Efficiency and Economic Fallacies." *Energy Policy,* March: 783–785.
5. Jevons, W. Stanley (1865). "The Coal Question—Can Britain Survive?" First published in 1865, reprinted by Macmillan in 1906. (Relevant extracts appear in *Environment and Change,* February 1974.) My thanks to Leonard Brookes for this citation.
6. Saunders, Harry D (1992). "The Khazzoom-Brookes Postulate and Neoclassical Growth." *The Energy Journal* (forthcoming).
7. Beginning with Solow, Robert M. (1956). "A Contribution to the Theory of Economic Growth." *The Quarterly Journal of Economics* 52: 65–94.
9. Hogan, William W., Dale W. Jorgenson (1991). "Productivity Trends and the Cost of Reducing CO_2 Emissions." *The Energy Journal* 12(1): 67–85.

19 Economics and the Greenhouse Effect: Some Early Implications for Coal

Stuart Beil, Quentin Croft, Mike Hinchy, and Brian S. Fisher

ECONOMIC ISSUES

The Nature of the Greenhouse Problem

The enhanced greenhouse effect is an externality caused by the failure of markets to price or grant property rights for the use of the atmosphere. This externality occurs because, to a large extent, the atmosphere is a free good to which everybody has uncontrolled access, and individuals generally bear only a small proportion of the costs associated with their activities. Without some signal to users of the atmosphere that their activities are imposing costs on others, the way in which the atmosphere is used will not be optimal. In some instances the quality of the atmosphere will be degraded and in the case of the greenhouse effect there may be global consequences.

Policies to alleviate any adverse consequences of the greenhouse effect will require multilateral action. Unilateral action to counter the increased greenhouse effect is unlikely to be effective because the benefits from reducing greenhouse emissions cannot be captured by the instigating country alone although it would bear the costs of whatever actions it undertakes. The net costs of any unilateral action, like the imposition of a carbon tax, will fall on the economy of the country instigating such independent policies. Overall, this will probably have a negligible impact on global emissions unless other countries follow with similar policies. Consequently, efforts by one group to restrict greenhouse gas emissions will have little effect on the quality of the atmosphere when all other groups retain uncontrolled access to the resource.

Multilateral action is necessary because of such free access to the atmosphere. With free access to the atmosphere, individuals have little, if any, financial incentive to maintain its quality at any level of operational efficiency. Solutions to this problem range from creating or simulating a market in the use of the atmosphere and allocating property rights in this market to regulating the use of the atmosphere as a sink for greenhouse gases. However, access rights cannot be based on the resource itself, since the atmosphere cannot be captured by individual countries. Access rights need to be linked to the services provided by the resource. In this case the service is the atmosphere's ability to absorb greenhouse gas emissions without unacceptable results. It is of course inevitable that some degree of climate change will be optimal in the sense that it is consistent with achieving the best intertemporal allocation of global resources.

Possible Solutions

Any policy response to the greenhouse effect must take into account the cost of reducing greenhouse gases and the costs imposed by the greenhouse effect. The optimal response will minimize both of these costs by limiting greenhouse emissions up to the point where the net cost of reducing emissions by a marginal tonne is equal to the marginal benefit obtained by doing so. There are uncertainties surrounding the exact calculation of optimal emission levels and the time frame involved, but there is no doubt that the problem is a very long-term one. Consequently, the use of policies like carbon taxes and tradable emissions rights needs to be evaluated in a long-term framework. Over such a long-term period, the development and use of new and more efficient energy technologies can also be expected to mitigate greenhouse emissions.

One solution to the concerns about the level of carbon dioxide emissions from coal use lies in the development of new coal burning technologies. The conversion efficiency of conventional plants is technologically constrained to between 30 and 40 percent. Clean coal technologies can achieve an extra 10 to 20 percent increase in efficiency compared with conventional plants, with considerably less environmental impact.

To achieve commercially viable clean coal technologies, substantial financial commitment to research and development programs is required. Already, significant funds have been committed to clean coal technologies in countries like the United States and Japan. This investment is in response to a projected worldwide market for coal technologies of over A$70 billion a year by the year 2000. Australia recognizes the importance of clean coal technology development, and to date has focused on brown coal and coal preparation. While it is clear that these technologies will improve the efficiency of coal consumption and lower costs, it is less certain that their introduction will result in lower coal consumption and reduced carbon dioxide emissions overall.

Economic policies designed to allocate access rights to the atmosphere can take two broad forms. These include a charge or tax placed on activities that use and degrade the atmospheric resource, or a quota allowing certain amounts of greenhouse emissions. A charge or tax amounts to payment in return for the privilege of using the atmosphere for waste disposal on a short-term basis while a quota or tradable emission right is a permanent asset with a value (assuming that the quota is binding). Such approaches could be applied at either a national or international level.

Tradable Emission Rights

A tradable emission right amounts to a marketable right to a proportion of the atmospheric resource. To be effective, desired annual global greenhouse emissions would have to be agreed upon in a multilateral forum. The rights to emit given quantities would then be granted to governments of sovereign nations which would be free to enforce or otherwise influence the level of emissions as they saw fit. If such a system is to succeed, it would first be necessary to resolve any question of equity associated with the initial allocation of emission rights. The initial allocation, and any necessary monitoring system, would most likely require extensive international negotiation.

Trade of emission rights would need to be possible to ensure that countries with the highest value uses could acquire the right to emit from those involved in lower valued uses. Furthermore, a country wishing to emit more carbon dioxide than it was initially allocated would be able to purchase the extra emission quota from a country willing to sell. A more efficient distribution of emissions would result with such a market in place.

If a workable tradable emissions scheme is to be developed, a number of major problems would have to be overcome. The first problem concerns the coverage of the scheme in terms of both gases and activities. It is estimated that during the 1980s the increasing concentration of carbon dioxide in the atmosphere was responsible for 57 percent of the increase in global warming potential, with the remaining 43 percent accounted for by methane, nitrous oxide, chlorofluorocarbons, and tropospheric ozone.[2] However, the relative importance of greenhouse gases other than carbon dioxide is expected to increase in future decades.[2] Further, deforestation is estimated to contribute 20 to 25 percent of the increased global warming potential due to carbon dioxide emissions.[3,4]

If the least cost solution for world control of the greenhouse effect is to be found, it is desirable to permit trade-offs between all activities that contribute to the effect. The difficulty is that there are varying degrees of understanding about the sources of emissions. The ease of controlling and monitoring these sources differs. Carbon dioxide emissions from the burning of fossil fuels may be one of the best understood and most easily monitored sources of emissions. However, limiting a scheme to carbon dioxide emissions would not achieve a global least cost allocation of resources for control of the greenhouse problem.

Afforestation and deforestation should also be covered by the scheme. Positive afforestation could earn emission credits and deforestation debits. The position of Brazil (as a seller or buyer of rights) under any scheme would be profoundly affected by the treatment of deforestation.[5]

If all gases and activities were to be covered by the scheme, a decision would have to be made whether to set a quota for different gases or a quota for a composite of greenhouse gases. A difficulty with both approaches is that there is some scientific disagreement about the relative contribution of different gases to global warming as the contribution depends on both the radiative capacity of the gas and the atmospheric life of the gas.

To obtain agreement on the size of quotas is a further problem. Agreement will be difficult since the quota will impose different costs on the participating countries and there will be uncertainty about the benefits. There may be a 20 year lag between changes in greenhouse gas concentrations and the full effect of global warming, with the possibility of a cumulative feedback effect compounding the warming.[6]

A major economic problem is the "free rider" problem. Countries not joining the scheme and remaining free to set their own emissions may benefit from reduced emissions from countries that join the scheme. In fact, the problem may be even more difficult since some countries may actually benefit from the greenhouse effect. In the absence of any form of world government forcing participation, a tradable emissions scheme to control the greenhouse effect would be voluntary. Thus, the free rider problem appears to be a potentially serious difficulty.

To be induced to participate in the scheme, a country would have to believe that the net benefits of participating exceeded the net benefits of not participating. The direct net benefits of participating would consist of the perceived benefits (or costs) of the reduction in greenhouse gas concentrations that would be achieved and the costs (benefits) obtained from the purchase (sale) of emission rights. Assuming competitive conditions, at the margin the price paid for the last quota bought (sold) would reflect the marginal value of the economic activity permitted (forgone).

Included in the costs of participating in the scheme (perhaps financed as a percentage of the price of quotas when exchanged) would be the costs of monitoring adherence to quotas. The incentives to violate quotas would be essentially the same as those not to participate in the scheme. These could be substantial. Hence monitoring costs for the scheme may also be substantial.

The net benefits of not participating would probably consist of a probability weighting of two states. One state would be where there was no scheme and a country would compare the costs (benefits) of the greenhouse effect with the benefits of no controls on its emission levels. The second state would occur where there was a partial scheme among other countries and benefits and costs would be estimated under these conditions.

There may also be indirect benefits and costs from participating in the scheme. Countries taking action to reduce their emissions may reduce their international competitiveness. Such action may benefit both participating countries that are not reducing their emission levels and non-participating countries. On the other hand, if the large majority of trading countries decided to participate in such a scheme, it is not inconceivable that the majority might decide to impose trade sanctions on those that did not participate.

It is clear that the initial allocation of quotas will have a major bearing on the assessment by a country of the net benefits of participating in the scheme. A large number of criteria have been suggested for the initial allocation of quotas.[5,7,8] However, only a limited number of criteria may be economically relevant. To be economically relevant, criteria would have to induce a sufficient number of countries to participate in the scheme so that progress in controlling the greenhouse effect is made.

Some recent theoretical work[9] suggests a solution to the initial allocation problem. It has been shown that in a model of an economy with a public good and agreement about the desired level of production of this good, there exists a mechanism for sharing the costs of its production that makes everyone better off after participation, rather than either relying on the limited action of others or not taking part at all. There is a major jump from this simplistic model to the more complex problem of a tradable emissions scheme. Nevertheless, there is some hope that a solution has been found to a somewhat analogous problem.

If a tradable emissions scheme were established, it would be after a period of protracted bargaining. Each detail of the scheme such as the coverage of gases and activities, the size of the quota, monitoring procedures, and the initial allocation of this quota will affect the costs and benefits of each participating country.

In spite of the difficulties, a tradable emissions scheme represents a market-based approach to the greenhouse problem. As such, it provides a way of adjusting rapidly to new information about the greenhouse effect that becomes available as research progresses.

Carbon Taxes

Carbon dioxide has been calculated to be the predominant contributor to greenhouse gas emissions (Fig. 19.1), responsible for about 55 percent of total emissions.[10] About eight percent of this can be attributed to coal combustion for electricity generation.[11] A tax on the carbon content of fossil fuels has received significant international attention as a policy option to reduce greenhouse gas emissions. In effect, this policy imposes a charge on the polluting

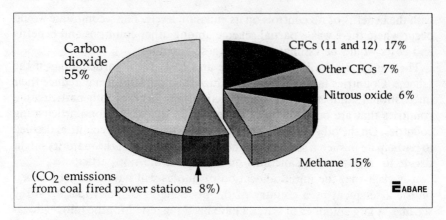

Fig. 19.1. The estimated contribution from each of the greenhouse gases to the change in radiative forcing from 1980 to 1990. The contribution from ozone may also be significant, but cannot be quantified at present.

activities of fossil fuel users. A carbon tax raises the cost of using fossil fuels, thus raising the price of the energy services provided by fossil fuels. With such a tax in place, markets should respond by beginning to conserve energy and seek areas of efficiency gains, for example, through inter-fuel substitution and technological developments. However, questions remain about the effectiveness of such a tax and whether it is possible to implement such a tax on a global basis. The revenue implications of a tax and the effects of the way in which the tax revenue is dispersed by governments also need to be considered.

Governments wishing to impose a carbon tax require simultaneous multilateral cooperation. That is, countries that are first to impose a carbon tax and increase the cost of using fuels with a high carbon content could be at an economic disadvantage in international competition should others be slow to reciprocate.

Some Scandinavian countries have introduced formal carbon taxes. Finland has agreed to a tax equal to US$6.10 per tonne of carbon emitted, while Sweden has made an even greater tax commitment in the order of US$39 per tonne.[12] However, these tax levels are relatively small and at this stage have not substantially affected the relative prices of different fuels.

The real test of the carbon tax policy is its effectiveness in achieving reduced greenhouse emissions. Clearly, international harmonization of the tax is necessary if the environmental cost is to be properly reflected. The purpose of a carbon tax is defeated if fuel taxes are lowered simultaneously, for example by 50 percent as proposed by the Swedes. In this case, it appears that carbon taxes are merely being substituted for fuel taxes as another means by which governments can raise substantial amounts of revenue, while simultaneously minimizing the net effect on their own economies. It is therefore inconsistent if countries adopt such policy mixes while trying to be seen as actively participating in reducing greenhouse emissions.

The notion that countries could not manipulate their tax regimes so easily if a carbon tax were truly international begs further discussion. If the proceeds from a carbon tax were directed to an international body, what would the proceeds be used for, how would decisions be made, and would nations be willing to contribute significant amounts of their income in the first place?

Haynes, Fisher and Jones[7] report that current global consumption of fossil fuel produces over five gigatonnes (Gt) of carbon a year with over 75 percent coming from just 12 countries. To achieve the Toronto target, given a low price elasticity of demand for fossil fuel, an emission charge of 50 percent on present price levels was estimated. Assuming a four Gt carbon emission, the tax could yield annual revenues of about US$400 billion. (This estimate does not account for substitution between fuels, or between fuels and capital, nor does it allow for increased demand as a result of population growth and per person GDP growth.)

Australia's contribution would be just over one percent or US$5 billion, which is almost two percent of GDP. It is evident that the financial payments by some of the larger carbon dioxide emitting countries could be quite significant. It is therefore difficult to imagine countries being willing to support a policy with such large payments, unless they perceive at least commensurate benefits. As yet, considerable uncertainties still surround the benefits from greenhouse mitigation.

A key issue in this debate is the estimates of price elasticities of demand for fossil fuels. A partial analysis has been undertaken by the Australian Bureau of Agricultural and Resource Economics (ABARE), including calculations of international coal own-price and cross-price elasticities of demand and elasticities of demand for Australian coal to changes in the relative prices of coal from competing suppliers. Data from 1978 to 1988 on the use of fuels in the electricity generation, iron and steel and industrial sectors in Europe and Japan and the OECD countries as a group have been used to derive estimates of the elasticity of demand for coal. Preliminary results of this research are presented later in this paper.

Australian Energy Demand Projections and Greenhouse Targets

In October 1990, the Australian government adopted an "interim planning target" for 2005 to reduce greenhouse gas emissions by 20 percent below 1988 levels. The means by which this target is to be achieved are as yet unclear, though several policy options are available. The Australian government has announced that it will not consider measures which have a net adverse economic impact nationally or on Australia's trade competitiveness in the absence of similar action by major greenhouse gas producing countries.[13]

ABARE regularly publishes long-term domestic energy supply and demand projections. The most recent[14] includes a "business as usual" projection and, for the first time, a greenhouse gas reduction scenario.

The "business as usual" scenario estimates energy consumption and supply in the absence of government action to reduce greenhouse gas emissions. It represents a baseline from which the extent of action needed to achieve a reduction planning target can be measured.

The results under this scenario are presented in Fig. 19.2 for total energy production by fuel type and in Fig. 19.3 for total energy consumption by fuel. Total Australian energy production is projected to increase to 13,961 PJ in 2004–05, or at an average rate of 3.0 percent a year from 1989–90. Black coal and uranium are projected to show strong production growth. All uranium and about two-thirds of black coal produced is projected to be exported in 2004–05. Overall, in energy terms, 69 percent of Australian production in 2004–05 is projected to be exported, while imports are expected to represent about eight percent of production.

Total energy consumption is projected to grow at an average annual rate of 2.1 percent between 1989–1990 and 2004–05. Black coal and crude oil are projected to remain the dominant fuels consumed in Australia. In 2004–05, about 63 percent of the energy input to thermal electricity generation is projected to come from black coal consumption. This represents a growth of 5.7 percent from the year 1989–90. Natural gas consumption is also projected to continue growing, particularly in the manufacturing and electricity generation sectors.

To achieve a 20 percent reduction in carbon dioxide emissions from 1987–88 levels, 1989–90 emissions would have to be reduced by 27 percent—roughly equal to the emissions resulting from 80 percent of all black coal consumption (Fig. 19.4). This point illustrates the size of reductions required to achieve the "interim planning target." If the target is to be met, fundamental changes to energy markets will have to take place. Broadly, the options available include:

- increasing the efficiency of energy use;
- inter-fuel substitution to lower carbon dioxide emitting fuels per unit of energy;
- reducing the demand for services provided by energy; and
- trapping emissions at source to prevent them from entering the atmosphere.

Ideally, greenhouse gas emissions targets should be achieved without reducing society's net welfare. However, emission reduction by lowering the demand

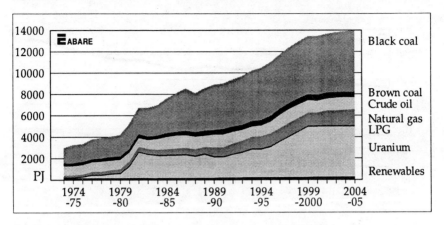

Fig. 19.2. Total Australian energy production, by fuel.

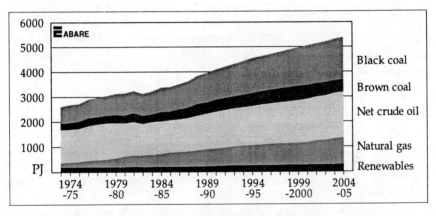

Fig. 19.3. Total Australian energy consumption, by fuel.

for services provided by energy could impose substantial costs on society. The first two options appear most feasible, while the last option is very expensive and not yet well developed.

Analysis by Jones et al[14] of options for meeting the "interim planning target" considers a greenhouse gas reduction scenario based on determining the potential of the first two options. The use of these options makes assumptions that represent historically unprecedented rates of change in the way energy is used in Australia and the most cost-effective way of achieving this change. Examples of some assumptions include 80 percent of hot water heating to be achieved by using solar energy and efficiency improvements of 25 percent for other residential appliances; 80 percent of black coal used in the cement and basic nonferrous metals industries substituted by natural gas; and for

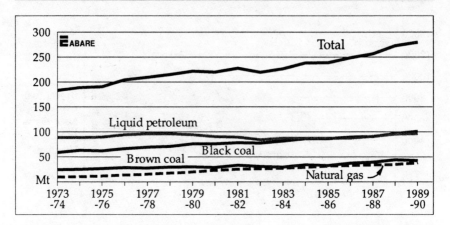

Fig. 19.4. Australian carbon dioxide emissions from the energy sector.

all other industries efficiency improvements of 30 percent for primary fuels and 20 percent for electricity; a 20 percent efficiency improvement in the average fuel use of fleet cars; and the assumption that no new black coal fired electricity generating capacity would be commissioned after 1989–90, and that all additional electricity demand would be met by natural gas combined cycle units.

The results of these historically unprecedented energy efficiency and conservation assumptions, however, go only halfway from the "business as usual" scenario to meeting the government's emission reduction interim target (Fig. 19.5). Total compliance with the target would appear to be difficult in the absence of major energy price changes or government intervention. Achievement of the full target by relying on cost-effective gains in energy efficiency alone would seem to be improbable.

The difficulty in meeting the target is compounded by population and income growth projections which will add upward pressure to energy demand unless there are continual efficiency gains sufficient to offset this tendency. Any efficiency gains might reduce the cost of energy and increase consumers' demand for energy services. Thus, efficiency gains alone are unlikely to reduce energy consumption per person proportionally, as assumed in the above analysis. Finally, no assessment of the effects on Australia's energy exports of actions taken by other countries in meeting their greenhouse targets has been made. The effects of these actions could be considerable.

It has been suggested that a major area for concern in the energy sector is that of market failure in the provision of information. This form of market failure differs from the problem of free access to the atmosphere. However, it is related because solving market failure within energy industries will have an effect on total greenhouse gas emissions and hence the quality of the atmosphere.

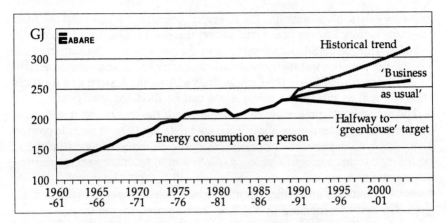

Fig. 19.5. Projected Australian energy consumption per person.

Commentators have argued that many energy-related technologies in use worldwide are far less efficient than the best available. This poses the notion that the market has failed to provide the information or incentive for adoption and use of the most efficient energy-related technologies. Unilateral action to overcome this market failure is feasible as is evident by the use of pulverized coal injection in steel making and more fuel-efficient cars and lighting. Hence, additional unilateral energy conservation measures could reduce the costs of using energy and therefore the amount of greenhouse gas emissions per unit of energy.

Whether market failure exists in a number of Australian markets for energy and energy-using products is an open question. At present there is considerable government intervention in energy pricing that may discourage the establishment of an efficient pattern of energy consumption.

Irrespective of the degree of failure in energy markets, adopting policies to reduce domestic market failure will not overcome the fundamental problem of free access to the atmosphere.[7] There is still no mechanism to prevent the growth of greenhouse emissions after new technologies have been installed. Overcoming intra-country market failures may lower the base from which the growth of greenhouse gases is measured, but it would not necessarily prevent global emission growth.

The adoption by Australia of policies to mitigate the greenhouse effect will affect the structure of the Australian energy sector and economy. In the process of analyzing policy it is important to ascertain the least cost combination of technology and policy options. An energy sector database is being compiled and MENSA (Multiple Energy Systems in Australia), an Australian regionalized version of the MARKAL model, is being used for policy evaluation. MARKAL is a large-scale linear programming model of the energy sector which was developed by the International Energy Agency during the 1970s and now exists in versions specific to several countries. It has been the basis for many national energy policy studies over this period. The Australian regionalized version, MENSA, was developed in the early 1980s. The dispersed nature of the largely capital city centered electricity loads and future patterns of electricity transmission interconnections among the eastern and southern states as well as interstate gas pipelines can be modeled specifically.

The model is comprehensive in its treatment of the energy sector and therefore requires an extensive database. Base case data for 1990–91 include production, imports, exports, and consumption for primary energy sources, in addition to technologies available for conversion to secondary energy sources. Objective functions can be specified which will compute least cost combinations of technology and policy options to best meet greenhouse emission targets. The results generated by MENSA can be used by the ORANI model of the Australian economy to evaluate the impact of greenhouse policies and technologies on key variables in the Australian economy.

IMPLICATIONS FOR COAL

Coal is an important source of energy worldwide (see Table 19.1). In OECD countries, for example, it currently accounts for 21 percent of primary energy use. Coal provides much of the energy necessary for the production of steel and generation of electricity. As a result, its consumption has been inextricably linked to the economic growth of many countries.

ABARE projections[15] indicate that world seaborne steaming coal trade will almost double to just over 330 megatonnes (Mt) by 2004–05 (Fig. 19.6). This is in contrast with the seaborne coking coal trade which is expected to increase only slightly to around 165 Mt. Given the many uncertainties associated with the extent and type of regulations that will be adopted to reduce greenhouse gas emissions and the extent of global commitment to redress the problem, these projections to 2004–05 assume that environmental policies will have only a minimal impact on coal demand.

The projected large increase in world steaming coal trade reflects an expected rise in demand for electricity, particularly in the newly industrialized and developing countries of Asia, due to:

- strong economic growth projections;
- the continued expansion in coal-fired power generation stations as a major source of power in many countries;
- the rationalization of high cost coal production in several industrialized countries; and
- the continued use of steaming coal as a primary source of energy by industries outside the power generation sector.

Table 19.1. Major coal producing and consuming countries, 1988 (Mt)

Country	Production	Domestic consumption
China	940.5	926.4
United States	783.5	699.3
Soviet Union	526.4	498.9
Poland	193.0	161.8
India	188.3	188.3
South Africa	178.2	135.6
Australia	141.0	48.6
United Kingdom	103.8	114.1
Germany (Western)	79.3	81.8
Republic of Korea	24.3	47.9
Japan	11.2	112.4

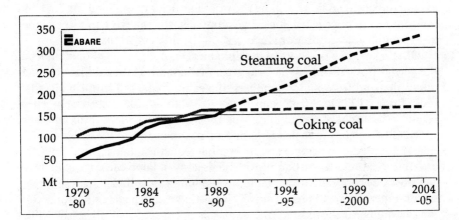

Fig. 19.6. World seaborne coal exports.

Total Asian seaborne steaming coal imports are expected to rise from a forecasted 81 Mt in 1990–91 to around 160 Mt in 2004–05. Over the same period, western European seaborne steaming coal imports are projected to rise from 74 Mt to 136 Mt.

These projected increases in steaming coal trade will continue to be of major importance to the Australian, South African and U.S. economies. Over the projection period, developing countries and steaming coal exporters such as Colombia and Indonesia are also expected to benefit from the projected increases in steaming coal trade. Both of these countries could expand their coal trade by about 20 Mt over the projection period.

One example of a study that at this very early stage has attempted to predict the effect of greenhouse policies on seaborne steaming coal trade is that of Price.[16] He first projected world seaborne steaming coal trade for 2004–05 to be about 340 million tonnes of coal equivalent (Mtce)(similar to ABARE's projection) and then presented a range of outcomes for world seaborne steaming coal trade that assumed significant substitutions to natural gas, and after 1995 a severe carbon tax. Results indicate that greenhouse policies could reduce trade anywhere in the range of up to 115 Mtce in 2004–05. This is a very large range, equivalent to one-third of trade, and highlights the uncertainties surrounding greenhouse policy choices.

Coal Elasticities and Carbon Taxes

As previously mentioned, there are difficulties in deciding on the level and form of carbon taxes. One of the important pieces of information required to decide at what level to set a tax on coal, in order to gauge its effect on carbon dioxide emissions, will be the price elasticity of demand for coal and inter-fuel cross-price elasticities. The more inelastic the estimates, the higher a tax would need to be to reduce carbon dioxide emissions.

ABARE research on short to medium term elasticities based on data from the period from 1978 to 1988[17] suggests that conditional own-price elasticities of demand from major suppliers of steaming coal in Europe and Japan range from −1.775 to −0.469 and from −0.364 to −0.205, respectively. These results indicate coal demand in Europe and Japan can be quite price inelastic.

Overall though, the inelastic nature of coal demand in these regions implies that in order to achieve any substantial reductions in coal consumption, and thus coal-related carbon dioxide emissions, a large carbon tax or price rise would be required. Such a policy would impose significant losses in terms of consumer surplus. Those relatively inelastic steaming coal importing economies would bear the most significant losses in consumer surplus. Any reductions in steaming coal trade would also adversely affect steaming coal exporting countries.

The implications of a carbon tax for coal in the future are likely to be significant because coal emits a higher proportion of carbon dioxide per unit of energy in comparison with other fossil fuels such as oil and gas. Coal emits approximately 25 kilograms (kg) per gigajoule (GJ), which is twice that of gas and about four kg/GJ higher than oil. As a result of coal's relatively high carbon content, the adoption of carbon taxes will tend to adversely affect coal more than other fossil fuels. (For a detailed discussion of these issues, see Thorpe, Sterland, Jones, Wallace and Pugsley.)[18]

As alluded to earlier in the paper, if fuel taxes are reduced in the same proportion to a carbon tax increase, coal again will be the most adversely affected because current fossil fuel taxes raise more revenue in petroleum related industries as opposed to the coal industry. A switch away from fuel taxes will reduce petroleum prices and therefore increase petroleum's inter-fuel competitiveness and demand relative to coal.

CONCLUSIONS

The greenhouse effect is potentially the biggest challenge facing all fossil fuel energy markets, including coal. Coal's contribution to total greenhouse emissions is relatively small, but nevertheless the coal industry will face significant challenges in a policy environment where options such as carbon taxes are being considered.

Carbon taxes have been extensively discussed over recent years. There are some vagaries, such as the specificity and treatment of the revenue raised by such a tax, which require clarification. Carbon tax research indicates that tax rates needed to meet the carbon dioxide emission targets under consideration will need to be high to be effective. Therefore, such a tax is potentially of major consequence for economic activity. Additionally, since the accumulation of carbon dioxide is a global concern, measures such as a carbon tax will require multilateral action.

A considerable degree of uncertainty remains as to the nature, extent, and time frame involved in the greenhouse effect. What is clear, though, is that the problem is a global one requiring global cooperation. The more complete the global commitment toward greenhouse reductions, the more effective policy solutions will be.

REFERENCES

1. J. Stocker, "The Impact of Clean Coal Technologies," CSIRO paper presented at the National Coal Week Conference, Sydney (April 15, 1991).
2. D. A. Lashof and D. R. Ajua, "Relative Contribution of Greenhouse Gas Emissions to Global Warming," *Nature* **344**, 529 (1990).
3. D. W. Pearce and R. K. Turner, "Economics of Natural Resources, and the Environment," BPCC Wheatons, Great Britain (1990).
4. U.S. Department of Energy Multi-laboratory Climate Change Committee, *Energy and Climate Change*, Lewis Publishers, Chelsea, MI (1990).
5. G. Bertram, "Tradable Emission Permits and the Control of Greenhouse Gases," Paper presented at the Conference on the Economics of Environmental Policy, Canberra (Oct. 11, 1990).
6. A. Ravel and V. Ramanathan, "Observational Determination of the Greenhouse Effect," *Nature* 342, 758 (1989).
7. J. Haynes, B. S. Fisher and B. P. Jones, "An Economic Perspective on the Greenhouse Effect," *Agriculture and Resources Quarterly* 2 (3), 307, ABARE, Canberra (1990).
8. M. Grubb, "The Greenhouse Effect: Negotiating Targets," Royal Institute of International Affairs, London (1989).
9. S. Weber and W. Wiesmith, "The Equivalence of Core and Cost Share Equilibria in an Economy with a Public Good," *Journal of Economic Theory* **54** (1), 180 (1991).

10. Intergovernmental Panel on Climate Change, "Climate Change: the IPCC Scientific Assessment," Report to IPCC from Working Group I, University Press, Cambridge, Great Britain (1990).
11. World Coal Institute, *Coal and the Greenhouse Effect,* World Coal Institute, London (1990).
12. The Economist, "Green Taxes; Where There's Muck There's Brass," p. 54, London (March 17, 1990).
13. R. Kelly and J. Kerin, "Joint Statement—Government Sets Targets for Reductions in Greenhouse Gases," Press release, Commonwealth of Australia, Canberra (Oct. 11, 1990).
14. B. P. Jones, S. Bush, A. Kanakaratnam, M. Leonard and P. Gillan, *Projections of Energy Demand and Supply: Australia 1990-91 to 2004-05,* AGPS, Canberra (1991).
15. D. A. Muir and S. J. Beil, "Outlook for World Coal Trade," ABARE paper presented at the National Agricultural and Resources Outlook Conference, Canberra (Jan. 29-31, 1991).
16. D. Price, "The Impact of Potential Environmental Measures for the Steam Coal Trade and Prices," WEFA paper presented at the National Coal Week Conference, Sydney (April 15, 1991).
17. K. Ball and T. Loncar, "European and Japanese Demand for Australian Coal: A Systems Approach to Import Demand," ABARE paper presented at the Conference of Economists, University of New South Wales, Sydney (Sept. 24-27, 1990).
18. S. Thorpe, B. Sterland, B. P. Jones, N. A. Wallace and S-A. Pugsley, *World Energy Markets and Uncertainty to the Year 2100: Implications for Greenhouse Policy,* ABARE Discussion Paper 91.9, AGPS, Canberra (1991).

20 The Clean Air Act Amendments of 1990: Implementation of the Acid Rain Provisions

Leonard L. Coburn

INTRODUCTION

The U.S. President signed the Clean Air Act Amendments of 1990 on November 15, 1990, and industries regulated by this new law confronted an entire new scheme for controlling their industrial emissions.[†] The sweeping nature of the new clean air law will mean significant changes in the way many industries do business. None will be more affected than the electric power industry. For the first time, acid rain caused in part by sulfur dioxide (SO_2) emissions from electric generating power plants will be the subject of a nationwide reduction effort.

The acid rain provisions of the new Clean Air Act Amendments (CAAA) require the reduction of SO_2 emissions by about one half by placing a cap on electric power industry SO_2 emissions. By the year 2000, this industry will be limited to 8.9 million tons of SO_2 emissions per year. The acid rain provisions also seek to control nitrogen oxide (NO_x) emissions by reducing them in 2000 by 2 million tons per year.

The acid rain reduction program relies upon a unique emissions trading system to implement the SO_2 reduction program.[‡] Allowances, representing

---

[†] The emissions include sulfur dioxide (SO_2), nitrogen oxides (NO_x), carbon monoxide, volatile organic compounds (VOCs), hazardous pollutants (toxics), and minute particulates less than 10 microns known as PM-10.

[‡] Two previous papers by the author provide additional perspective on the emissions trading system. "Emissions Trading: A Market-Based Solution for Environmental Problems in the Electric Power Industry," in Conference Proceedings of 13th Annual International Conference, IAEE, Copenhagen, Denmark, June 19–21, 1990, Vol. I, and "The Clean Air Act: Energy and Environmental Interactions," in Conference Proceedings of 12th Annual North American Conference, IAEE, Ottawa, Ontario, Canada, October 1–3, 1990, pp. 6–17.

the right to emit one ton of SO_2 per year, will be distributed to existing power plants up to certain defined SO_2 emission levels.† Electric generating units will have the choice of meeting the emission limits through a variety of strategies—technology, fuel switching, conservation—or buying additional allowances, as necessary. Since each generating unit is given only enough SO_2 allowances each year to meet the statutory emission limits, power plants wanting more allowances will have to buy them on the open market from other holders of allowances. Allowances become the currency of the emissions trading system. This approach encourages least cost compliance for SO_2 reduction since companies either will make investments to control emissions or buy allowances, whichever is cheaper.

The CAAA establishes tight deadlines for the implementation of emissions trading. The rules for auctions and sales of allowances by the Environmental Protection Agency (EPA) are due within one year of enactment or by November 15, 1991. All the remaining rules are due within 18 months of enactment or by May 15, 1992. These deadlines impose substantial burdens upon the EPA to develop the rules quickly with as much consensus as possible in order to expedite the publication of the rules.‡

THE IMPLEMENTATION PROCESS IN GENERAL

To implement the CAAA, EPA has two primary goals: the reduction of SO_2 by 10 million tons and the design of the emissions trading system. EPA's role in the implementation of the law is to make sure that all the various pro-

---

†This trading system is divided into two phases with Phase I lasting from 1995 to 2000 covering 111 of the nation's largest electric power plants that emit SO_2, all located east of the Mississippi River. Phase II begins in 2000 and runs indefinitely and will reach all electric power generating units greater than 25 megawatts. The electric generating units affected by Phase I must meet a limit of 2.5 pounds of SO_2 emissions per million BTUs of heat output (lbs/mmBTU). In Phase II, the limitation is lowered to 1.2 lbs/mmBTU.

‡The EPA decided early in the developmental process to build as much of a consensus during the rulemaking procedure as possible in order to reduce the risks of extensive litigation over the end result. The EPA created the Acid Rain Advisory Committee (ARAC) composed of 44 members drawn from all the various interests affected by the acid rain legislation, including electric power companies (investor owned companies, public owned companies, and independent power producers), coal and gas suppliers, public utility regulators, state environmental and consumer agencies, environmental and consumer groups, and labor unions. With this cross-section of interests, the EPA hoped to be able to find common ground on many issues. Where common ground could not be achieved, the process of debate might lead to better understanding of the issues with less likelihood of court challenge. Moreover, it was hoped that the personal interaction of such diverse interests might lead to better understanding of the interests and positions of each group represented at the table, greater personal investment in the final outcome, and increased chance that the end result would be acceptable to more interests. This was a high risk enterprise since it was possible that the entire process could bog down in acute parochialism with little or nothing gained. After five meetings of the ARAC by mid May, it can be said that the gamble has paid off since ARAC accomplished a great deal through its examination of many issues and by reaching consensus on many of them.

visions of the CAAA are addressed in a thorough and timely manner. But the EPA can do more. It can create an environment where the participants believe the EPA is serious about making the emissions trading system work. The EPA's role in creating the perception of workability is as important, if not more so, than getting the details right.

The emissions trading system is the largest experiment to date in the use of market incentives for environmental compliance. What the EPA does here will represent the model for future market-oriented efforts. For too long environmental compliance has relied upon command and control regimes. The acid rain program strikes out in a different direction, relying instead on market forces to produce results in the least costly manner. The implementation process must create the perception of workability for this market-oriented approach. It must develop rules of both certainty and flexibility that promote the use of market forces rather than merely trying to write regulations that make it more difficult to introduce market-based concepts.

Since this is a new market, the rules of allowance holding and trading must be clear, explicit, and free from ambiguity. Certainty in the system can foster the development of a large market for the trading of allowances. The bigger the market the more likely it is that participants will be able to derive the efficiency gains expected from allowance trading. Moreover, a robust market will foster growth as new units readily find that allowances are available for compliance purposes.

The EPA's role is limited, however. The EPA cannot make companies participate nor make state agencies implement rules to foster market development. Even if the EPA is serious about encouraging a market-based system and creates a perfect environment for allowance trading, each individual participant will approach the allowance trading system in a way that maximizes its unique interests. Similarly, each state agency will approach the new system in a way that maximizes its economic and social interests. But the EPA's intent will go a long way towards building an environment conducive to allowance trading. The success of the acid rain program depends upon the EPA's creating the appropriate perception of workability.

METHODOLOGY FOR ISSUE ASSESSMENT

There are two overarching goals of the acid rain program: the reduction of SO_2 by 10 million tons and the reliance upon market forces to accomplish this goal. The reliance upon market-based mechanisms should minimize compliance costs, maximize economic efficiency, and permit strong economic growth. A subsidiary goal that flows from the first two is the development and use of new technologies and strategies for pollution prevention and increased electric generation growth.

From these two goals flows a methodology for analyzing the various issues that arise in the implementation of the acid rain program. The SO_2 reduction goal can provide the foundation for an analytical approach to issues that examines whether SO_2 reductions are achieved to the fullest extent possible or whether too much flexibility is provided undermining the achievement of the reduction goal. Therefore, one way to look at issues is the environmental impact associated with the issue. Thus, if one interpretation of an issue will result in a delay in implementing the program, a strict reduction position would opt for an interpretation that would limit or eliminate the delay. If an issue leads to the potential for additional emissions or creates uncertainty over this potential, then a strict reduction approach would argue for an interpretation to limit this potential.

The second goal of introducing market incentives for environmental compliance relies upon an analysis that does not consider environmental impact. The issue should be analyzed from the viewpoint of whether it reduces compliance costs and maximizes economic efficiency.

There are a large number of issues concerning CAAA implementation. This paper discusses only a few of the more controversial or important issues since an analysis of all issues raised by the CAAA is beyond its scope.

ISSUES WITH ENVIRONMENTAL IMPACT

SO_2 Monitoring

An issue with a significant environmental impact is the implementation of monitoring techniques for SO_2 emissions. The statute calls for the use of a continuous emission monitoring system (CEMS), an in-stack monitoring device for SO_2 emissions that produces a high level of accuracy and precision in counting SO_2 emissions. The approach that achieves the highest level of environmental compliance would need a 98-99 percent level of accuracy for the CEMS (and equally effective alternative mechanisms), that obtained and reported data hourly, and with incentives to minimize data gaps and maximize the maintenance of CEMS at high levels of accuracy. The more flexible approach to achieving the same levels of SO_2 reductions argues that this is a yearly SO_2 emissions program. In addition, while the same degree of accuracy is required for CEMS, and even though data are collected on an hourly basis, the level of reporting does not call for hourly reporting of data (reporting a daily average of the 24 data points would be sufficient). Moreover, alternative monitoring systems do not have to be as detailed in their reporting requirements as CEMS; for example, an oil-fired plant could rely upon a calculation that measured the sulfur content of the oil and the time it takes to empty a tank—flow rate—rather than use an in-stack monitor. The issue revolves around the degree of certainty the monitoring systems impart to the level of SO_2 emissions, with those desiring the maximum reduction arguing for the highest level of accuracy and the others arguing for a degree of confidence commensurate with the overall goals of the program—a yearly accounting of SO_2 emissions. The difference is really one of degree. Since the trading system must rely upon a high level of confidence in measuring SO_2 emissions, it would be wise for the EPA to require a tighter system of monitoring initially. If the EPA determines in the future that more flexibility will achieve the same result with the same level of confidence in measurement, then the EPA can relax its rules at later date.

Phase I Extensions

The CAAA provides in section 404(d) that during Phase I any power plant may receive a two year extension of time to comply with the Phase I emission limits, if the power plant agrees to install a scrubber or some other technology that reduces SO_2 emissions by 90 percent. In addition, the power plant will receive bonus SO_2 allowances in the remaining three years of Phase I. The statute imposes a 3.5 million allowance limit on the number of allowances that can be distributed for power plants qualifying for this extension. The allowances are to be distributed by the EPA "in order of receipt" of each proposal. While the statutory language appears quite clear, one issue developed that created controversy: the manner by which allowances would be distributed in the event of an oversubscription.

It is expected that the allowances available for the Phase I extensions will be oversubscribed, most probably on the first day that applications are accepted. How the allowances are distributed can make a big difference in the number of utilities that obtain these bonus allowances and the amount of scrubbing that will be undertaken. There is the potential for a significant impact upon the environment if more high sulfur coal is used versus other compliance alternatives.

There were two major reasons why the Phase I extension was included in the legislation. First, there was a concern on the part of those representing high sulfur coal interests that they would be adversely affected by the CAAA because of the likelihood that many utilities would switch to low sulfur coal, or switch to gas, or take other measures to comply rather than install scrubbers that would continue the use of high sulfur coal. If economic incentives could be provided for scrubbing, the loss of high sulfur coal due to the use of these other measures would be mitigated.

The second reason for the Phase I extension was to provide additional economic assistance to Midwest utilities. The biggest burden of the Phase I program falls upon utilities in the Midwest. By creating an incentive to install scrubbers by distributing bonus allowances, these utilities could have additional allowances to sell and, thereby, reduce their overall cost of environmental compliance.

Two basic methods were proposed for distribution: first come, first served and pro rata. The first come, first served approach would require distribution according to the date and time of the application. The pro rata approach would distribute allowances on a first come, first served basis until the day of oversubscription and then allowances would be distributed pro rata among the remaining qualifying units. A third method—a lottery—did not receive much support or discussion.

An examination of the number of units that could install scrubbers differed markedly depending upon whether a strict first come, first served approach (or lottery) was used or whether a pro rata approach was used. With the first come, first served approach, about 20 to 25 power plants would qualify for scrubbing. With a pro rata approach, about 35-50 power plants could qualify, a substantial increase in the number of units eligible for bonus allowances, and a potentially larger environmental impact.

The question of how these allowances are distributed should be judged on the merits of what will advance the goals of the CAAA and at the same time lead to a fair result. Environmentally, it is possible that the first come, first served approach may promote less use of technology and more fuel switching and possible conservation with a consequent positive environmental impact. Alternatively, this approach may reduce incentives to overcontrol SO_2 emissions, meaning less early reductions of SO_2 emissions. If more and early SO_2 reductions are the goal, the pro rata distribution method should be preferred.

Use of more scrubbing may be a more cost-effective compliance strategy than fuel switching or other compliance mechanisms and should not be relegated to a lesser alternative by choosing a first come, first served approach. While the pro rata approach gained general support in the Acid Rain Advisory Committee (ARAC), the EPA eventually decided through the White House dispute resolution process to implement a telephone first come, first served application process for the distribution of Phase I extension allowances.

Reduced Utilization

Another issue with substantial environmental consequences is reduced utilization. The obscure provision in the statute covering reduced utilization of power plants generated more discussion than almost any other issue. Section 408(c)(1)(B) states that if a power plant chooses to reduce its utilization (or shut down) as part of its compliance strategy, then the unit must designate the other unit or units that will be supplying the compensating generation. The consequence to the unit so designated is that it becomes a Phase I unit for SO_2 and NO_x emission limitation purposes. The SO_2 limitation is a serious problem; however, the NO_x limitation could cause substantial compliance problems. The reduced utilization is not a problem in Phase II when all units are part of the program; but it is a problem in Phase I when only some units are covered and some are not.

This is the crux of the problem. If a Phase I power plant chooses to reduce its utilization (an RU unit) and designates a Phase II unit to supply the compensating generation, the RU unit would receive its share of allowances in its annual distribution. Its emissions would decline as a result of reduced utilization and consequently they would be freed up for sale or banking, but emissions would increase at the Phase II unit that had increased its capacity to make up for the lost generation at the RU unit. The combination of the increase in emissions at the Phase II unit and the freed up allowances at the RU unit could lead to an overall increase in emissions beyond those allowed by the CAAA. The statute solves the problem by forcing the RU unit to designate the other unit and by limiting the number of allowances distributed so that total emissions equals total allowances distributed or purchased on the open market. This solution is imperative since without it as many as one million additional allowances could be added to the system, posing severe problems for the Phase I SO_2 reduction goal.

This statutory solution poses serious problems, however. For example, how would a company deal with an unplanned forced outage of a power plant where no unit was designated in the compliance plan? How would a company deal with a situation where it was very small and did not have other units to designate or could not find other units to designate because they did not want to become Phase I affected units because of difficulty in complying with NO_x limits? How would growth in electric generation by a Phase II unit be dealt with between 1985 and 1995, since the baseline for the Phase II designated unit is 1985 and many Phase II units may have increased their capacity and emissions as a consequence of natural growth? If the designated unit's baseline relied upon its 1985 emissions, this natural growth would be penalized if it became a designated unit.

Two general solutions evolved from the ARAC discussions. The first solution would look at the entire five year Phase I period and permit the RU unit to average its emissions over the five year period. The RU unit would carry forward any excess allowances to cover any emission increases at other units. Careful calculation of emissions would be necessary so that at the end of the five year period the RU unit would have to surrender any excess allowances to the EPA so that they could not be used in Phase II and, thereby, increase overall emissions.

A second approach permitted the RU unit in the unplanned situation to obtain compensating *generation* from other units without bringing them into the Phase I program with all its consequent limitations. Also, provision would be made for growth by the units providing compensating generation by setting threshold levels so that they would not penalized in this regard. Any additional allowances created by the reduced utilization would be surrendered at the end of each year maintaining environmental neutrality. The five year approach was criticized because it permitted too much emission variation within that period even though it was environmentally neutral over the entire Phase I period because of the surrender of allowances.

The second approach received widespread support in the ARAC since it permitted enough flexibility for the small systems or those with few Phase I units without creating the potential for large emission variations of the averaging method. Those opting for maximum SO_2 reductions favored the second approach.

Repowering

The repowering issue is definitional, but it may have significant environmental consequences. Section 409 permits power plants to extend their Phase II compliance by four years to the beginning of 2004 if they apply for and receive an extension for a qualified repowering project. Repowering is defined in section 402(12) to mean the replacement of an existing coal-fired boiler with six named clean coal technologies or, as approved by the EPA with consultation with the Department of Energy, a derivative of one or more of these technologies capable of meeting certain criteria. The dispute centers on whether the EPA has seven choices of derivative technologies, the six named and boiler replacement, or six choices if boiler replacement must be accompanied by one of the six named technologies. If the boiler replacement is considered separately from the six named technologies, then the scope of repowering is widened and more power plants may opt to repower and apply for the extension. This delays compliance for those units by four years and thus delays the achievement of the SO_2 reductions by four years. If boiler replacement must accompany one of the six technologies then the number of power plants that may apply for the extension may be reduced with an improvement in SO_2 emission reduction.

Needless to say, those wanting to maximize SO_2 reductions argue that the statute requires the coupling of boiler replacement with the six named technologies. The ARAC took the general position that boiler replacement should be considered separately from the remaining six; however, there was a strong minority position against this interpretation.

The statute is ambiguous. The underlying intent of the provision was to make accommodation for emerging technologies in addition to the six named in the statute. A flexible interpretation is to read the statute so that boiler replacement and the six technologies are separate.

ISSUES WITH ECONOMIC IMPACT

Allowance Allocation, Trading, and Tracking

The goal of reliance upon market-based forces to achieve compliance with the SO_2 reduction goal is achieved through the emissions or allowance trading program. How the EPA deals with the many issues involved in allowance trading will have a significant impact upon reducing compliance costs and maximizing the efficiency of the program.

Allowance Ownership

The most simple design is for the EPA to permit any person to own or hold allowances. This provides access to the allowance market by the largest number of participants and simplifies the EPA's role since it does not have to examine the qualifications of holders. In the draft proposed regulation on auctions and sales issued April 12, 1991, this is what the EPA has done—it has opened up the holding of allowances to any person.

Allowance Tracking

Similarly, allowance tracking should provide the most information to the public in the most accessible form. Creation of accounts also is essential if each holder is to be identified easily. The creation of accounts should be a simple application process and this is what the EPA has decided. If public knowledge of ownership of the account is troublesome to some holders, then the use of street names or broker names should be permissible. Computerization of the tracking system is essential. Access to the tracking system also should be available, although this will require safeguards on the system so that people accessing the system cannot destroy or create information.

An important part of the tracking system is the identification of allowances. This issue generated more interest than one would have expected. The EPA indicated that it will identify each allowance by year and to whom it was allocated initially. Beyond that the EPA was searching for reasons why it should number allowances individually. The EPA was fearful that individual numbering would lead to recording errors and time consuming efforts to clarify ownership. But individual numbering had many supporters for varying reasons. Tax accounting rules would opt for individual numbering. For example, the tax basis of allowances distributed to a holder would be zero, while the basis of a purchased allowance would be the transfer price. Upon sale of the allowance the gain would vary substantially depending upon the basis. Regulatory accounting rules also would push for individual numbering since the cost of allowances would be important for regulators trying to determine the original cost of the investment necessary for the setting of rates. Finally, the development of commodity markets for the trading of allowances also would want easy identification of individual allowances through individual numbering. These are sufficient reasons for individually numbered allowances.

Allowance Transfer

An allowance trading system implies that allowances can be traded easily among holders. The EPA's rules for the transfer and recording of allowances must be clear. The EPA indicated that if transfers are made but not recorded with the EPA as they are required to be by statute, then the EPA cannot count those allowances for compliance purposes as belonging to the transferee. Thus, the transfer system must have an explicit way for transfers to be officially recorded so that they can be effective for compliance purposes.

A serious question is the degree of information available about transfers. Will the quantity, price, ownership, and other information about the transfer be made public? In discussions on this issue there were considerable differences in viewpoint. The state regulators desired that the system be as open and transparent as possible to ease their burden of regulation and to provide as much information as possible to the market. Others, who also wanted the market to work efficiently, were less sure that everything about each transaction had to be made public. For example, price and quantity certainly should be made public, but the name of the purchaser may not be necessary for an efficient market. Commodity markets operate quite efficiently without ownership disclosure. In the context of transfers, however, it is necessary that the market see quantity, price, and other conditions of sale (for example, the sale of allowances of different vintages or a stream of allowances over a period of years) without the necessity to disclose the parties to the transaction if the parties choose not to make the disclosure. Giving this option to the parties involved preserves the information function of the market and at the same time preserves transactional confidentiality when it is essential.

Auctions and Sales

The statute requires that the EPA hold both auctions and fixed price sales starting in 1993. The auctions and sales will be for current year or spot allowances (allowances sold in 1993 and 1994 can be used in 1995 and thereafter) and for future year or advance allowances that can be used seven years after the auction or sale. The statute calls for two types of auctions, a public auction by the EPA of the allowances that the EPA reserved from each distributee (the CAAA requires that the EPA withhold 2.8 percent of each allocation for this purpose), and a private auction whereby the EPA sells allowances given it by allowance holders. The CAAA also requires fixed price sales of allowances at a price of $1,500 per allowance. The $1,500 value was chosen since it was thought that allowances would sell in the $500 to $800 range and that $1,500 would be a last resort price for those unable to purchase allowances from any other source. In Phase I, the EPA will auction

150,000 allowances and in Phase II, it will auction 200,000 allowances. In the Phase I direct sales, the EPA will sell 25,000 advance allowances, while in Phase II, it will sell 25,000 spot allowances and 25,000 advance allowances.

The auction and sale rules raise a number of issues. For instance, when should the public auction be held? The generally preferred view is to hold the auction as early in the year as possible so that it provides an early indication of the value of allowances to market traders and also gives unsuccessful bidders sufficient time to make trades in other forums. The EPA is proposing to hold the auction on or before March 31 of each year which is sufficiently early in the year for planning and informational purposes.

Should the EPA conduct a multiple price or discriminative price auction, or should it use a single price auction? The statute states that "auctioned allowances shall be allocated and sold on the basis of bid price, starting with the highest-priced bid and continuing until all allowances for sale at such auction have been allocated." Most observers have interpreted this language to mean a multiple bid auction. At least one observer has argued that this language could just as easily mean a single bid auction and that single bid auctions are more efficient. While there is nothing in the Conference Report language on this issue, one participant in the legislative process understood the intention of the staff working on the language was for the EPA to hold a multiple bid auction. Most of the participants in the ARAC process recommended a multiple bid auction since that was easier to implement and to understand. The EPA, in its recently issued draft proposed rules on auctions and sales, did opt for the multiple bid auction, which is a preferable way to implement the auction rules, at least in early years when bidders are getting used to the system.

With respect to bidding, the statute says that any person can bid and the EPA is proposing to follow this requirement. The statute requires that bidders submit sealed bids three days prior to the auction. The EPA should also require that each bid state the quantity of allowances bid upon, the price, the type of allowance (spot or advance), to whom the allowances will be sold (the designated representative), and the account information, accompanied by certified funds for the full price of the bid. The number of sealed bids that any person wants to submit should be unrestricted as should the varying prices that each bidder wants to make. The EPA has followed this approach in its recent auction and sales proposal. The EPA proposes to deal with tie bids by using a lottery, which is preferable to a pro rata approach in this instance.

The CAAA requires that the "nature, prices, and results" of each auction should be made public. This language creates some ambiguity about what should be disclosed. It is clear that with successful bids the quantity and price of the bids should be disclosed. Should the quantity and price of unsuccessful bids be made public? There is no harm in publishing a range of prices that did not meet with success; however, it is less clear what would be gained by making known the name and price associated with each losing bid. It is also less clear what is to be gained through the disclosure of the names of successful and unsuccessful bidders.

The names of the successful bidders present the same issues that arose with respect to allowance transfers. Again, the publication of names should be made optional. The EPA has chosen the full disclosure of the names of all bidders and their bids as well as the publication of the lowest price for which allowances were sold. The EPA argues that disclosure adds additional information to the market that may make it more efficient. Other markets work quite efficiently without the disclosure of the names of traders. Furthermore, it argues that there is no confidentiality provision in the statute and, therefore, the information would be made available under Freedom of Information Act requirements. One could argue that the EPA has sufficient general authorities to keep proprietary information confidential if it wants to do so.

The design of the private auction has engendered a substantial amount of discussion. This is the auction where the EPA sells allowances turned back to it by allowance holders. The views on this auction ranged from doing the minimum amount required by law to holding a completely different kind of auction from the public one that would maximize market participation. One set of views claimed that the private market will provide suitable markets for trading and that the EPA should not try to substitute the private auction for the development of private markets. Those holding this view indicated a desire that the EPA do as little as possible in the private auction with the minimum being merely to mirror what it was doing in the public auction.

At the other end of the continuum, there was the view that the EPA should not wait for the development of private markets, but should provide an innovative private auction, at least in the initial years, with the expectation that private markets eventually will substitute for the EPA's efforts. Two ideas emerged from this viewpoint. One was for a catalogue type auction where the offering party would indicate all the terms and conditions of the allowances it wants to sell, whether single year, multiple year, single price, multiple price, etc. Bidders would use the EPA catalogue as a way of learning about offers to provide the information to the EPA or make contact outside EPA purview, with the successful bidder announced by the EPA. If done privately, the EPA would be notified by the successful bidder. Another type of auction could be a bulletin board type auction, again with a range of allowances being offered, and with the EPA playing a lesser role than in the catalogue. Either form of private auction would be more than just a straightforward pick-a-winner auction for current year allowances.

In its draft proposed rulemaking on auctions and sales dated April 12, 1991, the EPA indicated that it was seeking comments on its initial proposal to establish a private auction that mirrored the public auction, but with the possibility of establishing a voluntary, catalogue auction where the EPA would compile the information on the bids and submit the information to the offering party. It also proposed a bulletin board auction where the EPA would be an electronic intermediary with negotiations held privately. After considerable discussion on the pros and cons of choosing one type of private auction over the other, the ARAC recommended that the EPA consider establishing both types of auctions—a discriminative price sale of spot and advance allowances, and a catalogue type approach for those wanting greater flexibility. The EPA would do well to consider this alternative since it solves the problem of trying to design a private auction that satisfies all constituencies. It adds to market efficiency and, as the private market develops, it could be displaced and eventually phased out.

The direct sales provisions are rather straightforward. Many of the issues associated with auctions are relevant here. One question is when to hold the sale. The EPA proposed to hold it on or before July 1 of each year. This is a good time since it should be after the auction so that information is available on the range of prices allowances were sold for. It also allows sufficient time to implement the IPP guarantee provisions that require the EPA to issue guarantees to IPPs who are unable to buy allowances at auctions or elsewhere and must rely on the last resort direct sales. The EPA also is proposing to permit sales to be made any time after the initial date of direct sales and to continue up until the last day that trading is permitted (through the end of the grace period, see below). Sales should be made on a first come, first served basis, which the EPA has chosen to do. The EPA has decided to implement a waiting list for oversubscriptions rather than use a lottery or pro rata and this is an acceptable approach to the distribution allowances in the direct sales program.

Grace Periods

The grace period issue concerns the period of time after the close of the year that power plants would have to make final trades in order to come into compliance. The grace period would allow units to "true up," that is, acquire sufficient allowances so that their emissions did not exceed the number of allowances held. Since there is a penalty for not having a sufficient number of allowances to cover emissions ($2000 per ton plus the requirement to offset the excess in the next year), the grace period is a critical period of time for power plants to maintain compliance.

In the Conference Report accompanying S. 1630 (the bill that was signed by the President) the conferees indicated their intent with respect to the permissibility of a grace period; "[t]he conferees do not intend that any affected unit or affected source be subject to any penalty for 'exceeding' its allowances for a given calendar year until that year has ended and all transfers of allowances applicable to that year have been completed within a reasonable time after the end of that year." Most observers have interpreted this language to mean that the Congress contemplated a period of time after the close of the year for trades to be made to maintain compliance.

The issue is not so much the appropriateness of the grace period, but its duration. There are some statutory constraints. The CAAA requires that any power plant that does not have enough allowances to cover its emissions submit its compliance plan for offsets and payment of penalty within 60 days after the close of the year. The outside limit on the grace period is considered to be 60 days.

The EPA proposed a 15 day grace period within which trades could be made, with the remaining time available for the EPA to record trades, correct any trading errors, and provide sufficient time for power plants to submit their offset plans. Virtually everyone else who analyzed the problem indicated that 15 days was far too short a period of time for trades to take place and suggested that 30 to 45 days would be appropriate. The arguments for longer time periods were that the complexity of trades requires more time, and the recording of trades will require time and the perception of workability. Because 15 days is such a short time, it was felt that the EPA was not serious about making the program work.

It is clear that a 15 day time period is insufficient to make trades and have them recorded by the EPA to ensure that power plants will comply with the statute. At least 30 days should be provided if the system is to be flexible and workable from the viewpoint of the participants.

SUMMARY

The creation of a model for the analysis of implementation issues divided the issues into those with an environmental impact and those with no environmental impact, but with an economic impact. Issues that had an environmental impact usually were divided along the lines of strict environmental compliance leading to maximum SO_2 reduction or additional flexibility in the achievement of the SO_2 reduction goal. The issues with economic impact were divided between those that could reduce compliance costs and increase the efficiency of the market compared to those that discouraged the development of the market for allowance trading or somehow increased compliance costs. This model worked well in the analysis of issues and made the debates over these issues more understandable.

7 2 2 5